Biopolitics and Structure in Legal Education

Taking up the study of legal education in distinctly biopolitical terms, this book provides a critical and political analysis of structure in the law school.

Legal education concerns the complex pathways by which an individual becomes a lawyer, making the journey from lay-person to expert, from student to practitioner. To pose the idea of a biopolitics of legal education is not only to recognise the tensions surrounding this journey, but also to recognise that legal education is a key site in which the subject engages, and is engaged by, a particular structure—and here the particular structure of the law school. This book explores that structure by addressing the characteristics of the biopolitical orders engaged in legal education, including: understanding the lawyer as a commodity, unpicking the force relations in legal education, examining the ways codes of conduct in higher education impact academic freedom, as well as putting the distinctly Western structures of legal learning within a wider context.

Assembling original, field-defining essays by both leading international scholars and emerging researchers, it constitutes an indispensable resource in legal education research and scholarship that will appeal to legal academics everywhere.

Luca Siliquini-Cinelli is Reader in Law at Cardiff University, UK.

Thomas Giddens is Chair of Jurisprudence at the University of Dundee, UK.

Biopolitics and Structure in Legal Education

Edited by Luca Siliquini-Cinelli
and Thomas Giddens

Routledge
Taylor & Francis Group
a GlassHouse Book

First published 2023
by Routledge
4 Park Square, Milton Park, Abingdon, Oxon OX14 4RN

and by Routledge
605 Third Avenue, New York, NY 10158

Routledge is an imprint of the Taylor & Francis Group, an informa business

a Glasshouse book

British Library Cataloguing-in-Publication Data
A catalogue record for this book is available from the British Library

ISBN: 978-1-032-00692-5 (hbk)
ISBN: 978-1-032-00695-6 (pbk)
ISBN: 978-1-003-17519-3 (ebk)

DOI: 10.4324/9781003175193

Typeset in Bembo
by Deanta Global Publishing Services, Chennai, India

Contents

Contributors

Bruce Baer Arnold is Associate Professor of Law at the University of Canberra.

Kim Barker is Senior Lecturer in Law at The Open University.

Carlo Caprioglio is Postdoctoral Researcher and Aggregate Professor in the Legal Clinic on Migration and Asylum at Roma Tre University.

Jane Ching is Professor of Professional Legal Education at Nottingham Trent University.

Filippo Contarini is Lecturer in Legal Theory at the University of Lucerne, and a Postdoctoral Fellow at University Paris 2.

Peter Čuroš is Assistant Professor at the Institute of Political Studies, Polish Academy of Sciences in Warsaw.

Eric Deibel is Lecturer in Science, Technology and Society (Engineering Faculty), and Assistant Professor (Political Science Faculty) at Bilkent University.

Talya Deibel is Assistant Professor of Law, and Chair of Legal History at Bilkent University.

Thomas Giddens is Chair of Jurisprudence at the University of Dundee.

Olga Jurasz is Senior Lecturer in Law at The Open University.

Omar Madhloom is Senior Lecturer at the University of Bristol.

Martina Millefiorini is an independent researcher.

John R Morss is Honorary Fellow in Law at Deakin University.

Cosmos Nike Nwedu is Lecturer at the Federal University Ndufu-Alike Ikwo.

Fernando del Mastro Puccio is Professor of Legal Ethics and Law and Psychoanalysis at Pontificia Universidad Católica del Peru.

Francine Rochford is Associate Professor at La Trobe University.

Sergio Iván Anzola Rodríguez is Research Coordinator at CEEAD (Centro de Estudios Sobre la Enseñanza y el Aprendizaje del Derecho) in México, and Adjunct Professor at Universidad de los Andes in Colombia.

Chin Chin Sia is Programme Director at Taylor's University.

Luca Siliquini-Cinelli is Reader in Law at Cardiff University.

Luana Mathias Souto is an independent researcher.

Giulia Walter is a PhD candidate at the University of Zurich.

Introduction

Luca Siliquini-Cinelli

Critics of biopolitics might say that it is *à la mode*, in the sense that it is but a fashionable field of inquiry which has lost most of its original analytical appeal. At first glance, such criticism would appear to strike the right chord: over the past few years, biopolitical thinking has come to encompass such a diverse and extensive spectrum of political-philosophical reflection that it inevitably leaves one to wonder whether it is as effective and valuable as it once was believed and shown to be. In this sense, popular and wide-ranging definitions of biopolitics such as that set forth by internationally renowned biopolitical philosopher Roberto Esposito, according to whom, *qua* '*living thought*'—that is to say, thought in action, involving as well as being constantly defined and shaped by practical concerns[1]—biopolitical thought preoccupies itself with the domains of, and multiple interactions between, 'politics and life… history and nature',[2] might give the impression that biopolitics is indeed a rather intangible and inconsistent intellectual endeavour and practice unworthy of being pursued.

Biopolitics might also be criticised by those who think that biopolitical thinking is not as special as it is generally assumed to be. In particular, it could be argued that the whole of philosophical reflection as such, rather than just biopolitics as a specific philosophical strand, is, ultimately, thought *in action*. For since its inception on Ionian shores,[3] (Western) philosophical inquiry has never been merely contemplative. To the contrary, the argument could continue, it has always concerned itself with practical matters, too. From Socrates' epistemic and political search for 'an eternal moral truth',[4] to Plato's merging of *episteme* (knowledge) and *teckne* (practical skills),[5] to the therapeutic orientation

1 Esposito (2008), Ch 5; (2012), Ch 4.

2 Esposito (2017), p 19, cited, critically, in Portinaro (2018), p 9. My translation. Italian political philosophy is very much divided over the analytical valence of its relatively recent biopolitical turn. In addition to Portinaro's critique, see Cacciari (2019).

3 Severino (2010); Rovelli (2011).

4 Jaeger (1986a), p 89. See also ibid., p 64.

5 Jaeger (1947), p 369.

DOI: 10.4324/9781003175193-1

of Cicero's and Boethius' philosophical ponderings,[6] to Dante's similar praising of philosophical knowledge for being capable of 'free[ing] the soul from grief'[7] and conception of the speculative intellect as an extension of the practical one,[8] all the way down to phenomenology, the practical philosophy *par excellence*,[9] examples abound.

It is not our intention to defend the biopolitical cause, so to speak. Yet, presenting to the market two edited collections on the biopolitics of legal education[10] requires that we clarify what we mean by 'biopolitics' for present purposes and, most importantly, why we believe that there is much to be gained by exploring vexed themes such as the nature, aims, dynamics, flaws, and present and future challenges of the teaching, learning, and practising of law through biopolitical lenses.

To that effect, let us start with a reminder that, as just noted, 'biopolitics' is indeed a broad term which cuts across not only various disciplines and topics, but also cultures and ages. Traditionally, it refers to that branch of political-philosophical thought which places life and its social expressions at the centre of intellectual considerations concerning how identities are construed, shaped, constrained, voided, and freed. More specifically, as its very name suggests, biopolitics can be defined 'as the expression of a kind of predicament involving the intersection, or perhaps reciprocal incorporation, of life and politics'.[11] Biopolitics, then, investigates what, in his commentary on Esposito, Timothy Campbell has aptly defined as '*qualified* form of life'[12]—that is, a biological life (*zoē*[13]) that is bestowed *institutional*[14] recognition and qualification through the means of politics (*bíos*[15]) as a regulatory, disciplinary, and ultimately technocratic system and practice of order. Order the achievement, promotion, and protection of which depends upon specific and increasingly pervasive epistemic-ontological and societal instruments of production, subordination, alteration, destruction, and, eventually, re-creation, of identities.

6 See, respectively, *Tusculan Disputations*, *De Divinatione*, 2.40.83, and *On Obligations*, 1.153f, 2.5-6; *The Consolation of Philosophy*.
7 Gilson (1963), p 96.
8 *Monarchy*, I.III.9.
9 De Monticelli (2018), p 10.
10 This volume and the related volume titled *Biopolitics and Resistance in Legal Education*, also published by Routledge.
11 Campbell and Sitze (2013), p 2. See also Esposito (2008), Ch 1, also featuring in Campbell and Sitze (2013), Ch 17.
12 Campbell (2008), p xxix. Emphasis added.
Cf. Agamben (1998), p 7, 124.
13 '[T]he simple fact of living common to all living beings (animals, men, or gods)': Agamben (1998), p 1.
14 Cf. Esposito (2022).
15 '[T]he form or way of living proper to an individual or a group': Agamben (1998), p 1.

Biopolitics' broad analytical spectrum makes it a fertile field of inquiry for critical reflections regarding the educational enterprise in all its official declinations and veiled nuances. That political-philosophical analysis is well-suited for meaningfully inquiring into the educational dimension is, of course, not new. In fact, it can be safely said to be one of the key tracts of the Western tradition understood as a cultural-ethical experience of *critique*. Werner Jaeger's studies on Ancient Greece's *paideia*,[16] to name but one classicist Anglophone literature is acquainted with, illustrate this remarkably well. From the Sophists' intellectual revolution,[17] to Aristotle's reporting, not coincidentally in the *Politics*, of continuous political disagreement over what, at his time, had to be taught and how,[18] to Emperor Frederick Barbarossa's 1155/1158 *Constitutio Habita*,[19] to Humanism's educational renaissance,[20] to the crucial role that education has had in the origins, development, and spread of modern economics and contextual forms of polity,[21] all the way down to more recent stances on education's emancipatory and revolutionary power (arguably best epitomised by Nelson Mandela's famous 1990 remark that 'education is the most powerful weapon which you can use to change the world'), examples abound to show that education is, among other things, a *political* matter.

What makes education (also) a political matter is the fact that one of its main aims is to craft identities, human as well as professional. Needless to say, this objective also underpins *higher* education as well—the pedagogical laboratory *par excellence*, where, since its inception in medieval Italy, individuals are systematically[22] moulded via the means of a training that functionally turns students into 'experts'[23] for socio-political and economic purposes.[24] Accordingly, when scholars reflect on the nature, aims, benefits, limits, and challenges of the educational enterprise biopolitically, they ask (and, eventually, answer) pivotal questions as well as examine central and pervasive themes concerning the place of *both* the human as a general epistemic-ontological, socio-political, and economic category of thought, and singular, living and lived individualities within a wide range of teaching and learning activities, at both the undergraduate and postgraduate levels.

Unfortunately, while the academic discourse on the biopolitics of education is well-established generally,[25] *legal* scholars are yet to inquire into it and explore

16 Jaeger (1965, 1986a, 1986b).

17 Taylor and Lee (2020).

18 *Politics*, 1337ª 33ff.

19 Cavallar and Kirshner (2020), p 47f.

20 Ciliberto (2017); Cacciari (2019).

21 Mokyr (2016).

22 On the establishment of 'systematic' (or 'advanced') higher education and practice in the Middle Ages, see Honoré (1978), p xiii; Berman (1983), p 121; Brundage (2010), p 1, 80, 219, 223.

23 Kennedy (2016), p 277.

24 See, e.g., Brown (2015), Ch 6; Deneen (2019), Ch 5.

25 See, e.g., Peters (2007); Bourassa (2011); Boundy (2012); Pierce (2013); Lewis (2013); Bazzul (2017); Jasinski (2018).

the potential of its multiple declensions effectively. While there are valuable accounts in legal literature on such biopolitically oriented topics as, say, the role of emotions in the classroom,[26] there is a clear shortage of consistent and adequate investigations into the biopolitics of legal education (and practice). This is all the more unfortunate if one considers, first, that law *qua* regulatory and coercive artefact of power is biopolitics' preferred operational means; and second, the historical role that jurists (and legal studies) played in the successful inception and diffusion of the higher education model. Accordingly, rather than being a fashionable intellectual exercise as some detractors believe, questioning the legal education dimension biopolitically is a *necessity*.

That said, neither this volume nor the *Biopolitics and Resistance in Legal Education* one aims to offer readers a definitive appraisal of legal education's (and practice's) biopolitical dynamics—which, due to life's fluidity, would not only be impossible to provide, but also pointless. Rather, their aim is much more modest—namely, to take the first, introductory steps into a delicate topic with clear and meaningful practical implications that can no longer be overlooked. The volumes pursue this difficult task by collecting original and much-needed essays by internationally renowned scholars as well as emerging researchers from several jurisdictions globally, which not only offer sensible theoretical evaluations on various biopolitical themes relating to the educational sphere, but also share their personal experiences as individuals, students, educators, and practitioners.

This volume in particular, explores the ways in which the lives of law students, teachers, and professionals are formed, shaped, nullified, and re-created by the structures which make up today's law school. It is divided into three thematic Sections which address the book's overall theme from specific analytical angles and pedagogical experiences—namely, *Producing Lawyering Subjects*; *Relations*; and *Meta-Structures*. The first Section explores the biopolitical imperatives and logics animating the identitarian, institutional formation of the figures of the 'law teacher', 'law student', and 'legal professional'. Taking one step forward, the second Section delves into the (international) relations that make up the biopolitical substratum of both the law school and classroom as the primary *loci* of higher education's institutional dynamics. Finally, the third Section looks at the biopolitical structures of legal education's nature, aims, and operations from a meta-structural point of view, providing key insights that feed back into the other chapters' analyses, arguments, and trajectories of inquiry. This tripartition, however, is not rigid and some of the chapters could well have appeared in other Sections. Overall, the volume aims to contribute to a contextual understanding of the intricate biopolitical dynamics which underpin both the life of the classroom and that of the places where the managerial decisions which direct the pedagogical experience are made. It offers a rich

26 Jones (2019).

biopolitical appraisal of a whole series of pedagogical themes in a great variety of jurisdictions, including the nature and purposes of the office of the law teacher; the Solicitors Qualifying Examination; the biopolitical logic of foreign professional qualifications; the teaching of international law; the precariousness of women in legal academia; lawyers' self-identity as legal professionals; clinical legal education both within and outside the West; the impact of codes of conduct on academic freedom; the politics of responsible social media use in universities; the ability of today's academic system to cater to the needs of our knowledge-based economy; lifelong learning; the spread and implications of loneliness in legal education and practice; the link between sovereignty and the teaching, studying, and practising of law; the digitalisation of the teaching and learning experience and the related tyranny of metrics; and the role that transformative legal technologies can play in increasing access to higher education.

References

Giorgio Agamben (1998) *Homo Sacer: Sovereign Power and Bare Life*, trans. Daniel Heller-Roazen, Stanford University Press.

Jesse Bazzul (2017) 'Biopolitics and the "Subject" of Labor in Science Education' 12 *Cultural Studies of Science Education* 873.

Harold J Berman (1983) *Law and Revolution. The Formation of the Western Legal Tradition*, Harvard University Press.

Gregory N Bourassa (2011) 'Rethinking the Curricular Imagination: Curriculum and Biopolitics in the Age of Neoliberalism' 41 *Curriculum Inquiry* 5.

Wendy Brown (2015) *Undoing the Demos: Neoliberalism's Stealth Revolution*, Zone Books.

James A Brundage (2010) *The Medieval Origins of the Legal Profession: Canonists, Civilians, and Courts*, The University of Chicago Press.

Jessica Bundy (2012) 'Rendering (Gender) Invisible: Early Childhood Education and Care in Ontario as a Biopolitical Social Investment Apparatus' 33 *Discourse: Studies in the Cultural Politics of Education* 591.

Massimo Cacciari (2019) *La Mente Inquieta. Saggio sull'Umanesimo*, Einaudi.

Timothy Campbell (2008) '*Bíos*, Immunity, Life: The Thought of Roberto Esposito' in Roberto Esposito (ed)*Bíos: Biopolitics and Philosophy*, trans. Timothy Campbell, University of Minnesota Press.

Timothy Campbell and Adam Sitze (2013) *Biopolitics: A Reader*, Duke University Press.

Osvaldo Cavallar and Julius Kirshner (2020) *Jurists and Jurisprudence in Medieval Italy: Texts and Contexts*, University of Toronto Press.

Michele Ciliberto (2017) *Il Nuovo Umanesimo*, Editori Laterza.

Patrick J Deneen (2019) *Why Liberalism Failed*, Yale University Press.

Roberta De Monticelli (2018) *Il Dono dei Vincoli. Per Leggere Husserl*, Garzanti.

Roberto Esposito (2008) *Bíos: Biopolitics and Philosophy*, trans. Timothy Campbell, University of Minnesota Press.

Roberto Esposito (2012) *Living Thought: The Origins and Actuality of Italian Philosophy*, trans. Zakiya Hanafi, Stanford University Press.

Roberto Esposito (2017) 'Anacronismi' 31 *Filosofia Politica* 13.

Roberto Esposito (2022) *Institution*, trans. Zakiya Hanafi, Polity Press.

Étienne Gilson (1963) *Dante and Philosophy*, trans. David Moore, Harper & Row.
Tony Honoré (1978) *Tribonian*, Duckworth.
Werner Jaeger (1947) 'Praise of Law' in PL Sayre (ed), *Interpretations of Modern Legal Philosophies: Essays in Honour of Roscoe Pound*, Oxford University Press.
Werner Jaeger (1965) *Paideia: The Ideals of Greek Culture, Volume I. Archaic Greece: The Mind of Athens*, trans. Gilbert Highet, Oxford University Press.
Werner Jaeger (1986a) *Paideia: The Ideals of Greek Culture, Volume II. In Search of the Divine Centre*, trans. Gilbert Highet, Oxford University Press.
Werner Jaeger (1986b) *Paideia: The Ideals of Greek Culture, Volume III. Archaic Greece: The Mind of Athens*, trans. Gilbert Highet, Oxford University Press.
Igor Jasinski (2018) *Giorgio Agamben: Education Without Ends*, Springer.
Emma Jones (2019) *Emotions in the Law School. Transforming Legal Education Through the Passions*, Routledge.
David Kennedy (2016) *A World of Struggle: How Power, Law, and Expertise Shape Global Political Economy*, Princeton University Press.
Tyson E Lewis (2013) *On Study: Giorgio Agamben and Educational Potentiality*, Routledge.
Joel Mokyr (2016) *A Culture of Growth. The Origins of Modern Economy*, Princeton University Press.
Michael A Peters (2007) 'Foucault, Biopolitics and the Birth of Neoliberalism' 48 *Critical Studies in Education* 165.
Clayton Pierce (2013) *Education in the Age of Biocapitalism: Optimizing Educational Life for a Flat World*, Springer.
Pier Paolo Portinaro (2018) *Le Mani su Machiavelli: Una critica dell'«Italian Theory»*, Donzelli Editore.
Carlo Rovelli (2011) *Anaximander*, trans. Marion Lignana Rosenberg, Westholme Publishing LLC.
Emanuele Severino (2010) *La Filosofia dai Greci al Nostro Tempo. La Filosofia Antica e Medioevale*, BUR.
CCW Taylor and My-Kyoung Lee (2020) 'The Sophists' *Stanford Encyclopedia of Philosophy*, https://plato.stanford.edu/entries/sophists/.

Part 1

Producing Lawyering Subjects

Chapter 1

The Office of Law Teacher

Thomas Giddens

The office of law teacher includes an 'obligation to be complicit'[1] in the reproduction of legal form. It is a pedagogic office, constituted under the authority of the academy, and thus its jurisdiction includes the inculcation of certain characteristics of mind and body in the students whose education it facilitates. These characteristics are drawn from the traditions of legal practice and study and become those of the law graduate; should the law graduate become a professional lawyer, they also help to constitute their subsequent conduct of lawyerly office alongside the characteristics gained through any further skills-based training required for admittance to practice.[2] The law teacher thus administers an important, albeit not sole, site of institutional reproduction, and is implicated in the qualities and contours of that reproduction and of what is reproduced. The obligations and privileges of the law teacher encompass the administration of the subject formation of lawyers and professionals, playing a substantive part not just in facilitating the intellectual development of students, but in institutional iteration—of the transmission of the conceptual or, as framed in this chapter, *imaginary* forms of legal understanding and method that shape law's institutional evolution. The law teacher's privileges and obligations thus extend beyond the educational journey of their students, encompassing a custodianship of the lawful relations enabled by the legal forms their execution of office helps to reproduce within the unfolding traditions of law and its practice.

Law teachers take responsibility for the reproduction of the legal institution: the forms of life produced through the legal education process and the subsequent legal and living forms they engender. This is an unavoidable responsibility that comes with the office of law teacher. As Shaun McVeigh explains: 'How obligations of office are understood depends in large part on

1 This turn of phrase comes from McVeigh (2016), p 194.

2 In England and Wales, for example, a law degree traditionally covered legal knowledge, with postgraduate training and work experience developing the vocational competencies required for legal practice. The reforms of the Solicitors Qualifying Examination (SQE) have obviously changed this somewhat, but for those studying on law degrees the focus remains on legal knowledge. On the SQE, see Madhloom (this volume).

DOI: 10.4324/9781003175193-3

the authority under which it was created and the attendant formulation of the responsibilities, rights and privileges'.[3] The contours of the office of law teacher are determined by the institutional frameworks and material forms of the university, and are oriented towards the pedagogic practices of higher learning. In legal education, this higher learning involves the development of characteristics fit for a certain type of office:

> The vocational training of the contemporary lawyer is more or less explicit in its cultivation of a *persona* and training in a conduct of office. Such a training might cultivate an openness to the proper administration of justice or a disinterest in pursuing political ideologies whilst in office, or an awareness of the responsibilities of living within a tradition of law as well as a training in reasoning and procedure.[4]

McVeigh, talking of common law jurisprudence in general, reframes the complicity with legal forms in terms of office: being a jurisprudent of the common law, McVeigh claims, includes being complicit in the production of lawful relations through the interpretation and development of the common law tradition—however uncomfortable or uneasy that might be in the context of the tradition's track record.[5] Thus, to be a jurisprudent is to be complicit: it is a term of office. It is also a term shared by law teachers in general, for via the shape and content of what they teach law teachers are unavoidably complicit: they curate the educational journey, and thus train students for a particular conduct of office, within the tradition of which the office is a part.

While much of the training in legal education is explicitly for the capacities of lawyerly office, and thus the production of specifically legal form, the imaginary structures and processes and their habitual manifestation in praxis that are engendered also provide resources for conducting oneself in other settings. The training of the law graduate helps constitute conduct in a range of professional contexts, thus with a range of social consequences beyond the production of specifically legal institutions and the lawful relations they administer. Recognising the broader effects of the subject formation in law schools, as well as the unavoidable involvement of law teachers in this subject formation, means that attached to the office of law teacher is an obligation not only to be complicit in the production of legal form, but also, at least in part, in the production of social form—via both the legal forms produced and the conduct of law graduates in other contexts. To take up the office of law teacher is to recognise and discharge these obligations, to acknowledge and work with the

3 McVeigh (2016), p 192.

4 Ibid., p 192.

5 The colonial treatment of indigenous populations is a major example—see McVeigh (2016); or, more generally, see, for example, Watson (2014)—but there are of course many others.

effects of the power of the office and the forms of life it enables—the subjects it forms and the effects of that formation.

The *imaginary* quality of legal understanding was mentioned above, and this quality is the focus of the first section of this chapter. Overall, the argument rests on a vision of law as method, and more specifically as an invisible method that dwells beyond the material forms of institution upon or through which that method plays out. If law is in large part a question of method—even if it might be said that is not necessarily all it is—then the development of understanding and competence through the execution of pedagogic office becomes in large part the inculcation of law's hallmark methodological practices, rather than any particular substance or objective content. In an attempt to capture the distinctly conceptual qualities of legal understanding and method—that is, the intellectual habits associated with legal proficiency, rather than the mere reliance on a particular kind of institutional source or the rote repetition of supposedly static rules—this chapter focuses on the way legal education works to shape the minds of individuals. In doing this, it characterises the development of subjecthood through legal education as a journey of imagination and play, and—significantly—as one administered or facilitated by the execution of the office of law teacher, and for which those who inhabit that office take responsibility. The second section, accordingly, will outline the playful qualities of legal learning, before the final section focuses in on the processes of subject formation administered by the office of law teacher.

Law as Imaginary Method

The main methodological practices of law include close reading, categorisation, conceptual working, an ethical, social, or utilitarian praxis, and the unresolved oscillation between particular cases and abstract rules and principles. Law is a method of conceptualisation and praxis characterised by a concern with community and 'just' worldly living, achieved through social and moral governance via the constitution and administration of lawful relations and the practical resolution of specific disputes. Law is an imaginary schema that effects structure and change in society and culture, in national identity and in the psycho-social development of citizens and subjects. It is where imagination begets governance; where the invisible, abstract, timeless, or divine dogmas of legality take effect in the material world; where formlessness takes form, binding the subject.[6] Law has broad constitutive functions for how individuals relate, how communities exist. It is because of this trajectory towards community and the articulation of relation that law takes on general and abstract forms, seeking a particular form of fairness or equality in application that aims to transcend indi-

6 See Legendre (2019). On the formation of legal speech in the context of community, see also Matthews (2017).

vidual bias or bespoke, differential treatment. In terms of its method, then, law becomes a way of conceptualising and working with moral, ethical, social, and practical problems in oscillation between both general and individual levels.

If law is not something to be known, but is instead a way of knowing, then legal education is characterised by an indoctrination of students into a particular epistemological framework, their induction into a particular 'geography of mental spaces'[7] and the application of these to specific instances of human living. Through the course of a traditional law degree, those who study law are taught substantive subjects, but overall are seeking not substantive knowledge but the capacity to read, understand, and work with legal materials and processes. Law is not something to 'know' but something that is done, represented by the skill and expertise required to work with legal materials and divine their logic and meaning, and thence undertake their application to the vicissitudes of life within a tradition of administering lawful relations. To learn the law, one must develop the skills and habits of mind to be able to conceptualise the world in a way that enables the construction and manipulation of general categories, evidenced by written and linguistic descriptions. This manipulation may have various ends (justice, the client's interest, the public interest, a personal desire for order, and so on), but 'learning the law' inculcates the skills and methods of legality—not the rote memorisation of static rules.

To be a lawyer requires a peculiarly limited form of imagination. It requires an individual to imagine law in a way that is deemed appropriate to the institution, as anchored to institutionally sanctioned material sources. Goodrich, for instance, observes that 'the printed word is simply another figurate sign … [that lawyers] interpret and unpack'.[8] One might imagine or 'discover' law via other material forms of culture, but such sources do not have the appropriate institutional provenance to be recognised as authoritative evidence of legal principles. One might interpret institutional materials in a range of ways, but only some of these will have institutional propriety as producing *legal* meaning.[9] To be a lawyer is to live and work in this conceptual geography, to inhabit law's imaginary spaces, to navigate its complex structures that are accessed through, or enabled or evidenced by, law's material imprint or codification.

To become a lawyer is a movement of investiture, of occupying the uncertainty of invisible realms that are tethered to human encounter by their material forms.[10] Law's resources are shared within the lawyerly community, but are only accessible through the sources and practices that illustrate or evidence them. In legal education, these material forms also include those of the uni-

7 Goodrich (1995), pp 9–10.
8 Goodrich (2013), p xxviii.
9 See, for example, Fish (1982). For a fuller account of the genre of legal writing and its tensions and relations with literature more broadly, see Goodrich (2021).
10 On this structure of material 'investiture', see Goodrich (2012).

versity institution and the particular pedagogic resources provided within the jurisdiction of the law teacher. For an individual to move into a mode of life that is understood to be that of 'a lawyer', the features and requirements of that life need to be disciplined into them—through pedagogic play and the reward, and the concomitant organisation of their mental habits. To explain the law to a client, to read a case, to stand before a judge, to apply a doctrine, to make a case in a tribunal—these are daunting and complex tasks that involve a vast array of expert knowledges and skills and an expansive plethora of imaginary resources. In moving towards a state of proficiency, students must undergo a rich journey of play and practice, of trial and error, within a space that is safe and that has both material and immaterial dimensions, and that inducts them into the immaterial strata of legal thought. To approach the capacity to take up lawyerly office, to attain the skills and competencies necessary, requires rehearsal.[11] But not just any rehearsal. Because law is an epistemic rather than substantive art—a praxis and method characterised by particular ways of framing and working with concepts and understandings within the improvised setting of an instant case,[12] rather than the memorising and mechanical application of set knowledge[13] or working with clearly delineated material objects—it is the capacity to imagine, to work on a conceptual level, that needs to be inhabited and cultivated through the practical activities undertaken. One must play at being a lawyer to develop the imaginary habits of thinking with principles and norms, and the ability to manifest their effects in the unfolding praxis of casework.

The play inherent in legal education (indeed, one could make the case for many areas of education) is a particular form of conceptual or imaginary play. To study law is to play with the imagination, to inhabit roles and modes of thinking that—once they reach a certain degree of sophistication and cohesion with a normative standard—represent professional competence. This competence can be evidenced through material objects and their manipulation (the clear-sighted navigation of a law report, the laminated argumentation of a moot court, the concise and effortless rounding of analysis in a typed essay or client letter, embodied performance in a debate), but the competence itself is immaterial or unavailable for direct scrutiny. Only the material evidence of legal

11 Examples of common playful activities found on law degrees include identifying and retrieving legal sources, drafting client letters, preparing case notes, performing in debates and moots, giving oral presentations, discussing legal complexities with peers, inhabiting different argumentative positions, and proposing principled solutions to problem scenarios. The outcomes of this play then result in variable 'rewards', in the forms of affirmative feedback, grades, or—perhaps—the existential pleasures of performing activities well. While this may seem simplistically Pavlovian, in practice grades do act as gatekeepers for accessing continued training and pathways to legal practice and other professional trajectories.

12 On the broadly improvisational nature of law, see Ramshaw (2013).

13 On the problems with imagining law as a 'machine', see White (1996).

proficiency, not the proficiency itself, can be witnessed. And the development of lawyerly subjecthood emerges not through a simple transfer or shift in identity, but through complex rituals of play and imaginary development, of the unfolding of a potential enabled by the structures of the law school, and—importantly—administered by law teachers. Legal education is a key site of the subject formation of the profession, where the academic and vocational apparatuses of the discipline collide and work to shape individuals into lawyers. It is thus, also, the central place of legal reproduction and evolution, where the future of law as a social and governmental force is wrought. And is wrought on the planes of imagination, where it has the most power to endure and have ongoing effects as law graduates take up legal offices, professional positions, and various other roles in society.

Pedagogy, Play, and Imagination in Law

Knowing requires movement outside the material: narration, development, interpretation, unfolding, conceptualisation. As Della Volpe puts it: 'What is it that enables us to *know* something … if not our ability to penetrate beyond the immediacy of brute matter …?'[14] To know is to hold, elaborated in the mind, an imaginary schema—a set of categories and their virtual contents, of ideas and their operators and relations, through which we may (or may not) filter experience. To learn, then, necessarily involves the cultivation of the imagination. Indeed, the discontinuity between an object and what we know about it—its epistemic features—reveals the operations of the imagination.[15] And caught up with the imagination, and thus with pedagogy, are the ludic practices of play. As Nilsson observes in her reading of Gunilla Lindqvist's pedagogy of play:

> play is imaginative, that is, a creative process of interpretation in action where, through fantasy, a real situation is given a new and different meaning … [this] capacity to create an imaginary or fictitious situation in play makes play a vehicle for developing abstract thinking.[16]

Play cultivates the imagination, and the ability to conceptualise and unfold abstract thought that comes with it. To play is to learn; to know is to imagine.

While we might associate play with childhood (as Lindqvist did), this notion of learning through play, with an appropriate shift in the sophistication of the game, can also be applied to those seeking to learn the complex competencies of legal office in higher education environments. A child's imaginary play, for example,

14 Della Volpe (1978), p 20. Emphasis in original.
15 See Nilsson (2009), p 18.
16 Ibid., p 16.

might be understood as the elaboration and inhabiting of a virtual world, triggered or inspired by material objects or 'props'. But such play is not limited to childhood: 'As adults we continue to use props in a more advanced manner, for instance by using a novel to experience a fictional world'.[17] Framed more generally, it is clear that the 'characteristics of learning and playing games are closely correlated: curiosity, persistence, risk-taking, reward, attention to detail, problem-solving, and interpretation'.[18] Indeed, some games are played by grown-ups with deadly seriousness. Tans, for example, sets out the ways in which law—as a system lacking in any available foundations for its normative authority—is at root a

> game of make-believe. As props [legal subjects] use the material that can be found in legal sources, such as codes, statutes and jurisprudence ... [which] function as objects that trigger the imagination of an ultimate normative foundation[19]

which is not actually accessible.

The imagination tends to be overlooked in the history of Western education, which instead focuses on inculcating rational capacities as a means of developing the humanity of the subject—even though imagination is deeply involved in reasoning processes.[20] Although law 'simulates reality in a cut-down model ... [and] constructs its own "virtual reality" ... which is passed off as truth under the authority of law',[21] the authorising power of reason is taken with full seriousness[22] and the imaginary is commonly (if naïvely) suppressed in favour of the purely rational.[23] This legal game may be played in a knowing way, with awareness of its artificiality and wider normative or ethical implications,[24] but what is generally preferred over imaginary play is a capacity for 'critical thinking' about the law after buying into its fictional premise, in terms of a combative interrogation of legal sources and the arguments of others. A certain mode of this 'critical thinking' might be characterised as involving the forceful attack of texts and propositions: a kind of academic aggression that rewards students able to thrive in the combative arena of intellectual debate, and preparing for the crucible of the adversarial common law court. But this version, while operating on an imaginary or conceptual level in terms of the intellectual capacities involved, misunderstands the nature of critical learning and the imagination.

17 Tans (2014), p 133.
18 Abbott (2019), p 82.
19 Tans (2014), p 134.
20 See Wang and Huang (2018).
21 Beattie (2007), p 489.
22 See, as an extended and exemplary analysis of how legal reasoning procedures might authorise legal decision-making, MacCormick (2005).
23 On the rich non-rational qualities of law, put in terms of the aesthetic, see Manderson (2000).
24 See Tans (2014).

Hayes notes that classrooms do not need 'the adoption of a critical distance in relation' to the sources and doctrines under scrutiny, because an average student 'already begins at a distance from them': 'what is more challenging and fruitful is to try to take up a position of *interest*'.[25] Indeed, while an aggressive mode of critical attack might be characterised as 'critical thinking', as Hayes does in his relatively limited characterisation of the practice,[26] this really only reflects a certain masculine way of approaching critical pedagogy, which can also unfold via less combative or antagonistic procedures. Critique, in a different version, arguably involves simply the capacity to question, and this dissolves any necessity of inter-personal aggression and becomes more reflective of the critical project in general. And we must, as Hayes says, develop an *interest*: we need to get close to and inhabit our sources and principles and propositions, because, as students, we need to understand them. We must attune to their details in order to unpack their effects and possibilities. But the trick, the habit to inculcate, is not to get lost or comfortable inside once we have learned to inhabit, but always to keep open a space of questioning. Always, that is, to imagine an outside, to imagine alternatives, to thereby recognise that *this* is contingent because we can imagine *that*.

If to critique is to question, then this means to enter and inhabit a text, a source, a doctrine—and imagine a way out. As Adam Gearey has described the critical imagination in his study of Bill Ayers's critical pedagogy: 'One has to "work the gap" or remain within the "contradiction" of what is and what might be'.[27] On one level this might appear to be a version of a transformative imagination in law, which Mark Antaki clarifies comes with an associated trepidation at an unbounded imagination wedded to radical contingency.[28] But in its call to inhabit, to occupy and develop interest, to 'remain within' the distinction between this and that, this critical imagination is not merely transformative. Antaki might frame it as 'nostalgic'. As he explains:

> where transformatives, by way of imagination as invention, include the post- or hyper-modern, embracing wholly the cult of the now or the new, of the made, nostalgics, by way of imagination as attunement, ask us to let go, and to cultivate the capacity to be struck.[29]

A critical legal imagination requires one to attune to the law, to spend time coming to understand and live within its imaginary forms and their practical

25 Hayes (2015), p 322. Emphasis added.
26 See ibid., pp 318–20.
27 Gearey (2020), p 297.
28 See Antaki (2012), pp 11–13.
29 Ibid., p 15.

manifestations—to acknowledge that one is living within a tradition, to put it in McVeigh's officious terms. It means being 'struck' by an encounter with law: to stay in the 'gap', dwelling and playing in law's virtual world with one foot in another world, knowing that law's world is virtual and that playing there is in no way a flippant activity.

To play at law is to learn to work with the imagination in particular ways. It is not merely learning the rules of the game—the details of law's foundational fiction, the premises of the 'validity game', as Tans describes it[30]—but the imaginary techniques that enable movement between worlds. Framed pedagogically—as a question of what capacities of office are inculcated—gameplay teaches 'how to use one's imagination to read *across boundaries*... to bridge the gaps and boundaries between worlds to provide a more complete understanding of both the virtual and the physical world the player inhabits'.[31] It is a 'disposition', 'a way of not only seeing the world but of seeing ourselves in it' and the 'various possibilities' to which a world opens up.[32] And, with law, its imaginary or fictional quality requires precisely this kind of world-shifting disposition: 'the imaginary foundation of legal systems is related to a type of social action, namely legal reasoning and ordering, in which participants appear to switch between two separate and mutually exclusive realities'.[33] And playing the game of law works on a synthesis of the construction of legal reason on one hand, and an imagined source or origin on the other.[34] For the system to operate on its imaginary foundations, we must construct and apply legal principles in the material world as if they have reality in law's virtual world.

Thus, by keeping one foot in another world, players retain agency within the games they play. In a virtual world, players 'are neither authors nor readers, but they are, themselves, a new conceptual blend: both author and reader, both player and character, both virtual and physical'[35]—both lawyer and subject. Play inculcates the 'ability to recognize, reflect on, and incorporate those reflections back into those worlds',[36] providing the pedagogic space for critical learning as the cultivation of the imagination. While we might inhabit the virtual space of the game, we can maintain critical awareness that it has an outside—that this imagined space and its associated habits of mind and interpretive practices are contingent, that there are many other realms—and concomitantly remain stuck in the gap between our different worlds.

30 Tans (2014), p 135, and generally.
31 Thomas and Brown (2007), p 150. Emphasis in original.
32 Ibid., p 156.
33 Tans (2014), p 130.
34 See ibid., p 140.
35 Thomas and Brown (2007), p 168.
36 Ibid., p 168.

Imagining the Lawyerly Subject

Legal education is a key site of the reproduction of the legal institution. It is where lawyers of the future are shaped and trained. Legal education is also a relatively protracted moment, extending beyond the vocational inculcation of methodical habits as evidenced by concrete practical skills (client interviewing, letter writing, following procedural regulations) and the understanding, analysis, and application of substantive legal knowledge. Law teachers, working within the institutional frameworks of universities and higher education, de facto administer and oversee significant portions of lawyerly training, with professional regulatory bodies more firmly taking up the baton the closer one gets to being deemed fit for practice. In the history of legal training, the relationship between the legal academy and the legal profession has often been fraught, with the vocational apprenticeship model of the Inns of Court existing in tension with the academic study of law away from its sites of practice. Indeed, David Sugarman examines how this tension resulted, ultimately, in the particular style of knowledge and legal method associated with the academic study of law, epitomised by the elaboration of 'doctrine' in the form of the modern student textbook.[37] This historic tension means that the jurisdiction of the office of law teacher is where the jurisdiction of the office of jurisprudent, with its obligation to be complicit in the legal tradition and the care of lawful relations, overlaps with that of the office of educator, with its obligations and privileges associated with overseeing the development of an individual's capacities and knowledge for the wider benefit of society.

But in terms of its duties to develop critical capacity and depth of understanding, the administration of the office of law teacher—like other academic offices—finds itself undermined by recent neoliberal shifts in higher education environments. These shifts are anathema to the duties of the academic office upon which the university rests, and promote a focus on 'employability skills' as dictated by the short-term needs of the market in place of the wider personal, social, cultural, and economic benefits traditionally associated with higher learning.[38] The model of legal understanding administered by the law teacher is thus part of the processes of subject formation that produce *university* law graduates and feed into legal practice and the reproduction of legal form, with particular imaginary effects on the legal minds wrought through higher education and their subsequent execution of lawyerly office, understood within—and often in tension with—a wider context of capitalist exchange.

In her examination of the subject formation at work through leading examples from the heyday of US Critical Legal Studies (CLS), Penny Pether highlights some of the limitations or problems with these effects—and, notably,

37 See Sugarman (1991).

38 See, for example, Bendixen and Jacobsen (2017); Canning (2019). See also Giddens (2021), pp 39–41.

issues that much of CLS does not manage to escape or overcome despite its claims to educational activism against, particularly, the capitalist ideologies of modern law. Doctrine, she notes, despite being 'a self-serving legitimation invention by the emergent cadre of professors of the common law in the late 19th century' was presumed to be all that legal education involves, even though theory, skills, and methods can and often do form part of the legal curriculum.[39] Such a 'radically narrow conception of lawyering, let alone the law'[40] in the context of legal education and the 'high stakes involved in practising critical legal scholarship and pedagogy',[41] overlooks not only a wider imaginary of what legal understanding and learning can be, but also the embodied dimensions of legal and pedagogic praxis. Pether's concern, then, is not just with how future lawyers are shaped—how law teachers should exercise their office—but with 'the body, and specifically the body of the law student and what is written in and on it in the practices of professional subject formation found in the law school'.[42] Legal education is a question of the exercise of power,[43] feeding into the administration of lawful relations in general by law graduates. It concerns the subjects or forms of life that are produced or enabled through pedagogic processes and the wider social, political, and economic impacts of this. As Pether puts it: 'We are talking here of questions of institutional power and of the power wielded in a legal system that shapes the nation and impacts profoundly on the lives of its citizens'.[44] And if the jurisdiction of the office of law teacher is a site of the reproduction of the legal institution—it is also a site of resistance.[45]

One response is for law teachers to deny responsibility: to claim that one is simply repeating or teaching law and legal forms determined elsewhere. Reform and change, if needed, should take place under the purview of professional bodies or the enactment of legislation. To teach, ideally, is to be a transparent conduit for knowledge and understanding, and students can make up their own minds how to comport themselves in their future professional activities. The law teacher, on this understanding, seeks to erase themselves from the process—to deny their complicity in the power structures of the university and the public and private institutions it feeds.[46] But teaching is a form of signification: 'the signifier is in relation to the signified in the same way that

39 See Pether (1999), p 219.
40 Ibid., p 230.
41 Ibid., p 221.
42 Ibid., pp 225–6.
43 Compare with the more general understanding of pedagogic power and the responsibilities of those who hold academic office: see Freire (2005).
44 Pether (1999), p 231.
45 See, for instance, Goodrich (1999) for some examples and purported failures in this regard.
46 See Bingham (2007), p 18, who notes (with Derrida) that this desire for erasure is more generally entrenched.

the teacher is in relation to whatever is being taught … the practice of teaching is a system of representation'.[47] As Derrida frames it: 'The teaching body, as *organon* of repetition, is as old as the sign and has the history of the sign'.[48] And this pedagogic assumption that the teacher's role is to erase themselves so their topic or knowledge can speak for itself thus attracts all the problems of accessing 'true' or transcendental meaning, or of representing meaning in a transparent manner.[49] But, as Bingham interprets Derrida, 'there can be no true erasure of the teacher'.[50] Nor can there be an erasure of the student, since it is 'the student who interprets, who understands, who is integral to both the teacher and the taught, as the teacher is integral' to what they teach.[51]

This Derridean pedagogy thus recognises the insight of critical education shared by Pether: that there is no neutral place of teaching, and that power is always at work in the signification practices of education institutions.[52] 'Derrida's deconstructive understanding of teaching indicates that teaching, itself, always enacts power effects that are in some ways oppressive'.[53] 'Teaching' is not neutral, but exercises power, it works to form subjects—in law, the subjects formed are likely lawyerly or at least professional, and feed into the wider social reproduction of institutions of power. Thus, to deny the agency of the law teacher is to be either naïve or knowingly complicit in the reproduction of problematic legal forms. But Derrida's insights point to an acknowledgement that it is not as simple as 'resistance of oppression' versus 'championing liberty'. The 'activist teacher signifies *against* the power she wants to fight, while the "ordinary" teacher signifies *for* the content she wants to teach', yet both are 'enmeshed in an economy of erasure', striving 'to get out of the way so that their work can be done'.[54] But the teacher always has effects on the power that is signified,[55] and thus, in all cases, 'new variations of social power emerge from within the pedagogical act'.[56] Aims like 'liberty' or 'social empowerment' are contingent forms, and represent different configurations of oppression.

This acknowledgement is not necessarily fatalistic, however, but can lead instead to 'a re-doubled commitment to the political possibilities of teaching'.[57] In law, this commitment becomes an enhanced consideration of the role of the office of law teacher within the activities of legal education and train-

47 Ibid., p 19.
48 Derrida, quoted in Bingham (2007), p 20.
49 See Bingham (2007), p 20.
50 Ibid., p 21.
51 Ibid., p 22.
52 See ibid., pp 25–7. See also, of course, Freire (2005).
53 Bingham (2007), p 27.
54 Ibid., p 27.
55 Ibid., pp 27–8.
56 Ibid., p 29.
57 Ibid., p 29.

ing, and the professional conduct for which students are being trained. If law teachers cannot avoid leaving a mark, if they necessarily inscribe something on the body of the emergent lawyerly subject, shaping their habits of intellectual and practical conduct—through the subjects selected, the contours of their framing, the attention paid to reading lists, the selection of core texts and seminar topics, or even through explicit attempts to inspire critical activism or dogmatic methodical adherence—then responsibility for the modes of conduct inculcated similarly cannot be avoided. It is the law teacher's execution of their office that enables and facilitates the effects of pedagogic power within legal education. Those who occupy this office, consciously or not, hold this obligation—the obligation, as noted at the outset, to be complicit in the reproduction of legal form. To be a legal educator thus comes with a privilege of agency, of the capacity to shape the processes of production. Indeed, this cannot be avoided—but it provides opportunities for a self-conscious and reflexive consideration of the way this shaping is done, of the imaginary forms and processes into which the minds of students are moulded and the resultant fashioning of their conduct, and the complicity of law teachers in the wider effects produced as graduates, having followed a certain course of training, take up lawyerly office or other social roles.

Conclusion

The office of law teacher is constituted under the authority of the academy, and includes duties to care both for the administration of lawful relations and the intellectual development of students within a tradition of law. Embedded in the increasingly marketised logics of higher education, its capacity for overhauling legal pedagogy is not unlimited, and itself has certain contingencies and contours associated with higher education policy, sectoral and institutional resources, and the differential qualities between specific academic organisations.[58] Accordingly, although it includes an obligation to be complicit in the reproduction of legal form, the role of the law teacher is not solely determinative in the formation of lawyerly subjects and law graduates, with multifarious other factors playing their part. But within this milieu, the administration of specific courses and materials, the conduct of lectures and seminars, and other functions of the law teacher remain core aspects of academic legal training. How one conducts the office of law teacher within this increasingly limited jurisdiction manifests in the numerous practical decisions made in administering a course of higher learning, to which attention should be paid in light of the obligation to be complicit: whether to resist or not particular intellectual or political positions, how to manage and respond to different influences on teaching practice and legal reform, which capacities or qualities to foreground

58 See, for example, Giddens (2021).

and background in course materials and assessments, whether to acknowledge or not the traditions of which a course, doctrine, or principle is a part, whether students encounter or not law's ideological qualities, the extent to which students are knowingly prepared for their future roles and potential social effects. Overseeing such activities within the context of legal education is no small thing, and cannot be done lightly.

Acknowledgements

I would like to thank Mark Antaki, Jacques Hartman, Sarah Hendry, and Timothy Peters for reading and constructively commenting upon an earlier draft of this chapter. Thank you, also, to Luca Siliquini-Cinelli and the peer reviewer for their inputs. Any errors in the work remain my own.

References

Daisy Abbott (2019) 'Game-Based Learning for Postgraduates: An Empirical Study of an Educational Game to Teach Research Skills' 4 *Higher Education Pedagogies* 80.

Mark Antaki (2012) 'The Turn to Imagination in Legal Theory: The Re-Enchantment of the World?' 23 *Law and Critique* 1.

Scott Beattie (2007) 'Voicing the Shadow—Rule-Playing and Roleplaying in *Wraith: The Oblivion*' 3 *Law, Culture and the Humanities* 477.

Carsten Bendixen and Jens Christian Jacobsen (2017) 'Nullifying Quality: The Marketisation of Higher Education' 23 *Quality in Higher Education* 20.

Charles W Bingham (2007) 'Derrida on Teaching: The Economy of Erasure' 27 *Studies in Philosophy and Education* 15.

John Canning (2019) 'The UK Teaching Excellence Framework (TEF) as an Illustration of Baudrillard's Hyperreality' 40 *Discourse: Studies in the Cultural Politics of Education* 319.

Galvano Della Volpe (1978) *Critique of Taste*, New Left Books.

Stanley Fish (1982) 'Working on the Chain Gang: Interpretation in the Law and in Literary Criticism' 9 *Critical Inquiry* 201.

Paulo Freire (2005) *Pedagogy of the Oppressed*, Continuum.

Adam Gearey (2020) 'The Parable of Bill Ayers: Comics, Allegory, and Critical Legal Thinking' in T Giddens (ed) *Critical Directions in Comics Studies*, University Press of Mississippi.

Thomas Giddens (2021) 'A Series of Unfortunate Events *or* The Common Law' 33 *Law and Literature* 23.

Peter Goodrich (1995) *Oedipus Lex: Psychoanalysis, History, Law*, University of California Press.

Peter Goodrich (1999) 'The Critic's Love of The Law: Intimate Observations on an Insular Jurisdiction' 10 *Law and Critique* 343.

Peter Goodrich (2012) 'The Theatre of Emblems: On the Optical Apparatus and the Investiture of Persons' 8 *Law, Culture and the Humanities* 47.

Peter Goodrich (2013) *Legal Emblems and the Art of Law: Obiter Depicta as the Vision of Governance*, Cambridge University Press.

Peter Goodrich (2021) *Advanced Introduction to Law and Literature*, Edward Elgar Publishing.

David Hayes (2015) 'Against Critical Thinking Pedagogy' 14 *Arts and Humanities in Higher Education* 318.
Pierre Legendre (2019) *God in the Mirror: A Study of the Institution of Images (Lessons III)*, Routledge.
Neil MacCormick (2005) *Rhetoric and the Rule of Law: A Theory of Legal Reasoning*, Oxford University Press.
Desmond Manderson (2000) *Songs without Music: Aesthetic Dimensions of Law and Justice*, University of California Press.
Daniel Matthews (2017) 'From Jurisdiction to Juriswriting: At the Expressive Limits of the Law' 13 *Law, Culture and the Humanities* 425.
Shaun McVeigh (2016) 'Jurisprudent of London: Arts of Association' 20 *Law Text Culture* 189.
Monica E Nilsson (2009) 'Creative Pedagogy of Play—The Work of Gunilla Lindqvist' 17 *Mind, Culture, and Activity* 14.
Penny Pether (1999) 'On Foreign Ground: Grand Narratives, Situated Specificities, and the Praxis of Critical Theory and Law' 10 *Law and Critique* 211.
Sara Ramshaw (2013) *Justice as Improvisation: The Law of the Extempore*, Routledge.
David Sugarman (1991) '"A Hatred of Disorder": Legal Science, Liberalism and Imperialism' in P Fitzpatrick (ed) *Dangerous Supplements: Resistance and Renewal in Jurisprudence*, Pluto.
Olaf Tans (2014) 'The Imaginary Foundation of Legal Systems: A Mimetic Perspective' 26 *Law and Literature* 127.
Douglas Thomas and John Seely Brown (2007) 'The Play of Imagination: Extending the Literary Mind' 2 *Games and Culture* 149.
Tsung Juang Wang and Kuo Hung Huang (2018) 'Pedagogy, Philosophy, and the Question of Creativity' 23 *Teaching in Higher Education* 261.
Irene Watson (2014) 'Re-Centring First Nations Knowledge and Places in a Terra Nullius Space' 10 *AlterNative: An International Journal of Indigenous Peoples* 508.
James Boyd White (1996) 'Imagining the Law' in A Sarat and TR Kearns (eds) *The Rhetoric of Law*, University of Michigan Press.

Chapter 2

Educating into Aware Subjects Instead of Unaware Objects

Peter Čuroš

Introduction

It was an image of a lawyer that started this chapter's idea. The same image that many law students express when thinking about their image of their future, an image of professionalism and success in appearances. It is not only a disciplinary influence on the individual's body. However, the more complicated concept of biopower shapes individuals' identities into the form needed to perform the most efficient outcome. The identity of lawyers is shaped by their position as subjects in a social structure. The law school is an instrument to deliver a lawyer as a product for this structure. Lawyers' position within the structure is to function as a hindrance towards any dramatic change, or more positively, they are guardians of the status quo.

So how are lawyers' appearances always very similar despite the various environments, personalities, and influences from which the law students come? Valid for such an explanation of lawyers' unified behaviour is the habitus theory of Pierre Bourdieu.[1] However, the question goes even further than Bourdieu's theory of habitus—as a hybrid theory of agency and structure. The question is beyond the observation of shared patterns of behaviour of lawyers. How do these behaviour patterns within a specific community mirroring the community's prevailing social and cultural conditions appear in the consciousness? How does the power grip the human body to make it a cog in a chain in a functional machine of modern society? How is it that despite the claimed uniqueness of every consciousness, we all become subjects sharing the same desire?

This chapter will present a structuralist method of explaining the subjectivity of lawyers. Instead of the dominant view of individuality as a subject moulding the world around itself, structuralism builds on the relational approach used in

1 Habitus is a subjective, but not individual, system of internalised structures, schemes of perception, conception, and action common to all members of the same group or class. See Bourdieu (1977), p 86. See Kryss MacLeod's chapter in *Biopolitics and Resistance in Legal Education*, 'The Role of Legal Educators in Digital Disruption of Hierarchies within Education and the Profession', on Bourdieu, habitus, and theory of cultural capital.

DOI: 10.4324/9781003175193-4

the linguistics of Ferdinand de Saussure. In this approach, a language is a system of interdependent terms. The value of each term results solely from the simultaneous presence of the others.[2] In the same way, the subject's value is determined not by its intrinsic qualities but by what it is not, by its relation to others.[3]

In addition to Saussure's structuralism, the Lacanian psychoanalytic approach appears. Structuralism in psychoanalysis presupposes that consciousness does not constitute language, but language constitutes consciousness. Therefore, the subject is the construction of the discourse that surrounds it. The structuralist view works in two ways. First, the subject is determined by the position within the structure where the subject occurs. Second, the subject is constituted by the language, which constitutes reality and how the subject perceives it.

According to structuralism, the signifiers and signifieds do not respond to external objects.[4] Moreover, the Lacanian approach would possibly follow the impossibility of any relation between signifier and signified.[5] Behind every signifier is nothing more than another signifier without any rigid connection to the signified. Any kind of connection between them is illusory. The consciousness is a subject to this system of signifiers. It is entirely constituted by the system of signifiers—the Other, as the Other is the only medium through which the subject can enunciate itself.

There is no other reality outside the system of signifiers.[6] Language precedes our understanding of the world: 'Words seem to be symbols for things because things are inconceivable outside the system of differences which constitute the language'.[7] In other words, the consciousness perceives the world only through language, and it is created and taught how to perceive the world around itself by language.

This approach has no space for an autonomous, free agency of consciousness. On the contrary, consciousness is wholly embedded in the system of signifiers. Such an approach is antihumanist.[8] As echoed in Nietzsche:

> We are not the consequence of a special intention, a will, a goal; we are not being used in an attempt to reach an 'ideal of humanity', or an 'ideal of happiness', or an 'ideal of morality' – it is absurd to want to divert our essence towards some goal. We have invented the concept 'goal': in reality, goals are absent.[9]

2 Saussure (1959), p 114.
3 Kang (2018), p 71.
4 Saussure (1959), p 68.
5 Lacan (1993), p 185.
6 Like in Derrida's 'there is nothing outside the text'.
7 Belsey (1980), p 46.
8 See Luca Siliquini-Cinelli's chapter in the *Biopolitics and Resistance in Legal Education* volume for more on post-humanism as a method.
9 Nietzsche (1997), p 36.

Unlike humanism, which builds on the human agency, moral responsibility for an individual's action, and the free subject, antihumanism refutes the possibility of the subject as a free agent. It emphasises the determinacy of the subject by its surroundings.

While other chapters suggest ways to avoid the influence of biopolitics and make legal education more humane and students less alienated, this chapter will negate such a thesis. It will focus on how biopolitics naturally uses subjectivity to language to maintain the stable status quo, and the subjects cannot avoid it. However, it does not root for social revolution against biopower. It aims only to point to the inevitable outcomes of biopolitics in the capitalist economy and the persistent incapacity of lawyers to contribute to fundamental change.This chapter explains how a unique consciousness with a free undetermined agency is a myth.

Therefore, suppose human action is determined by the structure of chains of signifiers governed by impersonal power relations aiming at the efficiency of life. Any attempt at a change would be predetermined by the language and the outcome mediated by these power relations. For this reason is proposed a way to recognise what governs our thoughts, speech, and actions. Such an approach would enable students and future lawyers to recognise their determination within the signification system and help them understand their subjectivity to the language they use and the ideology reflected in their utterances. Introducing the lessons on Foucault, Lacan, Zizek, or Althusser into the curriculum would be essential. In this way, it can still aspire to make lawyers' education more humane in the way of the Hegelian emancipatory project of subject attaining freedom. It does not mean it would create happier people. It may bring just the opposite result. Moreover, it would not bring more freedom to an individual's life. It would just explain its unfreedom.

The Origins of Biopower—From Violence through Normalcy to Efficacy

In the pre-modern society, the power operated from the top down. When criminal behaviour disrupted order and sovereign power was challenged, an execution symbolically re-established order. The audience was essential to the execution, as symbolic power needed to be seen.[10] However, society disapproved of such atrocious punishments at the beginning of the 18th century. The sovereign needed to detach themselves from the condemned. Foucault claimed that the shifts in punishment practice do not indicate greater humanity but rather a desire to punish more effectively.[11] The change from scaffolding a body to disciplining a soul was part of what Foucault called the 'power economy'.[12]

10 Foucault (1995), p 10.
11 Ibid., p 80.
12 Ibid., p 303.

The new power put the individual's behaviour under the microscope of the scientific method. The method that inspired the sentencing system can be observed in ideological state apparatuses, like schools and hospitals. The normalisation of the individual soul became essential.[13] Thanks to this shift, society grew more unified by categorising normal and abnormal. Focusing on the repentant soul instead of the condemned body, the concept of an individual possessing agency became popular. An individual was seen as having the capacity to make decisions and thus also be responsible for their actions.

By repeatedly analysing the individual, disciplinary power gives the individual identity that constitutes a self within society. One can say: 'I am a son, a husband, a father, a judge, and a golfer'. When claiming these identities, one also says, '*I have duties, and I obey rules as a son, as a husband, a father, a judge, and a golfer*'. Foucault claims that this shift towards identity classification, through the analysis of delinquents and establishment of limits between normalcy and abnormality, followed the creation of the subject.[14] While discipline creates the concept of normalcy, which leads to stable identities, simultaneously emerging with the discipline, biopower aims at the efficacy of life based on rationality and knowledge. How we live has become the object of interest. Therefore, it became subject to knowledge and effective control.[15]

While disciplinary power worked through the strict organisation of time and space by controlling which activity occurs at a particular time at a particular place, biopower organised what was considered a knowledge.[16] Biopower is a component of power that aims to make life more efficient—expanding, organising, and reproducing the life that is 'worthy'.[17] It manifests itself as the discipline of bodies when the body is seen as productivity and economic utility and as the regulation of bodies by which human capital is to be reproduced for efficient use in society. Besides focusing on the mechanics of life, births and mortality, the level of health, life expectancy, and longevity, biopower aims to govern life most productively.

13 Ibid., pp 20–1.

14 According to Deleuze, power both individualises and collectivises in the process of creating a subject; that is, it incorporates members of the system into a body and moulds the individuality of each member. Deleuze (1992), p 4. It is interesting to compare the notion of the subject among Descartes, Foucault, and Deleuze. When we label a person—a subject of law—we imagine an active standpoint—a consciousness that has agency and freedom. However, in the Foucauldian sense, a person is a body reduced to the identity of the subject and subjected to the set of rules under threat of sanction.

15 Foucault sees this power emerging in the topic of sexuality, that was scientific through the institution of confession. Foucault (1980), p 25.

16 For the 'tyranny of metrics' of knowledge and how knowledge works, see Bruce Baer Arnold's chapter, 'A Tyranny of Metrics in the Age of Legal Big Data'.

17 'Worthy' in relation to the concept of necropolitics. For a detailed explanation of necropolitics, see Foluke I Adebisi's chapter in the *Biopolitics and Resistance in Legal Education* volume.

The goal is a stable, disciplined, efficient, and regulated population that creates appropriate conditions for social stability. The beginning of the Enlightenment is associated with the rise of capitalism, to which Foucault gives main credit for the increase of biopower.[18] Biopower distributes the bodies within the system due to the system's needs. The power aims to preserve and multiply. Biopower became a powerful instrument for the maximisation of the potential of life. With the emergence of capitalism, the human body came to be seen as a working instrument. Capitalism is a perfect system that furthers efficacy and creates subjects. It does not require violence from the authority, as every individual is directly or indirectly forced to cooperate. The subject that does not fulfil his role in the structure is put aside. Such a political and economic system does not need enforcement and violence, as the individuals are prone to follow the anticipated goals—enjoy the race for economic success by multiplying the capital for their benefit.

Therefore, modern subjects desire the same way while being convinced they decide to think and desire so.[19] If the individuals' desire gets subjected to the same system of signification, the subjects of power relations are born. There is no need to be coerced or under surveillance to act preferably. With the wide acceptance of normalcy within the majority of how they should act, the subjects will happily follow the preferable behaviour voluntarily, as they desire in the same way as everybody else. By then, the subjects' behaviour appears to be an act of free will because the despot or ruler did not command it.

Willing accepting of the desire of the Other as own became an instrument of biopolitics, a *modus operandi* of the biopower that leads a life to rational calculation. The dispersed power leads the subject's desire towards maximising the potential of life together with the personal inclination of the individual. In other words, it creates a matrix that guides the subject to desire for a particular object (owning a big house, car, having enough money in the account to feel secure), which corresponds with economic and political growth and furthers the stability of the community, creating more capital for the creation of even more capital.

The desire that defines the subject is determined via ideology—a stable chain of signifiers that overcome the instability of the fragile illusory connection between signifier and signified. The subject is moved like a puppet towards behaviour and choices by the dispersed power of which it is mostly unaware. Moreover, it considers these choices as its own, and in the illusion of being a free agent of its own choice, it supports this choice/determination as the rational outcome based on what is considered knowledge at that time.[20]

18 Foucault (1998), p 140.

19 See Forzani's chapter in the *Biopolitics and Resistance in Legal Education* volume, where the structured desire is portrayed in the picture of 'learning society'.

20 See Puccio and Rodriguez's chapter (this volume) for the great explanation of knowledge: knowledge 'is not product of a passion for knowing that would help us see the world objectively, but a necessity to give it meaning: it does not aim to comprehend but allows to control' (p 121).

The crucial instruments for furthering this goal are ideology and personnel that will bar any ideological change of how subjects desire. Ideology is an instrument of making individuals think that what they do is their choice. Biopolitics drives ideology because of its efficiency: 'each mass ejected en route is practically provided with the ideology which suits the role it has to fulfil in class society'.[21]

What Does It Mean to Become a Subject?

When Foucault retrospectively announces his goal: to find out the way an individual becomes subjectivised, he notices that there are two popular usages of the word 'subject': subject to someone or something else by control and dependence, or subject as an attachment to one's own identity by a conscience or self-knowledge.[22] This contradiction is visible in the Enlightenment thought of a subject as an active, unique consciousness,[23] ruptured by historical subject and the structuralist view, which contested the individual consciousness' unique perception. While the 'Enlightenment' subject as a free autonomous agent is defined through phenomenal (self)experience, the structuralist view proposed that all human behaviour is regulated by the unconscious flow of chains of signification existing outside consciousness.[24] Such a change of view would move the human subjectivity into an object acted upon by the Other. Lacan sees a problem with the Cartesian subject in the vagueness of the term's usage: 'What do we call a subject? Quite precisely, what in the development of objectivation is outside the object?'[25] For Lacan, the notion of the subject is in the very uniqueness of subjectivity. However, where is this uniqueness located?

When looking for the difference between subject and object, in Hegel, subjectivity is a reason, and the reason is purposive activity. This reason is unmoved, and as well as moving, it is not moved by the Other but moves itself. So the reason actualises itself via self-movement. Otherwise, it would be an object actualised by the Other. The subject is not caused by something else, by definition. To move, it must negate itself, as it cannot be moved by the Other. So when moved by the Other, the subject ceases to be the subject.[26] Hegel prophets the emptiness of the subject, claiming that the modern subject is not a 'light' of the modern Enlightenment, but this 'night', this empty nothing.[27]

Lacan used the Hegelian outcome in the psychoanalytical method to explain the problem of the Cartesian subject via the notion of the split subject. Lacan's

21 Althusser (2014), p 251.
22 Foucault (1982), p 781.
23 The Cartesian subject 'I' in 'I think therefore I am'.
24 Lacan (1988a), p 188.
25 Lacan (1988b), p 194.
26 Hegel (2018), p 12.
27 Sinnerbrink (2016), p 1.

point is that the fundamental fantasy of the self-experience of ego is illusory, and the subject is split between unconscious and consciousness.[28] One should claim that what 'characterises human subjectivity properly is the gap that separates the two, namely, the fact that fantasy, at its most elementary, becomes inaccessible to the subject'.[29] Lacan criticises the Cartesian subject, whose 'I' corresponds to the level of the ego, a constructed self, taken to be the master of its thoughts and whose thoughts are believed to correspond to external reality. This Cartesian subject is characterised by what Lacan calls a 'false being'.

Lacan replaced the standard notion of the subject, which experiences itself directly via its inner states, with the dichotomous empty—non-phenomenal subject of the unconscious and phenomenal subject of ego constituted by the former. Ego is constituted as a representation of the unconscious subject, incapable of assuming its inner experience. Ego represents the subject—it is rather the object than the subject.[30]

Ego is not aware of the possessed knowledge that it is just a construct of the Other and the utterances and behaviour are nothing more than the construction of unconscious subject that is the result of the discourse of the Other. Lacan's point on the split subject, which is governed and conditioned by the signifiers of language, is quite gloomy: 'I am deprived of even my most intimate subjective experience, the way things really seem to me... the fundamental fantasy, that constitutes and guarantees the core of my being, since I can never consciously experience it and assume it'.[31] When ego asks: how might I be myself? Sadly, the answer is that it cannot because it is a construct of the subject that tries to enunciate the desire via the system of signifiers it received from the Other. Ego is a double reflection of otherness, a signifier representing the subject, while the unconscious subject mirrors the otherness. In other words, ego is always determined by its position in the structure and the part of otherness it reflects. The constitution of the ego works through the self-recognition of the ego as a free agent, where the ego is ignorant of the mechanism that produces itself. It depends on the unconscious subject that provides thinking—sliding on the chain of signifiers. Ego is an outcome of the signifying chains reflected in the unconscious subject when entering the Other.

Lacan claims that the Real is the unconscious subject. Unlike Freud, he did not imagine the unconscious like repressed wishes and desires.[32] Instead, he thought of the unconscious as the language itself that creates these wishes and desires. The unconscious is not about repression or trauma but the very essence of thought: 'The unconscious is neither primordial nor instinctual, and

28 Fink (2017), p 45.
29 Žižek (2012), p 96.
30 Lacan (1953), p 11.
31 Žižek (2006), p 53.
32 Freud (1922), p 291.

what it knows of the elemental is no more than the elements of the signifier'.[33] Unconscious 'we only grasp when it is explicated, in that part of it which is articulated by passing into words'.[34] Therefore, the unconscious subject passes through and reflects the Other that comes from the 'outside'. 'The unconscious is that of concrete discourse qua transindividual',[35] which implies that individuals are not prior to the social, but the reverse is true. The chain of signifiers conditions the unconscious: 'the unconscious (thinking) is structured like a language'.[36] The impression that the unconscious seems interior is an effect of the Imaginary order, which blocks the relationship between the subject and the Other and inverts the message of the Other. The unconscious is an articulation of the signifying chain; for the ego, it represents the 'unknown known'.[37]

The unconscious subject is initially negative, defined by the lack emerging at the entrance to Symbolic order. At that moment, the Real register was suppressed by entering the realm of language, where words and signs cover the Real and signify everything that does not resist signification: 'The symbol first manifests itself as the killing of the thing, and this death results in the endless perpetuation of the subject's desire'.[38] This lack became structured by the system of signifiers. The need existing in the Real was transformed into desire, which slides on the signifiers of Symbolic order.

In Lacanian theory, desire is a drive, castrated *jouissance*, conditioned by what the Other desires. The subject seeks completeness but cannot be satisfied by its agency alone. Hence, the desire points to objects which the ego assumes will comfort it. However, these are connected to signifiers only illusorily, which the subject recognises. The desire is insatiable because it only covers the lack that appeared after the subject's entrance into the Symbolic, and the signifiers of the Symbolic cannot fill the lack. The desire slides over constant slippage of signifiers. None of the acquired objects is the 'thing in itself' it seeks.

When looking for the uniqueness in the subjectivity, it must be an element in the subject that is not originated in the Other. Thus, subjectivity is the drive behind desire. Outside the drive, the split subject is always a subject to the Other—the language as the system of signifiers: 'It is the language that speaks and interpellates the individual as a speaker …, the subject is subjectified by the language it speaks'.[39] The process of subjectivisation is constant. Every time the subject 'thinks' or 'is', it is possible only through Symbolic order. It is a constant process, and the subject seems like a passive and determined receiver

33 Lacan (2006), p 434.
34 Lacan (1992), p 32.
35 Lacan (2006), p 214.
36 Lacan (1999), p 48.
37 Žižek (2006), p 52.
38 Lacan (2006), p 262.
39 Lecercle (2006), pp 164–5.

mirroring the otherness. What may seem like the very core of the unique individuality—the thought—may be seen simultaneously as the not unique otherness. Subjectivity is the 'discourse of the Other'.

The drive becomes subject via entering the otherness—the language, social norms, and everything signified by the system of signifiers. The impersonal relations of power that struggle for the effectivity of power connect the signifiers into chains creating what is considered to be knowledge that determines the subject into what will be presented as ideological fantasy.

Ideology

Two contemporary approaches to ideology are: first, announcing the end of the ideology that economic capitalism, political liberalism, and legal democratic constitutionalism is the best system that will not be overcome. The second which wants to reassert the pertinence of ideology as liberal capitalism does not sufficiently put its values under critique.[40] The former perceives ideology as some deformation of the reality, humanly devised mechanisms of the ideological constitution of the subject. Moreover, the ideologies were portrayed as unnatural, harmful, and misleading, trying to change the individual's view of the world. As if some primordial untouched subject was mystified by 'propaganda-like-ideology' that distorts reality for the benefit of some government. As if behind the ideology was a particular individual or state body governing it, and with the withering of this control over individuals, the ideology will disappear.

However, the ideology does not work like propaganda. The influence of state institutions on ideology is certain. However, it is only one of many influences. Not even totalitarian states at the peak of their existence could eliminate other sources of influence on the subject. If the state occupies the whole symbolical order, it is possible to talk about the state as the only language controller. On the other hand, we can see a competition of various sources that create the ideology that constitutes the subject. A state is one of them. In some periods, it becomes a more substantial source of ideology due to control and intervention into ideological apparatuses than in other periods.

The concept of ideology has a long history. It started with Tracy's 'ideology (as) the science of ideas and their origins', followed by Marx's theory of ideology as false consciousness, a mode of maintaining subservient classes obedient to a superior class, despite their actions not being in compliance with their best interest, to Althusser's process of interpellation.

For Marx, it is the being of the men, the material base, that constitutes their consciousness.[41] The falsity of the worker's consciousness lies for Marx in the

40 Glynos (2001), p 192.
41 Marx (1859), p 5.

misrecognition of the oppression and inequality stemming from the dictate of the ruling class, supported by the bourgeois superstructure. The superstructure that is structured to maintain the status quo of the base works to maintain the consciousness of subjects to be 'false', not to undermine the status quo. Althusser moved Marx's thesis further. He considered both relations of production and the political and legal order as the determinants of consciousness.[42] Ideology is not determined exclusively by the superstructure or base. His concept overcomes the dichotomy. He also uses the Lacanian linguistic approach to reflect the Symbolic—the whole system of signification.[43] The reception of the system of signifiers and following the constitution of the subject happens through the process of interpellation, a process of acquiring the ideas from the outside world but perceiving them as their own.[44] Symbolic order determines the split subject. The subject is defined by the relation to its place in the overall social, symbolic structure, including the family structure.[45]

Ideology resides in the Symbolic—the big Other. It is dispersed in the signifying chains. However, it is observable in the subject's Imaginary that constitutes the ego and its utterances. Specifically, it is visible in the ego's quest for the answer to What does the big Other want from me? The formation of ideology is mediated by 'the material existence of representations of the Symbolic order'.[46] Ideology is a chain of signifiers stemming from the Symbolic in an imaginary relationship to the real conditions of existence.[47] If it complies with the subject's real conditions, in other words, if the question '*Che vuoi?*' is answered by enough options to fill the desire, then the subject should feel at 'home in the world', non-alienated.

Ideology presents itself fully in the Imaginary register, fuelled by the signifying chains of the Symbolic, and operates on its own materiality of the utterances of ego. Just like Symbolic is the system of representations, ideology reflects this Symbolic in the Imaginary, in the subject's fantasy about itself. Ideology is the guess of the answer to the question: 'What do you want from me, big Other?' It is a blind guess to that unanswered and unanswerable question: *Che vuoi?* The subject guesses and constantly asks: Is that what you want? Ideology is a system of unconscious mass representations.[48] It is the unknown known—'we do not know, that we already know' as the ego presents itself in a particular way, based on the signification stemming from the unconscious subjects, that is, the discourse of the Other. They are the disavowed beliefs and suppositions we are unaware of adhering to ourselves but which determine our

42 Althusser (1996), p 143.
43 Kang (2018), p 69.
44 Althusser (2014), p 191.
45 Kang (2018), p 72.
46 Althusser (1971), p 172.
47 Ibid., p 162.
48 Althusser (1971), p 231.

acts and feelings.[49] The split subject does not know it performs the determined pattern, even though it might be aware of its existence.[50]

The ideology can be seen in the utterances of the subject. It is noticeable how the subjects, despite the non-existent anchor of signifiers, use the signifiers in the same way. In order to maintain the same meaning behind signifiers, ideology overcomes the meaning of the metaphor. Metaphor gives the subject an odd feeling of insecurity in the meaning. Lacan celebrates metaphor as it represents a place for the liberation of the subject.[51] Where Lacan sees the moment of celebration, it is the task of ideology not to let the subject get stuck in the chain.

The chain of signification is a metonymic line of signifiers the subject misrecognises as standing for particular signifieds or material objects. Every once in a while, there is a metaphor within the metonymic chain. This metaphor manifests the object cause of desire, as desire shows itself as incomplete. This provides a moment of insecurity for the subject. In the metaphor, at least for a short moment, the subject can see the essence of the signifier, its non-relatedness to any signified. This metaphor is called a quilting point (*point de capiton*). The movement of the signifier is a movement of desire. The quilting point or anchoring point is the part of the chain where the signifier is not attached to any signified but can be replaced with other signifiers. However, for the efficacy of the social existence of the subject, this *point de capiton*—the metaphor must be knotted to a particular meaning.[52] The desire sliding on the chain of signifiers must follow despite the unstable moments of metaphor. 'The result of the paternal metaphor is to tie a specific meaning to particular words without regard to an absolute referent'.[53] The quilting point is where the signifier seems to be attached to the meaning,[54] although this connection is just illusory. It is a task for ideological fantasy to establish quilting points.

Subjects are always within ideology because they understand and construct reality via language. They see what they have learned to see. Subjects accept this ideology in Althusser's theory via the system of interpellation. A way of incepting ideological concepts to subjects' minds through a series of practices within social institutions produces obedient citizens unaware of the fallenness in the ideology. These practices might be represented either by coercion and violence, in the form of repressive state apparatuses (RSA), such as police, the court system, and prisons, or ideological state apparatuses (ISA), such as schools and cultural institutions, and media. While the RSAs seem weak nowadays,

49 Žižek (2006), p 52.
50 For example, in thinking about own behaviour and asking why 'I' behave in the same way as the others.
51 Lacan (2006), p 423.
52 Lacan (1993), p 268.
53 Fink (1999).
54 Žižek (2008), p 112.

they still exist and come to work in a moment when the ISAs fail. The repression appears to restore the order only when there is a rupture within obedience to power stemming from an ideological conviction. Both RSAs and ISAs have the same goal—maintaining the stability of the social order by protecting the status quo.

According to Althusser, the primary purpose of ideology is in 'constituting' concrete individuals as subjects: as he puts it,

> the individual is interpellated as a (free) subject in order that he shall submit freely to the commandments of the subject, i.e., in order that he shall (freely) accept his subjection, i.e., in order that he shall make the gestures and actions of his subjection 'all by himself'.[55]

Subjects do not perceive this influence as artificial or secondary but natural, authentic, or apparent.[56] Because subjects believe these ideas to be self-evident, they act upon them and reproduce the status quo. With every word, utterance, or performative act, the subject confirms itself to be a subject to ideology.[57] The fact they do not recognise this action as ideological shows that 'one of the effects of ideology is the practical denegation of the ideological character of ideology by ideology: ideology never says, 'I am ideological'.[58]

Ideology should not be reduced to the false consciousness as it was before because it is the whole consciousness—how subjects interact, communicate, and understand each other. Ideology is inescapable and essential for everyday life. Even when we think we are outside the ideology, we are very much in it.

The Role of the Lawyer

Lawyers' role in every structure of political and economic systems is to maintain the current social institutions. Currently, the legal professionals in the Western world of political liberalism and economic capitalism are experts in protecting the principles of the rule of law 'as a restriction on arbitrary power by the state, that no man, including officials, is above the law'.[59] The word *currently* appears on purpose, as lawyers are constantly protecting the system of rules in which they are embedded.

The role of lawyers as guardians of the law is also visible in cultural texts. One example is William Shakespeare's *Henry VI*, where in one scene, Jack Cade says, 'I thank you, good people: there shall be no money; all shall eat

55 Althusser (1971), p 182.
56 Ibid., p 172.
57 Ibid., p 174.
58 Ibid., p 175.
59 Dicey (1915), p 110.

and drink on my score; and I will apparel them all in one livery, that they may agree like brothers and worship me their lord'. Following this, Dick the Butcher declares, '*The first thing we do, let's kill all the lawyers*'. It is not a call for justice, nor is it driven by revenge. Instead, the coup must destroy the current system's pillars, the guardians of the law, to accomplish its goals.[60] Jack Cade is announcing the political regime change, and Dick, perhaps unconsciously but very well, knows what needs to be done to make it possible.

Lawyers play an essential role in society by maintaining the institutions. This means reproducing the system of rules and protecting stability and the status quo. Therefore, lawyers are not expected to be catalysers of social change. Law as a social order has one incredible quality—it maintains the meaning. It creates stable connections, even though illusory, between signifier and signified. Lawyers are trained, unaware of this illusion of the connection, not to allow any considerable doubt about the stable meaning of legal terms to enter the discourse. It is evident that lawyers are not expected to doubt the legal pillars of the democratic community, such as private ownership, legitimacy of the state power, or fundamental rights. Of course, lawyers often appeal against the particular law, question rights in individual cases, or criticise the current administration. However, lawyers seldom attack the concept of law, rights, or legitimacy in general. They do not claim there is no law, rights, or legitimacy. The reason is simple. Lawyers perceive signifiers and signifieds—symbols and concepts—as connected. They are convinced and prove it in everyday practice that they can say what the signifiers written in codes signify.

Moreover, they not only think they know, but they can also convince others about this connection. The language of the law does not allow floating signifiers that do not stand for any signifieds. Lawyers must perceive the meanings as stable. Otherwise, social stability fades away.

Such an attitude is acquired in how lawyers adopt the language of law in legal education and practice that helps the power to use their bodies to reproduce itself and maintain the status quo and stability.[61] Lawyers are therefore always led by the Master discourse: the 'Lawyer is the one able to abstract himself from immediate experience and relate directly to the knowledge of written law to translate the formless real into the structured reality of legal language'.[62] It seems that 'to be good at "doing law", one has to have serious blind spots and stunningly selective sense of curiosity'.[63]

The legitimacy of lawyers is rooted in rationality and knowledge embedded in their education and appearances that guarantee knowledge via the scientific

60 See W Shakespeare, *King Henry VI*, pt. II, Act IV, scene 2, line 72.

61 See Kate Galloway's chapter on the role of the lawyers in promoting the interests of the growing middle class and the national economy with the rise of capitalism (in the *Biopolitics and Resistance in Legal Education* volume).

62 Cercel (2014).

63 Schlag (1998), p 140. See also Omar Madhloom's chapter in this volume.

method. This shift towards the scientification of law started in the 18th century with the rise of the school of exegesis that treated law in very positivistic terms. The way the law has been practised is perceived as knowledge. The legal service has the scientific method of application, and therefore the lawyers are supposed to follow this method. The method is formalistic because the form distinguishes law from other normative systems. Therefore, the form of the law, formal chains of signifiers, must be followed. The form of law is what the lawyers learn to follow and distinguish from other normative orders.

Legal education aims to teach lawyers to adopt the position of the pure instrument of the big Other's Will: 'it is not my responsibility, I am not the one who is effectively doing it, I am merely an instrument'.[64] Moreover, legal service generally acts purely on the client's command or fulfils the will of the law. The position of lawyers conditions them to be a tool, either in the hands of clients or the law. In other words, lawyers are told what the big Other expects. They know the answer to the question: *Che vuoi?* Answering the question of what the law means and requires: 'I conceive of myself as exculpated for what I am doing: I am able to inflict pain on others with the full awareness that I am not responsible for it, that I merely fulfil the Other's Will'.[65]

'They do not know they are doing it', unconsciously, by necessity. Their position within the structure of society, the network of social expectations and rules regulating their profession, but also norms such as grammatical rules, conditions them to follow norms and master them to function in society. Their identity as lawyers stemming from their position determines them as subjects. It is 'unknown known', or they are unaware that they already know.[66] Law is an ideal instrument for maintaining the order of the status quo. Moreover, law schools are the best way to create the personnel that will take care of the proper application of this instrument. With disciplinary power and biopower at school and in legal practice, lawyers are unaware of fulfilling this duty by determination and not by choice. The formal law is their Symbolic order that structures their reality. Lawyers are the subjects *par excellence.*

Conclusion

The most humane thing education can do is to allow subjects to be aware of the subjectification.[67] As the subject always speaks via ego, and the ego reflects the otherness, the most we can do about subjectivity is recognise how subjected to the language we are. Without awareness of this subjectification,

64 Žižek (2006), p 105.

65 Ibid., p 105.

66 Kang (2018), p 72.

67 See Cassandra Sharp's chapter in *Biopolitics and Resistance in Legal Education*: 'Conversation as Pedagogy: The Use of Popular Stories in the Identity Projects of Law Students', that also discusses biopolitical awareness.

the subject acts based on foreign influence, therefore being an object. There is no way to escape the Other. In conclusion, understanding is the furthest the subject can get. There would be no benefit in fighting the system by several individuals in monopoly capitalism, as it would only lead to their loss and punishment. I do not see any possibility for breaking the wheel of the prevailing capitalist and liberal ideology or any kind of ideology. Individuals are always determined in acting, thinking, and even resisting.

Lawyers are inherently the guardians of the status quo, servants of the ideology—of stable meanings. Their education is very ideological, as it teaches the very essence of the Symbolic order—the rules for action. The lawyers, trained executioners of law, play the inherent role in the maintenance of the Symbolic.

They speak the language of law regardless of how repressive and authoritative it is. As Raz puts it, the rule of law's virtue is like the virtue of a sharp knife; it enables the law to fulfil its function, whatever the function might be.[68] Lawyers are conditioned to sharpen that knife.

References

Louis Althusser (1971) *Lenin and Philosophy and the Other Essays*, New Left Books.

Louis Althusser (1996) *Writings on Psychoanalysis: Freud and Lacan*, Columbia University Press.

Louis Althusser (2014) *On the Reproduction of Capitalism: Ideology and Ideological State Apparatuses*.

Catherine Belsey (1980) *Critical Practice*, Methuen.

Pierre Bourdieu (1977) *Outline of a Theory of Practice*, Cambridge University Press.

CosminCercel (2014) *Discourse of the Master, Discourse of the University: An Archaeology of Modern Legal Education in Romania*. Presented at the workshop entitled 'Legal Education In Europe.Challenges and Prospects' organized by the International Institute For the Sociology of Law, 1–2 May 2014, Oñati, Spain.

Gilles Deleuze (1992) 'Postscript on the Societies of Control' 59 *October* 3.

Albert Venn Dicey (1915) *Introduction to the Study of the Law of the Constitution*, Macmillan.

Bruce Fink (1999) *A Clinical Introduction to Lacanian Psychoanalysis: Theory and Technique*, Harvard University Press.

Bruce Fink (2017) *The Lacanian Subject: Between Language and Jouissance*, Princeton University Press.

Michel Foucault (1980) *The History of Sexuality: 1 : An Introduction*, Vintage.

Michel Foucault (1982) 'The Subject and Power' 8 *Critical Inquiry* 777.

Michel Foucault (1995) *Discipline and Punish: The Birth of the Prison*, Vintage.

Michel Foucault (1998) *The Will to Knowledge: History of Sexuality, Vol 1*, Penguin Books.

Sigmund Freud (1922) 'The Unconscious' 56 *The Journal of Nervous and Mental Disease* 291.

Jason Glynos (2001) 'The Grip of Ideology: A Lacanian Approach to the Theory of Ideology' 6 *Journal of Political Ideologies* 191.

GWF Hegel (2018) *Hegel: The Phenomenology of Spirit*, Oxford University Press.

68 Raz (1979), p 223.

KD Kang (2018) 'Language and Ideology: Althusser's Theory of Ideology' 70 *Language Sciences* 68.
Jacques Lacan (1953) 'Some Reflections on the Ego' 34 *International Journal of Psycho-Analysis* 11.
Jacques Lacan (1988a) *The Seminar of Jacques Lacan: The Ego in Freud's Theory and the Technique of Psychoanalysis, 1954–55, Book 2*, WW Norton.
Jacques Lacan (1988b) *Freud's Papers on Technique, 1953–1954*, WW Norton.
Jacques Lacan (1992) *The Seminar of Jacques Lacan. Book 7, The Ethics of Psychoanalysis: 1959–1960*, Routledge.
Jacques Lacan, & Jacques-Alain Miller (Ed.). (1993). *The seminar of Jacques Lacan, Book 3: The psychoses 1955–1956.* (R. Grigg, Trans.). W. W. Norton & Company.
Jacques Lacan (1999) *Seminar XX, On Feminine Sexuality: The Limits of Love and Knowledge, 1972–1973*, WW Norton.
Jacques Lacan (2006) *Ecrits: The First Complete Edition in English*, WW Norton.
Jean-Jacques Lecercle (2006) *A Marxist Philosophy of Language*, Brill.
Karl Marx (1859) 'Preface to a Contribution to the Critique of Political Economy' 2 *The Marx-Engels Reader* 3.
Friedrich Nietzsche (1997) *Twilight of the Idols*, Hackett.
Joseph Raz (1979) *The Authority of Law*, Oxford University Press.
Ferdinand de Saussure (1959) *Course in General Linguistics*, Philosophical Library.
Pierre Schlag (1998) *The Enchantment of Reason*, Duke University Press.
Robert Sinnerbrink (2016) 'The Hegelian "Night of the World": Žižek on Subjectivity, Negativity, and Universality' 2 *International Journal of Žižek Studies* 1.
Slavoj Žižek (2006) *How to Read Lacan*, Granta.
Slavoj Žižek (2008) *The Sublime Object of Ideology*, Verso.
Slavoj Žižek (2012) *Organs without Bodies: On Deleuze and Consequences*, Routledge.

Chapter 3

Biopolitics and the Solicitors Qualifying Examination

Omar Madhloom

Introduction

The Solicitors Regulatory Authority (SRA), which is the statutory body responsible for regulating solicitors in England and Wales, has modified the route to qualifying. This new pathway, referred to as the Solicitors Qualifying Examination (SQE), was introduced on 1 September 2021. This chapter examines the pedagogy of the SQE, namely SQE stage 1 (Functioning Legal Knowledge),[1] through the lens of biopolitics.

In general terms, biopolitics is a form of politics which prioritises the production and management of life.[2] It alludes to the fact that life can be manipulated and owned. In social theory, biopolitics is used to describe the institutions, bodies of knowledge, and administrative techniques used for 'measuring, regulating and controlling people and behaviour in order to ensure that states get the most out of their human resources'.[3] Applying biopolitics and Freire's theory of education, this chapter argues that the SQE's pedagogy promotes lawyer amorality and risks limiting solicitors to the conventional lawyering model whereby lawyers act as zealous agents for their clients in exchange for a fee. A supplemental egalitarian pedagogical model[4] is proposed which enables future solicitors to challenge the dominant hegemony and address societal inequalities.

Foucault is credited with introducing the concept of biopolitics in his book *The History of Sexuality*,[5] where he argues that the economic and political regulation of society, in addition to 'discipline' of the body, plays a key role in power relations within the modern nation state. Foucault applies analytical and

1 Functioning legal knowledge requires candidates to 'apply their knowledge of the law to demonstrate the competences required to the level of a newly qualified solicitor', see Solicitors Regulation Authority, 'Assessment Specification for SQE Stage 1 pilot', www.sra.org.uk/sra/policy/solicitors-qualifying-examination/pilot/sqe-assessment-specification/

2 Saltman (2018), p 50.

3 Danaher, Schirato and Webb (2008), p 80.

4 Giroux (2010).

5 Foucault (1990).

DOI: 10.4324/9781003175193-5

historical evaluation of the various mechanisms of power and suggests that, since antiquity, new mechanisms of 'biopower'[6] have emerged in Western societies.[7] This chapter examines biopolitics as a pedagogic power in solicitor education and training and seeks to address two key questions in relation to the SQE: whether the SQE empowers aspiring solicitors with the necessary conceptual tools to engage in critical reflection, namely examining issues of power and control[8] of juridic institutions; and whether the SQE's pedagogy promotes justice. For present purposes, justice is conceived as the 'confluence of law and morality'.[9] Justice is a valuable conception in education because it enhances analysis of the law through moral considerations,[10] while moral education is useful for evaluating the law according to a set of principles.[11]

There are three reasons for incorporating moral discourse into legal education and training. First, lawyers are expected not to merely act competently but also morally.[12] Second, the law curriculum ought to include moral education in order to equip future lawyers with the skills required for 'good moral counsel'.[13] Third, moral education, which includes legal ethics, facilitates the evaluation of not just law, policies, and principles, but also values and the professional codes of conduct.[14] As members of the legal profession, solicitors owe a moral duty to the common good which requires them to be more than 'passive servants of the state, of capital, of firm, the client, or even the immediate general public'.[15] Lawyers in a liberal state are a vital institution for 'changing rules and norms, for resisting the use of legalized violence on individuals, and for encouraging trust in the system'.[16] Solicitors, and lawyers in general, also have an obligation to advance the common good of the community.[17] To do so requires their education and training to equip them with 'deep learning and critical thinking'.[18] The following section outlines the pedagogy of the SQE.

The SQE

In April 2017, the SRA announced that it would introduce an independent assessment, the SQE, to ensure that 'all solicitors meet consistent, high

6 Foucault uses the terms 'biopower' and 'biopolitics' interchangeably.
7 Foucault (1990), p 135.
8 Brookfield (2009), p 298.
9 Schehr (2009), p 13.
10 Madhloom (2019).
11 See Hart (2012); Fuller (1969); Finnis (1980); Dworkin (1986).
12 Swygert (1989), p 807.
13 Ibid., p 814.
14 Janoff (1991); Madhloom (2022).
15 Freidson (2001), p 217.
16 Boon (2001), p 156.
17 Demack (2003), p 27.
18 Morrison (2018).

standards at the point of entry to the profession'.[19] Prior to the SQE, aspiring solicitors were required to successfully complete two stages of training: the academic and the vocational. Two options were available in relation to completing the academic stage: one route for law graduates, and one for non-law graduates. The former involved completing a qualifying law degree, while the latter required successful completion of the Common Professional Examination (CPE) or Graduate Diploma in Law (GDL). The academic stage was followed by the vocational part which consisted of the Legal Practice Course (LPC) and a two-year period of recognised training (training contract) carried out in a law firm or in-house legal department in an organisation. Replacing these stages,[20] the SQE will have four elements which candidates must complete to qualify as solicitors:

- Have passed SQE stages 1 and 2 to demonstrate their knowledge and skills
- Have been awarded a degree or an equivalent qualification, or have gained *equivalent experience*
- Have completed at least two years of qualifying legal work experience
- Be of satisfactory character and suitability[21]

SQE stage 1 will eventually replace the academic stage, while SQE stage 2 (Practical Legal Skills), which tests skills such as client interviewing, drafting, and advocacy, replaces the LPC. Candidates will still be required to complete a period of pre-qualification legal work experience known as Qualifying Work Experience (QWE). QWE can be gained within one role or placement or within several (provided it is in no more than four organisations).[22]

SQE 1 is a computer-based 'single best answer' multiple choice questions (MCQ) test.[23] Each single 'best answer' question is followed by five possible answers.[24] However, an examination of the SRA's sample MCQs reveals that most questions do in fact have a single correct answer. Ethics, namely professional conduct, are examined pervasively. Candidates are required to apply legal principles and rules, at the level required of a newly qualified solicitor, to realistic client-based and ethical problems and situations. The focus, therefore, is on the conventional lawyering model and not on equipping candidates to

19 Solicitors Regulation Authority, 'SRA announces new solicitors assessment to guarantee high standards', www.sra.org.uk/sra/news/press/2017/sqe-ensure-high-consistent-standards/
20 Students will have until 31 December 2032 to qualify under the previous route.
21 Solicitors Regulation Authority, 'SRA announces new solicitors assessment to guarantee high standards', www.sra.org.uk/sra/news/press/2017/sqe-ensure-high-consistent-standards/
22 Solicitors Regulation Authority, 'Qualifying work experience for employers', www.sra.org.uk/trainees/qualifying-work-experience/qualifying-work-experience-employers/
23 Solicitors Regulation Authority, 'Assessment information', www.sra.org.uk/sra/policy/solicitors-qualifying-examination/sqe1-functioning-legal-knowledge-assessment-specification/
24 For critique of the SRA's MCQ assessment method, see Mason (2018); Morrison (2018).

engage in law reform and challenge power relations. This is evidenced by the fact that in relation to the application and analysis of legal authorities, the SRA has confirmed that '[c]andidates will be tested on the law as it stands at the date of the assessment', nor will they be assessed on the development of the law.[25]

SQE 1's pedagogy suffers from three fundamental limitations which can hinder the development of future solicitors in relation to law reform. First, apart from limited circumstances where candidates need to demonstrate knowledge and application of primary sources of law, aspiring solicitors are not be assessed on legal skills such as recalling specific case names, or citing statutory or regulatory authorities.[26] Second, candidates are not examined on the development of the law.[27] They will be only tested on settled law and not what the law *ought* to be. By limiting functioning legal knowledge to the application of settled law, namely legal principles and rules, the SQE adopts a positivist approach to legal training. This not only gives future solicitors the false impression that law is autonomous but fails to provide them with conceptual tools, such as moral and political theories, to analyse and critique the law.[28] The SQE focuses on 'What is the law?', which is a question of fact, and ignores normative questions such as 'What is good law?'. To avoid this 'thin' notion of legal education, it is important that the SQE, and legal education generally, 'moves beyond the merely descriptive towards the explanatory and analytical'.[29] Third, excluded from the definition of functioning legal knowledge are secondary sources of law. This is a significant omission for a number of reasons. Secondary sources reflect the prevailing opinion on how courts interpret primary sources of law. They are authoritative because courts have been known to rely on secondary sources.[30] Secondary sources such as academic peer-reviewed articles highlight the potential implications of the law and suggest avenues for reform. By omitting analysis of primary and secondary sources, and focusing on a narrow version of the doctrinal approach to legal education, SQE 1 fails to equip candidates to engage in critique of the law and analysing its development. It also risks producing solicitors who are unable to critically reflect on juridic institutions. The positivist and primary sources-centric pedagogy of the SQE gives rise to the risk that future solicitors, namely

25 Solicitors Regulation Authority, 'Assessment information', www.sra.org.uk/sra/policy/solicitors-qualifying-examination/sqe1-functioning-legal-knowledge-assessment-specification/

26 Ibid.

27 Ibid.

28 O'Donovan (2014), p 140.

29 Guth and Harvey (2018), p 353.

30 *Gapper v Avon & Somerset Constabulary* [1998] EWCA Civ 1146 (2 July 1998) citing Professor John Smith; *R v Woollin* [1998] UKHL 28; [1999] AC 82 citing John Smith, Glanville Williams, and Andrew Ashworth; *R v A* [2001] UKHL 25 citing Neil Kibble at [29]; *R v Golds* [2016] UKSC 61 citing Professor Mackay at [48].
R v Ali Syed [2018] EWCA Crim 2809 citing David Ormerod at [89].

those who have not completed a law degree, may be ill-equipped to critique the law. The biopolitics of the SQE will be examined in the next section.

Biopolitics and the SQE

Lemke suggests three essential dimensions of biopolitics which are useful in analysing the biopolitics of the SQE. First, biopolitics entails 'a systematic knowledge of "life" and of "living beings"'.[31] The SQE's uniform curriculum and a standardised form of testing can devalue aspects of an individual. Such methods of assessment focus on types of experience that can be empirically measured and quantified.[32] In other words, the SQE focuses on characteristics of the individual which can be controlled. Thus, what constitutes a 'good' solicitor is not one who can apply reasoned legal and political analysis or relate claims to truth to historical power struggles,[33] but rather one who successfully completes the SQE and complies with the SRA's vision of the conventional lawyering model. Second, Lemke argues, 'the regime of truth cannot be separated from that of power, the question arises of how strategies of power mobilize knowledge of life and how processes of power generate and disseminate forms of knowledge'.[34] The 'truth' promoted by the SRA is that there is one right answer to a legal question and that law is an autonomous and neutral concept free from political and moral evaluation.[35] Lemke's third dimension of biopolitics involves:

> [F]orms of subjectivation, that is, the manner in which subjects are brought to work on themselves, guided by scientific, medical, moral, religious, and other authorities and on the basis of socially accepted arrangements of bodies and sexes.[36]

Subjectivation is used to assess how the regulation of life processes affect individual and collective actors and gives rise to new forms of identity.[37] By focusing on the application of a standardised body of knowledge to resolve a client's legal issues, the SQE's pedagogy subjects future solicitors to the ideology of corporate culture which measures success according to billable hours calculated in six-minute increments.[38] Therefore, the SQE is a process of knowledge production and a form of subjectivation.

31 Lemke (2011), p 119.
32 Saltman (2018), p 51.
33 Ibid., p 51.
34 Lemke (2011), p 119.
35 Mason (2018).
36 Lemke (2011), p 120.
37 Ibid., p 119.
38 Waller-Davies (undated).

Unlike law schools where teachers interact with students, challenge, and motivate them using different pedagogies and teaching methods such as the flipped classroom approach,[39] SQE 1 entails using MCQs to assess candidates' knowledge of existing rules and principles. In this sense, the SQE is analogous to Freire's 'banking' concept of education in which he equates teachers with bank-clerks 'depositing'[40] information into students rather than drawing out knowledge from individual students. Thus, minimal responsibility lies with the student other than passively acquiring knowledge through deposits of information. The banking model echoes the SQE's doctrinal approach which focuses on 'superficial' legal knowledge and learning.[41] The banking concept of education regards students as an 'adaptable, manageable being' with limited 'critical consciousness', and thus, unlikely to play a significant role in transforming their world.[42] Through the banking model, the SRA risks turning future solicitors into 'automatons'[43] who are educated to accept their role in society without challenging or questioning it. The harm produced by the banking concept of education is the production of 'passive'[44] individuals who are adapted and obedient to their world.

Freire's critique of the banking model which turns students into passive, obedient automatons is reminiscent of Llewellyn's description of the first year of law school at Columbia University, where the aim is to encourage the student into 'thinking like a lawyer'.[45] However, according to Huxley-Binns, thinking like a lawyer involves understanding complex data quickly and having the ability to 'distil principle to apply to a novel problem'.[46] For present purposes, 'thinking like a lawyer' incorporates Huxley-Binn's definition as well as the ability to judge unjust laws according to set of values such as those contained in the Universal Declaration of Human Rights (UDHR).

Returning to Llewellyn's analysis of legal education, he warns students that '[t]he hardest job of the first year is to lop off your common sense, to knock your ethics into temporary anaesthesia'.[47] Llewellyn continues his critique:

> You are to acquire ability to think precisely, to analyze coldly, to work within a body of materials that is given, to see, and see only, and manipulate, the machinery of the law. It is not easy to thus to turn human beings into lawyers. Neither is it safe. For a mere legal machine is a social danger.[48]

39 McGowan (2012); Butler and Madhloom (2016).
40 Freire (1993), p 45.
41 Morrison (2018), p 468.
42 Freire (1993), p 46.
43 Ibid., p 47.
44 Ibid., p 49.
45 Llewellyn (2008), p 107.
46 Huxley-Binns (2011), p 309.
47 Llewellyn (2008), p 107.
48 Ibid., p 107.

Law as a machine is synonymous with the idea that the law is a form of social control.[49] By focusing on the application of rules, students may be led to believe that 'thinking like a lawyer' entails subduing their compassion, idealism, and pursuit of truth and justice.[50] This process of temporary moral numbing can be found in today's law schools in England and Wales. Moral detachment can be attributed to the prevalence of the positivist approach in legal education,[51] has also contributed to law and morality being kept separate.[52] However, it is acknowledged that law schools, unlike the SQE, incorporate other approaches into legal education such as socio-legal studies,[53] critical legal studies,[54] and clinical legal education.[55] The SQE's doctrinal approach to legal learning may be detrimental to aspiring solicitors because 'without an understanding of the nature of law, or the conflicting views on the nature of law, the social context and normative nature of the law cannot be grasped'.[56]

The SQE's pedagogy, as a process of knowledge production, consists of three elements. First, it adopts Freire's 'banking' model, where aspiring solicitors are not required to engage in critical analysis and reflection on the law and its social implications but simply to memorise information. Second, it embraces a positivist approach to legal education which is devoid of any moral or political considerations. Third, 'thinking like a lawyer' within this positivist approach teaches students to ignore their emotional responses to the case facts, to ignore the consequences of their clients' actions, and instead to focus on achieving their clients' objectives. Accordingly, the SRA's implicit message, through the SQE, is that solicitors should respond to legal, political, and social problems, not as human beings but as 'legal machines' devoid of moral considerations. In other words, as legal practitioners, they should ignore not only the moral and political dimensions of the case and focus instead on the 'legal' aspects, but also the moral implications of their actions.[57] The next section considers the potential impact of the SQE on legal ethics.

Biopolitics, Governmentality, and Legal Ethics

Foucault describes two models of political power: the pre-modern model of juridical power and the modern normalising power.[58] In the former, the

49 White (1996), p 33.
50 Wizner (1998), p 587.
51 Cownie (2003), p 159.
52 Nicolson and Webb (1999), p 66.
53 Hunter and Cowan (2012).
54 Thomson (1987); Anderson (2004).
55 Madhloom and MacFaul (2022).
56 Huxley-Binns (2011), p 301.
57 Wizner (1998), p 588.
58 Foucault (1990), pp 135–9.

sovereign had the rights to take the life of those who threatened the order of the state, or to demand subjects surrender their lives in defence of the state. The normalising model, however, is concerned with power over life. In other words, the administration of bodies rather than seizure or negation. Normalising power, according to Foucault, evolved in two 'basic forms': discipline and biopower.[59] The former operates on individuals found in institutions such as prisons, schools, and hospitals through the use of surveillance and control aimed at the efficient distribution and use of power in order to increase their 'usefulness and docility'. Biopower, on the other hand, is aimed at the administration and production of life. While legal education can promote values committed to human rights and social justice,[60] the vocationalisation of solicitors' training, through the SQE, risks separating solicitors from the social implications of their actions, the consequences of their client's actions on third parties, and the role of the state. By falsely placing law as a neutral and technical concept, devoid of any moral or political considerations, the SQE risks being viewed by future solicitors as being valuable only for its market application.

According to Foucault, the new techniques of government that developed in the modern period were distinct from the traditional forms of juridical governance such as those found in the work of classical legal positivists such as Hobbes,[61] Bentham,[62] and Austin.[63] According to these theorists, in every society sovereign power rests with a definitive person or group and that all laws, which are recognised as such by courts, are to be regarded as the commands of the sovereign. For example, Austin insists on sanctions as a mark of law and a necessary element of the sovereign's command. His view regarding the role of sanctions has been objected to on the ground that it distorts the true character and function of law in a society.[64] Sanctions do not explain why law is changed, and exaggerate fear.[65] This thesis omits the possibility that law may be accepted by the community as binding, irrespective of the threat of sanctions.[66] His conception of the sovereign's authority suggests that 'obedience is rendered by one person to another because the former recognises that the latter has a right to obedience'.[67] This hierarchal subordination between citizens and the sovereign can be contrasted with the willingness to follow a rule or law because it is considered as appropriate to govern conduct between members of 'peer groups'.[68]

59 Ibid., p 139.
60 McKeown and Ashford (2018); Antonopoulos and Madhloom (2021).
61 Hobbes (2017).
62 Bentham (1996).
63 Austin (1995).
64 Freeman (2016), p 211.
65 Ibid., p 211.
66 Goodhart (1947), p 283.
67 Freeman (2016), p 211.
68 In social theory, the term 'peer group' denotes a social group whose members have interests, social class, and age in common.

The argument that the application or threat of sanctions plays a tangential feature of law is found in the experiments of Milgram regarding the effect of authority on participants and their willingness to obey instructions even in the absence of sanctions. It is worth noting that in some instances participants also carried instructions which conflicted with their moral beliefs.[69] The phenomena of obedience and the training for persons to obey are known to the social sciences, from Foucault's[70] work on governmentality and the construction of disciplinary societies to Jacques' representation of the worker as an expert in obedience.[71] Foucault defines governmentality as a specific form of power which 'has as its target population, as its principal form of knowledge political economy, and as its essential technical means apparatuses of security'.[72] Governmentality is associated with the modern liberal state and capitalist economy 'as the means by which population and individuals are managed so that individuals can become the self-governing subjects of the liberal legal order'.[73] Governmentality, for present purposes, focuses on the SRA's practices that shape the subject (the solicitor). Cunha et al. outline four reasons as to why participants in Milgram's experiments conformed to authority.[74] First, most individuals are conditioned to obey authority figures such as parents, teachers, and police officers. Second, participants were conditioned through gradual demands. Third, the source of information was limited, and the situation was novel. In other words, individuals may increase their obedience to the source of information, the authority figure. Fourth, participants were not assigned any responsibility and, therefore, they were not accountable for their actions. The fourth reason, with its focus on the absence of responsibility and acting on instructions from an external source, is similar to the 'amorality theory' which has become the prevalent and 'standard conception' of legal ethics.[75] According to this view, a lawyer's actions must be guided by two principles:

- The principle of *partisanship*, according to which lawyers must zealously defend the interests of their client, everything that is not technically illegal in order to further these interests, even when the result clearly thwarts the aims of substantive law
- The principle of *neutrality*, according to which lawyers must represent their client regardless of their own view on the justice of the cause, and are consequently absolved of any moral responsibility for acts done in the name of the client[76]

69 Milgram (1974).
70 Foucault (1979).
71 Jacques (1996).
72 Foucault (2000), p 220.
73 Veitch, Christodoulidis and Goldoni (2018), p 278.
74 Cunha, Rego and Clegg (2010), p 293.
75 Arjona (2013), p 52.
76 Ibid., p 52.

While partisanship requires lawyers to zealously pursue their clients' ends, the principle of neutrality shields lawyers from considering issues relating to morality or justice[77] in achieving their clients' ends. Nicolson and Webb argue that the neutrality principle involves two related notions:[78] the first is based on the theory that the lawyer is not responsible for the consequences of their client's decisions:

> It is the client, not the advocate, who decides whether—and how—to enforce his legal rights in a democratic society. If such conduct causes unfairness to others, it is the client, not the advocate, who should be criticised.[79]

This consequentialist and passive approach ignores duties to third parties and the responsibilities that lawyers have towards society. The second idea holds that lawyers are entitled to zealously pursue their clients' objectives irrespective of how immoral or unjust they are or the means necessary to achieve them may be.[80] Thus, while neutral partisanship is predicated on the assumption that moral neutrality promotes a 'better legal defence for the citizen and the client',[81] it ignores the impact a client's actions can have on third parties and the environment. For Holmes and Rice, who reject the consequentialist approach in favour a contextual method to legal ethics, lawyers need to 'recognize the global effect of their conduct, and to take responsibility for it'.[82]

The potential adverse effects of neutral partisanship on society is illustrated by the recent controversy surrounding the appointment of David Perry QC, a British lawyer, who agreed to prosecute, on behalf of the Hong Kong government, nine pro-democracy activists.[83] Perry eventually stepped down following condemnation from the legal profession and the United Kingdom government. For example, he was described as a 'mercenary' by the Foreign Secretary, Dominic Raab.[84] This notion of a lawyer zealously pursuing their client's ends was recently brought to the attention of solicitors by the SRA's report, *Balancing Duties in Litigation*.[85] While maintaining that solicitors must advance their clients' cases, the report warned that they are not 'hired guns' whose sole duty is to their clients.[86] The 'hired gun' metaphor bears a striking similarity to Raab

77 The term 'justice', for present purposes, refers to both procedural and substantive justice.
78 Nicolson and Webb (1999), p 163.
79 Pannick (1992), p 168.
80 Nicolson and Webb (1999), p 163.
81 Arjona (2013), p 53.
82 Holmes and Rice (2011), p 121.
83 Slingo (2021a).
84 Slingo (2021b).
85 Solicitors Regulation Authority, 'Balancing Duties in Litigation', www.sra.org.uk/risk/risk-resources/balancing-duties-litigation/
86 Ibid.

describing Perry as a 'mercenary'. The 'hired gun' or standard conception can be contrasted with Luban's conception of the lawyer as a moral activist, 'in which the lawyer who disagrees with the morality or justice of a client's ends does not simply terminate the relationship, but tries to influence the client for the better'.[87] 'Moral activism', as conceived by Luban, involves law reform.[88] Luban's model requires the lawyer knowing what justice is in order to engage in law reform. However, justice has no universally accepted definition. The different conceptions of justice include Aristotle's theory of justice as virtue, legal justice (substantive and procedural), and distributive justice. It is worth noting that the SQE does not assess knowledge of legal theory or jurisprudence. The relevance of this omission becomes apparent when we consider that an unjust law is a valid rule which conflicts with the values by which it is judged.[89] One possible source of values for evaluating positive law is the UDHR.

Adopting Lasswell and McDougal's anti-positivist model for legal education, Antonopoulos and Madhloom suggest sourcing universal values from the UDHR due to its commitment to dignity.[90] Human dignity is the nexus between human rights-based legal pedagogy and the 'supreme value of democracy'.[91] Democracy includes:

> [T]he dignity and worth of the individual; hence a democratic society is a commonwealth of mutual deference – a commonwealth where there is full opportunity to mature talent into socially creative skill, free from discrimination on grounds of religion, culture, or class. It is a society in which such specific values as power, respect, and knowledge are widely shared and are not concentrated in the hands of a single group, class, or institution—the state—among the many institutions of society.[92]

Regarding 'respect', they distinguish between 'positive respect' and 'negative respect'.[93] The former is defined as 'equality of access to opportunity for maturing latent capacity into socially valued expression'.[94] While the latter involves promoting a person's right to self-determination and the absence of interference with their choice.[95] However, the 'hired gun' or the standard conception requires the lawyer to zealously pursue their client's instructions regardless of the consequences on third parties. In other words, the standard conception

87 Luban (1988), p 160.
88 Ibid., p 174.
89 Lloyd (1991), p 131.
90 Antonopoulos and Madhloom (2021), p 116.
91 Lasswell and McDougal (1943), p 212.
92 Ibid., p 212.
93 Ibid., p 223.
94 Ibid., p 223.
95 Ibid., p 223.

treats law as autonomous, free from moral and political considerations, and, thus, can lead to situations where the client's instructions undermine a person's or a group's right to self-determination.

The negative impact of the standard conception on third parties' right to self-determination is seen in *Day and another (Appellants) v The Government of the Cayman Islands and another (Respondents)* JCPC 2020/0033, where the Judicial Committee of the Privy Council was asked to decide whether the Bill of Rights in the Constitution of the Cayman Islands provides a right for same-sex couples to access the institution of marriage. The controversy surrounding this case concerned the appointment of Dinah Rose QC, a barrister practising in England and Wales, to represent the Cayman government. This appointment raises two important questions in relation to legal ethics: the role of a lawyer, in this case a barrister, in the administration of justice, and the value of the 'cab rank rule'. In relation to the first issue, the lawyer for the Cayman government has two options available to them. First, to represent the client according to the standard conception. This approach involves a commitment to Hart's concept of legal positivism, namely the 'separation of law and morals'.[96] Hart, according to Fuller, was recommending that 'law must be strictly severed from morality'.[97] Second, to adopt Luban's lawyering model requires the lawyer to take on the role of a moral activist and engage in law reform. The SQE, through SQE 1 and/or QWE, can play a role in promoting Luban's approach by educating aspiring solicitors to engage with democratic values such as citizens' right to self-determination.

One of the factors attributed to the continued dominance of the standard conception is legal positivism.[98] In general terms, legal positivists focus on authority when determining legal validity, only consider laws imposed by valid human machinery, and are only parenthetically concerned with justice. Within the realm of legal positivism, '[t]he legislator is conceived as an independent authority, and the judge as a dependent authority, whereas the lawyer has no authority at all'.[99] Contributing to the lawyer's lack of authority and the success of the standard conception is the separability thesis,[100] which claims the existence of a conceptual separation between law and morality. Thus, for a legal positivist, determining normative validity involves deductive reasoning once the official authority has been identified. Unlike natural law theory, however, legal positivism maintains that moral reasoning does not have a role in this process.[101]

96 Hart (1957).

97 Fuller (1957), p 656.

98 Arjona (2013) contends that two other factors, in addition to legal positivism, concern the continued success of the standard conception: the adversarial system and the agency model of the lawyer–client relationship.

99 Ibid., p 56.

100 The other two theses are the pedigree thesis and the discretion thesis. See Wacks (2005), p 69.

101 Arjona (2013), p 57.

The impact of the separation thesis on legal education, and legal practice, is that ethical dilemmas are viewed as a tension between legal and non-legal considerations.[102] In the context of the SQE, there is a risk that future solicitors are being educated to view ethical dilemmas as a clash between their duty to zealously pursue their clients' ends against moral considerations that might negatively impact on securing the desired outcomes for their clients. Viewing ethical dilemmas through a positivist lens reinforces the standard conception and limits the lawyer's role to that of an agent who acts on the principal's instructions. A consequence of acting as the client's agent is that the lawyer adopts a passive role involving the provision of options and acting on the client's preferred choice. The separation thesis in legal education does not promote the alternative lawyer–client model whereby the lawyer explains the different legal options to their client and the potential ethical and legal consequences of those options on both the client and third parties. Thus, the SQE's positivist approach educates solicitors to be zealous amoral lawyers, committed to achieving their clients' objectives irrespective of the consequences these might have on third parties.[103] A supplemental egalitarian model is proposed to address the limitations of the SQE.

An Egalitarian Approach to Solicitor Education and Training

The SQE is criticised by Macleod for its

> focus on traditional knowledge acquisition and the static approach to skills where an increasingly dynamic approach is required, leaving a vacuum for where this should be positioned.[104]

Given the above and the limitations highlighted in this chapter, an alternative approach is to reject the SQE's 'banking' model in favour of educating students to become what Freire terms 'more fully human',[105] by which he meant a 'conscious being'[106] and a subject. The Freirean individual, understood as a subject, is one who can 'relate to the world' and can change it.[107] An individual's subjectivity, therefore, informs how they perceive the world and assess right from wrong. To do so requires individuals to be integrated in their world as opposed

102 Ibid., p 57.

103 The SRA's Standards and Regulations contain prevision in relation to duties to the court, third parties, and the wider public interest. However, these are either limited in scope or lacking detail.

104 Kryss Macleod, in the *Biopolitics and Resistance in Legal Education* volume.

105 Freire (1993), p 47. Emphasis in original.

106 Ibid., p 48.

107 Ibid., p 5.

to merely being passive actors.[108] This highlights that lawyer amorality is insufficient for the purposes of training solicitors to challenge and change the world around them. To achieve 'integration' requires 'the capacity to adapt oneself to reality *plus* the critical capacity to make choices to transform that reality'.[109] This would involve incorporating a critical and egalitarian model to learning and development.[110] In this model, learners are no longer 'docile listeners' but 'critical co-investigators in dialogue with the teacher'.[111] Critical reflection and exposure to problems relating to students and their world obliges them to respond to these problems.[112] For reflection to be considered critical it must engage in:

> [U]uncovering, and challenging, the power dynamics that frame practice and uncovering and challenging hegemonic assumptions (those assumptions we embrace as being in our best interests when in fact they are working against us).[113]

Unlike the SQE's 'banking' model, critical reflection creates an awareness of how dominant ideologies such as capitalism and patriarchy shape beliefs and norms that justify and maintain economic and political inequality. Thus, if future solicitors, especially those who have not successfully completed a law degree, are to become critically reflective practitioners, it is essential that the SQE, and legal education in general, incorporates normative ethics[114] and critical theory.[115]

Conclusion

This chapter has examined the pedagogy of the SQE through the prisms of biopolitics and Freire's 'banking' model, in order to address two main questions: whether the SQE empowers future solicitors with the necessary conceptual tools to examine and critique issues of power and control in relation to juridic institutions, and whether the SQE's pedagogic approach promotes justice. It would appear that while the biopolitics of the SQE will produce solicitors who are able to identify settled law, there is a risk that this form of

108 Ibid., p 4.
109 Ibid., p 4.
110 Ibid., p 53.
111 Ibid., p 54.
112 Ibid., p 54.
113 Brookfield (2009), p 293.
114 Madhloom (2019).
115 Neither the SQE not the current qualification regime requires future solicitors to have grounding in normative ethics and critical theory. See Bar Standards Board and the Solicitors Regulation Authority (2014).

education and training will also create solicitors who are amoral lawyers not equipped to address normative questions such as 'What *should* the law be?'

Ching, writing in this volume, argues that in addition to caring about the law and justice, law students and junior lawyers are also concerned about 'resilience, about equality and about the planetary future'.[116] The inclusion of an egalitarian pedagogical model which is underpinned by normative ethics and critical theory can address some of the limitations of SQE 1, namely in relation to producing solicitors who are able to shape the world around them and respond to social, political, and environmental problems.

References

Jerry L Anderson (2004) 'Law School Enters the Matrix: Teaching Critical Legal Studies' 54 *Journal of Legal Education* 201.

Irene Antonopoulos and Omar Madhloom (2021) 'Promoting International Human Rights Values Through Reflective Practice in Clinical Legal Education: A Perspective from England and Wales' in E Sengupta and P Blessinger (eds) *International Perspectives in Social Justice Programs at the Institutional Level*, Emerald.

Cèsar Arjona (2013) 'Morality Explained: Analysing the Reasons that Explain the Standard Conception of Legal Ethics' 4 *Ramon Llull Journal of Applied Ethics* 51.

John Austin (1995) *The Province of Jurisprudence Determined*, WE Rumble (ed), Cambridge University Press.

Bar Standards Board and the Solicitors Regulation Authority (2014) *Academic Stage Handbook*, www.sra.org.uk/globalassets/documents/students/academic-stage/academic-stage-handbook.pdf?version=4a1ac3.

Jeremy Bentham (1996) *An Introduction to the Principles of Morals and Legislation*, JH Burns and HLA Hart (eds), Oxford University Press.

Andrew Boon (2001) 'Cause Lawyers in a Cold Climate' in A Sarat and S Scheingold (eds) *Cause Lawyering and the State in a Global Era*, Oxford University Press.

Stephen Brookfield (2009) 'The Concept of Critical Reflection: Promises and Contradictions' 12 *European Journal of Social Work* 293.

Nicolette Butler and Omar Madhloom (2016) 'Teaching Company Law to Business Students: An Effective Framework' 50 *The Law Teacher* 160.

Fiona Cownie (2003) 'Alternative Values in Legal Education' 6 *Legal Ethics* 159.

Miguel Pina e Cunha, Arménio Rego and Stewart Clegg (2010) 'Obedience and Evil: From Milgram and Kampuchea to Normal Organizations' 97 *Journal of Business Ethics* 291.

Geoff Danaher, Tony Schirato and Jen Webb (2000) *Understanding Foucault*, Sage.

Alan Demack (AO) (2003) 'Public Interest or Common Good of the Community: Bringing Order to a Dog's Breakfast' 6 *Legal Ethics* 23.

Ronald Dworkin (1986) *Law's Empire*, Harvard University Press.

John Finnis (1980) *Natural Law and Natural Rights*, Oxford University Press.

Michel Foucault (1979) *Discipline and Punish*, Penguin.

116 Jane Ching, this volume.

Michel Foucault (1990) *The History of Sexuality: An Introduction, Volume 1, Trans Robert Hurley*, Vintage.
Michel Foucault (2000) 'Governmentality' in JD Faubion (ed) *Essential Works of Foucault 1954–1984: Volume III Power*, New Press.
Michael Freeman (2016) *Lloyd's Introduction to Jurisprudence*, 9th Edition, Sweet & Maxwell.
Eliot Freidson (2001) *Professionalism; The Third Logic*, Polity Press.
Paulo Freire (1993) *Pedagogy of the Oppressed*, Penguin Classics.
Lon L Fuller (1957) 'Positivism and Fidelity to Law – A Reply to Professor Hart' 71 *Harvard Law Review* 630.
Lon L Fuller (1969) *The Morality of Law*, Yale University Press.
Henry Giroux (2010) *Youth in a Suspect Society: Democracy or Disposability?*, Palgrave.
Arthur L Goodhart (1947) 'An Apology for Jurisprudence' in P Sayre (ed) *Interpretations of Modern Legal Philosophies*, Oxford University Press.
Jessica Guth and Tamara Hervey (2018) 'Threats to Internationalised Legal Education in the Twenty-first Century UK' 52 *The Law Teacher* 350.
Herbert L A Hart (1957) 'Positivism and the Separation of Law and Morals' 71 *Harvard Law Review* 593.
Herbert L A Hart (2012) *The Concept of Law*, 3rd Edition, Oxford University Press.
Thomas Hobbes (2017) *Leviathan Christopher Brooke* (ed), Penguin Classics.
Vivien Holmes and Simon Rice (2011) 'Our Common Future: The Imperative for Contextual Ethics in a Connected World' in R Mortensen, F Bartlett, and K Tranter (eds) *Alternative Perspectives on Lawyers and Legal Ethics*, Routledge.
Caroline Hunter and David Cowan (eds) (2012) *Integrating Socio-Legal Studies into the Law Curriculum*, Palgrave.
Rebecca Huxley-Binns (2011) 'What is the "Q" for?' 45 *The Law Teacher* 294.
Roy Jacques (1996) *Manufacturing the Employee: Management Knowledge from the 19th to 21st Centuries*, Sage.
Sandra Janoff (1991) 'The Influence of Legal Education on Moral Reasoning' *Minnesota Law Review* 76: 193.
Karl N Llewellyn (2008) *The Bramble Bush*, Oxford University Press.
Harold D Lasswell and Myres S McDougal (1943) 'Legal Education and Public Policy: Professional Training in The Public Interest' 52 *The Yale Law Journal* 203.
Thomas Lemke (2011) *Biopolitics: An Advanced Introduction*, NYU Press.
Dennis Lloyd (1991) *The Idea of the Law*, Penguin.
David Luban (1988) *Lawyers and Justice: An Ethical Study*, Princeton University Press.
Omar Madhloom (2019) 'A Normative Approach to Developing Reflective Practitioners: Kant and Clinical Legal Education' 53 *The Law Teacher* 416.
Omar Madhloom (2022) 'A Kantian Moral Cosmopolitan Approach to Teaching Professional Legal Ethics' 23 *German Law Journal* 1139.
Luke Mason (2018) 'SQEezing the Jurisprudence Out of the SRA's Super Exam: The SQE's Bleak Legal Realism and the Rejection of Law's Multimodal Truth' 52 *The Law Teacher* 409.
David McGowan (2012) 'Making Law School More Useful' (San Diego Legal Studies Working Paper No 13-102) http://papers.ssrn.com/sol3/papers.cfm?abstract_id=2181793.
Paul McKeown and Chris Ashford (eds) (2018) *Social Justice and Legal Education*, Cambridge Scholars Publishing.
Stanley Milgram (1974) *Obedience to Authority: An Experimental View*, Harper & Row.

Doug Morrison (2018) 'The SQE and Creativity: A Race to the Bottom?' 52 *The Law Teacher* 467.

Donald Nicolson and Julian Webb (1999) *Professional Legal Ethics: Critical Interrogations*, Oxford University Press.

Darren O'Donovan (2014) 'Legal Education in the Era of Globalisation: What Makes for Market Failure?' in W van Caenegem and M Hiscock (eds) *The Internationalisation of Legal Education: The Future Practice of Law*, Edward Elgar.

David Pannick (1992) *Advocates*, Oxford University Press.

Kenneth J Saltman (2018) *The Politics of Education: A Critical Introduction*, 2nd Edition, Routledge.

Robert Schehr (2009) '"The Lords Speaks Through Me": Moving Beyond Conventional Law School Pedagogy and the Reasons for Doing So' 14 *International Journal of Clinical Legal Education* 9.

Jemma Slingo (2021a) 'Lawyers Condemn QC Prosecuting Pro-democracy Activists', *The Law Society Gazette*, 14 January 2021, www.lawgazette.co.uk/news/lawyers-condemn-qc-prosecuting-pro-democracy-activists-/5107032.article.

Jemma Slingo (2021b) 'QC Instructed for Hong Kong Prosecution Steps Down', *The Law Society Gazette*, 21 January 2021, www.lawgazette.co.uk/news/qc-instructed-for-hong-kong-prosecution-steps-down/5107109.article.

Michael I Swygert (1989) 'Striving to Make Great Lawyers- Citizenship and Moral Responsibility: A Jurisprudence for Law Teaching' 30 *Boston College Law Review* 803.

Alan Thomson (1987) 'Critical Legal Education in Britain' 14 *Journal of Law and Society* 183.

Scott Veitch, Emilios Christodoulidis and Marco Goldoni (2018) *Jurisprudence Themes and Concepts*, 3rd edition, Routledge.

Raymond Wacks (2005) *Understanding Jurisprudence: An Introduction to Legal Theory*, Oxford University Press.

Rebecca Waller-Davies (2014) 'What are Billable Hours and What Do Students Need to Know About Them?', *The Lawyer*, www.thelawyer.com/what-are-billable-hours/.

James Boyd White (1996) 'Imagining the Law' in A Sarat and TR Kearns (eds) *The Rhetoric of Law*, University of Michigan Press.

Stephen Wizner (1998) 'Is Learning to Think like A Lawyer Enough?' 17 *Yale Law & Policy Review* 583.

Chapter 4

The Biopolitical Perspective in Women's Legal Education

Luana Mathias Souto

Introduction

Women are underrepresented in senior positions in legal systems throughout the world, and this starts in legal education based on a patriarchal project to continue the status quo. To demonstrate the plausibility of this statement, this chapter uses the case of Brazilian as an example.

In 2019, a case study was undertaken by the Law School of the University of São Paulo (FDUSP) which identified that there is a *hidden curriculum* from which professors and female students are affected in their process of teaching–learning[1].

This study concluded that the professor's gender, as well as the students' gender, interfere in how they teach; how they learn; how they interact with each other; how they build their authority as a professor, and; how they physically occupy the classroom when they are learning and when they are teaching. It also revealed historical and symbolical aspects inside FDUSP that demark that this is a male-dominant space.

Besides this, in Brazil women are also underrepresented in the judiciary system, as well as in the legislative and executive branches of government, which reflects on the decisions about women's rights, as well as their effectiveness, in the country.

All these facts in the reality of Brazil express what Giorgio Agamben describes in his theories about bare life and *homo sacer*. Using Michel Foucault's theory of biopolitics, Giorgio Agamben explain that in modern societies biological life has more value than a person's rights.

Updating his theory, mostly following Thomas Lemke's reviews of Giorgio Agamben's work, we aim here to demonstrate that women's exclusion in the Brazilian legal system started with a *hidden curriculum* and developed into underrepresentation in the judiciary system, and exists as a biopolitical project with the purpose to capture female lives as bare lives from the beginning of their legal education throughout the legal system, where judiciary decisions about women bodies and rights are ineffective.

1 Neder et al. (2019)

DOI: 10.4324/9781003175193-6

Biopolitics: The Biological Body in the Sovereignty Power

Thomas Lemke in *Biopolitics: An Advanced Introduction* describes biopolitics as a buzzword because 'it is used today in many different disciplines and discourses'.[2] The term was first designed by Rudolf Kjellén and it is formed by two words: 'bio-', which means life in Greek, and 'politics'.

In its relationship, these two words provide several combinations, and 'each definition of biopolitics must sharpen its analytical and critical profile against the blind spots and weak points of competing suggestions'.[3]

According to Thomas Lemke, Rudolf Kjellén was the first to employ the term 'biopolitics' in a context in which he understands the state as a living being. His theory emerged from 'a general historical and theoretical constellation'[4] that followed the *Philosophers of Life*—Arthur Schopenhauer, Friedrich Nietzsche, and Henri Bergson—who re-evaluated life 'and its adoption as a fundamental category and normative criterion of the healthy, the good, and the true … [and] was opposed to the "dead" … the concept of life served as a standard by which processes perceived as adversarial to life, such as processes of ratio-nalization, civilization, mechanization, and technologization, were subjected to critical examination'.[5]

From this idea, Rudolf Kjellén is designated as an organicist because he comprehends the state as an organism, from where all aspects of life (individual and social) come, and 'only a politics that orients itself toward biological laws and takes them as a guideline can count as legitimate and commensurate with the reality'.[6]

However, 'in the 1960s and early 1970s, the meaning of biopolitics assumed another form. It was not so much focused on the biological foundations of politics but rather disclosed life processes as a new object of political reflection and action'.[7] The population growth and the ecological transformations meant that 'the concept of biopolitics acquired a new meaning. It came to stand for the development of a new field of politics and political action directed at the preservation of the natural environment of humanity'.[8]

As we can see, biopolitics designates more than one idea. In this study, however, the definition of biopolitics that will be adopted is that of Michel Foucault[9], who, according to Thomas Lemke, 'broke with the naturalist and

2 Lemke (2011), p 1.
3 Ibid., pp 2–3.
4 Ibid., p 9.
5 Ibid., p 9.
6 Ibid., p 10.
7 Ibid., p 23.
8 Ibid., p 23.
9 Foucault (2008).

politicist interpretations'[10] previously discussed and 'describes biopolitics as an explicit rupture with the attempt to trace political processes and structures back to biological determinants … biopolitics denotes a specific modern form exercising power'.[11]

For Michel Foucault, biopolitics is, in fact, a reformulation of what sovereignty means. Because 'for millennia man remained what he was for Aristotle: a living animal with the additional capacity for a political existence; modern man is an animal whose politics calls his existence as a living being into question'.[12]

From this perspective, Michel Foucault understands that human life, in its biological aspect, became a mechanism of state power. A life that can be managed by the state as a weapon to increase its powers of sovereignty, powers that were no longer measured by territorial extent but by how many biological lives the sovereign has at its disposal to decide who lives and who dies[13]. 'It is as managers of life and survival, of bodies and the race, that so many regimes have been able to wage so many wars, causing so many men to be killed'.[14]

Foucault's analysis also considers what the word 'life' means for the Greeks. They had not one single term to express life, but two: *zoē* and *bios*.[15] *Zoē* is the biological life, the reproductive life 'common to all living beings (animals, men, or gods)';[16] *bios* is 'a qualified life',[17] a political and social life that only those who are included in the *polis* can live. In Ancient Greece, women, slaves, and children were excluded from the *polis*. All these concepts are also found in Giorgio Agamben's *Homo Sacer: Sovereign Power and Bare Life* where the author aims to unveil 'this hidden point of intersection between the juridical–institutional and the biopolitical models of power'.[18] In *Homo Sacer*, Agamben also intends to finish Michel Foucault's works, something that Roberto Esposito agrees with when he affirms:

> Foucault never fully answered the question; or better, that he always hesitated to choose from among different responses, responses that were for their part tributaries of different modes of approaching the question that he had raised. The opposite interpretations of biopolitics, the one radically negative and the other absolutely euphoric that today lead the field, do

10 Ibid., p 33.
11 Ibid., p 33.
12 Foucault (1976), p 127.
13 Foucault (2008a).
14 Foucault (1976), p 137.
15 Agamben (1998), p 9.
16 Ibid., p 9.
17 Ibid., p 9.
18 Ibid., p 11.

> nothing except make absolute (by spreading them apart) the two hermeneutic options between which Foucault never decided.[19]

Agamben, in his opinion, completes Foucault's work when he introduces the concept of *homo sacer* and permits that 'the paradox of biopolitics is that to the same degree to which the security and the amelioration of life became an issue for political authorities, life is threatened by hitherto unimaginable technical and political means of destruction'[20].

Homo sacer is a Latin expression that means the sacred man, 'who may be killed and yet not sacrificed'.[21] It's 'an obscure figure of archaic Roman law, in which human life is included in the juridical order [*ordinamento*] solely in the form of its exclusion (that is, of its capacity to be killed)'.[22] This related to a person who committed a horrible crime that could only be punished by God, and because of this they had to be banned from the community.

This notion that someone could be excluded from political life without being killed is updated for the modern world by Agamben when he introduces the possibility of human life as a biopolitical organism. When human beings could be allocated in spaces without the respect of their rights, where we can find 'the bare life of the citizen, the new biopolitical body of humanity'.[23]

This analysis of exclusion indicated in Agamben's theory is the main modern political problem when the exception becomes the rule[24] and the 'own bare life … maintains himself in relation to that bare life in an inclusive exclusion'[25] creating 'a zone of irreducible indistinction … [where] the state of exception actually constituted, in its very separateness, the hidden foundation on which the entire political system rested'.[26]

In this new political order based on sovereignty standards 'the problem of sovereignty was reduced to the question of *who* within the political order was invested with certain powers, and the very threshold of the political order itself was never called into question'.[27] Using Schmitt's definition of sovereignty that 'sovereign is who decides on the state of exception',[28] Agamben concludes, in the end, that *some* lives will be chosen by the sovereign power to be excluded from the *polis*, excluded from the political life (*bios*), maintained on their own bare life, living as *homo sacer*.

19 Esposito (2008), p 8.
20 Lemke (2011), p 39.
21 Agamben (1998), p 12.
22 Ibid., p 12.
23 Ibid., p 13.
24 Benjamin (2012), p 13.
25 Ibid., p 12.
26 Ibid., p 12.
27 Ibid., p 14.
28 Schmitt (2005), p 5.

Agamben establishes this analysis from his observation of the intensification of biopolitics in the Nazi concentration camps where the bare life of the prisoners was exposed without limits. The same situation occurred with the prisoners of Guantanamo. Places where under the rule of law human lives were put in a zone of indetermination between *zoē* and *bios*; *nomos* and anomie; law and fact.

After these terrible episodes of human history, Agamben affirms that 'in our age, all citizens can be said, in a specific but extremely real sense, to appear virtually as *homines sacri*',[29] because 'inside every human life … Bare life is no longer confined to a particular place or a definite category. It now dwells in the biological body of every living being'.[30]

It can be difficult to understand all these concepts, mostly because some aspects of our political, social, economic, and historical life are veiled from us. Hidden from us by the sovereign with this precise purpose: unable us to understand how inside the rule of law citizens can be considerate *homines sacri*.

Aware of this, this study aims to understand more clearly what Michel Foucault and Giorgio Agamben created, using women's lives as models, from which we will be able to conclude that they are *homines sacri*. They are *homines sacri* because they are excluded from the *polis*; because their biological bodies have more value than their human rights; and because when the decisions about their lives are made, they are not consulted.

The Sacredness of Women's Lives

According to Lemke, Agamben did not 'investigate to what extent the production of "bare life" is also a patriarchal project, one that codifies gender difference through a strict and dichotomous apportionment of nature and politics'.[31] Nor, it should be noted, did Lemke.

But we have to consider that Lemke was partially right in this. Indeed, Agamben did not investigate the relationship between bare life and patriarchalism; however, his conclusions on *homo sacer* are valuable to understand how women's lives remain only in the *zoē* dimensions even today. His theory can be used to explain several situations when some people (not everyone) have their bodies more valuable than their rights. Agamben points out this possibility in such works as the essay 'State of Exception and Genealogy of Power'.[32]

From this biopolitical perspective, women become *homines sacri* when the state apparatus controls their lives and avoid the fruition of their rights. To

29 Agamben (1998), p 111.
30 Ibid., p 140.
31 Lemke (2011), p 63. Cf. Deuber-Mankowsky (2002).
32 Agamben (2014).

understand this, the work developed by Roberto Esposito in *Bíos: Biopolitics and Philosophy* will be used to demonstrate through several historical facts how life became a political measure. Esposito mentions the Chinese 'single child' policy, which imposed on Chinese families a limited number of children as a way to reduce the Chinese population. However, this Chinese policy also created the 'legalisation of female foetus abortion' and 'made the former traditional practice in the countryside, of drowning female infants upon birth, unnecessary, but it was bound to augment the numerical disproportion between males and females'.[33] As a result of these practices 'it has been calculated that in less than 20 years it will be difficult for Chinese men to find a wife if they do not tear her away from her family as an adolescent. Perhaps it's for this reason that in China the relation between female and male suicides is five to one.'[34]

Another historical episode exposed by Roberto Esposito is the mass ethnic rapes that occurred in Rwanda, when 'ten thousand babies of the same age'[35] were born after the 'genocide that the Hutu committed on the Tutsi'.[36] According to Esposito this situation 'is an example of "positive" eugenics that is not juxtaposed to the negative one practised in China or elsewhere, but rather constitutes its counterfactual result'.[37]

In these two examples, only one gender was violated: the female. Abortion in China as a public policy results in the death of the female foetus; the imbalance of gender created by the 'one-child' policy also indirectly permits child marriage as a way to restore it. Women were raped in Rwanda as a war practice. Women carried and love babies conceived from rape. In all these cases, women's bodies are what connects politics and life. And mostly because 'we are faced here too with a sort of undecidability, or a double-faced phenomenon in which life and politics are joined in a relation whose interpretation demands a new conceptual language',[38] which is biopolitics.

The control of women's bodies through a biopolitics agenda also happens in 'less' invasive ways than rape, which 'can be seen in the intensity of resistance to laws and social changes that put control of women's bodies in women's hands: reproductive rights, freedom of sexuality whether heterosexual or lesbian, laws that criminalize rape in marriage, etc.'.[39] A control that only those with decision-making powers can exert. But unfortunately, this is not a woman, because they are a minority in these spaces.

All these aspects demonstrate that women's bodies, minds, and lives are always controlled and captured by a patriarchal dimension inscribed inside the

33 Esposito (2008), p 6.
34 Ibid., p 6.
35 Ibid., p 6.
36 Ibid., p 6.
37 Ibid., p 7.
38 Ibid., p 7.
39 Bunch (1990), p 8.

state and society. And this happens from birth, and sometimes before. A life that 'may be killed and not yet sacrificed'.[40] Women's reality is surrounded by a patriarchal culture that imposes many rules on women—'social, economic, political, and biological—which control every single aspect of their lives'.[41]

This patriarchal project that arbitrarily divides the world into two (male and female) and creates a dominant and submissive gender, acts across a wide spectrum of aspects of life; so far we have illustrated only a few.

So, this study aims to demonstrate how the existence of the biopolitical exception tarnishes the notion of the rule of law[42] inside the legal system. When half of the population is excluded from the decision-making spaces, such as the constitutional courts and the judiciary system, where decisions about their rights are made, it reveals a biopolitical perspective that is created through legal education and perpetuated through the legal system to preserve women's bare life.

Legal Education: Women's Hidden Curriculum

In 2019, the Research Group and Studies of Inclusion in Academia (GPEIA) from the Law School of the University of São Paulo, Brazil (USP), with the support of UNESCO, published some important results about gender and legal education in their research: 'Gender interaction in the classroom of Law School of University of São Paulo: A hidden curriculum?'

The research group created in 2015 is composed of a professor, graduate, and undergraduate students of USP Law School (FUSP), and intends to investigate the dynamics of inclusion and exclusion inside the university environment.

The main study object of GPEIA is the gender aspect, in which legal education is deeply involved, and to evaluate how gender inequality shapes law and the judiciary system in Brazil. Qualitative methods, participant observation, and ethnographic methods have been used inside the FDUSP classroom to demonstrate that there is a *hidden curriculum* shaped by gender aspects.[43]

The researchers warn that legal education in Brazil is a very complex object of study because there are a large number of law schools in Brazil and also because legal education methodology varies from one region to another. The main observations of this research remain generic, and there are some reasons for this.[44]

The FDUSP and the Olinda Law School were the first two law schools in Brazil. For a long time, both law schools monopolised legal education in the

40 Agamben (1998), p 12.
41 Souto (2020), p 162.
42 Agamben (2005).
43 Neder et al. (2019), p 10.
44 Ibid., p 14.

country and shaped the mentality of a large number of legal experts, who likely helped to build other law schools in the country and bring to them the same mentality developed in the FDUSP where the study was developed.[45] The notability of FDUSP is still remarkable even after almost 200 years of existence. Another reason is because, according to the authors, besides the variety of methodological approaches inside Brazilian legal education, in any law school it remains difficult to appropriately deal with gender diversity.[46]

Some specific aspects of FDUSP's history and reality also reflect how gender demarks differences in legal education. When the data was collected, just one woman was a director there. Besides this, all the classrooms are named after honoured male professors. 'These tributes reflect an Academy that seems to erase the trajectory of the women who were part of its history'.[47]

The data collected also concluded that the number of female professors is lower than male professors, and qualified professor positions (assistant or titular) are dominated by men. In 2018, the FDUSP had 152 professors and only 26 women. In the highest professorship position, there were 36 professors and only 4 were women.[48]

To understand how these data can impact legal education, the researchers used the *hidden curriculum* theory.[49] It is an educational theory that understands that some content provided outside of regular teaching methods can also interfere with the teaching–learning process.

> This refers not to those activities which are deliberately planned for pupils and students to engage in, but rather, to those unplanned—and perhaps unintended—messages which are transmitted to pupils via the institutional structures of our educational establishments and the—often unacknowledged—attitudes of those, teachers and others, who serve such establishments (see deschooling). Such messages have been thought important in the field of moral education but they have also been the focus for many critics of the educational establishment[50] who see such messages as, by and large, detrimental to the interests of pupils and students and society generally.[51]

So, the gender aspect in which legal education is shaped can interfere with how women and men learn or teach.

The way a professor approached a student during learning-teaching experiences interferes in the gender interactions inside the classroom increasing or not the gender inequalities and this also impacts legal education, because it's mostly based on debates and arguments.

45 Ibid., p 15.
46 Ibid., p 13.
47 Ibid., p 25, translated.
48 Ibid., p 26.
49 Ibid., p 11.
50 Winch and Gingell (1999), p 54. Cf. Bowles and Gintis (1976); Kleinig (1982).
51 Winch and Gingell (1999), p 54.

According to GPEIA's research, the professor's gender is not the only aspect of the teaching–learning dynamic, but it is a meaningful one: numerically and symbolically law school is a male-dominated space. The researchers analyse that when the professor is a woman the female students consider that she is more open to talking. The data also indicate that the influence of external and pre-existent contexts of gender oppression can interfere with this relationship.[52]

Although the professor being a woman doesn't guarantee that the female students will be more participative, this nonetheless indicates an external factor that interferes inside the classroom, demonstrating the applicability of the *hidden curriculum* theory.[53]

Another aspect that was studied is how each gender builds its professorship authority. For women, acquiring a position of authority is a difficult endeavour. It is surrounded by cultural stereotypes that shape interactions with students. Female professors who crafted their authority in a rigid measure are negatively viewed by their students, mostly because being a stern person is socially understood as a male characteristic.[54]

When women use affection as a teaching tool this is naturalised as a female characteristic. Yet, when men use this kind of approach the students don't look at this as a negative characteristic, which reflects that male professors can build their authority more freely than female professors using a multidimensional approach, simply because it's implicitly understood that being a law school professor is a man's job.[55]

The study materials used also impact the teaching–learning process: the professor's openness to debate gender issues; the use of female authors; and the awareness of misogyny or chauvinists behaviours in the classroom are some of the methodological approaches that made female students more comfortable inside the classroom and to participate in debates.[56]

How each body (female and male) physically occupies law school's spaces is also defined by gender aspects. Male students feel more comfortable sitting in the back of the classroom; they speak louder; are more spontaneous; and come and go inside and outside of the classroom more often. Female students, however, prefer to sit in the front of the classroom; stay closer to each other; occupy small spaces; and speak more often when they are already prepared for what to say.[57] The same reflection appears in the female professor's body language: they occupy less space when teaching and limit their interaction. Their gestures are shorter and closer to the table or the blackboard.[58]

52 Neder et al. (2019), pp 59–78.
53 Ibid., pp 59–78.
54 Ibid., pp 62–7.
55 Ibid., pp 62–7.
56 Ibid., pp 73–5.
57 Ibid., pp 42–6.
58 Ibid., pp 68–71.

The research also evaluates that there is an intersectionality aspect between gender and age in which the analyses reveal interesting data: older male students often participate more orally, sometimes disrespect younger students, and are more likely to voice misogynistic opinions.[59]

The data collected from this study case is valuable. Not only for the Brazilian case but to understand how legal education worldwide can include or exclude women from the legal system.

The biopolitical perspective revealed in the women's process of teaching–learning in this Brazilian law school is problematic.[60] Mostly because legal education is a prerequisite for occupying the legal system as lawyers, judges, and prosecutors. Under the rule of law, rules are created, executed, and interpreted by those who occupy these positions. So, directly or indirectly preventing women from holding these positions affects the diversity of decisions and rules as well as the democratic process.

Even today, women are in the minority in the superior courts and the judiciary system in Brazil, and this unfortunate fact impacts how the decision-making process within the rule of law is conceived and is a reflection of how the state perpetuates women's bare lives.

Clarice Paiva Morais, in her book *Gender Inequalities in Superior Courts in Brazil: Analysis of Judicial Neutrality from the Perspective of the Question of Women*, argues that women's underrepresentation in Brazil's Supreme Court and legal system prevents women from exercising their rights—in particular their reproductive rights. Currently, the Brazilian Supreme Court is composed of 11 judges and only two of them are women.

Analysing the Brazilian Supreme Court's decision regarding the abortion of anencephalic foetuses, she demonstrates, using the standpoint theory, that the legal hermeneutic approach conducted in Brazil is far away from women's point of view. She concludes that women are invisible there. They are underrepresented in the decision-making spaces and when decisions are made, women's life experiences and points of view aren't taken into account, even when it is women who are deciding. Because all their juridical knowledge is shaped by men and for men.[61] And, as we see, this is the heritage of legal education.

Preventing legal abortion is the foremost aspect of biopolitics that captures women's bodies. It is also representative of how a *hidden curriculum* in the legal system undermines women's rights in general as they contribute to excluding women from the decision-making spaces where their rights are shaped.

59 Ibid., pp 75–7.

60 For more information about a reformulation of the teaching–learning process through feminist and queer perspectives, see: Chris Ashford, Laura Graham, and Samantha Rasiah, 'Centring Feminist and Queer Experiences in the Law School: Legal Zines as a Humanising Pedagogy' in the *Biopolitics and Resistance in Legal Education* volume.

61 Morais (2020), pp 189–92.

These two studies analysed here demonstrate how the biopolitical aspect of legal education has led to women being excluded from the *polis*.

Being aware of this reality is just the first step to changing this. And these studies are meaningful in the construction of an equal world where everyone has the same opportunities. Because this data makes clear that even though women have formally the same educational, political, and juridical rights as men, they still being far away from the effectiveness of their rights. This is how biopolitics works, the women's rights exists only in the paper and they remain as *homines sacri*.

Conclusion

The Brazilian case study analysed here allows us to reflect on the biopolitics structures that surround us. It also demonstrates how biopolitics shapes the learning–teaching process and undermines women's rights through the legal system.

At the same time, this Brazilian case study has indicated how we can change this. Because when we see, from data, that women and men have different interactions in their learning process, we understand that this is more harmful than we might have imagined before. There is an exclusionary process in legal education that prevents women from learning, interacting, and expressing their opinion inside the classrooms. But being aware of this and seeing how this happens is an important tool for change.

This exclusion can be minimised by professors' approaches and methodologies, that instead of reaffirming these exclusions and prejudices start a new way of teaching and constructing legal knowledge that changes not just the legal education but the entire legal system.

Giving female students in law school a space where they will be heard is a first step to starting a new world, where all women's lives will be effectively *bios*.

Acknowledgements

This study was financed in part by the Coordenação de Aperfeiçoamento de Pessoal de Nível Superior—Brasil (CAPES)—Finance Code 001.

References

Astrid Deuber-Mankowskz (2002) 'Homo Sacer, das bloße Leben und das Lager: Anmerkungen zu einem erneuten Versuch einer Kritik der Gewalt'. *Die Philosophin* 25: 95.

S Bowles and H Gintis (1976) *Schooling in Capitalist America*, New York, Basic Books.

Giorgio Agamben (1998) *Homo Sacer: Sovereign Power and Bare Life*, trans. Daniel Heller-Roazen, Stanford University Press.

Giorgio Agamben (2005) *State of Exception*, trans. Kevin Attel, The University of Chicago Press.
Giorgio Agamben (2014) 'Estado de Exceção e Genealogia do Poder' 108 *Revista Brasileira de Estudos Políticos* 21.
Carl Schmitt (2005) *Teologia política*, trans. Luiz Moreira, Del Rey.
Charlotte Bunch (1990) 'Women's Rights as Human Rights: Toward a ReVision of Human' 12 *Human Rights Quarterly* 486.
Roberto Esposito (2008) *Bíos: Biopolitics and Philosophy*, trans. Timothy Campbell, University of Minnesota Press.
J Kleinig (1982) *Philosophical Issues in Education*, Beckenham, Croom Helm.
Michel Foucault (1976) *History of Sexuality, Volume I: An Introduction*, trans. Robert Hurley, Random House.
Michel Foucault (2008) *Nascimento da biopolítica: curso dado no Collège de France (1978–1979)*, trans. Eduardo Brandão, Martins Fontes.
Michel Foucault (2008a) *Segurança, território, população: curso dado no Collège de France (1977–1978)*, trans. Eduardo Brandão, Martins Fontes.
Thomas Lemke (2011) *Biopolitics: An Advanced Introduction*, trans. Eric Frederick Trump, NYU Press.
Clarice Paiva Morais (2020) *Desigualdade de gênero nos Tribunais Superiores no Brasil: análise da neutralidade judicial sob a ótica da pergunta pela mulher*, Lumen Juris.
Sheila Christina Cerezetti Neder et al. (2019) *Interações de gênero nas salas de aula da Faculdade de Direito da USP: um currículo oculto?* Cátedra UNESCO de Direto a Educação/ Universidade de São Paulo (USP).
Luana Mathias Souto (2020) 'Life-narratives and Human Rights: Reflection about Women's Rights and State of Exception' 6 *Anamorphosis—Revista Internacional de Direito e Literatura* 151.
Christopher Winch and John Gingell (1999) *Key Concepts in The Philosophy of Education*, Routledge.
Walter Benjamin (2012) *O anjo da história*, trans. João Barrento. Autêntica.

Chapter 5

Lawyer as Biopolitical Asset

Jane Ching

Introduction

Professional licensure as a lawyer has, as the ABA Taskforce has put it, both a public and a private 'value'.[1] Without the latter, the capitulation of the self and assault on personal autonomy occasioned by acquisition of the professional habitus[2] would not be tolerable. Licensure and secure employment[3] both confer, and are contingent on, economic, cultural and social capital.[4] Although the individual lawyer is not of course bought and sold in the Marxian economic sense of a commodity, the right to practise is inalienable from the human lawyer who exercises it. Consequently, the bundle of capitals and licensures possessed by that lawyer is tradable in the legal services market and, for the purposes of this discussion, constitutes them as a biopolitical asset. There is, however, a dialectic in operation in this relationship, between qualifications as indicators of competence, and as symbols emphasising status, social and cultural capital recognised, if at all, as a 'halo'[5] in the labour market. This is especially visible for the foreign legal qualifications that are the subject of this chapter.

The chapter is in three parts. First it considers the technology of power[6] present at the regulatory macro-level where compromises are made between evaluation of competence and symbolic credentialism.

It then moves to the micro-level to discuss two ways in which individuals seek to constitute themselves as competitively valuable assets by acquiring credentials (cultural capital).[7] They hope to translate these into economic or

1 ABA Task Force (2014).

2 Bourdieu (1977), p 2. See, for example, Hilary Sommerlad (2008).

3 This chapter focuses on employment rather than self-employment, particularly as, in most jurisdictions, a period of employment is required for licensure and this is normally controlled by law firm recruitment practices.

4 Bourdieu (1986).

5 See Ballakrishnen (2011), p 2445.

6 Foucault (1982), p 781.

7 Bourdieu (1986), p 241. Bourdieu treats educational qualifications as 'cultural capital' capable of translation into economic capital through employment. Cultural capital also includes the advantages of elites in cosmopolitan experience, etiquette and multi-lingualism.

DOI: 10.4324/9781003175193-7

social capital, or remedy deficits in elite capital.[8] The first represents attempts to bypass barriers in local routes to licensure. In the second the emphasis is on implicit (employer-defined) recruitment criteria using foreign qualifications as a 'halo'. Whilst in some cases the value of such qualifications has to be individually negotiated, in others they are *de facto* quasi-regulatory requirements.

The chapter therefore ends with a novel call to Gramsci's concept of subalternity[9] for the aspirant lawyer, in autonomously co-developing a disruptive proposal for a supra-jurisdictional programme. This would transcend regulation through the 'technology of the self'[10] to rebalance the opposing poles of the dialectic.

For simplicity, in this chapter, 'local' refers to the receiving jurisdiction and 'foreign' to jurisdictions outside it.

Macro-Level

Here, professional bodies[11] engage with the state, each other and supra-national agencies to determine who can practise where and in what. Legal services are the subject of international negotiations through the GATS[12] and similar instruments[13] which ostensibly prioritise competence.[14] The professional bodies, however, determine operationalisation and their bargaining position is influenced by reciprocity, post-colonialism, hierarchy and pragmatism. This trading is enabled because licensure is on a jurisdictional basis and therefore 'among the most restricted' in the global economy.[15] It perpetuates legal professions as closed groups, anxious to preserve their own monopolies and to limit outsiders' access to them.

Foreign lawyers are often permitted to advise on their own, foreign law:[16] this does not trespass on the sensibilities of local lawyers.[17] Challenges arise

8 See Ballakrishnen (2011), p 2473 describing a qualification as a replacement for social capital in India.

9 Green (2002).

10 Foucault (1988).

11 And sometimes law firms: see Faulconbridge et al. (2008), p 461.

12 World Trade Organisation (2021). See also Collins (2018); Terry (2013). The details of the GATS, other than as a technology of power, are outside the remit of this chapter. See for general discussion, however, Hutchinson (2005); Sereno (1995) Terry (2010); Udobong (2012).

13 As, for example, Directive 98/5/EC which, like the GATS, controls the extent to which foreign lawyers can be re-tested. For discussion, see Blitz (1999).

14 Hill (2006).

15 Collins (2018), p 8.

16 Possibly through a bilateral trading agreement: Law Society of England and Wales (April 2021). India has been a notable outlier: Eisen (2011); Desai (2018).

17 Partnership with local lawyers may open up opportunities for those local lawyers: Collins (2018), p 10. Outsourcing can provide high-status opportunities for individuals when local jobs are scarce, see Ballakrishnen (2012).

when they seek to practise local law, compete with local lawyers[18] and, in principle, exercise a power to hold the local state to account through litigation.

It is here that credentialism conflicts with competence. It may be, politically, difficult to refuse to acknowledge academic credentials from high-status foreign institutions, from a former colonial power or legal family hub,[19] particularly where these are acquired by members of powerful, high-status local groups. Consequently, which universities obtain accreditation, and which students, with which capital, have access to them, is a microcosm of the wider transactional picture. Negotiations for recognition may be significant and de-recognition is possible.[20]

The stakes are higher for the grant of licensure. A jurisdiction's political stance may be protectionist; anxious to establish itself as a preferred international financial or legal centre, or to enhance the tradable value of its own licensure. The result may involve compromise about the assessment of competence, tempered by questions of reciprocity: how local lawyers are treated when they attempt to requalify elsewhere.[21]

One response is principled prohibition,[22] so that, subject to nationality requirements, a determined aspirant would have to complete the entire local qualification system, so preserving what Flood calls a 'monocentric' approach.[23] This treats competence of local and foreign lawyers equally,[24] but is unattractive if the country wishes to be perceived as an international player or trade its qualifications in the international market. One British regulator has, for example, moved away from its initial position that its new examination would be universal, to providing exemptions.[25]

At the opposite end of the scale are systems where even local licensure is necessarily dependent on foreign or multi-national qualifications. These include the consciously multi-jurisdictional 'West Indian system' licensing for practice in any of the CARICOM nations.[26] Guernsey requires prior qualification

18 'The practice of law by foreigners ... can lead to resentment by local lawyers who feel that their own control over the profession is at risk': Collins (2018), p 11.

19 Roberts (2017), p 53, notes that student flows are hierarchical and largely unidirectional into Western states.

20 See, for example, Legal Profession Qualifying Board, Malaysia (1995). India explicitly 'facilitate[s]' Indian students in foreign study, with many recognised law degrees: Bar Council of India (2021).

21 Australian lawyers can requalify as solicitors in England and Wales through a special assessment (with exemptions) but the reverse is a case-by-case assessment. This is being renegotiated: Law Society of England and Wales (June 2021).

22 There are some 40 countries where (some) foreign lawyers cannot requalify: International Bar Association (date unknown).

23 Flood (2011), p 14.

24 No assessment can fully replicate legal practice in the real world, but if all take the same assessment, it is flawed consistently, even if it only tests a subset of competent practice.

25 Solicitors Regulation Authority (March 2022, April 2022).

26 Wooding et al. (1965).

in England and Wales.[27] Until recently Bhutanese lawyers could *only* qualify elsewhere.[28]

The middle ground is where the risks lie. First, the receiving jurisdiction must monitor the continued existence of accredited foreign qualifications. Second, attention must be paid to the gap between foreign and local education.[29] Assessment of individual competence on a case-by-case basis is possible, albeit resource-intensive.

Another approach is a special entry route for foreign lawyers. This pluralism represents what Flood calls a 'polycentric' model[30] and may emphasise only distinctive elements of local practice such as land law or the local constitution, taking on trust the foreign assessment of everything else.[31] It is emblematic of the dialectic that the foreign lawyers whom a jurisdiction wishes to attract are unlikely to practise in such fields.[32] Consequently, there is a risk of a race to the bottom in defining the lowest common denominator that will (a) satisfy the regulator in relation to competence, (b) not deter high-status foreign lawyers or operate as 'a disguised restriction on international trade',[33] but (c) not debase the local qualification system by creating attractive bypasses for those with elite capital. Symbolic value is of even greater significance when recognition moves from *de jure* to *de facto* in the employment market.

Micro-Level

The availability of foreign qualifications coupled with the effects of trading at the macro-level permits lawyers to 'creatively eliminate or penetrate … educational and licensing barriers'[34] to acquire licensure and status-enhancing credentials. Of course, gaps in local regulation may demand foreign qualifications or licensures[35] or may, as in Guernsey, deliberately depend on them. Some lawyers genuinely wish to practise in the foreign jurisdiction. It seems unlikely, however, that all the foreign-educated lawyers who take the New

27 Guernsey Bar—Barreau de Guernsey (2018).
28 Law (2018).
29 In India, welcoming of foreign law degrees, there is a mandatory bridging course: Bar Council of India (2016).
30 Flood (2011), p 14.
31 At one stage, a number of local competences were not assessed by one British regulator which assumed that incoming foreign lawyers would have acquired them in work-experience. However, the route was open to lawyers from jurisdictions without work-experience requirements.
32 See, however, suggestion of a 'corporate' route that would disregard the aspects of local law that corporate lawyers would not be likely to practise: Law Society of England and Wales (2015), p 34.
33 Collins (2018), p 21.
34 Liu (2013), p 678.
35 For example, a Chinese lawyer practising in China but working for a foreign law firm required a foreign licensure, see Silver (2011), p 42.

York Bar exam actually plan to practise in New York,[36] and almost half of students on the bar course for England and Wales have been non-UK/EU domiciliaries.[37] A particularly contentious recent example has been the post-Brexit rush by British lawyers to preserve their EU practice rights by dual qualifying in the Republic of Ireland[38] but not desiring to establish in Ireland. Reciprocity appears to have been a component of the negotiated response.[39]

Despite efforts by institutions to offer courses online[40] and overseas,[41] acquiring those licensures and symbols is, however, dependent on economic, linguistic and cultural capital that facilitates study abroad[42] and licensure assessments.[43] It may therefore embed, rather than address, inequality. Here we consider two aspects of the micro-level demonstrating the dialectic: bypasses of local qualification routes and the position of foreign qualifications as a 'halo' for recruiters.

Bypasses

As we have seen, recognition of foreign *degrees*, particularly if high-status, and from a high-status jurisdiction, is widespread. Foreign qualifications leading to *licensure*, however, may be thought easier,[44] or more straightforward[45] than local equivalents. Recruitment is competitive and its processes may be inequitable. Consequently, the impetus to bypass is stronger when it can avoid mandatory work-experience. Until recently, Italian students could avoid the *pratica forense* by qualifying in Spain (the *via spagnola*)[46] returning under EU freedom of movement provisions. US bar preparation courses have been marketed to

36 New York State Board of Law Examiners (2020).

37 Bar Standards Board (2021), p 21. Virtually all those who then commenced the mandatory work-experience (in order to practise in England and Wales) were UK/EU domiciliaries. Bar Standards Board (2021), p 79 and 93.

38 Croft (2018).

39 Law Society of England and Wales (March 2021).

40 Receiving jurisdictions often do not accredit more accessible and cheaper part time and online degrees. See, for example, Nigeria Bar (2020).

41 Backer and Stancil (2012); Flood (2011), pp 6–10. For the symbolic capital acquired by the university in so doing, see French (2015).

42 Silver (2011), p 47; Ballakrishnen (2011), fn 125 but contrast Lazarus-Black (2017), p 467. See also the Dutch English-language law degrees with lower tuition fees than in England: studylaw.nl (undated) and those British universities offering two-year LLBs targeting Canadians: Across the Pond (2021).

43 Which may have to be taken in the territory of the jurisdiction concerned, increasing expense.

44 See Nicola (2018), p 252: 'those who … circumvented the local exam to pass the New York Bar took a shortcut trying to circumvent the more demanding French Bar Passage regime'. Japanese and South Korean students have taken similar steps: Silver (2006), p 158.

45 In Mauritius '[t]he difficulty in passing the Vocational Course examinations has resulted in those who can afford it continuing to qualify by being called to the Bar in the United Kingdom': Phillips et al. (2019), para 16.

46 See TitoliSpagna (2022).

aspiring British solicitors, who also believed US licensure would be a halo for local employers[47] who are, however, committed to local work-experience as authentic and essential.[48] Bypasses devalue local qualifications by prioritising credentials over competence, advantage those with elite capital and lead to an entrenchment of vulnerability in the employment market for the disadvantaged.

Halos

Even qualifications not contributing to licensure can enhance the value of lawyers as assets,[49] particularly if from a high-status institution[50] in a high-status country. In some cases, essentially in less high-status countries, foreign postgraduate qualifications are an expectation of high-status employers to the extent that they become *de facto*[51] and quasi-regulatory requirements. Their value is, however, fluid: differing between jurisdictions[52] and employers and, if ubiquitous, devalued.[53]

Nevertheless, such study may confer new intellectual perspectives,[54] cultural awareness,[55] potential referral networks,[56] specialist understanding that is underdeveloped in the local context[57] and linguistic[58] or other skills that enhance local practice. Foreign students may appreciate the intellectual challenge of new forms of reasoning and pedagogy,[59] or find them intimidating,[60] demanding reframing and unlearning,[61] just as some of them find aspects of foreign legal cultures inexplicable.[62]

47 Aldridge (2011) and the views of employers in Law Society of England and Wales (2015), p 33.
48 Law Society of England and Wales (2015).
49 Ballakrishnen (2011) is illuminating on this topic given India's lack of recognition of foreign licensures: p 2465, 2471, 2453, 2461.
50 Silver (2006), p 173; Silver (2011), p 32; Ballakrishnen (2011), p 2471, 2449.
51 For example, in China: Ballakrishnen (2011) note 17; Liu (2013), p 686; Roberts (2017), p 31; Silver (2011), p 41.
52 Dinovitzer and Hagan (2006), p 131 demonstrated this empirically in the context of movement within a federal state.
53 'As a purchaser of those individuals to come and work at your firm,... you're going to say to yourself "Well, everyone's got [the New York Bar], it's frankly not good enough to do this job so I'm not going to set that much store by it" and then people will stop taking it, and they'll be doing something else that employers consider more effective' (English solicitor quoted in Webb et al. (2013), para 2.114).
54 Silver (2011), p 20, 32; Ballakrishnen (2011), fn 38, p 2467, 2468.
55 Local students may, however, not mix with their international peers: Lazarus-Black (2017), p 473.
56 See Silver (2011), p 20, 38; Ballakrishnen (2011), p 2446, 2467.
57 Lazarus-Black (2017), p 467.
58 Silver (2006), p 20, 30, 156; Silver (2011), p 32; Lazarus-Black (2017), p 476.
59 Ballakrishnen (2011), fn 38, p 2467, 2468.
60 Lazarus-Black (2017), p 465, 471, 473, 475.
61 Ibid., p 466.
62 See ibid., p 462 on concepts such as the lay jury and plea bargaining.

In terms of the international trade in qualifications, however, the effect is more questionable. As Roberts demonstrates,[63] the flow of students is largely unidirectional, towards hubs such as the USA and UK (common law), France and Germany (civil law), and Russia (post-Soviet). It perpetuates, therefore, patterns of historical colonialism,[64] even where deliberate efforts have been made to create distinct local systems that are culturally and legally relevant, as in CARICOM. It also provides opportunities for new forms of legal colonialism, or, less pejoratively, leadership,[65] in which models of ethics, legal[66] and firm culture,[67] the rule of law or of legal education[68] are transmitted from powerful, high-status nations with confidence in their scholarship[69] and the resources to deliver to the less powerful.

Conclusion

The discussion above has shown that, in the context of the recognition of foreign qualifications, at both degree and licensure stage, legal education, at least for those who intend to practise, treads a difficult balance between credentialism and competence. The underlying jurisdictionalism of regulation should, as recognised in the GATS and similar instruments, allow recognition to focus on competence. In fact, in both education and licensure, there is an international market, in which status, protectionism and reciprocity all play a part in what is recognised, *de jure*, for licensure. Beyond this, there is an active *de facto* market, albeit one that privileges those lawyer-assets with the social and economic capital to study in established high-status centres. Both can be exploited by institutions offering courses designed to attract foreign students, and by regulators choosing which degrees to recognise and how to manage foreign re-licensure without deterring foreign investment or devaluing local qualification. An unintended result is that some foreign qualifications are more valuable outside their home jurisdiction than within it.[70]

63 Roberts (2017), p 54 (2018).

64 See Lazarus-Black (2008); Roberts (2017), p 61. See also Foluke I Adebisi's chapter in the *Biopolitics and Resistance in Legal Education* volume.

65 See Lazarus-Black (2017), p 480; Van Detta (2014).

66 Nicola (2018); Roberts (2018).

67 See, for example, Beaverstock (2004) and Silver (2011), p 9. The extent of global convergence within a firm may, however, be illusory: Faulconbridge (2008); or need to be fostered through organisational training and structures: Faulconbridge and Muzio (2009).

68 The obvious example is the global influence of the JD, particularly in Asia, for example Sato (2016). More unusually, its influence has been seen in other Western nations, such as Canada and Australia: Flood (2011), p 32. The trend might, perhaps, be more accurately described in those countries as a movement to position legal education as postgraduate rather than undergraduate, rather than a duplication of the US model.

69 See Garth (2015), p 75: 'the superiority of US legal scholarship in the global market is taken for granted within the US'.

70 See, for example, s 15(1A) of the Legal Profession Act 1986, permitting graduates of two British courses to qualify with six months' work-experience in Trinidad and Tobago, when one or two

These mechanisms can be exploited by individuals seeking bypasses or halos, although those attempts can be misconceived, failing to enhance the asset value of the lawyer to potential employers. This is not to say that foreign study cannot have metacognitive benefits for individuals, exposing them to different concepts and ideas, and benefits in social capital and international networks: but this would be the case as much for a Chinese lawyer studying in the UK or USA as it would for the (unlikely) US or UK lawyer studying in China.

Whilst, as Roberts has shown, foreign study tends to be within legal families and hence to a large extent within language groups, the impact of English as a *lingua franca* cannot be detached from the equation. An Australasian, British, Canadian or US qualification speaks not only to legal study but even more to a language competence that enhances the value of the asset in working with foreign lawyers and clients. Moving outside the legal family, as when Chinese lawyers seek Anglo-Saxon qualifications, signals cosmopolitanism and a readiness to compete in an international field dominated by Anglo-Saxon law firms (which can also establish and carry out legal work locally) more than it need signal competence in practice.

Whilst credentialism expands the global market for those with the economic and linguistic capital to take advantage of it, questions of (local) competence narrow it and are a legitimate concern of local regulatory bodies. This is disfigured except in truly monocentric jurisdictions by the competing interests of the status of foreign qualifications and those who hold them, reciprocity and the need to attract international business that obscure evaluation of actual competence.

There have been attempts to synthesise supra-national statements of shared competences,[71] though not on the scale of, say, accountancy.[72] To the extent that some qualifications, such as the New York Bar or call to the Bar of England and Wales, service a wide range of jurisdictions, their outcomes come to operate as such supra-national competences by default.

One response might be to retain the negotiated status quo for local practice and embark on a project of convergence of competence by focusing on supra- or international practice. In 'transnational law', provided by international treaties, soft law and 'effort[s] by the parties to create their own law'[73] by contract, the competences of lawyers may be more similar, but they are shared with those of diplomats and entrepreneurs. Legal licensure may not be required,[74]

years is required in England and Wales. Ironically, given its privileged symbolic position for foreigners, there are suggestions that the New York Bar examination does not assure local competence: see Task Force on the New York Bar Examination (2020), p 69.

71 Conseil des Barreaux Européens—Council of Bars and Law Societies of Europe (2007). The West Indian system operationalises this approach for CARICOM.

72 IAESB (2019).

73 Jones (2013), p 63.

74 See, for example, United Nations Commission on International Trade Law (2013), art 5.

rolled over from local licensure[75] or, rarely, separately granted.[76] Jones, however, has suggested a model for a qualification for such lawyers.[77] He conceives this conferring *de jure* licensure to operate internationally, including as advocate before international bodies, in general corporate advice and as arbitrator or mediator. Extension of the problems of regulatory hegemony to a supra-national level would, however, compound the credentials vs. competence dialectic. Jones' model is drawn from the US experience of courses necessarily based on general principles for students who might later practise in any state. It is worth noting in the context of course design that whether, for example, US legal education is most effective at securing skills in legal writing, some kinds of UK legal education in developing adversarial trial advocacy skills, or German education in conferring 'excellence in doctrinalisation'[78] remains sadly unevaluated, although practitioners in international firms know the comparative strengths and weaknesses of the products of different traditions.[79]

Jones' approach is to devise a curriculum—taught in English—based on 'jurisdiction-neutral' 'general principles' that recognise, by way of comparison, differences between legal traditions, or use international treaties or similar supra-national documents as primary sources, and on business and finance issues. It seems to prioritise, therefore, substantive knowledge. Whilst comparativism is pluralist and divergent in nature, it is difficult to treat each comparator, the one known and the one less known, with real equivalence and without 'othering' the less familiar.[80] Indeed, as Roberts points out, even amongst international lawyers, the concept of what international practice is differs, and is informed by local culture and training.[81]

This chapter closes, then, with an approach to a supra-national course that approaches the problem differently in seeking to remedy the problems of the dialectic. First, it builds, not on knowledge, but on active competences: values; ethics; models of practice; concepts of professionalism, metacognition and justice that are key to practice in local, foreign and supra-national contexts. Most significantly, it draws on a global resource as its designers: young lawyers themselves. Even though they are acutely conscious of the credential and status value of foreign qualifications, the research on foreign students in the USA referred to in this chapter has noted their ability to evaluate and critique foreign legal concepts and therefore to push back, even if silently, against the

75 International Criminal Court (date unknown).

76 European Patent Office (2019).

77 Jones (2013).

78 Roberts (2017), p 218.

79 Law Society of England and Wales (2015).

80 Even the double maîtrise degrees offered by some universities must involve an element of othering, as students will almost certainly be more familiar with one jurisdiction and its norms than the other and the pairing is often of one civil law and one common law jurisdiction.

81 Roberts (2017).

credentialism and colonialism inherent in the trade in qualifications. My call is to this group within Gramsci's concept of subalternity,[82] in co-developing a disruptive proposal. It would in concept be creative, disruptive, harnessing the technology of the self and reflecting the autonomy and ethics that should be the defining characteristics of a legal profession and freed of the need to consider licensure as a governing technology of power. It treats its students and creators not as assets, but as actors, asking what they need to be secure, effective and happy in their work.[83]

Whether law students and junior lawyers are able to articulate what they want and need is constrained by their biopolitical status. They want to obtain licensure and employment and for this, they want to comply, adopting the relevant habitus and status. They are, however, concerned about law and justice, but also about resilience, about equality and about the planetary future. These are topics that are addressed, on a local and sometimes an international basis, in student and young lawyer groups. Young lawyers may be more confident amongst their peers to argue and to transcend norms. They would be concerned, naturally, about the cost and delivery of such a course. It would need to be delivered online and make as many demands of the native English-speaker as it does of others.

I suggest that an appropriate pedagogy, extending the discipline-specific concept of comparative law, is that of 'variation theory'.[84] This focuses on the ways in which people experience the same phenomenon differently, and teaches that we learn by examining commonalities and differences. Doing so in the context of individual experience provides a clear link to autonomous practice. The flow of information should not be from legal hub towards developing country, or by perpetuating existing hegemonies and colonial cultures,[85] but by the creation of new knowledge amongst peers in a safe environment in which different legal families, including indigenous approaches, are valued and heard.

If effective, and if valued by employers, such a programme might come to acquire *de facto* or even *de jure* status and therefore capital in its own right, but would have evolved from a starting point that is distinct from treating lawyers as assets, trading in symbols or actively seeking to bypass regulatory structures. In the current environment, however, it remains no more than a thought experiment. What remains is the dialectic in which qualifications and licensures—and their holders—are traded. Perhaps the best we can hope for is that the young people expending their time and money on them can be made aware of what they can, and what they cannot, provide.

82 Green (2002).

83 See also Omar Madhloom, this volume.

84 See, for example, Marton and Ling (2012). And, in law, Åkerlind et al. (2010); Ching (2015); Steel (2019).

85 See Foluke I Adebisi's chapter in the *Biopolitics and Resistance in Legal Education* volume.

Reference list

Primary Sources

Directive 98/5/EC of the European Parliament and of the Council of 16 February 1998 to facilitate practice of the profession of lawyer on a permanent basis in a Member State other than that in which the qualification was obtained.

Legal Profession Act 1986 (Trinidad and Tobago).

Secondary Sources

Larry Cata Backer and Bret Stancil (2012) 'Beyond Colonization – Globalization and the Establishment of Programs of US Legal Education Abroad by Indigenous Institutions' 5 *Drexel Law Review* 317.

Swethaa Ballakrishnen (2011) 'Homeward Bound: What Does a Global Legal Education Offer the Indian Returnees' 80 *Fordham Law Review* 2441.

Swethaa Ballakrishnen (2012) '"I Love My American Job": Professional Prestige in the Indian Outsourcing Industry and Global Consequences of an Expanding Legal Profession' 19 *International Journal of the Legal Profession* 379.

Jonathan V Beaverstock (2004) '"Managing across Borders": Knowledge Management and Expatriation in Professional Service Legal Firms' 4 *Journal of Economic Geography* 157.

Brad K Blitz (1999) 'Professional Mobility and the Mutual Recognition of Qualifications in the European Union: Two Institutional Approaches' 43 *Comparative Education Review* 311.

Pierre Bourdieu (1977) *Outline of a Theory of Practice*, Cambridge University Press.

Pierre Bourdieu (1986) 'The Forms of Capital' in J Richardson (ed) trans. Richard Nice, *Handbook of Theory and Research of the Sociology of Education*, Greenwood Publishing Group.

Jane Ching (2015) '"Favourable Variations": Towards a Refreshed Approach for the Interviewing Classroom' 25 *Legal Education Review* 173.

David Collins (2018) *The Public International Law of Trade in Legal Services*, Cambridge University Press.

Vyapak Desai, Kshama Loya and Bhavana Sunder (2018) 'Entry Restricted Casually: The Supreme Court of India's Judgment on the Entry of Foreign Lawyers in India' 20 *Asian Dispute Review* 112.

Ronit Dinovitzer and John Hagan (2006) 'Lawyers on the Move: The Consequences of Mobility for Legal Careers' 13 *International Journal of the Legal Profession* 119.

Arno L Eisen (2011) 'Legal Services in India: Is There an Obligation under the GATS or Are There Policy Reasons for India to Open its Legal Services Market to Foreign Legal Consultants' 11 *Richmond Journal of Global Law and Business* 273.

James R Faulconbridge (2008) 'Negotiating Cultures of Work in Transnational Law Firms' (2008) 8 *Journal of Economic Geography* 497.

James Faulconbridge et al. (2008) 'Global Law Firms: Globalization and Organizational Spaces of Cross-Border Legal Work' 28 *Northwestern Journal of International Law & Business* 455.

James R Faulconbridge and Daniel Muzio (2009) 'Legal Education, Globalization, and Cultures of Professional Practice' 22 *Georgetown Journal of Legal Ethics* 1335.

Michel Foucault (1982) 'The Subject and Power' 8 *Critical Inquiry* 777.

Michel Foucault (1988) 'Technologies of the Self' in Luther H Martin, Huck Gutman and Patrick H Hutton (eds) *Technologies of the Self: A Seminar with Michel Foucault*, Tavistock Publications.

Jan Hoffman French (2015) 'At Play in the Field of Law: Symbolic Capital and Foreign Attorneys in LLM Programs' 22 *Indiana Journal of Global Legal Studies* 95.

Bryant G Garth (2015) 'Notes toward an Understanding of the US Market in Foreign LLM. Students: From the British Empire and the Inns of Court to the US LLM' 22 *Indiana Journal of Global Legal Studies* 67.

Marcus Green (2002) 'Gramsci Cannot Speak: Presentations and Interpretations of Gramsci's Concept of the Subaltern' 14 *Rethinking Marxism* 1.

Louise L Hill (2006) 'Services as Objects of International Trade: Bartering the Legal Profession' 39 *Vanderbilt Journal of Transnational Law* 347.

Terry Hutchinson (2005) 'The Transnational Lawyer: GATS, Globalisation and the Effects on Legal Education' 10/11 *Australia & New Zealand Journal of Law & Education* 93.

Colin PA Jones (2013) 'The International Commercial Solicitor: Proposing a New Legal Profession for Japan – and the World' 60 *Osaka University Law Review* 45.

David S Law (2018) 'Isolation and Globalization: The Dawn of Legal Education in Bhutan' 9 *Yonsei Law Journal* 41.

Mindie Lazarus-Black (2008) 'After Empire: Training Lawyers as a Postcolonial Enterprise' 12 *Small Axe* 38.

Mindie Lazarus-Black (2017) 'The Voice of the Stranger: Foreign LLM Students' Experiences of Culture, Law and Pedagogy in US Law Schools' in James AR Nafziger (ed) *Comparative Law and Anthropology*, Edward Elgar Publishing.

Sida Liu (2013) 'The Legal Profession as a Social Process: A Theory on Lawyers and Globalization' 38 *Law and Social Inquiry* 670.

Ference Marton and Lo Mun Ling (2012) 'Towards a Science of the Art of Teaching: Using Variation Theory as a Guiding Principle of Pedagogical Design' 1 *International Journal for Lesson and Learning Studies* 7.

Fernanda Nicola (2018) 'The Global Diffusion of U.S. Legal Thought: Changing Influence, National Security, and Legal Education in Crisis' in C Crawford and D Bonilla Maldonado (eds) *Constitutionalism in the Americas*, Edward Elgar Publishing.

Anthea Roberts (2017) *Is International Law International?*, Oxford University Press.

Anthea Roberts (2018) 'Cross-Border Student Flows and the Construction of International Law as a Transnational Legal Field' 3 *UC Irvine Journal of International, Transnational, and Comparative Law* 1.

Nobuyuki Sato (2016) 'The State of Legal Education in Japan: Problems and Re-Renovations in JD Law Schools' 3 *Asian Journal of Law and Society* 213.

Lourdes A Sereno (1995) 'GATT and GATS: Implications on the Legal Profession and Legal Education' 11 *World Bulletin: Bulletin of the International Studies of the Philippines* 58.

Carole Silver (2006) 'Internationalizing US Legal Education: A Report on the Education of Transnational Lawyers' 14 *Cardozo Journal of International and Comparative Law* 143.

Carole Silver (2011) 'The Variable Value of US Legal Education in the Global Legal Services Market' 24 *Georgetown Journal of Legal Ethics* 1.

Hilary Sommerlad (2008) '"What Are You Doing Here? You Should Be Working in a Hair Salon or Something": Outsider Status and Professional Socialization in the Solicitors' Profession' *Web Journal of Current Legal Issues*, www.bailii.org/uk/other/journals/WebJCLI/2008/issue2/sommerlad2.html.

Alex Steel (2019) 'Succeed, Question, Repeat: Threshold Concepts and Variation Theory in Understanding How Law Students Build Competency' 53 *The Law Teacher* 231.

Laurel S Terry (2010) 'From GATS to APEC: The Impact of Trade Agreements on Legal Services' 43 *Akron Law Review* 875.

Edna Udobong (2012) 'Trends in Cross-Border Lawyering: The GATS Ideal or the Indian Reality for U.S. Lawyers' 43 *California Western International Law Journal* 343.

Jeffrey A Van Detta (2014) 'Transnational Legal Services in Globalized Economies: American Leadership, Not Mere Compliance with Gats, through Qualifying LL Degree Programs for Foreign-Educated Lawyers Seeking State Bar Admissions' 13 *Journal of International Business and Law* 1.

Reports

ABA Task Force (2014) *Report and Recommendations American Bar Association Task Force on the Future of Legal Education*, American Bar Association, www.americanbar.org/content/dam/aba/administrative/professional_responsibility/report_and_recommendations_of_aba_task_force.authcheckdam.pdf.

Bar Standards Board (2021) *BPTC Key Statistics 2021 An Analysis of Students over Three Academic Years*, Bar Standards Board, www.barstandardsboard.org.uk/uploads/assets/e7d22219-ffb2-4f36-a206b21736e2d2d8/BPTC-Key-Statistics-Report-2021-All-parts.pdf.

John Flood (2011) *Legal Education in the Global Context: Challenges from Globalization, Technology and Changes in Government Regulation*, Legal Services Board, www.legalservicesboard.org.uk/news_publications/latest_news/pdf/lsb_legal_education_report_flood.pdf.

Law Society of England and Wales (2015) *Global Competitiveness of the England and Wales Solicitor Qualification*, Law Society of England and Wales, www.lawsociety.org.uk/topics/research/global-competitiveness-of-the-england-and-wales-solicitor-qualification.

New York State Board of Law Examiners (2020) *NYS Bar Exam Statistics*, New York State Board of Law Examiners, www.nybarexam.org/ExamStats/Estats.htm.

Nick Phillips et al. (2019) *Report of the Committee*, Government of Mauritius, https://attorneygeneral.govmu.org/Documents/ReportCommiteeLawPractitionersAct/FinalReportofCommittee.pdf.

Task Force on the New York Bar Examination (2020) *Report of the NYSBA Task Force on the New York Bar Examination*, New York State Bar Association, https://nysba.org/app/uploads/2020/03/Report-of-the-NYSBA-Task-Force-on-the-New-York-Bar-Examination-With-Appendix-compressed.pdf.

Julian Webb et al. (2013) *Setting Standards: The Future of Legal Services Education and Training Regulation in England and Wales*, SRA, BSB, CILEx Regulation, https://paulmaharg.com/letr/the-report/index.html.

Hugh Wooding et al. (1965) *Report of Committee on Legal Education*, University of the West Indies.

Electronic Sources

Across the Pond (2021) *LLB (Qualifying Law Degree)*, https://ca.studyacrossthepond.com/llb-uk-law-school.

Gerlese Åkerlind et al. (2010) 'A Threshold Concepts Focus to First Year Law Curriculum Design: Supporting Student Learning Using Variation Theory', https://unistars.org/past_papers/papers10/content/pdf/12B.pdf.

Alex Aldridge (2011) *Horses for Courses. Why US Qualification Doesn't Help in UK Job Market*, www.theguardian.com/law/2011/feb/11/law-student-suing-college.

Bar Council of India (2016) *Introduction of Bridge Course for Foreign Law Degree Holders*, www.barcouncilofindia.org/introduction-of-bridge-course-for-foreign-law-degree-holders/.

Bar Council of India (2021) *Foreign Universities Whose Degrees in Law Are Recognised by the Bar Council of India*, www.barcouncilofindia.org/about/legal-education/list-of-foreign-universities-whose-degrees-in-law-are-recognised-by-the-bar-council-of-india/.

Conseil des Barreaux Européens—Council of Bars and Law Societies of Europe (2007) *CCBE Recommendation on Training Outcomes for European Lawyers*, www.ccbe.org/fileadmin/user_upload/NTCdocument/EN_Training_Outcomes1_1196675213.pdf.

Jane Croft (2018) 'Brexit Concerns Push UK Lawyers to Register in Ireland', www.irishtimes.com/news/politics/brexit-concerns-push-uk-lawyers-to-register-in-ireland-1.3590701.

European Patent Office (2019) *European Qualifying Examination Guide for Preparation 19th Edition*, http://documents.epo.org/projects/babylon/eponet.nsf/0/AD1DEB5847E771FEC125764E0056D80B/$File/eqe_preparation_guide_9th_edition_2019_en.pdf.

Guernsey Bar—Barreau de Guernsey (2018) *Qualifying as a Guernsey Advocate*, www.guernseybar.com/students-careers/qualifying-as-a-guernsey-advocate-in-detail.aspx.

IAESB (2019) *Handbook of International Education Standards*, www.ifac.org/iaesb/publications/2019-handbook-international-education-standards.

International Bar Association (date unknown) *International Trade in Legal Services*, www.ibanet.org/PPID/Constituent/Bar_Issues_Commission/BIC_ITILS_Map.

International Criminal Court (date unknown) *Guide for Applicants to the ICC List of Counsel and Assistants to Counsel*, www.icc-cpi.int/iccdocs/PIDS/docs/ICC_GuideForApplicants_ENG.pdf.

Law Society of England and Wales (March 2021) *Irish Re-Open Door to English and Welsh Solicitors*, www.lawsociety.org.uk/contact-or-visit-us/press-office/press-releases/irish-re-open-door-to-english-and-welsh-solicitors.

Law Society of England and Wales (April 2021) *France Paves the Way for UK Lawyers to Continue Practising in Paris Post-Brexit*, www.lawsociety.org.uk/contact-or-visit-us/press-office/press-releases/france-paves-the-way-for-uk-lawyers-to-continue-practising-in-paris-post-brexit.

Law Society of England and Wales (June 2021) *Legal Profession Will Benefit from New Trade Deal with Australia*, www.lawsociety.org.uk/contact-or-visit-us/press-office/press-releases/legal-profession-will-benefit-from-new-trade-deal-with-australia.

Legal Profession Qualifying Board (1995) *New List of Recognised Law Degrees (LLB) from the United Kingdom*, www.lpqb.org.my/images/psag/infomation%20for%20prospective%20candidates/PRESS%20RELEASE-5%20dec%201999-NEW[1].pdf.

Nigeria Bar (2020) *Council of Legal Education Nigerian Law School Application for 2020 Bar Part I Course*, www.nigeriabar.com/2020/06/council-of-legal-education-nigerian-law-school-application-for-2020-bar-part-i-course#.YO1HyT2SkdU.

Solicitors Regulation Authority (April 2022) *SQE Assessment Exemptions*, www.sra.org.uk/become-solicitor/qualified-lawyers/sqe-exemptions/.

Solicitors Regulation Authority (March 2022) *Qualified Lawyers*, www.sra.org.uk/become-solicitor/qualified-lawyers/.

studylaw.nl (date unknown) *Study Law in Holland*, www.studylaw.nl/faq#:~:text=For%20EU%20students%2C%20the%20annual,15%2C000%2C%20depending%20on%20the%20programme.

Laurel S Terry (2002, revised 2013) *General Agreement on Trade in Services: A Handbook for International Bar Association Member Bars*, www.ibanet.org/PPID/Constituent/Bar_Issues_Commission/BIC_ITILS_Committee/Projects.aspx.

TitoliSpagna (2022) *Practicante a vita?* www.titolispagna.com/.

United Nations Commission on International Trade Law (2013) *UNCITRAL Arbitration Rules*, https://uncitral.un.org/en/texts/arbitration/contractualtexts/arbitration.

World Trade Organisation (2021) *Legal Services*, www.wto.org/english/tratop_e/serv_e/legal_e/legal_e.htm.

Part 2

Relations

Chapter 6

Care, Practices of Justice, and the Renewal of Legal Education in Italy

A Case from the Roma Tre Law Clinic

Martina Millefiorini and Carlo Caprioglio

Introduction: Clinical Legal Education in Italy—An Answer to the Social Question of Justice

Clinical legal education, by now a global movement,[1] has two primary objectives: training students in the practice of law and the acquisition of professional skills and abilities; and implementing its mission of social justice and public engagement.[2] The Italian case is no exception. Since their early stages of experimentation, Italian law clinics have been characterised by their mission to promote access to justice for disadvantaged groups and to protect public interests.[3] Due to the success of the clinical methodology, the Italian debate has by now gone far beyond definitional and methodological questions, refining the practice with critical reflections on its potential to renew Italian legal studies and on its epistemological implications regarding the production of legal knowledge.[4]

This is a rather broad debate situated around a social justice perspective, namely the determination to direct the clinics' activities towards those oft-neglected sectors of the legal system[5] that involve marginalised subjects. Indeed, there is a profound difference in the perspective one adopts when observing legal phenomena—and, why not, society itself—from a clinic that deals with commercial or banking law, perhaps offering services to large companies and banking institutions, versus a clinic that promotes access to justice for workers, migrants, or detainees. Dealing with subjects with less social power, and with the sectors of law that form the very foundation of the legal system, allows clinical scholars and students to develop a radically different perspective—one that questions certain cornerstones of the legal tradition, starting with the alleged

1 Bloch (2011); Wilson (2018).

2 Kruse (2011), p 2. See also Bloch (2008).

3 The first Italian legal clinics were activated in the departments of law at the University of Brescia in 2009, and at Roma Tre University and IUC Turin in 2010. For the Brescia Clinic, see Barbera (2012); for the Human Rights and Migration Law Clinic of Turin, see Stege and Veglio (2018); for the Roma Tre Clinic, see Asta et al. (2018).

4 See Barbera (2018); Blengino and Cuenca (2019).

5 Asta et al. (2018), p 210.

DOI: 10.4324/9781003175193-9

autonomy and neutrality of law (as well as that of academia and the legal professions), with respect to the interests and actors involved.[6]

The main interventions of the Italian law clinics, therefore, are not random or coincidental. They correspond with aspects of society strongly marked by the structural inequalities that expose the vulnerability of one of the parties in dispute: labour law, migration, prison law, the environment and the right to health, anti-discrimination, and so forth.[7] These are sectors of the legal system that are often interconnected, where multiple structural inequalities add up and place some subjects at a severe disadvantage with respect to access to justice and the exercise of rights: think, for example, of the relationship between environmental health and the right to health, or between labour law and migration.[8] Furthermore, these areas of intervention imply assisting with specific problems beyond those of a legal nature. These include, for example, the illegitimate practices of public administrations; regulatory and bureaucratic obstacles that hinder their access to justice; exclusion from access to welfare services; and possessing lower social and economic capital than their counterpart, be it a state administration or private entity.

If taken seriously as a teaching method based on the practice of law using real cases (live-client clinic),[9] the clinical methodology requires taking a clear stance amidst a context of many conflicting interests, by adopting a partial perspective that is able to uncover the role of the law in building, maintaining, or strengthening social hierarchies. At the same time, from this very position that is neither neutral nor external, but partial and internal to the conflict, one experiences at the clinic how the law can be used as a tool to promote rights and give access to justice. Thus, if the chosen stance is on the side of socially marginalised subjects, the law becomes the main tool to promote demands for justice and social change.

After more than a decade of austerity and regressive politics on minority rights, the current social and political crisis throws into question the role of the law—including the academy and the university as a public institution—in the face of local and global inequalities now being exacerbated by the Covid-19 pandemic[10] and its socio-economic consequences.[11] The global success of legal clinics appears as one possible answer to this question. In other words, the increasing popularity of legal clinics—in Italy as elsewhere—can be related to the growing demand for justice that comes from the social groups who are systematically excluded from accessing fundamental civil and social rights. Responding to the demand for social justice through the practice of

6 Berrey et al. (2012), p 8.
7 Bartoli (2015); Maestroni (2018a).
8 On this last aspect, see Caprioglio (2019).
9 Santoro (2019); Wilson (2018).
10 Singer and Rylko-Bauer (2021).
11 Della Porta and Portos (2020).

law, however, requires confronting the crisis of law as an instrument of social mediation. This is a crisis with multiple causes: the proliferation of secondary administrative sources and bureaucratic practices, for one, which often contrast with the formal rules, and which at a national level question the coherence of the legal system; and the increasing fragmentation of the law at the supranational level due to globalisation.[12]

As far as we are concerned, however, the crisis is above all a crisis of law as an instrument of emancipation,[13] of recognising new rights, and demands for justice. This is a theme connected to the so-called crisis of jurisdiction or, in the words of Maria Rosaria Ferrarese, of the 'escape from justice', whereby 'people use the channels of civil justice less and less to settle their disputes'[14] due to the structural deficiencies of the justice system, the high costs of legal representation, and the systemic limitations in access to justice. In this sense, taking legal action for a migrant person, for example, is very different from that of a citizen for multiple legal, social, and economic reasons: for an 'irregular migrant' to go to court means self-denunciation to the authorities, and irregular migrants often lack integration into the social fabric and knowledge of their rights.

From this perspective, Italian law clinics often face the question of how to offer legal support to socially vulnerable subjects in the face of the crisis of law as an instrument of emancipation. Clinics are thus called upon to experiment with legal guidance methods and strategies that go beyond the use of 'traditional' litigation tools. But not only this: they must also imagine original ways of understanding vulnerabilities, of promoting empathy to build trusting relationships such that clients feel safe revealing elements of their personal histories that may be useful for the recognition of their rights, and of creating collaborative networks with public bodies and associations in order to offer integrated legal assistance that considers the complexities of their clients' individual situations.

A distinctive feature of law clinics is therefore that both students and people from outside the university, usually from marginalised social groups, are involved in the educational experience. From this perspective, it is possible to highlight the biopolitical tension that runs through clinical legal education, which, starting with its name, explicitly refers to the field of medical science.[15] Since Michel Foucault theorised biopolitics (or biopower) as a form of power targeting the living population as a biological or 'natural' entity, the concept has found an application in various areas of the social sciences, including edu-

12 Teubner (2010).

13 de Sousa Santos (2005).

14 Ferrarese (1988–89), pp 168–9.

15 For a discussion on the topic in the Italian context, see Carrer (2018), p 24. The parallels between US universities and medical clinics during the early 1900s are discussed in the well-known work of Jerome Frank (1933).

cation.[16] Nevertheless, the biopolitical dimension of clinical legal education is still largely overlooked.[17] Yet, at least two aspects highlight the constitutively biopolitical nature of clinical methodology.

The first concerns the role of students in law clinics, particularly those engaged in the field of social justice. The ethical dimension of the commitment and the face-to-face contact with the people, bearers of rights and claims, require the mobilisation of emotions, empathic and relational skills, which enrich the educational experience.[18] The second is, instead, that the activity of legal assistance provided by the clinics often involves spheres of people's lives that have an accentuated biopolitical dimension: from the right to health—and reproductive health, for women—to access to welfare services—such as social housing and benefits—up to the condition of confinement in a total institution. Legal assistance can thus go beyond mere technical-professional advice on specific legal issues to become an actual practice of 'taking charge' of the lives of the assisted persons.

Therefore, biopolitics is part of the constitutive ambivalence of clinical legal education, or rather, as Marella and Rigo put it, it is part of the 'dark side' of law clinics as a tool to govern social conflict.[19] At the same time, however, this constitutive ambivalence has potential, as we show in this chapter. The biopolitical features of clinical legal education can be played against the governmental logic to build social alliances for social justice and political transformation. To the biopolitical approach of 'taking charge of life', we thus counterpose practices of situated justice that aim to support the paths of emancipation and autonomy of vulnerable subjects: in this case, migrant women and asylum seekers.

In the following sections, the chapter aims to reflect on these issues, based on the experiences at the Migration and Citizenship Law Clinic at Roma Tre University (hereafter, the Clinic). Drawing on the theoretical tools offered by feminist literature, the following analyses the practices of situated justice experimented with at the Clinic in supporting the paths of migrant women in their legal and social emancipation. Based on these practices, in the next section, we propose an interpretation of the Clinic as a *space of care*, counterposed to the biopolitical practice of 'taking charge of life' through control and management of the assisted persons, in which rethinking the methods of legal assistance of migrant women is key in promoting claims to situated justice.

16 Kraftl (2015); Simons (2006). For an analysis of biopolitics and racism in the US higher education system in light of the Covid-19 pandemic, see Suspitsyna (2021). For a critical survey of the multiple uses of the concept of biopolitics in STS scholarship in the last three decades, see Birch (2017).
17 About the impact of clinical legal education in non-Western countries, specifically in Nigeria, see Nwedu's chapter in this volume.
18 On emotions and empathy in clinical legal education, see Santoro (2019); Marella-Rigo (2015); Tushnet (1984).
19 Marella and Rigo (2015), pp 545–6.

Roma Tre Law Clinic and Legal Assistance for Migrant Women: A Feminist Approach to Justice

Founded in 2010, the Clinic opted for the 'live-client' model from its inception, choosing to deal with real cases brought to the clinic by migrants.[20] In January 2012, the Clinic opened a Front Office at the Roma Tre University, offering free legal assistance year-round. There, under the guidance of lawyers and teachers, students have the opportunity to relate directly and unmediated with migrants, themselves bearers of rights and legal battles. This gives students the opportunity to experience the 'relational aspect', crucial to training legal experts who are not only well-aware of social realities,[21] but who actively and critically reflect on the law and question its socially constructed paradigms: for example, the privilege of national belonging itself, which obscures the structurally excluding nature of the institution of citizenship.[22]

The Clinic quickly became an important point of reference for the city, assisting an average of 200 clients a year, filing about 70 appeals for international protection, and following dozens of cases concerning expulsion and detention, family reunification, and access to local services. These numbers help to give an idea of how the Clinic responds to the concrete demands for access to justice that come from the local migrant population. Indeed, due to barriers that are social, cultural, linguistic, and economic in nature, there are regulatory obstacles that discourage or prevent migrants from asserting their rights through the courts. The very absence of the statute of citizenship, for example, is in itself a structural limit to a migrant's ability to take legal action: in fact, going to court means acting as *a citizen* in the public sphere and doing so as an individual—that is, alone.

The Clinic's activities concern many aspects of migrants' daily lives, but legal assistance aimed at obtaining a residence permit is one of its central functions. The right to asylum quickly became the main area of intervention at the Clinic due to recent reforms of immigration law and the restriction of other legal access routes that have made asylum the main instrument for migrant regularisation in Italy.[23] Despite this, the continuity of the Clinic's service—ten years to date—and the free and thorough nature of its legal assistance, ensured not only by the presence of experienced lawyers but also by the commitment and enthusiasm of its students, have ensured that clients' other needs, such as access to health services, training, and navigating the reception system, are always attended to. To take up the famous words of Abdelmalek Sayad, if the migratory phenomenon is a 'total social fact',[24] then legal assistance to migrants

20 Asta et al. (2018).
21 Santoro (2019), p 125.
22 Ferrajoli (2007).
23 Caprioglio and Rigo (2020).
24 Sayad (1999).

must not fail to deal with the complexity of the migratory experience, or rather with the interdependence between seemingly distinct aspects of life and the complexity of the causes of exclusion from the exercise of rights that take shape far beyond the purview of immigration law.

Extending the scope of intervention at the Clinic has resulted in an enrichment in student training, and, more importantly, has led to a greater awareness of the numerous barriers that hinder migrants from accessing rights. This has stimulated a certain creativity in developing defence strategies and forming alliances with different actors, both public and private. In the interest of consistency, the present discussion will centre on the case of migrant women, and the key role of the Clinic's students in guaranteeing their legal assistance.

In recent years, female migration to Italy has increased significantly: between 2005 and 2020, the number of migrant women increased by 141%.[25] Amidst the so-called refugee crisis, between 2014 and 2019—in which arrivals along the central Mediterranean route reached a peak of over 181,000 people in 2016—the percentage of women increased steadily from 15 to 25% of the total arrivals.[26] In 2015 alone, over 21,000 women arrived in Italy by sea, compared to 18,000 in 2014, or 14% of total arrivals compared to 10% the year before; the majority of these women were from Nigeria.[27] According to the IOM, in the two-year period 2014–2016, the arrivals of Nigerian women, potential victims of trafficking, increased by more than 600%, from 1500 to about 11,000.[28] Eurostat data confirm the importance of the female component in forced migration to Italy: the first asylum applications submitted by women went from almost 5,000 in 2014 to over 20,000 in 2017, then dropped to 14,000 in 2018, corresponding with the overall decrease in arrivals by sea, settling at around 20–25% of the total.[29]

Unsurprisingly, the Clinic experienced an influx of migrant women at its front desk during this period. The Clinic thus proved to be a place for observing the transformations in the gender composition of so-called forced migrations to Italy and, at the same time, a space for experimenting with new practices to support migrant women, mainly of Nigerian nationality. Despite the drastic reduction in arrivals by sea in 2018, people of Nigerian origin still represent at least 5% of the migrant population in Italy, and a significant portion of these are women, both alone and with children.[30]

The increase of women clients—an average of over 40 women per year between 2015 and 2018—has impacted the legal approach of the Clinic's

25 ISMU (2020), single page.
26 Data obtained from the UNCHR, Regional Data Portal, available at data2.unhcr.org/en/situations.
27 IOM (2016a), pp 13–14.
28 IOM (2017), p 10.
29 Data obtained from the Eurostat Data Browser, available at ec.europa.eu/eurostat/web/main/data/database.
30 Ministero dell'Interno (2020), pp 1–9.

teachers and students. For one, the students are confronted—often for the first time—with the phenomenon of human trafficking for the purpose of exploiting sex work,[31] which in Italy mostly involves Nigerian women. The knowledge students gained on the subject therefore did not come from abstract study, but from their concrete experiences with women requesting legal support. In these cases, requests for legal support often go beyond the boundaries, in the strict sense, of professional legal assistance, and involve different but decisive issues in women's emancipatory paths: access to the health system and matters of reproductive health, housing, income, and childcare services. Furthermore, the relationships established with migrant women through daily support, as well as the alliances with *other women* who work in specialised services such as anti-violence centres and anti-trafficking organisations, have provoked a rethinking of the methodologies used in protecting rights and the adopting of a 'practical' and 'situated' approach to justice. Such approaches can be better analysed through the theoretical lens of legal feminism.

In 1982, Duncan Kennedy, one of the leading voices of Critical Legal Studies, highlighted how the legal education imparted in US law schools reproduced within it the structure of social hierarchies. According to Kennedy, places of legal training are 'intensely political place[s], in spite of the fact that the modern law school seems intellectually unpretentious, barren of theoretical ambition or practical vision of what social life might be'.[32] In the conclusions of his article, Kennedy expresses hope for a radical change in teaching law, with the inclusion of clinical courses that would help to reveal the hierarchies within the law and that would deconstruct the perception of these hierarchies as 'natural'.[33]

The issue does not only concern law schools. It is more generally the educational system that tends to reproduce the hierarchies of social order. According to Maarten Simons, in the neoliberal regime the commodification of education appears

> as an instrument to bring about a social form of individuality and self-understanding in which people see themselves as part of a broader bio-social and bio-economic totality. This also makes it possible to start thinking about the reproduction of the order and norms of society (through education) or about its optimisation through biological and/or economic selection.[34]

31 UNODC (2021), pp 133–8.
32 Kennedy (1982), p 591.
33 Ibid., p 597. From the different perspective of decolonial thinking, Foluke I Adebisi, stresses the role of Euro-modern legal education in perpetuating racial and colonial social hierarchies (in 'Educating for the End of a Necropolitical World: What Happens Beyond Decolonisation in Legal Education?', in the *Biopolitics and Resistance in Legal Education* volume).
34 Simons (2006), p 531.

Spaces of resistance to the exercise of neoliberal biopower in education can thus only be created by radically different approaches to teaching, also in the field of legal education.

Around the same time as Kennedy's reflection, feminist critique broke into US universities and became one of the main critical lenses in the analysis of law. Feminism critique is based on the theoretical assumption that there is no field of knowledge that can be defined as 'neutral', including the law. According to legal feminist scholars, the distinction between 'politics' and 'law', and the alleged impartiality of the latter, is a fiction pursued by the dominant ideology that maintains and perpetuates the social hierarchies of gender, and the condition of subordination of women.[35] The law is thus not considered for its formal validity but as a social product of the balances of forces and dynamics that unfold in society. The fundamental principles of the legal feminism may be summarised as: a theoretical approach that at the same time uses and reworks existing legal concepts and proposes new issues addressed by the legal feminism's critical perspective such as equality;[36] a method based on the indissoluble connection between theory and practice; and finally, an approach that aims at unveiling the ideological apparatus behind the alleged neutrality of the law.[37]

With regard to legal education, the 'revolutionary' approach to law advanced by feminist theory, aimed at understanding its concrete functioning at a social level, was not based on abstract theoretical notions (which Critical Legal Studies was often criticised for), but on the feminist concept of 'starting from oneself'. As Carrie Menkel-Meadow points out:

> the main difference between the two ways of looking at the world is that the feminist critique starts from the experiential point of view of the oppressed, dominated, and devalued, while the critical legal studies critique begins – and, some would argue, remains – in a male constructed, privileged place in which domination and oppression can be described and imagined but not fully experienced.[38]

In its approach to the study of some specific sectors of the legal system, feminist criticism therefore starts from the real experiences of women. Feminist theorists have shown how the law re-purposes the patriarchal schemes of society, underlining, for example, the pervasiveness of patriarchal paradigms in criminal law. Among these, Catharine MacKinnon highlights how US procedural law,

35 Smart (1992).

36 In Italy an example is the work of Letizia Gianformaggio (2005).

37 Smart (1992).

38 Menkel-Meadow (1988), p 61. About the adoption of feminist and queer theory in legal education, see also Chris Ashford, Laura Graham and Samantha Rasiah, 'Centring Feminist and Queer Experiences in the Law School: Legal Zines as a Humanising Pedagogy', in the *Biopolitics and Resistance in Legal Education* volume.

in assuming that consent to sexual intercourse necessarily excludes the possibility of forced intercourse, denies justice to women if the violence occurred after consent was initially given.[39]

Legal feminism thus demands a methodology that begins with the concrete needs and experiences of women. Its critique, therefore, is likewise aimed at the 'Socratic method', or the idea that the teaching of law must be based on an '"underlying logic" of the cases',[40] in which the resolution of the legal question takes place through an abstract, intrinsically rational, logical-deductive procedure, totally detached from the social and material conditions that characterise it. Instead, for legal feminism, the study of concrete cases and co-participated reasoning in the classroom with students are the privileged methods in building a shared knowledge of law, through an analysis of cases that starts from the individual experiences of participants.

In light of these considerations, the Clinic's experience with migrant women, in particular Nigerian women, has allowed it to cultivate among its students an awareness of the need to adopt a feminist perspective, both theoretically as well as in the actual practice of law aimed at legal support. In this way, the law is understood as a barrier and, at the same time, a tool to satisfy needs, recognise rights, and pursue the objective of the emancipation of women and of migrants more generally. In its ambivalence, the law is thus studied and utilised at the Clinic, criticised for its defects, of course, but also re-imagined, using new strategies where necessary that are based on the specific characteristics of each case.

An episode that occurred at the Clinic can be useful to better understand what is meant by a 'practical' and 'situated' approach to justice. Between 2017 and 2018, a group of female students from the Clinic worked alongside a legal expert at an emergency reception centre in a neighbourhood situated on the eastern outskirts of Rome. The centre housed, on average, 60 female asylum seekers and refugees of Nigerian nationality. The Clinic's students listened to the women's stories and supported them throughout the asylum process, for example by helping them prepare for their interviews with the Territorial Commission, the authority that decides on migrants' applications for international protection. These Nigerian women often had histories of being trafficked for exploitative sex work. To support their release from trafficking and recognise their right to international protection, the Ministry of the Interior and the UNHCR introduced the so-called 'referral' procedure.[41] According to this procedure, if potential indicators of trafficking emerge during a woman's asylum interview in ways that are *unclear* or *ambiguous*, the interview must be interrupted and the woman directed to an anti-trafficking body where she sits

39 MacKinnon (1987).
40 Menkel-Meadow (1988), p 67.
41 Commissione Nazionale per il Diritto di Asilo and UNHCR (2019).

through a series of meetings aimed at elaborating her personal experiences, which are then reported to the Territorial Commission.

The Commission's approach required that the women's stories clearly showed their lack of consent to situations of violence and exploitation related to trafficking. 'Consent' thus became a 'rigid' category, disconnected from the lived experiences of women and the context of their origins. Therefore, the potential consent of women, even if only initial, was interpreted by the court as their voluntary adherence to trafficking or was even used to exclude the possibility of coercion and exploitation. In reality, women usually have complex elaborations of their experiences of trafficking and subjective understandings of the trauma they suffered, which will differ from person to person. The Territorial Commission, however, sought explicit recognition of the victim status and full awareness of the trafficking process, without recognising the necessarily personal ways women processed the violence and trauma they suffered.

In collaborating with anti-trafficking groups, it became clear to the Clinic that if psychological and legal support is indeed necessary to help a woman re-elaborate her experiences, then a few interviews aimed solely at recognising her condition as a victim are not sufficient for supporting her in her quest for self-determination. Rather, the support provided must be broader and more integrated to include the different spheres of a woman's life. The students thus concluded that, regardless of the level of awareness women have of their own experiences, what they are looking for is protection and support in their paths to emancipation: it is therefore imperative that they are guaranteed services regardless of their 'self-narrations' or their understandings of their experiences. From this point of view, obtaining a permanent residence permit is critical, as it is an essential tool in escaping from violence and beginning the path to self-determination.

The Clinic therefore launched an intense series of appeals before the Civil Court of Rome against the decisions of the Territorial Commission which did not recognise international protection for women who had not explicitly declared themselves victims of trafficking. This litigation—and the high number of appeals won—had a transformative effect, contributing to the development of a gender-sensitive orientation in the jurisprudential interpretation of the right to asylum, in which a woman's self-identification as a victim is no longer decisive, but the social and cultural contexts that push women into the trafficking system are recognised by the court, as are the endemic spread of different forms of gender-based violence. Among these is female genital mutilation, which represents a persecutory act against women as a specific social group, and which is in itself sufficient for the recognition of asylum.[42] The Tribunal of Rome now recognises international protection to female victims of genital mutilation or

42 See UNHCR (2002), p 2. According to International Law, female genital mutilation constitutes torture and cruel, inhumane, or degrading treatment, as affirmed for example by the EHCR in the case *Emily Collins and Ashley Akaziebie v. Sweden*, Application n. 23944/05, 8 March 2007.

women at risk of trafficking (or re-trafficking) in the event of returning to their country of origin, regardless of their self-recognition as victims.

A feminist approach to legal assistance further entails listening to the migrants themselves and favouring non-normative and non-hierarchical methods in processing cases, such as directly collaborating with the assisted persons in determining their cases. For the Clinic, drawing inspiration from the feminist approach to law therefore means starting from the material conditions of the case rather than subsuming the concrete situation within certain predefined legal categories. As Orsetta Giolo puts it:

> from a methodological point of view, the most significant and irrefutable characteristic of legal feminism concerns its reconfiguration of the relationship between theory and practice within legal phenomena, strengthening the connections between theoretical elaboration, political activism, and the experiential complexity and plurality of human existence.[43]

Another important aspect of the Clinic's experience involves the effort to consistently view its legal assistance from a decolonial lens. Indeed, the professional approach to law risks standardising services and methods around the 'citizen paradigm'—that is, white and male—without deconstructing the coloniality that permeates immigration law and institutional practices. With reference to the critical tools of decolonial feminism, 'decolonial legal support' requires relational practices that are capable of freeing oneself from 'the colonial legacy founded on power, domination, exploitation and oppression'.[44] The Clinic thus seeks to assert a respectful approach to difference, and a non-judgemental and non-normative attitude towards the assisted persons, who can independently choose the level and methods of legal assistance they receive. To this end, it is of critical importance to build individual relationships of trust between students and clients, which explains why, over time, women sometimes ask to be able to always talk to the same female student(s). Indeed, relationships that can re-imagine forms of 'sisterhood',[45] while unusual for most law students undergoing training in the university context, are in fact central to effectively supporting migrant women's demands for justice.

The Clinic as a Space of Care and Justice

The Clinic is an academic project in which scholars, students, and migrant people, such as asylum seekers and trafficked women, interact with each other.

43 Giolo (2017), p 212.

44 Mohanty (2003), p 56.

45 'Sisterhood' is used here in intersectional and decolonial terms, distant from the essentialist approaches that tend to consider the relationships and experiences of all women as equal. On this point, see Bunjun (2010).

This inevitably makes it a social setting marked by class, gender, and racial differences. The daily relationships between clients and staff encouraged a critical reflection on the forms of legal support provided. Being aware of the social hierarchies that shape the Clinic as an institutional space pushed the staff and the students to experiment with forms of legal support based on 'taking care'—in a broad sense—of clients' circumstances, focused on their life experiences, needs, and goals. Read through the lens of feminist and decolonial thought, the Clinic thus constitutes a space for experimentation with practices of justice, centred on the care for individual situations that goes beyond the use of traditional instruments of litigation.

In a seminar held at the Sapienza University of Rome in 2019, Joan Tronto underlined how 'caring with' can be considered 'a strategy for revitalizing the foundation of democratic citizenship: the practice of caring not just for fellow citizens, but also for democracy itself'.[46] *In a Different Voice* by Carol Gilligan is considered the first essay dealing with the ethics of care. The author proposes a critical reflection on the subject starting from the relationship between parents and children, defined by an unequal power structure and by a limited range of choices for the latter. This contrasts with the predominant conception that relations are undertaken voluntarily by free and equal individuals.[47]

In the context of feminist legal studies, Virginia Held has pointed out that the predominant Kantian view—in which the individual is a subject capable of rational choices as an independent and autonomous agent—is contrasted by a feminist ethics of care that considers people as constituted, at least in part, by concrete relationships with others.[48] The Kantian vision of justice focuses mainly on the concept of equality and individual rights through the formulation of impartial and abstract principles that require 'only' application to the concrete case. Instead, the ethics of care focuses on social contexts and the needs of real people, giving importance to the complexity of concrete relationships. Care should thus be placed at the centre of public decisions, in the sense that the needs of individuals, intrinsically linked to their relationships with others, must be the subject of collective attention and therefore of the law.[49] However, on closer inspection, the relationship between the ethics of care and feminist thought has not always been linear. Some authors, including Nussbaum, have warned against those interpretations that tend to consider care as something naturally 'feminine', or in any case relegated to the 'private' sphere, arguing instead for the need to radically rethink space and gender roles in the collective care of citizenship.[50]

46 Notes taken by the authors at Joan Tronto's seminar 'Caring Democratically: A Response to Neopopulism', held on 6 May 2019 at the Sapienza University of Rome.

47 Gilligan (1982).

48 Held (2004), pp 145–50.

49 Ibid., pp 145–50.

50 Nussbaum (1999).

Beyond the complexity of care as a political practice, what is relevant is how in 'taking care' of cases, the Clinic experiments with shared strategies with those seeking assistance. These strategies do not always lead to litigation before the courts. While litigation is often necessary, as in the case of appeals against the illegitimate practices of administrative bodies that limit migrants' access to rights or that hinder their acquisition of a residence permit, a significant part of the care given actually requires other forms of action. These actions include, for example, accompanying migrants to their appointments at public offices to support them in accessing public services, overcoming language barriers, or handling the illegitimate behaviour of public officials; intermediating between migrants and local services, such as medical clinics; or again, referring them to anti-trafficking institutions, anti-violence centres, and specialised reception centres with which the Clinic has been collaborating for some time.

Using the various tools offered by the law and by the public system is therefore strictly connected to the objectives identified for each specific case and to the subjective conditions of each assisted person. The intention is to overcome that clear separation between client and professional, typical in relationships with lawyers, in which the latter, holder of technical and exclusive knowledge, identifies the strategy for 'resolving' the case and presents it to the assisted person. Instead, the clinical methodology aims—if not to eliminate, then at least to reduce—its distance with the assisted persons, recognising them as active collaborators in elaborating and solving their own problems.[51] After all, once the alleged neutrality of law in regards to those involved has been radically questioned, it is not difficult to recognise an active role for those who experience the problem first hand in defining the best strategy to deal with the case—especially if they occupy a marginal position in society.

Adopting a situated perspective, specific to those who must bring forth requests for justice from the margins of the social hierarchy, together with an approach charged with the transformative potential of the ethics of care, allows us to integrate the tools of legal assistance, alongside litigation, with other practices of situated justice. These practices widen the net of the law in order to include those needs, requests, and subjectivities otherwise excluded from the recognition and exercise of rights. In the case of the Clinic, not limiting the forms of care to the right to litigation implies looking after the concrete needs of those seeking assistance, trying, indeed, to 'take care' of the multiplicity of existing individual situations.

Taking care of migrant women's individual situations—especially when related to specific spheres of life, such as health or access to welfare—can be read as a form of biopolitical power. In other words, the risk is that 'taking care' may end up in 'taking charge of' the lives of the persons, through a professional service, based on specific knowledge and practices, which reproduces

51 Houh and Kalsen (2014), p 294.

governmental logics of control and administration of life. Nevertheless, in our perspective, what makes the Clinic different from other institutional spaces that work through the exercise of biopolitical practices of protection, control, organisation, and direction of life, is precisely the attention to the individual situations of the persons assisted, the construction of empathic relationships with them, and the aim of supporting their autonomy and emancipation.

In this perspective, the feminist concept of 'starting from oneself' (*partire da sé*) is key in constructing relations between the subjects involved, particularly with migrant women. This concept means first of all, as Tristana Dini puts it, 'a practice of de-identification, a way to go beyond a submissive subjectivity and focus instead on a free one', focused on the 'desire that starts with the self, independently of the trajectories of power, and inscribes itself in a political and relational dimension'.[52] To experiment with practices of situated justice within a space of care means dealing with the material conditions of life of the assisted subject's concrete needs and desires, in order to build relationships which, even if formally based on the 'counsel–client' framework, allow for shared and situated strategies of resolution of their legal problems.

Relationships of care between individuals can thus play a crucial role in redirecting—'from below'—biopolitical practices towards the (re)production of life in different directions than those imposed 'from above'.[53] From this point of view, the Clinic represents an attempt to go beyond the approach of 'taking charge of life'—widespread in the humanitarian and voluntary sector or legal aid services for migrants—towards a space of care centred on the self-determination of the assisted persons.

Conclusion

'Looking after' the cases of migrants—and in particular of women—in their complexity, that is, attending to aspects of life that have no immediate connection with immigration law but that directly or indirectly affect personal emancipation paths, can be traced back once again to the biopolitical aspect of clinics. As mentioned in the introduction, starting with the name, legal *clinics* signal a semantic connection with medical knowledge and practices. Using this analogy with reference to Foucauldian theory, Marella and Rigo highlight the 'dark side' of Italian legal clinics: their governmental function of 'care' for social conflict supports the access to justice of marginal categories 'through technical *expertise*, which is therefore essentially neutral, scientifically qualified, and produced by a prestigious third party such as the university institution'.[54] The same authors, however, recognise that this is not a doomed fate, and that

52 Dini (2017), p 234.
53 Lin et al. (2018), p 887. See also Kraftl (2015); Hardt and Negri (2009).
54 Marella and Rigo (2015), p 545.

the Italian practice has also resulted in different outcomes: promoting the transformative potential of teaching law in legal clinics, for example, and developing a critical approach to law and an awareness of the social role of legal experts in promoting social justice.[55]

By giving relevance to the empathic relationships that are developed within a law clinic, clinical legal education provides an opportunity to go beyond the 'taking care of' people needs as a technical-legal service, to counterpose it with concrete support for the self-determination of the persons assisted. A challenge for both the teaching and practice of law that can be well described in the words of Dini: 'life must not be, as in bio-politics, an object of government, but a reference point for the construction (molecular, microphysical, contingent) of other relations, common spaces oriented towards another economy, another citizenship, another labour'.[56]

In regard to the activities of the Roma Tre Law Clinic, this is precisely what is intended by the practice of situated justice as a method of looking after the cases of assisted migrants. Unlike the victimising and de-subjectivising practices that characterise, for example, the biopolitical dimension of the humanitarian apparatus,[57] the Clinic proposes a model of legal assistance focused on social cooperation, the enhancement of empathic relationships between people, and the exchange of knowledge and experiences situated according to the emancipation paths of migrants. In a period of profound social crisis, the Clinic, as a place for both students' training and migrant legal assistance, constitutes a space for experimentation with new practices of justice, whose stakes are not only the renewal of legal education, but the opportunity to rehabilitate law as an instrument for promoting the demands of situated justice. This must start from the needs and desires of those who experience the unjust processes of increasing social and legal exclusion for themselves.[58]

Acknowledgements

This chapter is the result of shared reflections between the authors. Nevertheless, for organising purposes, Carlo Caprioglio wrote the first and the last section; Martina Millefiorini wrote the second and third sections.

References

Primary sources

Emily Collins and Ashley Akaziebie v. Sweden, Application n. 23944/05, 8 March 2007.

55 Ibid., p 546.
56 Dini (2017), p 236.
57 Fassin (2012).
58 de Sousa Santos (2005).

Secondary sources

Francesca Asta et al. (2018) 'Il Ruolo delle Cliniche Legali Come Strumento di Insegnamento e Approccio al Diritto. L'Esperienza della Clinica del Diritto dell'Immigrazione e della Cittadinanza di Roma Tre' in A Maestroni et al. (eds) *Teorie e Pratiche nelle Cliniche Legali*, Giappichelli.

Marzia Barbera (2012) 'The Making of a Civil Law Clinic' in M Pedrazzoli et al. (eds) *Risistemare il Diritto del Lavoro. Liber Amicorum Marcello Pedrazzoli*, FrancoAngeli.

Marzia Barbera (2018) 'Il Movimento delle Cliniche Legali e le Sue Ragioni' in A Maestroni et al. (eds) *Teorie e Pratiche nelle Cliniche Legali*, Giappichelli.

Clelia Bartoli (2015) 'The Italian Legal Clinics Movement: Data and Prospects' 22 *International Journal of Clinical Education* 213.

Ellen Berrey et al. (2012) 'Situated Justice: A Contextual Analysis of Fairness and Inequality in Employment Discrimination Litigation' 46 *Law and Society Review* 1.

Kean Birch (2017) 'The Problem of Bio-concepts: Biopolitics, Bio-economy and the Political Economy of Nothing' 12 *Cultural Studies of Science Education* 915.

Cecilia Blengino and Andrés Gascón-Cuenca (eds) (2019) *Epistemic Communities at the Boundaries of Law: Clinics as a Paradigm in the Revolution of Legal Education in the European Mediterranean*, Ledizioni.

Frank S Bloch (2008) 'Access to Justice and the Global Clinical Movement' 28 *Washington University Journal of Law & Policy* 111.

Frank S Bloch (ed) (2011) *The Global Clinical Movement. Educating Lawyers for Social Justice*, Oxford University Press.

Benita Bunjun (2010) 'Feminist Organizations and Intersectionality: Contesting Hegemonic Feminism' 34 *Atlantis. Critical Studies in Gender, Culture and Social Justice* 115.

Carlo Caprioglio (2019) 'Rethinking Legal Education in Times of Crisis. Some Remarks from the Case of the Roma Tre Migration and Citizenship Law Clinic' 2 *Roma Tre Law Review* 333.

Carlo Caprioglio and Enrica Rigo (2020) 'Lavoro, Politiche Migratorie e Sfruttamento: La Condizione dei Braccianti Migranti in Agricoltura' 3 *Diritto, Immigrazione e Cittadinanza* 33.

Matteo Carrer (2018) 'Rileggendo Carnelutti sulla Clinica del Diritto. Problemi e Questioni Sui Fondamenti della Clinica Legale' in A Maestroni et al. (eds) *Teorie e Pratiche nelle Cliniche Legali*, Giappichelli.

Donatella Della Porta and Martín Portos (2020) 'Social Movements in Times of Inequalities: Struggling Against Austerity in Europe' 53 *Structural Change and Economic Dynamics* 116.

Tristana Dini (2017) 'Politics of Care vs. Biopolitical Care? The Feminist Cut on Neoliberal Saturation' 4 *Soft Power* 227.

Didier Fassin (2012) *Humanitarian Reason, A Moral History of the Present*, University of California Press.

Luigi Ferrajoli (2007) *Principia Iuris*. Teoria giuridica della Democrazia, Laterza.

Maria Rosaria Ferrarese (1988–89) 'Civil Justice and the Judicial Role in Italy' 13 *The Justice System Journal* 168.

Jerome Frank (1933) 'Why not a Clinical Lawyer-School' 81(8) *University of Pennsylvania Law School Review* 907.

Letizia Gianformaggio (2005) *Eguaglianza, Donne e Diritto*, A Facchi, C Faralli, and T Pitch (eds), ilMulino.

Carol Gilligan (1982) *In a Different Voice. Psychological Theory and Women's Development*, Harvard University Press.
Orsetta Giolo and Maria Giulia Bernardini (2017) *Le Teorie Critiche del Diritto*, Pacini Giuridica.
Micheal Hardt and Antonio Negri (2009) *Commonwealth*, Harvard University Press.
Virginia Held (2004) 'Care and Justice in the Global Context' 17 *Ratio Juris* 141.
Emily MS Houh and Katrin Kalsen (2014) 'It's Critical: Legal Participatory Action Research' 19 *Michigan Journal of Race & Law* 287.
Duncan Kennedy (1982) 'Legal Education and the Reproduction of Hierarchy' 32 *Journal of Legal Education* 591.
Peter Kraftl (2015) 'Alter-childhoods: Biopolitics and Childhoods in Alternative Education Spaces' 105 *Annals of the Association of American Geographers* 219.
Katherine R Kruse (2011–2012) 'Getting Real About Legal Realism: New Legal Realism and Clinical Legal Education' 56 *New York Law School Law Review* 295.
Chih-Chen Trista Lin, Claudio Minca and Meghann Ormond (2018) 'Affirmative Biopolitics: Social and Vocational Education for Quechua Girls in the Postcolonial 'Affectsphere' of Cusco, Peru' 36 *Environment and Plannig D: Society and Space* 885.
Catharine MacKinnon (1987) *Feminism Unmodified. Discourses on Life and Law*, Harvard University Press.
Angelo Maestroni (2018a) *Accesso alla Giustizia, Solidarietà e Sussidiarietà nelle Cliniche Legali*, Giappichelli.
Maria Rosaria Marella and Enrica Rigo (2015) 'Le Cliniche Legali, i Beni Comuni e La Globalizzazione dei Modelli di Accesso alla Giustizia e di Lawyering' 4 *Rivista Critica del Diritto Privato* 539.
Carrie Menkel-Meadow (1988) 'Feminist Legal Theory, Critical Legal Studies, and Legal Education or "The Fem-Crits Go to Law School"' 38 *Journal of Legal Education* 61.
Ministero dell'Interno (2020) 'Cruscotto Statistico Giornaliero', www.libertaciviliimmigrazione.dlci.interno.gov.it/it/documentazione/statistica/cruscotto-statistico-giornaliero, Cruscotto statistico al 31 dicembre 2018.
Chandra Talpade Mohanty (2003) *Feminism With-out Borders*, Duke University Press.
Martha C Nussbaum (1999) *Sex and Social Justice*, Oxford University Press.
Enrica Rigo (2020) 'La straniera. Mobilità, Confini e Riproduzione Sociale Oltre lo Straniero di Simmel' 10 *Teoria Politica* 263.
Emilio Santoro (2019) 'Cliniche legali e Concezione del Diritto' 3 *Questione Giustizia* 122.
Abdelmalek Sayad (1999) *La Double Absence. Des illusions de l'émigré aux souffrances de l'immigré*, Éditions du Seuil.
Maarten Simons (2006) 'Learning as Investment: Notes on Governmentality and Biopolitics' 38 (4) *Educational Philosophy and Theory* 523.
Merrill Singer and Barbara Rylko-Bauer (2021) 'The Syndemics and Structural Violence of the COVID Pandemic: Anthropological Insights on a Crisis' 1 *Open Anthropological Research* 7.
Carol Smart (1992) 'The Woman of Legal Discourse' 1 *Social and Legal Studies* 29.
Boaventura de Sousa Santos (2005) 'The Counter-hegemonic Use of Law in the Struggle For a Globalization From Beow' 39 *Anales de la Cátedra Francisco Suárez* 421.
Ulrich Stege and Maurizio Veglio (2018) 'On the Front Line of the Migrant Crisis: The Human Rights and Migration Law Clinic in Turin' in A Alemanno and L Khadar (eds) *Reinventing Legal Education. How Clinical Education is Reforming the Teaching and Practice of Law in Europe*, Cambridge University Press.

Tatiana Suspitsyna (2021) 'Internationalization, Whiteness, and Biopolitics of Higher Education' 11 *Journal of International Students* 50.
Gunther Teubner (2010) 'Fragmented Foundations: Societal Constitutionalism beyond the Nationstate' in P Dobner and M Loughlin (eds) *The Twilight of Constitutionalism?*, Oxford University Press.
Mark V Tushnet (1984) 'Scenes from the Metropolitan Underground: A Critical Perspective on the Status of Clinical Education' 52 *George Washington Law Review* 272.
Richard J Wilson (2018) *The Global Evolution of Clinical Legal Education: More Than a Method*, Oxford University Press.

Reports

Commissione Nazionale per il Diritto di Asilo and UNHCR (2019) 'L'identificazione delle vittime di tratta tra i richiedenti protezione internazionale e procedure di 'Referral'. Linee Guida per le Commissioni Territoriali per il riconoscimento della protezione internazionale', www.unhcr.org/it/wp-content/uploads/sites/97/2021/01/Linee-Guida-per-le-Commissioni-Territoriali_identificazione-vittime-di-tratta.pdf.
IOM (2016a) 'Migrant Vulnerability to Human Trafficking and Exploitation: Evidence from the Central and Eastern Mediterranean Migration Routes', https://publications.iom.int/es/books/migrant-vulnerability-human-trafficking-and-exploitation-evidence-central-and-eastern.
IOM (2017) 'La Tratta di Esseri Umani attraverso la Rotta del Mediterraneo Centrale: Dati, Storie e Informazioni raccolte dall'Organizzazione Internazionale delle Migrazioni', https://italy.iom.int/it/notizie/rapporto-oim-sempre-pi%C3%B9-giovani-e-sempre-pi%C3%B9-vulnerabili-le-potenziali-vittime-di-tratta.
ISMU (2020) 'In Italia l'immigrazione è donna', Press release 6 March 2020, www.ismu.org/in-italia-limmigrazione-e-donna.
UNHCR (2002) 'Guidelines on International Protection No. 1: Gender-related Persecution within the Context of Article 1A(2) of the 1951 Convention and/or its 1967 Protocol Relating to the Status of Refugees' (HCR/GIP/02/01), www.refworld.org/docid/3d36f1c64.html.
UNDOC (2021) 'Global Report on Trafficking in Persons', www.unodc.org/unodc/data-and-analysis/glotip.html.

Chapter 7

Better Read than Unread?

Books and the Teaching(s) of International Law

John R Morss

Books, Biopolitics and International Law

This chapter is about the teaching of international law and about the book, with which, through which and because of which this teaching happens. This chapter is therefore in part about the textbooks of international law but also about the book as master of discourse in the discipline more generally. As such it is a modest contribution to the pedagogical biopolitics of the book, and to the biopolitical pedagogy of international law. In respect of this aim, it is informed by the textualist poetics of Jean d'Aspremont, especially as articulated in his *After Meaning: The Sovereignty of Forms in International Law*.[1] It is important to note at the outset that d'Aspremont's approach is text-focused and influenced more by Derrida than by Foucault, and is thus to be differentiated from the mainstreams of scholarship in biopolitics.[2] However as will be suggested here, informative overlaps and shared concerns are to be found. For example, in discussing the role of the footnote and citation protocols, d'Aspremont observes that this apparatus is 'never benign' but rather partakes in the distribution of power across gender and other divides.[3] Thus d'Aspremont's reflective sensitivity to the effects of his own book, of 'this book *as book*'—in its purporting to convey or 'deliver' a coherent and totalising argument—is at least a gesture to the biopolitical.[4] The affective domain is not neglected, for '[t]he international lawyer always arrives after meaning has slipped away from the form'.[5]

There are closer connections between the discipline or sub-discipline of international law and the book than is the case for many other domains of law, at least within the Common Law world. Within the legal system of a typical 'municipality', as international lawyers somewhat condescendingly label the jurisdictions of mere sovereign states, the law is provided by statutes and case-law, and while

1 d'Aspremont (2021a).
2 McLoughlin (2012), p 686.
3 d'Aspremont (2021a), p 116.
4 Ibid., p 26.
5 Ibid., p vii.

DOI: 10.4324/9781003175193-10

authoritative textbooks guide both students and practitioners around that parochial lore, discursive and comprehensive narratives covering the whole domestic field rarely displace the more pedestrian loose-leaf services and their online descendants. Even in Civil Law jurisdictions, which with their Roman Law roots and university-centred training defer much more habitually to professorial contributions, this is broadly the case. Codified law of a Napoleonic or other brand does not neatly generate the magisterial grand narrative. And grand narrative is in many ways what international law, as taught to generation after generation of students, is all about. Thus a 2006 Report from the International Law Commission (a United Nations body), which diagnosed 'fragmentation' across the global regulatory landscape, had the consequence of constructing 'fragmentation' as a master discourse and launching a scholarly industry.[6] A reformist if not quite missionary zeal was discernible. The post-colonial and decolonising movements in contemporary scholarship in international law, in which the missionary zeal is amplified, again generate grand programmes aimed at setting the discipline on its feet as a virtuous and now expressly pedagogical enterprise.[7] Books that support such programmes are its lifeblood.

Beyond the confines of the self-consciously radical, scholarship in international law is strikingly attuned to the world of books, of book-writing and book-reading. Leading international law blogs such as *EJIL:Talk! Blog of the European Journal of International Law*, *Opinio Juris* and *Völkerrechtsblog* routinely include book symposia, and *EJIL:Talk!* itself annually features observations on an eclectic selection of books (old and new, fact and fiction, and in more than one language) recently read and recommended by the editors. The epistemic nature of the book as artefact in its disciplinary context is occasionally reflected on in this format. Thus d'Aspremont has raised the question of canonicality in the discipline, by reference to the arch-canonicalist of English high literature, Harold Bloom. The canon in any discipline, just like the 'grand canon' of western civilisational pedagogy as a whole, is a species of biopolitics, for it compresses power and knowledge into one apparatus, excluding inferior substitutes. In the same piece, d'Aspremont observes that 'there is no content that pre-exists its inscription… ideas, historical findings, stories, arguments, etc. are not extracted from a book but they are *experienced* as one wanders through the signifying space provided by the book'.[8] And signifying space is space of the trace.[9] With an arguably prurient account of Foucault's chemically enhanced sojourn in California as one of the books he discusses, d'Aspremont reflects on the voyeuristic dimension of reading as an illustration of its inherently interactive nature.

6 Study Group of the International Law Commission (2006); Peters (2017).

7 For thoughtful overviews see al Attar and Abdelkarim (2021); Burgis-Kasthala and Schwöbel-Patel (2022).

8 d'Aspremont (2021b).

9 d'Aspremont (2021a), p 123.

Such express recognition of the role of desire in reading, and of its biopolitical aspects more generally, is admittedly unusual in commentary on international law.[10] Yet we teachers of international law are in some ways particularly self-aware of our shared identity as such, and of the obligations as world citizens which may therefore attach. The international invasion of Iraq in 2003 gave rise to a notable intervention in that respect.[11] The meaning of the book and of the author in the context of international law are conditioned by this heightened version of *noblesse oblige*.[12] The book can function as a soap-box, and in an over-determined way international lawyers are people of the book.

Within international dispute resolution, book-writing has a recognised status. The international law of the current era can be said to have been in formal and institutional terms in place for roughly the last 100 years, if one takes the settlements of the Versailles era with its Permanent Court of International Justice (PCIJ) for example as a starting point and if one is prepared to trace such a continuity. One of the canonical sources of law within this tradition on which the International Court of Justice may at its discretion draw, albeit as a subsidiary genre, is 'the teachings of the most highly qualified publicists of international law'.[13] That provision is found in the Statute of the International Court of Justice, which forms part of the Charter of the United Nations and is closely based on the corresponding article in the Statute of the PCIJ. That recognition of the writings of the publicists is itself a reflection of the synthesis of the Civil and Common Law traditions that constitutes international law as we still know it.[14] In any event, textbooks written by the most authoritative of scholar-practitioners would clearly fit the description of 'teachings of the most highly qualified publicists'.[15] The recent editions of *Brownlie's Principles of Public International Law* authored by the late James Crawford are paradigms of such.[16]

International Law as Mythology and as Ideology

Any discussion of books and book-writing gives rise to considerations of authorship and of the fictional as well as of the power dynamics inherent in publication and teaching through books. A book that serves to educate

10 More directly on international law as such, d'Aspremont's account of the 'discursive splendour' of Customary International Law illustrates the same sensibilities: d'Aspremont (2021c).

11 Craven et al. (2004).

12 See Gaita and Simpson (2017).

13 Art 38(1)(d) of the Statute of the International Court of Justice, closely based on the corresponding article in the Statute of the PCIJ; the Court is the 'master of the sources': d'Aspremont (2020a), p 72.

14 The roots of Civil Law are entangled with the prehistory of international law in ways that those of Common Law are not: Koskenniemi (2021a).

15 See Helmersen (2021); Kumaran (2017).

16 Morss (2020).

connotes a particular effect of the authorial, and a book that serves to educate in law connotes particular consequences of the fictional in the sense that any prose with narrative flow inevitably does, but more so. Somewhat arch references to 'stories' and 'mythology' are to be encountered in describing the genre of a book on international law.[17] In any event the typical textbook of international law begins with a condensed narrative, as if catching up with earlier episodes of a fantasy saga, of the inexorable upward march of the discipline from darkness into light. 'Once upon a time', so to speak, a miracle occurred in what may seem symbolically like the very centre of Europe in a place called Westphalia (it might as well be Ruritania). One gathers a remarkable image of the achievements of the peace settlements of 1648 from textbooks of international law. A veritable United Nations of mutually respectful sovereign and mono-confessional states was, it appears, 'treated' into existence in those heady days in a *Mitteleuropäisch* microcosm of enlightened tolerance.[18] The most substantive consequence, other than financial compensation to the Swedish monarchy for its trans-Baltic adventure, was the establishment of France as the most powerful state in the western part of Europe—eclipsing Spain with which it remained at war until 1659—even if radical French plans for re-drawing the map of Europe were frustrated by the pragmatic Protestant princes of the Empire.[19] The 'nation-state' is a poorly defined entity at best but nation-states in a meaningful way can hardly be seen until the late nineteenth century despite the attractiveness of the 'Just So Story' of Westphalia.[20] The point of all this is that the 'General Assembly' scheme of independent sovereign states, like so many planets in a Star Wars federation, insinuates itself into the imaginations of students as a kind of Natural Law of global pluralist governance by means of this kind of Edenic origin myth. By the end of the first chapter, even if its few pages are only skimmed, the student reader is hooked into a worldview.

Examinations of the connection between international law and literature generally tend to the aesthetic, but fiction and international law have much more dense interrelationships.[21] As far as authorship is concerned, the authorial voice is far from concealed in the most influential textbooks of international law in contrast to the 'Macpherson on Torts' tradition of the municipal. The ventriloquism of a new author stepping up to helm the latest

17 Koskenniemi (2021b).

18 The upshot of the peace agreements was a redefinition of the Holy Roman Empire, thus ensuring its survival, albeit with constitutional tweaking: Greengrass (2014), p 643. This is not to underestimate the scale of the negotiations: 'At various stages, 176 plenipotentiaries represented 196 rulers' that is to say, more sovereigns were represented than there are now members of the General Assembly of the United Nations: ibid., p 641.

19 Greengrass (2014), p 642.

20 Ibid., p 642.

21 Simpson (2021).

in a continuing series of editions, rather like a new director for the latest *Bond* or *Mission Impossible*, seems if anything to highlight rather than to attenuate the personalisation of the product in the context of international law. Indeed it sometimes seems as if the global scale of the enterprise of international law, and perhaps the gravity of the misdeeds with which it has to concern itself, gives rise to a defensive retreat to the personal and the familial.[22] The personalisation of the pronouncement of international law is also conveyed by the individuation of the judges of the International Court of Justice. These individuals are familiar denizens of international conferences of international law, rubbing shoulders or at least Zoom screens with *hoi polloi* in a manner that would be relatively unusual for members of the bench of the Supreme Court even of supposedly egalitarian Australia. Moreover each has a personality expressed by their separate opinions: the rococo munificence of a Cançado Trindade could not be mistaken for the terse precision of a Joan Donoghue.[23]

Individual personality coheres with the role of the teacher, the master at whose feet the student sits, and remaining in the context of the International Court of Justice, expresses itself most forcefully in the Advisory Opinion when a general legal question of international norms is debated and pronounced on by that bench. Such Opinions are themselves in undisguised form, a pedagogic exercise as the representatives of the legal conscience of the globe step up to the blackboard, smile benignly and resignedly, and patiently instruct the princes of the world on their duties—without expecting them to take much heed.[24]

The relationship of the book of international law to a broader Critical Legal Studies(CLS) movement should also be noted. Book-scale resources have been of significance in the teaching of jurisprudence mainly for reasons of disciplinary connections to philosophy and other humanities disciplines, and CLS emerged from jurisprudence with the contributions of Roberto Unger and others very much in the form of books. The CLS of those times comprised some palatable, liberation-flavoured Marxism along with a healthy dollop of *épater les bourgeois*. The effect of CLS was that according to Unger, 'leftist lawyers' with their consciousness raised had become 'a priesthood that had lost their faith but kept their jobs… a priesthood turned to stone'.[25] Goodrich refers here to the Druids, in order to capture a presumably metaphorical sense of arcane wisdom transmitted by a wizard-like sect, but also in identifying a genealogy connecting the Druids with the earliest teachers of Common Law.[26] Setting such

22 Sands (2016); Simpson (2021), p 38.

23 On individualisation on the ICJ bench, see Haskell (2021), p 31.

24 As observed by Haskell, ibid., p 24, the obituary of the famed international lawyer of past eras is a genre in itself, admittedly generic in style yet at the same time a performance of individualisation.

25 Roberto Unger, cited by Goodrich (2007), p 4.

26 Ibid., p 6.

flights of fancy aside, much can indeed be learned from an interrogation of the accounts of Druids passed down by Julius Caesar among others.[27]

A key announcement of CLS, according to Goodrich, was an 'inaugural speech' by Unger published in 1983.[28] By 1985, another CLS luminary, Duncan Kennedy, was to announce the 'death of CLS'.[29] We will encounter again these florid tropes of the decease of disciplines or of approaches within disciplines, and also the more troubling image of the cadre of law teachers who have lost their faith. For alongside continuing contributions of Goodrich and others to a critical approach in legal studies more generally, CLS had belatedly spawned reflective work in international law itself. In part through the CLS influence of Harvard's David Kennedy, a scholar of international law whose journal articles are sometimes of book scale (even without the voluminous footnotes endemic to US law journals),[30] a star was born.

'In My Former Book, Theophilus': The 'Uttermost Parts' of Martti Koskenniemi

Attention will now be focused on the pedagogical phenomenon in the field of international law constituted by the writings of Martti Koskenniemi, one-time member of the Finland Government's team of advisors on Foreign Affairs. This will be done in part by means of a reading of Koskenniemi's magnum opus, published in 2021, *To the Uttermost Parts of the Earth: Legal Imagination and International Power, 1300–1870*.[31] For Koskenniemi looms large over the teacher of international law in the twenty-first century. Indeed with his first and still most influential book *From Apology to Utopia: The Structure of International Legal Argument* having first appeared in 1989 and his most recent in 2021, Koskenniemi has dominated the imagination of international lawyers for over a quarter of a century. The industry of secondary literature, dissecting and debating Koskenniemi's arguments, is very much a literature written by teachers of international law rather than practitioners.[32] Although this fact is a little ironic given Koskenniemi's firm grounding in the professional practicalities of the legal advisor of princes, his impact has indeed been pedagogical in a number of senses.

Most recently Koskenniemi has published a long-awaited treatise on historical aspects of what he calls 'the legal imagination', a work that he defines

27 Thus for the invading Romans, with a weather eye on politics back home, the Druids 'were educated and wise enough to represent a society worth including in the Roman Empire, organized enough to pose a serious potential political threat, and barbaric enough to make their conquest a mission of civilization': Hutton (2009a), p 4.

28 Goodrich (2007), p 4.

29 Ibid., p 5.

30 Koskenniemi (2005), p xv.

31 Koskenniemi (2021a).

32 From Beckett (2006) to Morss (2018) and beyond.

as 'not a history of international law' but a book 'about legal imagination in its relationship to power abroad'.[33] The phrase in the title, 'To the uttermost parts of the earth', is taken from John Donne's paraphrase of Acts 1:8 and was employed by Donne to urge a pacific and (within significant limits) tolerant approach of Christians toward the native inhabitants of the Americas.[34] Fittingly for such a book by such an author, Acts 1:1 says, 'In my former book, Theophilus, I wrote about all that Jesus began to do and to teach …', a beginning that also reminds one in its directness of the 'Tell me, Muse, of the man of many devices' that opens the *Odyssey*, and likewise conveys a mood of pedagogy. With its avowed circumscription to (male) writers and thinkers of 'Christendom', albeit across nearly six centuries, the focus on the peoples of one particular book, so to speak, makes practical sense even if more reference might easily have been made at least to Jewish thinkers, or even to women thinkers, of the places and times.[35] And just as Jesus of Nazareth was a teacher, so was teaching the self-image of the international law that emerged at the very end of Koskenniemi's chronology here; for if it was the international law of 1870 to 1960 that was indeed targeted at 'the gentle civiliz[ing] of nations'[36] as claimed by Koskenniemi in his 'difficult second' book, then this was an educative mission as much as a quasi-imperialist one.

Moreover given the role of written instructions and written guidance in the professional life of diplomats, in times present and times past, the book as pedagogic instrument of international law is an institution that can be traced to the writings of Grotius in the seventeenth century and of Vattel in the eighteenth, among many others.[37] Books of advice to sovereigns have an even greater lineage if one includes as well as Machiavelli's *The Prince*, books such as *A Mirror for Magistrates* of 1559 or the *Basilikon Doron* of King James VI and I, written for his son the Prince. Indeed Koskenniemi introduces readers early on to the *De Regimini Principum* of 'Augustinian friar and professor of theology at Paris', Giles of Rome, written for the instruction of the young Philip le Bel of France in the late thirteenth century.[38] The perturbations in the force-field that is power as understood since the contributions of Foucault, that arose from such

33 Koskenniemi (2021a), p 1, 954; 'abroad' functions as a synonym for 'outside the realm that is conventionally and flexibly imagined as the domestic' (ibid.), and with its meaning of 'at large' adding to the semantic mix, nicely extends the sense of that 'outside'.

34 Ibid, p 700; Donne's tolerance was selective, not being extended to the Jews of whom he declaimed that 'God precludes them from any hope… [they] must lose their rest, they must have no rest': Shapiro (1996), p 177.

35 Kemmerer (2021).

36 Koskenniemi (2001).

37 Koskenniemi (2021a), p 21.

38 Ibid., p 22, 361; the name of Giles' tract is a reminder that the sixteenth century *Monstrous Regiment of Women* of John Knox, a tract of chastisement through instruction, was likewise concerned with 'rule' (as in our modern term 'regime') and that instruction to princes may be condemnatory just as often as it is hortatory.

widely read works of instruction, are comparable to the effects of the proverbial Amazonian butterfly shaking its wings. To give but one example, there can be no doubt that the guidance encapsulated in the *Basilikon Doron* played its role in the self-formation of the 'spare' second son of James, who became Charles I and who by overplaying the hand of God's chosen monarch, especially in relation to the confessional prerogatives of the Scots, tipped the fragile military balance in favour of his parliamentary enemies. If the number of celebratory events, launches of and symposia for *Uttermost Parts* is anything to go by, the effects of this book are likely to be if less dramatic than such antecedents, certainly extensive and long-lasting, especially for the teacher of international law.

Indeed although as Koskenniemi generously notes many scholars have worked on the role of commerce in early modern times as key driver of the development of what we think of as international law, it is perhaps in his focus on the status of private property and hence in his dogged working through of the ways that property and authority have co-driven the erratic vehicle of the *ius gentium* over the centuries, one steering the front wheels and the other steering the back, that Koskenniemi's chief contribution lies in his new book. For example, the significance of private property rights in the clash between Pope Boniface VIII and Philip of France is both illuminating of larger processes and at the same time a vital component of a deeply legal and text-based contestation.[39] Books as private property, as well as themselves comprising property in chattel form, have also conferred exclusionary dominium over intellectual content either on the basis of elitist access to literacy or more latterly on the basis of statutory intellectual property protections. The moral rights of authors, rights most salient to the authors of books, bring into focus that deep affinity of the book and the spirit of exclusionary control, and indeed the feeling of entitlement and of propriety that lies so close to property. The book as instrument of teaching, for example the textbook of international law, may be mass produced and massively over-determined in its form by publishers and their machinery, yet it remains a pedagogical instrument and it remains an ethical intervention by its author. Even if authors do not profit directly from sales of their books to their own students, they may profit from sales to students of their colleagues near and far so that like the adviser to the prince, remuneration even at a modest rate and despite the cuts taken by intermediaries is intrinsic to the institution of academic authorship.[40]

Mass publication for mass teaching is a phenomenon that post-dates Koskenniemi's chosen period in *Uttermost Parts*, which terminates in 1870, but some things have not changed. Throughout the unfolding of the dialectical

39 Ibid., p 28.

40 Within the field of international law only one major figure stands out from the commercial crowd in that sense, like a prophet crying in the wilderness, frequently publishing books through unorthodox channels: the incomparable Philip Allott, e.g. Allott (2008).

processes with which he is concerned, Koskenniemi shows that the book-writers and the 'bookish' Doctors of Law in the Civil Law tradition, as well as theologians with their own favoured collections of texts, played their part as those who have 'attain[ed] positions of authority from which to tell people whom we address what they ought to believe or do'.[41] With these words Koskenniemi is making a broader point about professional expertise and its concomitant conceit to authority, but the application to law is clear. Conflicts over governance, resources, and 'the determination of the conditions of life of domestic or alien communities' while '[s]ometimes' taking the form of physical violence, '[m]ore often … took place among the prince's counsellors, among courtiers, judges, legal polemicists, ministers or professors, among a reading public or the relative security of the academy'.[42]

Koskenniemi is something of a methodological Foucauldian as a non-professional historian, in that he re-reads and re-synthesises published materials rather than searching out archival remnants. As with Foucault professional and specialised historians might quibble at some of the claims made, but in any event, the result of Koskenniemi's efforts is appropriately genealogical; 'a history "of the present"'.[43] Looked at in this way, the centrality of power as theme in *Uttermost Parts* is worked out in appropriately Foucauldian ways, albeit without fanfare, with the capillaries of power being traced and indeed anatomised through discourse and through discourses. Koskenniemi's empiricist and 'from the ground up' approach is described by him as *bricolage*, although as d'Aspremont observes, one may perceive a unifying presupposition that the examples partake of a shared relationship with legality.[44] The power of the Papacy in the middle ages, and even up to the seventeenth century, is routinely distorted in historical observations within today's textbooks of international law, and has been badly in need of such a re-think. Going well beyond the obvious and frequently noted point that except on rare occasions Popes controlled rather modest military forces, if any, instead relying on the military protection of one or other European power against one or more other European powers, not to mention the Ottomans, the might of the Papacy consisted of rhetoric and law above all. Teaching Christians how to live, whether princes or plebeians, is the papal mission, driving its biggest strategic decisions across the centuries, including the entente with Mussolini's Italy established in 1929 by which access to schooling and, through education, to the surveillance of family life across Italy was regained after nearly six lonely decades.[45] If a constant theme of *Uttermost Parts* is the search on the part of the advising class for descriptive

41 Koskenniemi (2021a), p 952.
42 Ibid., p 954.
43 Ibid., p 12.
44 d'Aspremont (2021a), p 43.
45 Morss (2015).

and even explanatory frameworks that go beyond Scripture, then that search involved a migration from the one book to a plurality of books, but of course like sovereigns, some books have always been more equal than others.

The Death of International Law and How to Teach It

Despite the fact that *Uttermost Parts* is concerned with the period from 1300 to 1870—the latter being the starting date for *Gentle Civilizer*—in discussing his book at the Annual Conference of the European Society of International Law in Stockholm in 2021 Koskenniemi re-asserted his claim made 20 years earlier that in some important sense international law as a coherent system of claims and enlightened liberal values came to an end somewhere around 1960.[46] Under this account, a clearly articulated and institutionalised international law, of expressly Christian cast, had been in place for the half-century before Versailles, but ran out of steam in the early 1960s.[47] Alert to the perils of dogmatic periodisation in historical scholarship, as much as to the pleasures of academic provocation, Koskenniemi reserves an ironic distance from too close a commitment to such observations, but the sensationalist 'take away' element of such claims persists.

The suggestion that international law 'died' around 1960—and has since been no more than a 'zombie'—is in part based on the historical emergence of a large cohort of post-colonial sovereignties at around that time, all with a formal equality with the long-established European powers and so on, in a worldwide process stimulated by the same forces that brought the United Nations itself into being 15 years earlier. As Koskenniemi implies, the international law of the early to mid-twentieth century as a rational construction predominantly of Christian, liberal-minded European statesmen and their social circles, culminating in the founding of the UN by a mere 50 or so state parties—a smaller number of members than the League of Nations at its height—was a system designed for a very different world than that numerically dominated by non-aligned or otherwise unbiddable nations as in the twenty-first century.

Notwithstanding the watershed moments of post-war decolonisation, the re-announcement of the supposed 'death' over 60 years ago of international law is a re-promulgation of a claim that taken at face value can hardly be said to be other than 'bad faith'. As Goodrich has put it in a different context,

46 Koskenniemi (2001), p 511; indeed *The Gentle Civilizer of Nations* is subtitled *The Rise and Fall of International Law 1870–1960*. The re-assertion was made in a recorded conversation with Sarah Nouwen, subsequently made available to ESIL Conference registrants. In 2021 Koskenniemi also announced the 'death' of the so-called historical turn in critical scholarship in international law.

47 Folklorist and historian Ronald Hutton has noted the ways in which a shared, unsophisticated Christian worldview determined many influential historians' construction of the past, observing in this connection that '[t]he generation which came of age in England in the 1950s and 1960s was probably the last to be schooled automatically in Bible stories': Hutton (2009b), p 329.

'[t]here is without question a dimension of paradox to the critical pedagogue's disavowal of the institutional and pedagogic power that they both represent and purvey'.[48] The message received by Koskenniemi's readership, a readership which undoubtedly includes leading as well as modest educators of students in some numbers worldwide in courses called 'International Law', is that there is a mainstream orthodoxy in place that is in some serious way a sham. The ways in which international legal disputes currently get settled, and indeed the ways in which they do not get settled, would be a front, indeed an affront.

The interrogation of international law's legitimacy is indeed a duty of scholars. Many scholars are pursuing this question with rigour as well as with flair.[49] But the magisterial pronouncement of vacuity of a discipline—this mainstreaming of nihilism—seems to be a somewhat different event, especially when seen from the perspective of the teacher of the subject. How does the teacher of international law justify having her university (directly or indirectly) charge students a fee for teaching them a discipline in which she does not in any sense 'believe'? How can we require students to buy a textbook on such a topic? How can we purport to grade students on their grasp of such a will o' the wisp?

This conundrum arises from broader developments than Koskenniemi's own contributions. A view that international law as we know it is pernicious seems difficult to square with a presentation of oneself as a competent teacher of the discipline, for example in applying for a university post or a promotion. Yet the enthusiastic identification of so-called 'structural' deficiencies in international law, like any faux nihilism, runs the risk of such problematic consequences. Are we all really 'working from the inside'?

End Matter: Books Do Furnish a Room

In years dominated by Zoom calls, the rooms from which scholars not only communicate with each other but also teach their students are dominated by bookshelves. Learnedness can be conveyed never so well as with this particular décor, with its partnership of *bricolage* and authority. The obstinate materiality of books seems to resist tidiness and corporate management. However if international law is all about connectedness and solidarity, and if teaching international law is all about empowering students to carry forward that project, then books are tricky allies. They always promise so much more than they can possibly deliver. Such promises are like the pastoral assurances of the sovereign or of the state. If each book is a genealogy as Derrida suggests then we are faced with multiple genealogies.[50] But books on international law are willy-nilly focused

48 Goodrich (2007), p 5.
49 Johns (2013); Tzouvala (2020).
50 On the 'bookish' Rousseau's confession as outlaw/werewolf, Derrida comments that 'we still need to know how to deal with the wolf. And to know what kind of chase we're dealing with, in what

on populations, on herds, packs and flocks, even if this focus is distorted by the prism of a modernist sovereignty; and like international law, books are biopolitics all the way down, so that is where we find ourselves.

Acknowledgements

Thanks are due to Ronald Hutton.

References

Philip Allott (2008) *Invisible Power 2: A Metaphysical Adventure Story*, Xlibris.

Mohsen al Attar and Shaimaa Abdelkarim (2021) 'Decolonising the Curriculum in International Law: Entrapments in Praxis and Critical Thought' *Law and Critique*, https://link.springer.com/article/10.1007/s10978-021-09313-y.

Jason Beckett (2006) 'Rebel Without A Cause? Martti Koskenniemi and the Critical Legal Project' 7 *German Law Journal* 1045.

Michelle Burgis-Kasthala and Christine Schwöbel-Patel (2022) 'Against Colonialism in the International Law Curriculum: Examining Decoloniality' *The Law Teacher [online]*, www.tandfonline.com/doi/full/10.1080/03069400.2022.2057755.

Matthew Craven, Gerry Simpson, Susan Marks and Ralph Wilde (2004) 'We Are Teachers of International Law' 17 *Leiden Journal of International Law* 363.

Jean d'Aspremont (2021a) *After Meaning: The Sovereignty of Forms in International Law*, Edward Elgar.

Jean d'Aspremont (2021b) 'Favourite Readings 2021 – Canonization, Toleration, Incarnation, and Masturbation' *EJIL:Talk!*, www.ejiltalk.org/favourite-readings-2021-canonization-toleration-incarnation-and-masturbation/.

Jean d'Aspremont (2021c) *The Discourse on Customary International Law*, Oxford University Press.

Jacques Derrida (2009) *The Beast and the Sovereign Volume 1*, University of Chicago Press.

Raimond Gaita and Gerry Simpson (eds) (2017) *Who's Afraid of International Law?*, Monash University Publishing.

Peter Goodrich (2007) 'Druids and Common Lawyers: Notes on the Pythagoras Complex and Legal Education' 1 *Law and Humanities* 1.

Mark Greengrass (2014) *Christendom Destroyed: Europe 1517–1648*, Penguin.

John Haskell (2021) 'A Case in the Politics of Form: Yearbooks of International Law' 50 *Netherlands Yearbook of International Law 2019* 21.

Sondre Torp Helmersen (2021) *The Application of Teachings by the International Court of Justice*, Cambridge University Press.

Ronald Hutton (2009a) *Blood and Mistletoe: The History of Druids in Britain*, Yale University Press.

Ronald Hutton (2009b) 'Modern Druidry and Earth Mysteries' 2 *Time and Mind: The Journal of Archaeology, Consciousness and Culture* 313.

we have called our genealogy of the wolf, our book of wolves, our genelycology'; and later, 'It is always a matter of the law and of placing the other outside the law. The law (*nomos*) is always determined from the place of some wolf': Derrida (2009), p 99, 140.

Fleur Johns (2013) *Non-Legality in International Law: Unruly Law*, Cambridge University Press.
Alexandra Kemmerer (2021) 'Martti Koskenniemi's (German) Legal Imagination and the Politics of Panorama', *Völkerrechtsblog*, https://voelkerrechtsblog.org/de/martti-koskenniemis-german-legal-imagination-and-the-politics-of-panorama/.
Martti Koskenniemi (2001) *The Gentle Civilizer of Nations: The Rise and Fall of International Law 1870–1960*, Cambridge University Press.
Martti Koskenniemi (2005) *From Apology to Utopia: The Structure of Argument in International Law*, Cambridge University Press.
Martti Koskenniemi (2021a) *To the Uttermost Parts of the Earth: Legal Imagination and International Power 1300–1870*, Cambridge University Press.
Martti Koskenniemi (2021b) 'Response: Storytelling', *Völkerrechtsblog*, https://voelkerrechtsblog.org/de/response-storytelling/.
Siva Kumaran (2017) 'The Influence of Teachings of Publicists on the Development of International Law' 66 *International and Comparative Law Quarterly* 1.
Daniel McLoughlin (2012) 'Giorgio Agamben on Security, Government and the Crisis of Law' 21 *Griffith Law Review* 680.
John R Morss (2015) 'The International Legal Status of the Vatican/Holy See Complex' 26 *European Journal of International Law* 927.
John R Morss (2018) 'Description Without Apology? On Structures, Signs and Subjectivity in International Legal Scholarship' 58 *Indian Journal of International Law* 235.
John R Morss (2020) 'Book Review: Hernández, *International Law*; Crawford, *Brownlie's Principles of International Law* 9th ed' 21 *Melbourne Journal of International Law* 230.
Anne Peters (2017) 'The Refinement of International Law: From Fragmentation to Regime Interaction and Politicization' 15 *International Journal of Constitutional Law* 671.
Philippe Sands (2016) *East West Street: On the Origins of Genocide and Crimes Against Humanity*, Weidenfeld & Nicolson.
James Shapiro (1996) *Shakespeare and the Jews*, Columbia University Press.
Gerry Simpson (2021) *The Sentimental Life of International Law: Literature, Language, and Longing in World Politics*, Oxford University Press.
Ntina Tzouvala (2020) *Capitalism as Civilisation*, Oxford University Press.

Reports

Study Group of the International Law Commission (2006) *Report on the Fragmentation of International Law: Difficulties Arising from the Diversification and Expansion of International Law*, finalised by Martti Koskenniemi, UN Doc. A/CN.4/L.682 13 April 2006.

Chapter 8

The Truth about Conceptions of Law in Latin American Legal Education

Fernando del Mastro Puccio and Sergio Iván Anzola Rodríguez

Introduction

One of the central critiques of legal education in Latin America is that it is based on a formalist and positivist conception of the law that is transmitted in class. The critiques are theoretically well grounded with clear, understandable arguments on why these conceptions are limited and problematic. There is, however, something that critics neglect despite its relevance: the difficulties faced by individuals within law schools (authorities, students, and teachers) in reflecting on the conceptions of law. We refer to this problem not as an academic, theoretical issue that could be fixed with better knowledge, but rather one that is related to the way individuals construct the truth about themselves as legal professionals.

From this perspective, we hold that the inquiry about the conceptions of law is also an inquiry about one's own way of living in the profession and the meaning of their own work as a lawyer. This approach allows us to better understand the anguish and risks the question raises and how it is avoided in law schools.

Employing Michel Foucault's theoretical framework, we propose two models by which individuals construct the truth about themselves. In the first model, that truth refers to humans and the world in general, and one must show it operating in one's own life without questioning it and passing through institutional rituals and proceedings, under the threat of losing status.[1] In the second model, the truth about oneself lies in an exploration of the meaning of one's own life that leads to examine one's way of living through a specific type of dialogue with the other.[2] We will call the first model the *established model* and the second the *inquiry model*. These names describe truth's central trait in both models: in the first, it is presented to the individual as a set reality, while, in the second, truth is a dynamic and open reality searched by the individual.

1 Foucault (2014a).
2 Foucault (2014b).

DOI: 10.4324/9781003175193-11

Taking into account the distinctive elements of both models, we attempt to explore the subjective experience of individuals in both cases. Basing ourselves in Foucault's ideas in dialogue with Castoriadis and Arendt, we hold that the first model serves to avoid the anguish of non-meaning and a confrontation with the status quo, while simultaneously affording the gratification of being part of something stronger than oneself. On the contrary, the second model demands that we face this anguish with courage and that we transform the desire for control into passion for interrogation and care for the self.

The contrast between these two models will enable us to approach the critiques from a different angle and contribute different criteria to understand the challenges faced by law schools in regard to the truth about the conceptions of law.

Critiques of the Conceptions of Law in Latin American Legal Education

A broad characterisation of Latin American Legal education suggests that, with a few exceptions, it is still largely based in legal formalism,[3] and is mostly taught and directed by practising lawyers who alternate between teaching and their professional practice of law.[4] A degree in law is still an attractive career path to many and the high demand for the career, along with the scarce regulation and monitoring of newly opened law schools and programmes,[5] makes Latin America a 'land of lawyers', even when in recent years lawyers have gradually lost ground to the economists in the high spheres of public power.

Perhaps a deeper and more nuanced characterisation of the teaching of law is that of Madrazo[6] in his article '¿Qué?, ¿Cómo? y ¿Para qué? Análisis y crítica al modelo tradicional de enseñanza del Derecho en México' ('What? How? and What For? Analysis and Critique of the Traditional Model for Teaching Law in Mexico'), which is about Mexico but can easily be carried over to other Latin American countries.

To the question 'What is taught?' Madrazo suggests that an analysis of the texts typically used to induct law students to the career reveals a conception of law as a mere 'set of rules' meant to regulate human conduct. This definition excludes any mention or analysis of the moral values or facts that impact their creation, interpretation and application. It states nothing about how the law is applied, that is to say what cultural, psychological and physical tools are used to achieve their compliance or the way those values determine the contents of the

3 Bonilla Maldonado (2013), pp 259–302; Montoya (2009), pp 545–66; Pérez Perdomo (2008), pp 730–42.

4 García Villegas and Ceballos Bedoya (2019); Pérez Hurtado (2009).

5 García Villegas and Ceballos Bedoya (2019); Pérez Hurtado (2009).

6 Madrazo Lajous (2006), pp 167–247.

law (values which, with good reason, often point towards different solutions and visions of what a good life is). This way, the object of study examined by the students is quite different from the real object of study in which facts and values play a dominant role, and where the scientificity, objectivity and neutrality of the law is questioned.

To the question 'How is it taught?' Madrazo replies based on the answer to the question: 'What is taught?' Given that formalism regards the law simply as a set of rules contained in texts (the constitution, codes, decrees, sentences, etc.) which span and contemplate the whole gamut of social reality, it suffices to know the rules, memorise them thoroughly and know how to look them up in order to apply them to the situation at hand by means of syllogism operation.

Madrazo refers to Capella[7] to suggest that if this is indeed the prevailing conception of law, then the learning method best suited to that conception is maintenance learning (as opposed to shock learning or innovative learning). The focus of maintenance learning is to transfer or install a series of content in the students that they will later apply mechanically to the situations that arise in their professional practice.

This learning assumes that legal rules and the regulation they enact as a whole contemplate the solution to any and all issues that arise in the professional practice. Because the rules contemplate all possible situations and there are no gaps or contradictions, the teaching process is vertical, authoritative, routinely repetitive and leaves little room for students' doubts or questions. Research is unnecessary in this teaching, as the object of the teaching is clearly identified and delimited. For Madrazo, because this teaching method is based on an erroneous premise about the nature of law, it becomes clearly insufficient and inconvenient for the students once they graduate and begin their professional practice. Once installed into their professional practice, lawyers substitute maintenance learning with shock learning, where they perceive as insufficient and useless their legal training, which does not seem adequate for solving legal issues. Regardless of whether shock learning works or if it works for many or few, it has many issues: first, it reveals the uselessness of legal training as a preparation for the professional world; second, it imposes an unfair burden on the recent graduate and their employer, for the individual isn't ready to perform competently, needing to undergo a process of tiresome and stressful empirical learning; third and finally, it is problematic because despite its obvious inconvenience, teaching the formalist vision of law would seem evidently coherent; in other words, to teach the formalist vision with an innovative method would seem contradictory in its own terms. As a result, pedagogic and didactic innovations are innocuous or even counterproductive as long as the formalist vision of law persists in legal education.

7 Capella (1998).

The effects of maintenance learning and the formalist vision of law are present not only in the style of teaching (authoritarianism, routine, knowledge transmission) but also in the structure of curricula and study plans. In their material presentation in brochures and law school websites, these curricula reveal a clear division of subjects and contents, each carefully bounded to its space without overlapping, mixing or brushing against the others. They also reveal the existence of a core comprised of hard, important, serious 'legal' subjects such as criminal law, contracts, obligations and properties, as well as other peripheral, auxiliary, filler and interdisciplinary subjects such as legal sociology, law philosophy, professional ethics, research methodology and so on. This curriculum structure evokes a professional world where the issues actually faced by individuals and their lawyers can easily be pigeonholed into a specific branch of the law without touching any other, and additionally where the peripheral subjects or contents play a secondary or decorative role to the way we think about and solve these issues. In alignment with Madrazo, Kennedy[8] argues that this way of designing and imagining study plans is erroneous and wrong because there is no actual centre-plus-periphery, but instead contradicting trends between a human vision centred on individualism, autonomy and self-sufficiency and another human vision based in altruism, solidarity and collectivism.[9] Traditional legal education conceals these contradictions, suppresses the altruistic current and privileges the individualistic current (although it always keeps an ace up its sleeve for when it irrationally needs to appeal to the altruistic, charitable project).

Lastly, in regard to the question 'What is it taught for?' Madrazo distinguishes two different kinds of motivation: explicit, accepted and celebrated motivations; and occult, but intensely pursued ones. One of the explicit motivations is to train jurists who will consolidate the Rule of Law and are respectful of the will of the majority that is expressed in the laws. In this regard, law graduates, by learning and applying the rules in a judicious, logical and mechanical manner, guarantee the predictability of the Rule of Law and respect the political agreements that are projected in the laws and other legal rules. This is of course, as Madrazo points out, only possible insofar as the conception of the Rule of Law that one adheres to is a minimalist vision where the Rule of Law is equivalent to knowing the rules beforehand and applying them with good judgement and stability.

The second explicit end pursued by law schools and legal education is to make science that can assist in the resolution of so-called difficult cases. In order for the solution to be legitimate, it needs to be based in science, not in subjective or contingent facts or opinions. The stamp of scientificity purges these impurities to ensure that the interpretation and decision in cases is respectful of the will of the majority and the Rule of Law.

8 Kennedy (1989), pp 1–16.
9 Kennedy (1976), pp 1685–778.

The implicit motivation of this legal research is to promote a 'paralysis of legal thought' that discourages a critique of the way the law is created, interpreted and applied. This favours the existence of a legal profession that is more docile and apologetic towards the way in which the law is utilised as a tool of political power by the status quo. The 'scientificity' of the law serves not to contradict, avoid, criticise and condemn the political use of law; it serves to actually conceal it. Legal research removed from empirical facts and disinterested in the way that moral values are at play in the creation, interpretation and application of the law is only good for legitimating the exercise of power by inquiring, observing and investigating only a minimal fraction of the law (legal rules) while leaving many other relevant aspects outside the scope of the investigation.

The answer offered by Madrazo to the question 'What is it taught for?' matches what Gómez Sánchez[10] suggests in an article written about the Colombian context, in which he examines the role that Colombian legal education plays in the tension between the different political projects that the country has simultaneously lived through since the 1990s. On one hand, the democratic aperture and better protection and guarantee of rights through a more involved and protagonist State that was embodied in the Political Constitution of 1991 versus the neoliberal project purveyed from the transnational sphere, which vouches for market logic to regulate more and more aspects of our lives. On the other hand, the development of a sophisticated constitutional jurisprudence that guarantees peoples' rights and is worthy of being acknowledged and celebrated in the international sphere versus the reality of an armed conflict that is bleeding out the country.[11]

Through his analysis, Sánchez suggests that different characteristics of the legal education taught in Colombia indicate that the theoretical assumptions under which the law is taught, the teaching method employed, the current regulatory practices of the hidden curriculum and meagre state regulation on the quality of law schools allows for the formation of 'drone lawyers', meaning prestigious and capable lawyers endowed with ample social, economic and cultural capital and a high technical capacity that is at the service of big corporations, with a high instrumental effectiveness to adequately represent their clients, but who simultaneously reproduce symbolic violence, insensitive to the needs, pain and suffering of others. In the existing tension between the different political projects, these 'drone lawyers' would tilt the scales in favour of neoliberal, individualistic and corporate projects at the expense of projects and visions of society that are more charitable, altruistic and compassionate to the suffering of others. Legal education, such as it is taught in most Colombian law

10 Gómez Sánchez (2016), pp 225–56.

11 At the time Gómez Sánchez published the article, the Colombian government and the FARC guerrilla were yet to sign the peace treaty that, while it did not put an end to violence in the country, did bring about a significant reduction thereof.

schools, would have a tendency to create servile and instrumental subjectivities for the status quo, with little critical capabilities and transformative power.

The bleak landscape evoked in Madrazo's and Sánchez's studies is complemented by Del Mastro's psychoanalytical approach to legal education, particularly to how it affects the construction of law students' professional identity. In his research, he examines the *ways of being* learned by law students in their relations with authority figures (before entering law school, with law professors and while being interns in law firms). One of those *ways of being* is that of an individual who doesn't reflect on his thoughts, feelings and actions, even while living situations that affect his rights, wellbeing and ethical behaviour. In that sense, students don't put into question their own way of living authoritarian relations, with professors and lawyers who act with unrestrained power. In these type of relations, students' need of recognition and fear of being undervalued frustrate their reflective process and leads their behaviour.

As well, in the case of Peru, Gonzales Mantilla's,[12] examines the role of legal education in Peru recounting the ups and downs of a reform project promoted from the Pontifical Catholic University of Peru's Law School (PUCP) in Lima through their integration seminars. The seminars, a specific component of PUCP's larger, more ambitious educational reforms, had the aim of opening a space for debate on a legal issue that was present in real cases by tackling the dissociation between theoretical knowledge and praxis that legal formalism stealthily upholds. Gonzales relates how, despite good intentions and the effort and boldness of several reformist teachers, the project did not have the desired impact due to the resistance of the professional guild, where stagnant legal formalism persists. This was further compounded by the social and political context of Peru in the 1990s, marked by a stark authoritarianism, intolerant towards any critique of the law. However, Gonzales does not necessarily believe that the defeat (or the ambivalent future) of reformist projects for legal education in Peru, and more specifically at PUCP, are finished. He warns that the success of didactic efforts such as the integration seminars rely on the university community (teachers and students) as much as the professional practice; in other words, when we inquire about the possibility of a reform in legal education, trying to solve the chicken or egg dilemma is useless. Changes in legal education require internal effort by teachers and students, and likewise require change from practising law professionals.

Two Models for the Construction of Truth about the Self

Late in his life, Michel Foucault devoted himself to examining different models by which individuals construct the truth about themselves. In this chapter, we focus on two of them in order to recognise their defining traits.

12 Gonzales Mantilla (2007), pp 51–96.

We can find the central characteristics of the *established model* in the classes and conferences taught by Foucault in 1980 and 1981, particularly in the introductory sessions to *Subjectivity and Truth*,[13] *On the Government of the Living*[14] and in *About the Beginning of the Hermeneutics of the Self*.[15] The example we take from these texts is baptism during the origins of Christianity. In this model, the truth about oneself is presented as inextricable from a discourse about humanity. Because man bites the apple, he falls from paradise and Satan acquires and reigns over his soul. Thus, in order to access the truth about God and salvation, Satan must be banished. This is the truth applicable to every human being and, to that extent, to oneself. It is a truth about who reigns over one's soul, how he does it, how can he be banished, what actions show that he no longer reigns and what other actions show that he's back, and so on.

In this model truth is given as a fact, it is not questioned nor is it the product of an inquiry: it is knowledge that the person must accept without caveats or questioning:

> there can be no uncertainty with regard to access to the truth, in the sense that one must be very sure and cannot doubt for a moment that the truth is true, that what one is taught is true, that the truth really has been revealed in Scripture, and here non-anxiety, certainty without confusion is absolutely fundamental.[16]

For Foucault, in this model truth is conceived as a 'system of obligations'[17] given that the individual, starting from acceptance without questioning, must follow a series of mechanisms, procedures and practices that derive from said truth and shape his way of living. The individual who sought baptism had to face multiple trials over time to demonstrate that he had died in his prior life, in which Satan was king. Through these trials and ways of living, the subject managed to become a part of the institution and maintain himself within to enjoy a certain status. Here the source of the truth isn't individual but institutional: it deals with the sacred scriptures and detailed procedures outlined and conducted by the church that one must accept and comply with.

The *inquiry model* is found in the final class taught by Foucault, *The Courage of Truth*,[18] and is represented by Socrates. In this model, the truth about oneself is not applicable to all human beings. Chaerephon asks the oracle if Socrates is the wisest man, which the pythoness confirms. What is at hand then is not the truth about man but that which defines, distinguishes and differentiates

13 Foucault (2020).
14 Foucault (2014b).
15 Foucault (2016).
16 Foucault (2020), p 127.
17 Ibid., p 28.
18 Foucault (2014a).

Socrates from the rest. It is, more precisely, the truth about the meaning of Socrates' life, for this trait marks his path, his occupation in life and his place in the world. Notice how, while the truth about the meaning of Socrates' life is personal, he shares it with the rest, those he dialogues with and those who become his disciples.

This truth is not an institutional product to which Socrates bows. Socrates indeed says 'I went to one of the people who had a reputation for wisdom, thinking there, if anywhere, to disprove the oracle's utterance and declare to it: 'Here is someone wiser than I am, and yet you said that I was the wisest'.[19] What follows is thus an inquiry process. Foucault lays emphasis on the Socratic *zetesis* as an inquiry and interrogation regarding what is said by the oracle. Therefore, he does not interpret the oracle's word and waits on, as do the rest, but he goes to the world and 'submits it to verification', finding the meaning through this process.

Inquiry is linked to motivation. One does not discover in order to know, but to deal with the truth about oneself. Meaning becomes purpose and therefore guides the care of the self. Socrates is the wisest because he acknowledges his ignorance, and this puts him—as well as others—on the path of constantly examining oneself and acknowledging one's own ignorance. In *Crito*, for example, when faced with the possibility of escaping prison and avoiding death, he replies:

> it is necessary to examine if this should be done or not, for I, not only now but always, have been so that I haven't yielded to none of my friends, but only to that reasoning which after reflecting appeared to me as the best.[20]

Meaning then generates an obligation insofar as it relates one's way of living and leads one to take care of oneself. The term analysed by Foucault at this point is *epimeleia*, the care of the self. In its etymology, he indicates that 'melos' can refer to melody and might have carried the meaning of 'calling chant', a chant that guides someone to their place. Answering that call and being in conformity with it is to move towards a beautiful, coherent, well-aligned life.

An inquiry into the meaning and care of oneself requires a constant practice—that of examination. This means practising the art of ethical *parrhesia*, the examination of one's way of living. It isn't an examination of knowledge or expertise in the sense of the *téckne*, that which one knows based on technical knowledge, nor is it an examination of the soul. It is an examination of 'the style of life, the way of living, the very way we give our life' so that what is good and what isn't good can be distinguished: 'To submit one's life to what he calls a touchstone, a test that allows to distinguish what has been done

19 Plato (2017).
20 Ibid., p 145.

right and wrong in existence'. We arrive then at the level of the *bios*, the vital experience, and the *ethos*, the form we give to our life.[21] This examination is conducted through earnest dialogue with the other, in which each one reveals the truth about their own thought, not to win or convince, but to account for one's own self.

The way of living that is examined deals with one's actions, the actions they have carried out as well as those they may carry out, as is the case in *Crito*, where Socrates examines his reasons for making a choice, but also examines the conceptions that underlie one's own doings, occupation and role in life. This way, for example, in Gorgias,[22] Socrates examines three other speakers' conceptions of rhetoric. When Gorgias says that rhetoric is the art of persuasion, Socrates asks what does that persuasion persuade of. With this, he opens a dialogue where he seeks to examine the conceptions related to the meaning and the way of living of Gorgias, Polo and Calicles.

There is something worth highlighting in *Gorgias*. At one point, Calicles questions Socrates and tells him that at his age he should no longer philosophise but have certainties; that philosophy is for the young and that he should dedicate himself to ruling. This way, he is questioning the very meaning of his praxis, his occupation. Socrates answers without stepping out of his life's very meaning: 'let us examine what you say, and if it is valid, I will change my way of life this moment'. This shows that the truth about meaning isn't set in stone; it isn't a frozen truth but can be constantly examined. To a certain extent in Socrates, the inquiry into meaning leads to the establishment of inquiry as meaning.

We can relate the above with Arendt's views in *The Life of the Mind*. For her, Socrates does not arrive at truths or thoughts to petrify them: he wasn't enticed by the 'desire to find results that would make it unnecessary to keep thinking'.[23] For Socrates, 'thinking means that each time that we face a difficulty in life, it is necessary to prepare the spirit again'.[24] Meaning, then, lies in the inquiry and therefore can also be questioned if the circumstances and reasons should lead to that.

Brief Notes about Individuals' Subjective Experiences in Both Models

What affects are experienced by individuals in each of these models? What do they feel, what attracts them and what makes them adhere to one or the other, and what anguishes or satisfactions are involved? Foucault does not address

21 Foucault (2014a), p 136.
22 Plato (2010).
23 Arendt (2010), p 199.
24 Ibid., p 200.

these questions, although in speaking about the ethics of truth, or elsewhere when he mentions the resistance of individuals to engage in Socrates' play, he does offer characterisations that border on the psychological.

We want to refer to another text by Foucault to establish our approach: *Truth and Juridical Forms*,[25] a conference where he addresses the nexus between man and knowledge, not directly to knowledge about oneself, but the knowledge about the world and its objects and things. Basing himself on Nietzsche, Foucault holds that we exercise power on the world through knowledge: it enables us to shape it, organise it, make it understandable, transparent and tolerable. Knowledge, therefore, is not product of a passion for knowing that would help us see the world objectively, but a necessity to give it meaning: it does not aim to comprehend but allows to control. He goes on to say that knowledge is a surface effect of inner conflicts, which allows us to negotiate and avoid inner tensions. It is not an objective truth-seeking activity—it is a necessity for control in the face of a conflict that the individual carries within and in his relation to his surroundings.

Through psychoanalysis, we can explore the psychic basis for this control. Castoriadis starts with the notion of a psyche marked by a need for meaning, that leads it to 'create an image of the world and its place in it'.[26] Since its inception, 'the psyche demands meaning; it demands the holding-together, for itself, of what presents itself to the psyche as apparently disordered and unrelated'.[27] A child, for example, may wonder where she comes from and develop a theory about birth. This is not due to mere curiosity or a budding passion for knowledge but is an attempt 'to try to instaurate the mastery of her thought over her origin, in other words, to sketch out a meaning for her history'. This is extended in life to the causes that we find for different phenomena and our own actions.

For the author, the lack of meaning generates discomfort and anguish, by frustrating a first-order psychic necessity. That for which meaning can't be found is thus removed from or forced to fit within the scheme. Simultaneously, the representations of reality that cause pleasure and tranquillity are the ones that have meaning, that is to say, those which allow for things to remain whole and ordained. These representations are thus regarded as reality.

We can connect the above to Nietzsche when he says that man 'yearns for the pleasant consequences of truth, those that maintain life; he's indifferent to pure knowledge without consequence, and even hostile towards truths susceptible to harmful or destructive effects'.[28] For him, then, that there is a desire for pleasant, functional consequences that fit into his image of the world; there is

25 Foucault (2018)
26 Castoriadis (2018), p 162.
27 Ibid., p 170.
28 Nietzsche (2015), p 25.

neutrality towards knowledge that bears no consequence on said image, and there is hostility to that which challenges it.

For Castoriadis, the psyche finds ways of enclosing itself in its significations, in what it has established as meaning: the shutdown of interrogation. This occurs in society or in specific socialisation environments that provide, by virtue of language itself and transmitted notions, visions of things that are not presented as questions or answers, but as truths, such as reality.[29] The shutdown of interrogation leads to eschew anything that is presented as non-meaning or that questions the meaning we give to things. This shutdown is a way to satisfy 'the desire to find results that would make it unnecessary to keep thinking'.[30]

We believe that an example of the shutdown of interrogation can be found in the works of Hannah Arendt, particularly in the idea of 'frozen thoughts' found in *The Life of the Mind* and the idea of 'stock phrases' found in *Eichmann in Jerusalem*. Frozen thoughts are unexamined thoughts that nonetheless sustain our way of life. These are the thoughts Socrates sought to defrost, as we've seen in the Gorgias example. As for stock phrases, Arendt identifies that these configured Eichmann's thought and speech, who at his trial offered no reasoning or elaborate ideas of his own to the questions, but only slogans and clichés. For her, this irreflexivity afforded him relief, satisfaction and consolation by enabling him to deny the reality of his criminal acts. For Brunner,[31] Eichmann in addition killed his own individuality, his quality of autonomous being, whereby he managed to fuse into a superior power, finding omnipotent satisfaction.

We can now suggest that in the *established model*, the individual avoids the confrontation with the question of meaning, the uncomfortable awareness of one's incoherence and the risk of losing position in the institution that provides the truth about oneself and the word. People operating in this model could use frozen thoughts and close any opportunity for interrogation. As well, by adhering to a larger and powerful institution, the individual can feel the satisfaction of taking part in its grandeur.

The Difficulty of Truth about the Conceptions of Law

We wish to give some general reflections on the result of our investigation.

First, we can apply the logic of the two models to the truth about the conceptions of law. In the *established model*, this truth is only knowledge about the world, the law and lawyers in general—a truth that law students must bow to, leaving behind their previous life. This is a truth about the object of study and has no vital consequence in the individual who knows it. In the

29 Castoriadis (2018), p 173.
30 Arendt (2010), p 199.
31 Arendt (2016).

inquiry model, the truth touches the self and is related to an inquiry into the meaning one wishes to bestow on their professional life and is linked to one's own history.[32] In this model, the question about the conceptions of law is also a question about the meaning of one's own praxis, an inherently ethical interrogation.

Second, we can suggest two modes of relating to said truth. In the first model, the truth about the conceptions of law is institutional, and what constitutes the law is taken for fact, bringing us into a system of obligations that shapes one's own praxis and allows them to stay within certain types of institution in certain sectors of legal practice. In the second model, the question about the truth of one's own professional meaning brings about a duty to examine one's own way of living (the way in which they have lived, live and want to live) by means of open dialogue with the other, with the motivation of taking care of oneself and moving towards the goal of a coherent life.

Notice how, in the *inquiry model*, the question about the conceptions of law does not lead to a shutdown of interrogation: it does not seek an answer that makes it unnecessary to keep thinking, but rather to open the interrogation in the face of new difficulties. Therefore, the question about the conception of law is dynamic due to its relation with the way we live the practice of law. On the contrary, in the *established model* students arrive to a conception of law not by inquiry, but by exposure to a truth that is not genuinely questioned or confronted with other truths. Once that conception surfaces their way of living the law, students would cease their interrogation and avoid reflecting on other perspectives.

Third, both models suppose a particular answer to the affects generated by the interrogation. The *established model* enables us to avoid the anguish that the second model demands that we face. Indeed, by providing meaning and avoiding interrogation, the first model enables individuals to avoid the issue of having to position themselves in the professional field according to what they deem righteous. It simultaneously removes from sight the conflict between different conceptions and prevents them from questioning the one they operate under. In this way one can work without noticing and examining the problematic consequences of one's own professional practice, not recognising the truth of their own motivations and incoherence. In the same vein, this model enables one to access professional fields and remain there without risk of losing status or being excluded. Far from it, *the inquiry model* demands attitudes necessary to sustain the question regarding one's own meaning and the examination of one's own way of living, such as humbleness, courage, coherence and the desire to care about oneself.

In this light, what do critical studies show in regard to the truth about the conceptions of law?

32 Del Mastro, 2020.

First, they show a relation between conceptions of law and the fields of professional practice. Certain conceptions are functional to certain roles and ways of practising the law. If the students were to approach the question as one dealing with their own meaning, they would then need to deal with the anguish of choosing their professional path critically, through an examination framed in open dialogue with those who hold different conceptions. This could narrow their options, possibly raising concerns about many paths they previously desired. In any case, given that often professional practice demands that one uses the most convenient conception without regard for what is correct, a clarification of one's own meaning would lead one to recognise panoramas in which they would need to practice the law against the grain.

On the teachers' side, whenever they're also practising lawyers, we can suspect that there's a difficulty in recognising the conceptions underlying their stance, given that these are strictly postures they take in their professional life. Examining them Socratically would entail the risk of stepping into contradiction with one's surroundings, generating uncomfortable dilemmas, examining one's own ways of life and recognising the incoherence. If this is so, then it is only natural that the question about the conceptions of law isn't raised at all and, if it is, it is not framed within a dialogue such as *parrhesia*, but as statements that teachers make as owners of the truth. The transition from the *established* to the *inquiry* can mean opening a Pandora's box that will unleash the anguish of non-meaning, the reality about one's own motivations, one's own incoherence and the weakness of frozen thoughts that upheld an unexamined student or professional life. This affair jeopardises the 'order' and 'image of the world' that one builds to justify one's own practice. If this image hasn't been subject to genuine interrogation it might be because meaning has been provided from the outside and can't be opened due to underlying risks. From this point of view, there is a tendency to construct a model of legal education that provides superficial answers and shuts down inquiry into meaning and the examination of one's own way of living the profession.

Along these lines, studies give an account of characteristics of Latin American legal education that are closer to the *established model*. They point out that, in the learning process, the formalist conception of the law is often presented as a determined truth that students acquire implicitly, without questioning. Even when there are peripheral courses that propose different, contradictory conceptions, the subject matter isn't presented to the students as an inquiry on their professional future, but in a theoretical light that deals with issues such as the role of law in society or the way judges must justify their decisions. In that sense, for students the issue does not relate to their vocation and decisions. This way, upon graduation, students choose a professional field without examining the conception of the law that is to underlie their practice. They could consequently choose to defend private or public interests but will do so without examining the conception that will steer the way they enact their defence. Thus, in both cases the professional could alternate between conceptions according to convenience and showing an incoherence between their discourse and the way they act within their organisation and in their relations with others. As we've seen, critics argue that the law is presented to students as a neutral collection of norms that excludes any reflection about the values and factors underlying different outlooks and, to that extent, it separates law from its reality. Consequently, it might be that, upon entering the professional field, students are protected from said reality thanks to the neutral conception of the law they were trained on, which curbs any questioning that might be raised against their practice from other standpoints. This acritical way of living the profession could be then reinforced by frozen thoughts operating at the professional level as unquestionable truths such as 'a good lawyer always finds a solution' or 'everything in law is open to interpretation'.

It is worth noting too that the students' past isn't relevant either to the teaching of law, for the conceptions of law are largely constructed as an attempt to separate the legal from other regulatory systems, such as that of family or school. Students must sever ties with their past and learn the new legal logic. This way, lived experience of previous rules and authorities, which have shaped ways of experiencing and living regulation, aren't acknowledged as relevant or worthy of examination. This makes it ever more difficult for the issue of the conceptions of law to be brought forth as an inquiry into meaning, for meaning is necessarily constructed from one's own history.

At this point, we can even argue that critical studies that question the objectivity and neutrality attributed to the law seem to suggest the issue of the conceptions of law as an objective one at its core, insofar as they do not recognise the subjectivity and truth of those who uphold in practice the very conceptions they criticise. Even from critical perspectives, the question about the conceptions of law does not appear to be explicitly associated with an inquiry into meaning or related to the individual's truth. We think, then, that many critics could fall under the *established model*, as they criticise conceptions different from their own from the standpoint of an individual who holds the truth. It would be no surprise, then, that their classes treat the issue not as a dialogue centred around meaning and an exercise in *parrhesia*, but as a critique that reveals the truth of law to those who must recognise and adopt it.

It is important to clarify that for us, the issue of the conceptions of law refers both to legal theory and practice. Moreover, it refers to an object of study, the law, which has multiple tangents. A reflection about it can't step outside this framework, though it can be dealt with as related to the students' life and to the inquiry about the meaning they want to bestow on their professional practice. We say this not only in regard to their role in the creation and interpretation of the law and the handling of legal issues, but also the way they experience the rules that are applicable to them as law professionals who are part of organisations, possess duties according to the roles they exercise, realise or contravene values in their relationships and who must follow the ethical principles of their profession.

The issue of coherence thus acquires a special place. Law professors may be quite articulate in purporting what conception of the law they regard as more accurate, but in their relationship with students may act in a way contrary to that conception. For students, to act according to the *inquiry model* would imply the practice of examining their own way of living in experiences such as internships or clinical education, both in relation to their approach to legal issues as well as their relationships to authority figures and rules. The question about the conceptions of law then entails a significant effort towards coherence on the side of lawyers, who would need to examine how and why they alternate between conceptions. This would curtail the options available to defend cases insofar as the question about what is right—in light of one's own conception—would guide one's practice. We suppose that in many cases frozen thoughts such as 'the duty is to defend the client' or 'it comes with the job', which haven't been examined, facilitate the continuity of an unexamined professional practice.

Students and teachers alike face another challenge in entering a scheme such as the *inquiry model*: the kind of relationships they have within the teaching context and the professional field. Far from a dialogue in line with *parrhesia*, we often find hierarchical relations, where an individual holds a position of power and thus controls truth. In this context, being able to examine one's own ways of practising the profession through dialogue, in light of the question about the conceptions of law, would seem very difficult to achieve. It would demand, along with the courage needed to open interrogations, an attitude of humbleness, the acceptance of one's ignorance and a search for the betterment of one's way of living.

References

Hannah Arendt (2010) *La vida del espíritu* [*The Life of the Mind*], trans. Carmen Corral and Josefina Birulés, Paidós.

Hannah Arendt (2016) *Eichmann y el holocausto* [*Eichmann and the Holocaust*], trans. Carlos Ribalta, Taurus.

Daniel Eduardo Bonilla Maldonado (2013) 'El formalismo jurídico, la educación jurídica y la práctica profesional del derecho en Latinoamérica' [*Legal Formalism, Legal education and the Professional Practice of Law in Latin America*] in H Olea (ed) *Derecho y Pueblo Mapuche*, Centro de Derechos Humanos Universidad Diego Portales.

Juan-Ramón Capella (1998) *El aprendizaje del aprendizaje. Una introducción al estudio del derecho* [*The Learning of Learning. An introduction to the Study of Law*], Trotta.

Cornelius Castoriadis (2018) 'Pasión y conocimiento' [*Passion and Knowledge*] in *Hecho y por Hacer*, trans. Laura Lambert, Enclave.

Fernando Del Mastro Puccio (2020) 'La enseñanza del derecho frente al pasado de sus estudiantes' [Law Students' Past and its Relevance for Legal Education] 84 *Derecho PUCP* 393.

Fernando Del Mastro Puccio (2018). 'Venga a nosotros tu reino: la justicia como fuerza anímica ausente en la enseñanza del derecho' [Let Your Kingdom Come: Justice as an Absent Driving Force in Legal Education] 81 *Derecho PUCP* 463

Fernando Del Mastro Puccio (2022). 'Pensar y sentir de estudiantes de derecho en su contacto con el mundo profesional'. [Thoughts and feelings of law students on their contact with the workplace] 81 *Themis* 135

Michel Foucault (2014a) *El coraje de la verdad. El gobierno de sí y de los otros, II* [*The Courage of the Truth. The Government of Self and Others, II*], trans. Horacio Pons, Akal.

Michel Foucault (2014b) *Del gobierno de los vivos* [*On the Government of the Living*], trans. Horacio Pons, Fondo de Cultura Económica.

Michel Foucault (2016) *El origen de la hermenéutica de sí* [*About the Beginning of the Hermeneutics of the Self*], trans. Horacio Pons, Siglo XXI.

Michel Foucault (2018) 'La verdad y las formas jurídicas' [*Truth and Juridical Forms*] in *Michel Foucault Obras esenciales*, trans. Miguel Morey et al., Paidós.

Michel Foucault (2020) *Subjetividad y verdad* [*Subjectivity and Truth*], trans. Horacio Pons, Fondo de Cultura Económica.

Mauricio García Villegas and María Adelaida Ceballos Bedoya (2019) *La profesión jurídica en Colombia. Falta de reglas y exceso de mercado* [*The Legal Profession in Colombia. Lack of Rules and Market Excess*], Dejusticia.

Gabriel Ignacio Gómez Sánchez (2016) '¿Abogados para la democracia o para el mercado?: Repensar la educación jurídica' [*Lawyers for Democracy or for the Market?: Rethinking Legal Education*] 46 *Revista de Derecho* 225.

Gorki Gonzales Mantilla (2007) 'Enseñanza del derecho y cultura legal en tiempos de globalización' [*Teaching of Law and Legal Culture in Times of Globalisation*] 60 *Derecho PUCP* 51.

Duncan Kennedy (1976) 'Form and Substance in Private Law Adjudication' 89 *Harvard Law Review* 1685.

Duncan Kennedy (1989) 'The Political Significance of the Structure of the Law School Curriculum' 14 *Seton Hall Law Review* 1.

Friedrich Nietzsche (2015). 'Sobre la verdad y mentira en sen*tido extramoral y otros fragmentos de* filosofía del conocimiento'. [On Truth and Lies in an Extra-Moral Sense] Tecnos.

Alejandro Madrazo Lajous (2006) '¿Qué?, ¿Cómo? y ¿Para qué? Análisis y crítica al modelo tradicional' [*What? How? And What For? Analysis and Critique to the Traditional Model*] 7 *Academia Revista sobre Enseñanza del Derecho* 167.

Juny Montoya (2009) 'The Current State of Legal Education Reform in Latin America: A Critical Appraisal' 59 *Journal of Legal Education* 545.

Luis Fernando Pérez Hurtado (2009) *La futura generación de abogados mexicanos: estudio de las escuelas y los estudiantes de derecho en México* [*The Future Generation of Mexican Lawyers: A Study of Mexican Law Schools and their Students*], Universidad Nacional Autónoma de México; Instituto de Investigaciones Jurídicas; Centro de Estudios sobre la Enseñanza y el Aprendizaje del Derecho.

Rogelio Pérez Perdomo (2008) 'Lawyers, Rule of Law and Social Justice: A Latin American Perspective' 5 *University of St. Thomas Law Journal* 730.

Plato (2010) *Gorgias, Fedón, El Banquete* [*Gorgias, Phaedo, The Symposyum*], trans. Luis Roig de Lluis, Austral.

Plato (2017) *Eutifrón, Apología, Critón, Fedón, El juicio y la muerte de Sócrates* [*Euthyphro, Apology, Crito, Phaedo, The Trial and Death of Socrates*], trans. Anacleto Longué y Molpeceres, Alastor.

Chapter 9

The Clinical Humanisation of Legal Education

From the Western Model to Emerging Practices in Non-Western Countries

Cosmos Nike Nwedu

Introduction

Today, legal education has navigated the conflict between professional and liberal training in many jurisdictions.[1] This progress is a manifestation of a legal evolution typically known as clinical legal education (CLE); a component of experiential legal education increasingly professed worldwide, which incorporates social ambition into the educational objective of traditional legal education. Remarkably, it represents a paradigm shift from the conventional approach of legal scholarship to the modern way of learning by doing,[2] like new wine in a new bottle. The concept of CLE has some biopolitical dimensions. Though accounts of biopolitics are contradictory in terms of its true origin, it has often been widely credited to Michel Foucault.[3] Biopolitics refers to a system of politics that places life at its centre.[4] Theoretical underpinnings of biopolitics have seen wide usage in different disciplines and discussions.[5] The social theory refers to biopolitics as bodies of knowledge, institutions, and techniques of administration employed for 'regulating, controlling, and measuring people and behaviour' in ensuring that the human resources of states are at best maximised.[6]

The biopolitics of law is concerned with how life is contextually managed, as a part of the knowledge production of law. Thus, it is a fundamental and normative index of modern legal education. In addition it is an attempt by higher education institutions of law seeking to apply 'morality' to make life more meaningful, as a renewal of natural law that underpins human rights, at least.[7] Further, it brings a new narrative to the 'power foundation of law' in

1 Sood (2017), p 2.
2 Wilson (2018).
3 Foucault (1979).
4 Saltman (2018), p 50.
5 Lemke (2011), p 1.
6 Danaher et al. (2000), p 80.
7 Swiffen (2012).

DOI: 10.4324/9781003175193-12

modern society.[8] Therefore, biopolitics invokes moral obligations to command legal obligations from individuals entrusted with or possessing legal authority in discharging certain legal roles or practising law.

While research has shown that CLE began first in the west, with the United States (US) and Canada as pioneers,[9] it has been widely adopted as a learning approach for reshaping legal education and reorienting lawyers and law students across many countries, including non-western countries. The modern significance of legal education, or specifically CLE, from its geo-biopolitical point of view, is not just for lawyers and students, but also for society in terms of social transformation.[10] Most of all, at the centre of CLE are the indigent and vulnerable citizens, as a primary legatee.

This clinical offshoot of legal education is an important legal development aimed at humanising legal education and engendering a transformative society from both an academic and social point of view. But biopolitically, emphasis on the power relation between law and human life is increasingly becoming more crucial.[11] Thus, key objective components of clinical education focus on 'academic and service' delivery.[12] Both components are anchored in training new generations of law students who would eventually become lawyers with a high level of professional competence, community service consciousness, and social and ethical values in society.[13] Being a modernised fragment of legal education, CLE stimulates global justice movements, promotes inclusive legal aid, access to justice, and social justice tailored in most cases to country- and individual-specific needs. Embodying unprecedented academic progress and supported by many universities and law school clinics, it is also gaining a visible place in law curriculum design as an experimental approach for engaging and equipping law students with practical experience and lawyering skills.[14]

There is, however, a lack of a comparative perspective on CLE, as a western model widely adopted in non-western countries. Developments or the impact of clinical education in various jurisdictions have not attracted much attention, at least in comparative single studies.[15] Most research tends to have focused on clinical progress within the west, particularly in the US, without effectively probing its corresponding developments, impact, and wide acceptance beyond a western context.[16] This mirrors criticisms that US higher education is still a perfect illumination of entanglement of the 'colonial past and neo-liberal neo-

8 Xiang (2014), pp 76–86.
9 Mammen (2020), pp 34–51.
10 Ibid., pp 34–51.
11 Swiffen (2012).
12 Ojukwu et al. (2013).
13 Ibid.
14 Nwedu (2017), pp 98–121.
15 Bloch and Ishar (1990), pp 92–120.
16 Peden (1992), p 503.

colonial present' without objective internationalisation.[17] This chapter fills the gap and is justified by a need for an understanding of the impact of a western clinical model of legal education in non-western countries, by comparing the US and South African (SA) experiences. These countries are selected given their longstanding, rich experiences in CLE. They are also both common law countries, which makes any comparison easier. The clinical programmes in both countries serve as models for a host of other jurisdictions worldwide.

The chapter has implications for stimulating clinical initiatives and reshaping legal scholarships that are more 'humane' and 'transformative' in society. Moreover, it will impact researchers, universities, law schools, lawyers, and law students in understanding the present-day need for law as a socio-legal tool driven by biopolitics. The chapter is comprised of four sections, to address a paradigm shift in legal education, in the context of CLE. The second section provides historical, comparative accounts of CLE in the US and SA. The westernisation of CLE with its various ranges of impact is discussed next. Essential humanistic principles of CLE are considered in the fourth section. Finally, a brief summary of key points and lessons is made.

Development of CLE in Western and Non-Western Countries: Comparison of Experiences in the US and SA

Brief Introduction

Early clinical models in western countries with early experience in legal education have arguably influenced CLE in non-western countries. Even so, western countries with no initial experience in CLE were also influenced by such early clinical models within some western jurisdictions before the eventual mainstreaming of the global clinical education movement. The foregoing argument is buttressed by axiomatic conflicting views on the historic accounts of CLE. For example, while a significant amount of existing literature traces the foundation of CLE to the US, more often than not, a different account has shown that, in 1495, King Henry VII had via legislation required judges to assign lawyers to persons from the underclass in need of justice.[18] This evidence, of course, has a British antecedence.

The claim is further strengthened by research indicating such a requirement was widely adopted in the British colonial empire, and, at least, taken to be one of the early efforts in mainstreaming the rule of law.[19] Though the King's legislation was meant to foster equality before the law, it was still symbolic of access to justice and legal aid. Legal aid and a need for reformation of legal education, aimed at bringing a more real-world method to legal scholarship, remain an

17 Suspitsyna (2021).
18 Winkler (undated), p 5.
19 Bloch and Noone (2010).

essential historical force behind the legal evolutionary process of CLE. Thus, one would assume it biopolitically spurred an initial idea of CLE, which afterwards inspired a subsequent call for redesigning university law school curricula across US universities, and diffused into Canada, Australia, etc.[20]

Even as legal clinics in non-western countries are perhaps a product of the western model, such has always been remodelled and tailored to particular contexts in meeting peculiar demands of a group or groups of individuals in different jurisdictions. The SA experience might have been greatly influenced by developments in the US, UK, Australia, and Canada, as evinced in existing historic accounts of CLE.[21] But SA has no doubt developed its own unique law clinics at different levels of law school and universities. The following accounts present a succinct, comparative history of CLE in the US and SA.

The US Experience

The evolution of CLE in the US is often analysed in three different stages of growth, more generally recognised as clinical waves. Literature has shown that the earliest wave occurred from the late 1890s to the early 1900s,[22] a nineteenth-century era. Then, law clinics were simply social justice-based, non-credit legal aid activities voluntarily undertaken by students required to learn lawyering skills and engender access to justice for the vulnerable citizens incapable of hiring attorneys.[23] There were detectable efforts from various stakeholders, such as individual academics, legal luminaries, non-governmental organisations (NGOs), law schools, and universities in fostering a US model of CLE.

Many of the earliest efforts reflect the individual works of John Bradway, Reginald Heber Smith, Jerome Frank, and Arthur von Briesen, just to mention a few legal luminaries. Bradway had reportedly been involved in a cause for a methodological CLE within in-house clinics from 1920 well into the 1940s.[24] He is well known for his passion and work at legal aid clinics at Duke University between 1931 and 1959. Both Bradway and Smith documented the early origins and the growth of the legal aid movement within the US context of legal education from 1893 to 1926.[25] Research indicates that one of early legal aid movements in New York City was led by von Briesen. Most notably, in 1933, Jerome Frank sparked a call for the reformation of legal education in the US, in a critique of Christopher Columbus Langdell's antediluvian ideas

20 Winkler (undated).
21 Wilson (2018).
22 Bloch (2010), p 5.
23 MacCrate (1997); Bradway (1930); Rowe (1917).
24 Amsterdam (1984), p 616.
25 Smith and Bradway (1936).

of teaching law.[26] Because Langdell's precedent of legal scholarship across US universities seemed unprogressive, a more radically, liberal system of practical legal education turned out to be highly needed. The early ideas of teaching and learning the law were hitherto overly doctrinal, both in the US and elsewhere. But of particular emphasis is that US legal education in the nineteenth century was primordially driven by three major methods: an apprenticeship-based system of skill training, a European legal education model-based general education approach, and a systematic and analytic law school lecture-oriented approach to law as mutual logical principles.[27] To boot, a learning theory known as 'Cone Experience', which was reportedly developed by Edgar Dale in 1946, proves learning is best achieved by doing. Dale has been quoted as considering both listening to lectures and text reading the least effective methods.[28] David Kolb and Roger Fry later expanded Dale's theory around the 1970s, as part of a second wave of developments.[29] By the 1950s, a significant number of accredited law schools had already established different clinical programmes based on different standards, most of which were voluntary.[30]

Efforts from NGOs were remarkable. First was the Carnegie Foundation for the Advancement of Teaching, whose funded study, known as the Reed Report, outlined general education, theoretical knowledge of the law, and practical skills training as crucial for preparing students for legal practice.[31] The Society, an NGO established in 1876, is, however, considered one oldest legal aid programmes in the US. Many clinics also received a boost with funding from the Ford Foundation, particularly with the establishment of Ford's Council on Legal Education for Professional Responsibility (CLEPR) in the 1970s. The seed money support from CLEPR is seen to have helped around 98% of accredited law schools to offer some kind of clinical legal programme in the 1980s.[32] Effectively, the Ford Foundation's significant funding for important clinical projects is believed to have helped integrate CLE programmes into the mainstream legal curriculum in the US.[33] The first wave of clinical education effectively replaced the casebook and Socratic methods that placed emphasis on decisions of the appellate courts to teach legal analytical skill.[34]

The second wave began in the 1960s, continuing well into the late 1990s, with increased development in civil legal services.[35] This period witnessed a new

26 Frank (1933), pp 907–23.
27 McManis (1981).
28 Du Plessis (2019), p 16.
29 Ibid., p 16.
30 Bloch (2010), p 5.
31 Sonsteng et al. (2007), p 42.
32 Schrag and Meltsner (1998), pp 5–7.
33 Bloch (2010), p 7.
34 Barry et al. (2000), pp 1–79.
35 Wilson (2018), pp 263–85.

dynamism and expansion of social movement and so attracted more states' generous, conscious efforts to inject a new, socially oriented methodical model of learning into the US system of professional legal education. By using law as an instrument of social change, clinical programmes were focused on the demand by law students for professional training relevance and passion to provide legal services to the poor people lacking access to justice.[36] Further, clinics were designed to equip students with lawyering skills, essential professional values, competent representation skills, promotion of justice, fairness, morality, professional self-development, as well as improvement of the legal profession. The US Office of Economic Opportunity created a Legal Services Programme, which roughly accounted for over $70 million a year of income in 1974, to provide grants to national non-profits groups of lawyers required to offer civil legal services.[37] This project, according to Richard Wilson, remarkably impacted US poverty law practice before its replacement with Legal Services Corporation in 1974.[38]

The final wave, beginning in the 1990s, was characterised by the rapid advancement of CLE programmes at different universities. The MacCrate Report of 1992,[39] with its impact, has become a reference point for the progress made during this time. More recently, in 2007, a report compiled by Carnegie Foundation focused on an integrated three-year curriculum based on theory and practice.[40] By far, it has impacted all universities with accreditation status in the US to engage in varying clinical initiatives. Therefore, mature systems of CLE such as the US no doubt provide a model for countries with evolving experience in CLE.

The South African Context

Early CLE courses began in SA with an introduction of full-time law programmes as far back as the 1970s, and afterwards inspired liberal academics to begin responding to social inequality.[41] There were both unfavourable political scenarios and a stark lack of government commitment to legal aid provision for the indigent citizens.[42] The first set of legal aid clinics were established at the University of Cape Town, the University of Witwatersrand, and the University of Natal, and law students were engaged in socially oriented clinical activities, in an attempt to fill the existing gaps.[43] More clinics evolved in 1973, following a conference sponsored by the Ford Foundation.[44]

36 Barry et al. (2000), pp 12–14.
37 Rhudy (1994), pp 231–2.
38 Wilson (2018), pp 263–85.
39 Findley (2006–2007), p 306.
40 Sullivan et al. (2007).
41 Mcquoid-Mason et al. (2010); Kentridge (1974), pp 87–9; Maisel et al. (2016), p 433.
42 Haupt (2006), p 229.
43 De Klerk (2006), p 930.
44 Mcquoid-Mason (1986), p 186.

Like the US context, university law clinics in SA increasingly focused on increased access to justice in the 1980s. They provided legal services for the vulnerable and poor citizens and dealt with human rights violations, and much live client activity was seen at the time.[45] Bad legacies of the apartheid government were a boost to clinical initiatives. The creation of the Centre for Applied Legal Studies and the Legal Resources Centre focused on litigation to deal with apartheid, and is one aspect of such improvement. By 1981, law clinics had already been established at 14 universities.[46] More so, in the 1990s, an increase in legal aid services was experienced.

There has been significant support for clinical programmes. An increase in state legal aid systems is presently widely applauded. However, funding is key to a sustainable clinical programme,[47] and lack of funding by states is a big threat to effective and inclusive legal aid delivery in many jurisdictions today. Many countries, such as the UK, have cut down on funding for legal aid. These are countries that generally do not provide legal support for certain offences, for example, criminal offences.

The accreditation of university law clinics by the South African Law Society in 1993, the establishment of the South African University Law Clinics Association (SAULCA), formerly the Association of University Legal Aid Institutions, in addition to funding from the Attorneys Fidelity Fund, are all seen to have boosted CLE within the country. The SAULCA is a primary body, which promotes broader clinical initiatives. The roles of law clinics in SA have increased over time to include broad areas of social justice, imparting practical skills to law students, in addition to filling a gap in legal aid services delivery.[48] There is now a focus on public law rather than private law, as inspired by an end to the apartheid regime.[49] Thus, addressing the bad legacies of an oppressive regime to strengthen a democratic transition has been important clinical progress made. SA appears to be the earliest country in Africa to embrace the global clinical movement. Therefore, it has arguably provided a model for most other African countries, such as Nigeria.

The Westernisation Impact of CLE

Overview

A country's legal education ought to, much like the legal system, reflect its national identity, values, and social, economic, and political contexts. This is because, as a supposedly integral part of legal education, it is instrumental

45 Du Plessis (2019), pp 12–34.
46 Mcquoid-Mason et al. (2010), pp 24–5.
47 Nwedu (2019), p 47.
48 Mcquoid-Mason et al. (2010).
49 Maisel et al. (2016), p 433.

to law student career pathways and ideological indoctrination.[50] The career objective of a lawyer could involve an engagement in socially oriented or self-interested legal practice, but both solely in pursuit of justice. Evaluating a particular legal education ideally depends on access to justice, which is also a biopolitical barometer for evaluating the rule of law and quality of governance, and embraces the nature, mechanism, and place of individuals in the 'judicial matrix and quality of justice' obtained in any society.[51]

Effectively, individuals' ability to pursue and receive remedy for grievances via informal and formal institutions, in line with human rights ideals, is globally held to be at the core of access to justice.[52] Both in theory and practice, access to justice is, in fact, a broad concept. From any lens of CLE, it underlines certain 'preconditions'.[53] Even access to justice, as broad as it is, entails activities that enhance access to the court, law, and information about legal rights and duties through an affordable, equitable, accessible, and liberal legal regime. More so, access to justice involves initiatives aimed at improving, protecting, and promoting the legal rights of every individual to avoid marginalisation and exploitation.[54]

Though CLE evolved from the west, it has become massively adopted in many jurisdictions, including non-western countries. This re-echoes an age-long fact that the 'law' is one area compatible with the westernisation process. However, critics' critiques of western education raise a critical concern about its legitimacy and universality of objective. For example, modern scholars have argued that internationalisation is an implicit neo-colonial process inherent in US education.[55] This neo-colonial philosophy impels non-western countries to internationalise via a parody of western laws, norms, and practices, as argued by Suspitsyna, and it reflects what Foucault meant by 'governmentality'.[56]

Biopolitics with its interplay of governmentality is a typical illumination of what and how western universities have come to re-invent, manage, and direct the cause of modern legal education, legal studentship, and professional practice of lawyers by placing individuals who are less privileged and society at large at the core of such a mission. This is a resurfacing of western colonisation used, in part, to convey subjugation, western knowledge production and systems of learning as superior and universal, and as a basis for modernity.[57]

50 Ball (2010).

51 Aliyu and Saleh (2018), pp 216–31.

52 United States Institute of Peace (USIP) (undated) 'Necessary Condition: Access to Justice', www.usip.org/guiding-principles-stabilization-and-reconstruction-the-web-version/rule-law/access-justice

53 Okogbule (2005), pp 94–113.

54 USIP (undated).

55 Suspitsyna (2021).

56 Suspitsyna (2015).

57 Stein and Andreotti (2017).

This tension has implications for how knowledge is produced and transmitted, and society controlled. One piece of research has demonstrated that a nexus exists between knowledge producers and their motives, which impacts what is perceived to be legitimate knowledge in society, politics, and economy in non-western backgrounds.[58] The western universities are, hence, perceived as characteristic of whiteness, modernity, and/or a colonial agenda,[59] and as such perhaps undermine local knowledge and ideas.

In any sense, clinical initiatives could be modelled to be adaptive or tailored to meet the specific needs of a country that its legal education generally, or legal clinics in particular, seek to address. But at the core of any model is justice, regardless. This is why it is perceived as a 'global justice crusade'. This perception has been its major catalyst, alongside democratic judiciaries, and professional bodies, especially in giving constitutional liberalism and impetus to it, in a way most beneficial to the most vulnerable and common citizens.[60] The case of *Gideon v Wainwright*,[61] in which the US Supreme Court unequivocally recognised a constitutional right to legal representation of defendants in criminal prosecution with serious charges and a possible considerable prison sentence, is a good illustration of CLE's constitutional credence. The constitutional right was further highlighted in *Argersinger v Hamlin*.[62] Typically, across many non-western jurisdictions, ensuring a defendant facing any criminal prosecution and who could not ordinarily afford a defence is provided with legal representation in a form of legal aid has become a mandatory requirement.

Equally, university and law school legal clinics as well as non-government organisations have also been fully supportive of clinical movement in different areas of activities, both in the US and around the world. Their activities have involved organising and sponsoring conferences, providing clinical training for university and law school student clinicians and staff, and pro bono services to the needy and society generally. The overall impact of CLE is felt in an umbrella area of justice, such as civic engagement, human rights, and environmental justice, as next detailed.

Civic Engagement

Many decades ago, universities, law schools, academics, and law students made infinitesimal impacts in society. Today, however, they are leading significant transformative impacts with civic engagement,[63] and are no longer seen as knowledge production places that turn human beings into a commodity

58 Akena (2012), pp 599–619.
59 Stein and Andreotti (2017).
60 Brown (1965), p 312; Cleary (1966), p 1; Monaghan (1965), p 445.
61 [1963] 372 US 335.
62 [1972] 407 US 25.
63 Brennan et al. (2004), p 72.

for competence and gain only. This development is, in part, driven by the massive adoption of CLE globally. Didactically, civil engagement with the community is well recognised as a part of academics' responsibilities within higher education environments.[64] Thus, it constitutes a salient, corresponding slice of university accountabilities and biopolitics in any society. Through law clinics, student clinicians and lawyers have proven commitments to promoting individual consciousness and capacity development with civil engagement worldwide. They have been instrumental for life-changing community outreach activities, which particularly benefit the indigent and uninformed citizens because such citizens gain legal knowledge and values.[65]

Clinical education is increasingly drawing much attention to societal problems, perhaps because legal knowledge and skills are essential for solving human challenges and making life better. The need for justice in the face of human challenges re-emphasises a need for efficient law clinic externship, which integrates democratic innovations as a basic feature, enabling law students or clinicians to develop a greater understanding of and alliance with dynamic relations existing in the familiarised clinical model and its actual use in the diverse communities in which they would work.[66] Legal clinics have also been a key driver of a number of sustainable development goals with the instrumentality of civic engagement across different parts of the world, including non-western countries.[67] For example, one seminal study has demonstrated that CLE is an aggressive tool for tackling 'poverty and ignorance'.[68] This revelation is in agreement with Narendra Modi's view that education is the best and most cost-effective approach to combat poverty,[69] and Nelson Mandela's view that 'education is the most powerful weapon which you can use to change the world'.[70] The impact of CLE as a system of education mirrors both observations. Essentially, it puts a restraint on social injustice and inequality, which brings about social change.

Human Rights

The instrumentality of CLE has helped in advancing human rights worldwide, as an underpinning of biopolitical law. There are different clinical initiatives

64 Guest (2015), paras 2–7.

65 MacQuiod-Mason (undated), pp 1–10.

66 Christopher et al. (2012), pp 380–91.

67 See United Nations General Assembly Resolution A/RES/70/1 (2015).

68 Iya (2000), pp 13–32.

69 See India Today Web Desk, 'PM Modi in Varanasi: Education is the Best Weapon to Fight Poverty', www.indiatoday.in/india/uttar-pradesh/story/live-pm-modi-in-varanasi-263551-2015-09-18, 18 September 2015.

70 This quote has always been attributed to Nelson Mandela who was former President of South Africa known for his extraordinary leadership, wisdom, and anti-apartheid revolution.

by which clinics support human rights, as well as related humanitarian services. Typically, street law is one example. Originated at Georgetown University Law Centre in Washington, 1972, street law is a programme crafted to help law students or student clinicians and others impart to the people an awareness of their legal rights and where to get help.[71] The scope of street law differs from clinic to clinic. However, students are usually assigned to some roles of legal concern. More broadly, street lawyering builds upon public interest law programmes with community outreaches. Typical programmes may focus on child rights education, community education, community support, freedom of information, environmental rights issues, and overall access to justice. Law student clinicians in Nigeria, for example, have continued to be engaged in street lawyering for the protection of prisoners' rights, securing bail for citizens unfairly detained, and mediating for women and child abuses.[72]

Most legal clinics specifically provide legal representation for citizens whose human rights have been violated. There are some clinics that enlighten citizens, usually poor and illiterate individuals, on what constitutes their fundamental human rights and how challenges affecting such rights can be overcome. Evidently, legal literacy has been argued to be a constituent of CLE with which clinicians increase legal knowledge in assisting illiterate citizens to become legally literate.[73] Therefore, with CLE, clinics have become instrumental in using public-oriented legal education or legal literacy to promote freedom of information on various human rights issues. By implication, clinics fill an existing knowledge gap that has prevented poor, rural illiterates from adequate access to legal aid services.[74] The application of human rights education to all levels of learning, including primary, secondary, and higher education, has received emphasis.[75] Even as the overall focus of any clinic is access to justice, it is a basic right per se, and means of defending and protecting other human rights and compelling accountability for abuse and related crimes of such rights.[76]

Growing domestic crises triggering abuse of human rights and internal displacement of victims of such crises is a remarkable trend, drawing humanitarian attention from legal clinics in many developing, non-western countries nowadays. The desire to boost human rights protection and enhance access to justice of internally displaced persons in the northeast part of Nigeria, where humanitarian crises are increasing,[77] has led to a call for clinics' intervention.[78] Legal clinics have also proved significant in providing free, legal advisory services to

71 McQuoid-Mason (undated), pp 1–10; Suhaimi and Zulkitli (2012), pp 218–26.
72 Aliyu and Saleh (2018).
73 Jha and Das (2015), pp 1–16.
74 Nwedu (2017), pp 98–121.
75 Smith and Bai (2015), pp 137–51.
76 Aliyu and Saleh (2018).
77 Abdulkadir (2019), pp 29–42.
78 Aliyu and Saleh (2018).

refugees or asylum seekers displaced under many conditions of crisis, both from a humanitarian and human rights perspective.

Environmental Justice

Environmental concern has drawn both national and global attention since the late twentieth century.[79] Like the history of CLE, university and law school clinics' interest in environmental justice first evolved in the US around the 1970s and has resulted in a specialised model of legal clinic known as the environmental law clinic.[80] There is a current call to mainstream environmental awareness via environmental education.[81] The environment has biopolitically become one of the key focuses of legal clinics. Law clinics in non-western countries have widely adopted an environmentally curated model legal clinic and sometimes general-purpose clinics for addressing injudicious and injurious actions of governments or corporations which impact humanity and the human environment. There are currently in existence some legal clinics with proven track records of practical performance in shaping environmental awareness and justice.[82]

There are different routes by which clinics seek to address social and global environmental justice and awareness. Typically, advocacy is one way, which has played a key role in fostering environmental justice. Law clinics engage in advocacy to enlighten the public on the consequences of certain actions on the human environment, and it is a remarkable manifestation of public legal education. They also engage in dialogue with governments, policymakers, regulators, and other stakeholders with the goal of influencing environmental policies or related governmental actions.[83] Engagement ideally supports inclusive contributions from local people.[84] Thus, the environmental crisis is deflected only when local people get involved in the policymaking process. Most of all, issues affecting local people are better resolved if a policy seeking to address such issues is driven by inclusiveness and deliberate participation. This assumption has been highlighted as a basic need for effective climate change adaptation,[85] and it is no surprise that climate change represents an environmental megatrend of our time. Litigation has also served as a route for legal clinics to pursue environmental justice and protect human lives.[86] This is par-

79 He et al. (2017), p 337.

80 Ibid., p 337.

81 Thapa (2021), pp 234–46.

82 See, for example, Ebonyi State University (EBSU) Law Clinic, http://ebsu-edu.net/history-overview/; Azim Premji University India, https://azimpremjiuniversity.edu.in

83 He et al. (2017), p 33.

84 Babich (2009), pp 11051–63.

85 Ayers (2010).

86 He et al. (2017), p 337.

ticularly a growing mechanism for seeking climate justice. However, the social impact of climate litigation has maintained a record low due to some technical and political issues climate change itself raises.

The Humanistic Principles of CLE

Principle of Inclusive Justice

There are certain core principles of CLE, which transmit biopolitical insights into how legal education is applied to advance human wellbeing and societal transformation. The principle of inclusive justice is one, which resonates as a modern concept evolved in response to inequalities and social injustice. Essentially, inclusive justice is a substratum for social justice. Both concepts underline 'common good' as a goal for which everyone in society has a moral duty or obligation to care for every other person.[87] Thus, social justice is a philosophical notion of fairness and equal access to social privileges, wealth, and opportunities in relationships existing between individuals and society.[88] The idea of CLE draws credence from early philosophical notions of 'justice as fairness' and 'justice' as impartiality.[89] Most interestingly, it is also in agreement with the principles of equal access, equality, participation, diversity, and human rights.[90] These hallmarks are at the forefront of inclusive justice, be it social, economic, or political justice.

Social justice has covered many spheres of human endeavours, including at least 'legal institutions and educational settings',[91] which reinforces the basis of CLE. The justification of inclusive justice as a principle of CLE is a true reflection of distributional justice and much of social work practice.[92] One would perhaps ask: inclusive justice for whom? Everyone in society needs justice at least in its most crude and strictest sense. But a certain group of people needs justice most, even in a wider sense, and it is the poor and vulnerable citizens who are most commonly marginalised. Most often, it is seen that gaps not addressed by the legal system and political system, and in particular legal aid and poverty programmes provided by governments, are mostly borne by the common people. Therefore, inclusive justice transcends conventional justice over rights and wrongs in civil and criminal cases. Both inclusive justice and social justice have weaved together as closely related, and, of course, as a focus of clinical activities worldwide.[93]

87 Kathleen Maas Weigert (2015).
88 Corporate Finance Institute (CFI) (undated) 'Social Justice: What Is Social Justice?', https://corporatefinanceinstitute.com/resources/knowledge/other/social-justice/
89 Rawls (1972).
90 CFI (undated); Kent State (2020).
91 Kazemi et al. (2015).
92 Staniforth (2015).
93 Nwedu (2018), pp 137–51.

The activities of clinics continue to focus on justice-based initiatives in providing poor and vulnerable people with free legal services. These services are at best expressed as legal aid. This is true as an index for receiving legal aid is determined by one's inability to provide it.[94] The truest reflection of this reality is Karl Marx's 'principle of needs'. The principle dialectically utilises the phrase 'from each according to his ability, to each according to his needs' to advocate for free access to and distribution of goods, capital, and services. Legal education institutions alongside law clinics somewhat advance needs principle via pro bono public or free legal aid services. There are different components of legal aid, including legal representation in criminal or civil matters, provision of legal advice, provision of financial aid, provision of public legal education or literacy. Law school and university legal clinics have been strongly instrumental in fostering these areas of justice globally.

Principle of Socially Responsible Profession

The legal profession arguably was not a very socially, responsible profession before a period preceding 1870s. Both lawyers and students were also not very open to take on and address problems that mainly affected poor people in society. Thus, it has been argued that the legal profession had overlooked interdependent relations because claims presented to court came from litigants under a supposition that independencies, and not interdependencies, personify society.[95] This means lawyers were overly addicted to a conventional adversary role or inclined to apply substantive and procedural rules,[96] perhaps across different common and civil law jurisdictions, respectively. In effect, much of a lawyer's responsibility had to be channelled to clients with almost no exposure to real life, societal relations, and problem-solving. The lawyer–client relationship is still unsurprisingly a focus of the legal profession as a defining age-long tradition.

The principle of the socially responsible profession is a changing narrative due to CLE influence from the lens of biopolitics. Granted, social responsibility should be seen as part of the modern lawyer–society relationship extending to students alike. Lawyers and law students have a social responsibility to society. The legal profession, law schools, and universities have a similar responsibility, however, in ensuring that students are trained and equipped with full mindfulness of the ethical and social duties of the profession.[97]

Both lawyers and student clinicians should be trained to influence policy and decision-making, and foster transparent and accountable judicial democracy

94 Nwedu (2017), pp 98–121.
95 Mandelker (1970), pp 355–63.
96 O'Connor (1985), p 659.
97 Ibid., p 659.

aimed at overall societal transformation. The impact of CLE is manifesting in how a lawyer's role is being reshaped and redefined in modern society. Law students have become much more active in such a societal role, however, in contexts permissible by governmental policy and rules of professional practice. Like never before, lawyers are increasingly becoming active, social actors and advocates of social justice and transformation, by engaging in public interest litigation and public legal education, for example. This development complements the professional role or educational goal of lawyers for which they are primarily trained and law schools established.

Principle of Social Transformation or Social Changes

Human society is deeply characterised by growing social tension and demands for major reformations in political institutions.[98] Even social institutions are in need of such transformations. Evidently, a significant pedagogical change in the social institutions of law and education reflects biopolitics. The biopolitical legal education is a transformative, social change that douses social tension and responds to societal demands. By itself, social transformation is a practical and strategic process embedded in the principle of inclusiveness for responding to human needs in society. Transformative social change encompasses socio-economic, political, and environmental indicators of sustainable human advancement and unity. The close relation between CLE and social transformation highlights the role of development law from a biopolitical lens, in particular.

Therefore, one of the law's objectives is to drive social change and enhance human life by biopolitics. The dynamic feature of law sustains the idea of CLE as its substratum. This legal dynamism is an enabler of social change because the law must first change itself in line with the desires of changing society. Thus, a core tenet of CLE should, among other things, be teaching an activist role in society. Through clinical pedagogy, a new generation of lawyers and law students should be trained to influence policy and decision-making, and foster transparent and accountable judicial democracy for overall societal transformation based on the notion of humanism. They should imbibe a sense of professional responsibilities towards engendering transformation.

Conclusion

This chapter has focused on the clinical westernisation of legal education, with a biopolitical, comparative analysis of its historical contexts in the US and SA. Effectively, it began as a progressive reform movement in response to students' passion to learn how the law could be used as an instrument of social change in providing legal representation for poor people in society, engendering societal

98 Mandelker (1970), pp 355–63.

transformation, in addition to helping the students gain practical and academic professional skills and knowledge of the law.

The adoption of a clinical model of western legal education in non-western jurisdictions is simply an attestation of its global advances and success. Most countries have become increasingly receptive to it, as an opportunity for reformation of legal education and legal systems. Though CLE has made a relatively significant impact in non-western countries, studies tend to focus on its success stories within the west. This reality gives strong credence to criticisms that US higher education remains a fragment of past and present colonial tendencies characterised by whiteness, supremacy, and dominion of western knowledge production, which are systemically encoded in biopolitics.

The roles of civil societies, NGOs, law schools, and university clinicians cannot be easily forgotten with regards to the global advancement of the clinical movement. They have had to engage in a wide range of clinical activities, as earlier highlighted. These activities aim to drive critical reformations and policies with a positive social and professional impact on society and law students. The legal profession itself has also been unprecedentedly well impacted. Both lawyers and law students are now more professionally responsible and receptive, both to their profession and society, with the wave of CLE.

References

Primary sources

Gideon v Wainwright [1963] 372 US 335.
Argersinger v Hamlin [1972] 407 US 25.

Secondary sources

Maryam Idris Abdulkadir (2019) 'Appraisal of the Role of Law Clinics in Internally Displaced Persons and Refugee Camps in Nigeria' 6 *Asian Journal of Legal Education* 29.

Francis Adyanga Akena (2012) 'Critical Analysis of the Production of Western Knowledge and Its Implications for Indigenous Knowledge and Decolonization' 43 *Journal of Black Studies* 599.

Anthony G Amsterdam (1984) 'Clinical Legal Education: A 21st-century Perspective' 34 *Journal of Legal Education* 612.

Jessica Ayers (2010) 'Understanding the Adaptation Paradox: Can Global Climate Change Adaptation Policy be Locally Inclusive?', PhD thesis submitted to the Department of International Development, London School of Economics and Political science.

Mohammed Babakano Aliyu and Mohammad Musa Saleh (2018) 'Enhancing Access to Justice to the Internally Displaced Persons (IDPS) in Borno State: The Role of Lawyers and the University Law Clinic' 5 *Unimaid Journal of Pubic Law* 216.

Adam Babich (2009) 'Illegal Permit? Who Are You Going to Call? Your Local Environmental Law Llinic!' 39 *Environmental Law Rep News & Analysis* 11051.

Mathew Ball (2010) 'Legal Education and the "Idealistic Student": Using Foucault to Unpack the Critical Legal Narrative' 36 *Monash University Law Review* 18.

Margaret Barry, Jon Dubin and Peter Joy (2000) 'Clinical Education for this Millennium: The Third Wave' 7 *Clinical Law Rev* 1.
Frank S Bloch and Igbal S Ishar (1990) 'Legal Aid, Public Service and Clinical Legal Education: Future Directions from India and the United States' 12 *Michigan Journal of International Law* 92.
Frank S Bloch and Mary Anne Noone (2010) 'Legal Aid Origins of Clinical Legal Education' in FS Bloch (ed) *The Global Clinical Movement: Educating Lawyers for Social Justice*, Oxford University Press.
Frank S Bloch (ed) (2010) *The Global Clinical Movement: Educating Lawyers for Social Movement*, Oxford University Press.
John S Bradway (1930) 'The Nature of a Legal Aid Clinic' 3 *S Cal L Rev* 173.
John R Brown (1965) 'The Trumpets Sounds: Gideon - A First Call to the Law School' 43 *Texas Law Review* 312.
Walsh Christopher et al. (2012) 'Strengthening Access to Justice Through Clinical Legal Education (CLE)' 6 *Transforming Government: People, Process and Policy* 380.
John J Cleary (1966) 'Law Students in Criminal Law Practice' 16 *DePaul Law Review* 1.
Geoff Danaher, Tony Sachirato and Jen Webb (2000) *Understanding Foucault*, Sage.
Willem De Klerk (2006) 'University Law Clinics in South Africa' 122 *The South African Law Journal* 229.
Morné A Du Plessis (2019) 'Forty-five Years of Clinical Legal Education in South Africa' 25 *South African Health Law Review* 12.
Keith A Findley (2006–2007) 'Rediscovering the Lawyer School: Curriculum Reform in Wisconsin' 24 *Wisconsin International LJ* 295.
Michel Foucault (1979) *The Birth of Biopolitics: Lectures at the Collège de France 1978–1979*, Volume 7, St Martins Press.
Jerome Frank (1933) 'Why Not a Clinical Lawyer-School?' 81 *U Pa L Rev* 907.
Frans S Haupt (2006) 'Some Aspects Regarding the Origin, Development and Present Position of the University of Pretoria Law Clinic' 39 *De Jure* 229.
Pei-Pei He et al. (2017) 'Environmental law Clinics in Collaboration with Environmental NGOs in China' 9 *Sustainability* 337.
Phillip F Iya (2000) 'Fighting Africa's Poverty and Ignorance through Clinical Legal Education: Shared Experiences with New Initiatives for the 21st Century' 1 *International Journal of Clinical Legal Education* 13.
Anamika Jha and Ankita Das (2015) 'Where is Clinical Legal Education Located Within Broader Discussions of Access to Justice in India?' 2 *International Journal of Legal and Social Studies* 1.
Ali Kazemi, Kjell Törnblom and Gerold Mikula (2015) 'Justice: Social Psychological Perspective' in James D Wright (ed) *International Encyclopedia of the Social and Behavioral Sciences*, Elsevier.
Felicia N Kentridge (1974) 'Lead-in Address' in D Mcquoid-Mason (ed) *Legal Aid in South Africa*, Proceedings of a conference held in the Faculty of Law, University of Natal, Durban, from 2–6 July 1973.
Thomas Lemke (2011) *Biopolitics: An Advanced Introduction*, trans. Eric Frederick Trump, NYU Press.
Peggy Maisel, Shaheda Mahomed and Meetali Jain (2016) 'Clinical Legal Education's Contribution to Building Constitutionalism and Democracy in South Africa: Past, Present and Future' 60 *New York Law School Law Review* 433.
Kathleen Maas Weigert (2015) 'Social Justice: Historical and Theoretical Considerations' in JD Wright (ed) *International Encyclopedia of the Social & Behavioral Sciences*, Elsevier.

Robert MacCrate (1997) 'Enhancing a Changing Profession: From Clinic to Continuum' 64 *Tennessee Law Review* 1099.

Rhea Roy Mammen (2020) 'Comparing Experimental Legal Education in Canada and India' 8 *Asian Journal of Legal Education* 34.

Daniel R Mandelker (1970) 'The Role of Law in Social Change' 8 *Osgoode Hall Law Review* 355.

Charles R McManis (1981) 'The History of First Century American Legal Education: A Revisionist Perspective' 59 *Washington University Law Review* 617.

David J Mcquoid-Mason (1986) 'The Organization, Administration and Funding of Legal aid Clinics in South Africa' 1 *Natal University Law and Society Review* 139.

David J Mcquiod-Mason (undated) 'Teaching Social Justice to Law Students through Community Service: The South African Experience', http://clarkcunningham.org/LegalEd/SouthAfricaMason1.pdf.

David J Mcquoid-Mason (2010) 'Clinical Legal Education in Africa: Legal Education and Community Service' in FS Bloch (ed) *The Global Clinical Movement: Educating Lawyers for Social Justice*, Oxford University Press.

David J Mcquoid-Mason, Ernest Ojukwu and George M Wachira (2010) 'Clinical Legal Education in African Legal Education and Community Service' in FS Bloch (ed) *The Global Clinical Movement: Educating Lawyers for Social Justice*, Oxford University Press.

Henry P Monaghan (1965) 'Gideon's Army: Student Soldiers' 45 *Boston Univ Law Rev* 445.

Cosmos Nike Nwedu (2017) 'Enhancing Legal Aid through University Law Student Engagement: A Case Study of EBSU Law Clinic Model' 24 *International Journal of Clinical Legal Education* 98.

Cosmos Nike Nwedu (2018) 'Taking Clinical Legal Education from Classrooms to Streets: A Practical Perspective to Solving Social Problems' 5 *Asian Journal of Legal Education* 137.

Cosmos Nike Nwedu (2019) 'Towards Clinical Sustainability from Evolution to Revolution: A Study of Sustainable Factors for Law Clinics' 6 *Asian Journal of Legal Education* 43.

Sandra Day O'Connor (1985) 'Legal Education and Social Responsibility' 53 *Fordham Law Review* 659.

Ernest Ojukwu, Sam Erugo and Charles Adekoya (2013) *Clinical Legal Education: Curriculum Lessons and Materials*, Network of University Legal Aid Institutions (NULAI).

Nlerum S Okogbule (2005) 'Access to Justice and Human Rights Protection in Nigeria: Problems and Prospects' 2 *Sur-International Journal on Human Rights* 94.

John R Peden (1992) 'Role of Practical Training in Legal Education: American and Australian Experience' 24 *Journal of Legal Education* 503.

John Rawls (1972) *A Theory of Justice*, Belknap Press.

Robert J Rhudy (1994) 'Comparing Legal Services to the Poor in the United States with other Western Countries' 5 *Maryland Journal of Contemporary Legal Issues* 223.

William V Rowe (1917) 'Legal Clinics and Better Trained Lawyers: A Necessity' 11 *University of Illinois Law Review* 591.

Kenneth J Saltman (2018) *The Politics of Education: A Critical Introduction*, 2nd Edition, Routledge.

Philip G Schrag and Michael Meltsner (1998) *Reflections on Clinical Legal Education*, Northeastern University Press.

Rhona Smith and Guimei Bai (2015) 'Higher Education in Human Rights within China: A Ten-year Review of the Peking University Model' 5 *Asian Journal of Legal Education* 137.

John O Sonsteng et al. (2007) 'A Legal Education Renaissance: A Practical Approach for the Twenty-first Century' 34 *William Mitchell Law Review* 1.

Mansi Sood (2017) 'Legal Education and its Outcomes: Digging Deeper into the Successes and Failures of India's National Law Schools', http://dx.doi.org/10.2139/ssrn.3062519.

Tatiana Suspitsyna (2015) 'Cultural Hierarchies in the Discursive Representations of China in the Chronicle of Higher Education' 56 *Critical Studies in Education* 21.

Tatiana Suspitsyna (2021) 'Internationalization, Whiteness and Biopolitics of Higher Education' 11 *Journal of International Students* 50.

Barbara Staniforth (2015) 'Communication Skills in Social Work' in James D Wright (ed) *International Encyclopedia of the Social and Behavioral Sciences*, Elsevier.

Sharon Stein and Vanessa de Oliveira Andreotti (2017) 'Higher Education and the Modern/colonial Imaginary' 17 *Cultural Studies-Critical Methodologies* 173.

Asnida Mohhd Suhaimi and Nur Farzana Mohd Zulkitli (2012) 'Street Law Based CLE: A Student Impact Assessment' 18 *International Journal of Clinical Legal Education* 218.

William M Sullivan et al. (2007) *Educating Lawyers: Preparation for the Profession of Law*, Jossey-Bass.

Amy Swiffen (2012) *Law, Ethics and Biopolitical*, Routledge.

Jwala D Thapa (2021) 'Spreading Environmental Awareness Through Environmental Education in Schools: The Case Study of a Sikkimese Green School' 8 *Asian Journal of Legal Education* 234.

Richard J Wilson (2018) *The Global Evolution of Legal Education: More Than a Method*, Cambridge University Press.

Richard J Wilson (2018) 'Legal Aid and Clinical Legal Education in Europe and the USA: Are They Compatible?' in O Halvorsen Rønning and O Hammerslev (eds) *Outsourcing Legal Aid in the Nordic Welfare States*, Palgrave Macmillan.

Xia Li'an Sun Xiang (2014) 'Towards a Biopolitical Law: On Foucault's Legal Thoughts' 44 *Journal of Zhejiang University* 76.

Reports / Resolutions

John Brennan, Roger King and Lebeau Yann (2004) 'The Role of Universities in the Transformation of Societies. Synthesis Report', Centre for Higher Education Research and Information and Association of Commonwealth Universities, UK.

Reginald H Smith and John S Bradway (1936) *Growth of Legal-Aid Work in the United States*, Bulletin of the United States Bureau of Labor Statistics, No 607.

United Nations General Assembly Resolution A/RES/70/1 on Transforming Our World: The 2030 Agenda for Sustainable Development, Adopted by Member States on 25 September 2015, www.un.org/ga/search/view_doc.asp?symbol=A/RES/70/1&Lang=E.

Emil Winkler (undated) 'Clinical Legal Education: A Report on the Concept of Law Clinics', www.academia.edu/40214205/Clinical_Legal_Education_A_report_on_the_concept_of_law_clinics.

News

Greta Guest (2015) 'Presidents Agree Engagement is Part of Academics' Obligation to Society', *Michigan News*, 14 May 2015, https://michiganross.umich.edu/rtia-articles/presidents-agree-engagement-part-academics-obligation-society.

Chapter 10

On the Biopolitics of Legal Education in Turkey

Eric Deibel and Talya Deibel

Introduction

Foucault's work is known for his discussions of power as exercised through intervention in the rate of birth, sanity, longevity, reproduction, and so on. While it might seem like a stretch to position legal education in modern Turkey alongside such observations on the transformation of power in the 19th century, it is very much a part of how the modern history of Turkey continues to be shaped by what Foucault called the 'problem of sovereignty' (in Society Must Be Defended). We are referring not only to the foundation of the Turkish republic and how it shaped legal education but also to the rule of law today, as it is most easily demonstrated by how the country continues to fall in each of the many rankings available on these issues.[1]

We refer to 'the biopolitics of legal education' with the understanding that it was only late in his life that Foucault started using the term 'biopolitics'. It was introduced in his lectures dealing with biopolitics found in *Society Must Be Defended* (1975/6) and *The Birth of Biopolitics* (1978/9), wherein he carefully distinguished this concept from conventional understandings of sovereignty in terms of the actions of nations as a foundational category or myth that can or should be identified with stable economic, political, and public interests.[2]

It is in this conventional sense that the origins of legal education in Turkey are easily shown to be tied up with the foundation of a new republic in the early 20th century, replacing the long-lasting Ottoman Empire's claim on divine and earthly rule with western style institutions. Accordingly, a system of law was literally imported from continental Europe (for example, civil law from Switzerland) in an attempt not only to recreate western institutions, but much more comprehensively it was a means to construct a new body politic. This included education, which is to say that legal history and legal education

1 See, for example, https://ecfr.eu/scorecard/2016/wider/37

2 See Foucault (2003); Foucault (2008). The general point is developed fully in Tamminen and Deibel (2019). For a clear and concise overview of how Foucault's concept of power matters for the field of law, see James (2018).

DOI: 10.4324/9781003175193-13

were key strategic vehicles whereby western values were to be incorporated into the body of the state—as its living embodiment of biopolitical strategies, as a foundation for its constitutional ordering of nature and culture, the basis of the stability and wealth of the unified nation.[3]

As is always the case with modern Turkey and the history of the Ottoman Empire, there is never a clear-cut line to be drawn in its relations to Europe or 'the west'. Its history, including that of its legal education, defies a simple designation as European or not, or whether it can simply be considered as identical to Eurocentric imperialist nation-states, or that it is, at its core, non-western and shares a predicament with countries that still experience the legacy of European colonisation acutely. This ambiguity goes back to the modern system of sovereign states, as based on cultural norms. Turkey, in this sense, has always been an insider in some senses and an outsider in others. Today is no different when it comes to Turkey's fraught relations with 'the west' and its attempts to establish cultural norms to accompany physical borders. This point extends to modern Turkey's relation to Eurocentric forms of law, which is to say that the country has consciously incorporated these into its educational system and, by extension, applied them to its students.

On the surface the suggestion is therefore one that is echoed throughout this volume, which is that the problem lies with positivist law and its close ties to neo-liberal/neo-colonial policies, inside and outside Europe and the US. Whether we see Turkey as an inside or an outside to Europe does not necessarily matter from the perspective of students of law, given that new generations of law students in western countries are experiencing a similar type of parody, one that echoes the principal features of any non-western attempts to resist the type of law that operates as neo-colonial vehicle—as 'a parody' wherein non-western countries are forced to internationalise European norms.[4]

Accordingly, the parody extends to how the Turkish relation to 'law' has always been ambiguous. It began with the founding of the modern nation, as a new republic, with European law as one of its ideological pillars. And yet that law is also nominally indigenous (e.g. the Byzantine influence on early modern Italy). Roman law, compiled in Byzantium, now İstanbul, influenced the laws of the Ottoman Empire. The best-known example would be the *Tanzimat* Reforms, as they ordered extensive changes to commercial, criminal, and procedural laws, which were modelled after France. However, it is the legal changes in the early period of the Turkish republic that took

3 See also Forzani, who points to how law, as the means to maintain order, is based on a premise of social cohesion (in the *Biopolitics and Resistance in Legal Education* volume).

4 The reference to 'parody' and neo-colonial practices refers to the text by Nwedu (this volume) while the neo-liberalisation of European law faculties comes out most clearly in the text by Walter and Contarini (this volume) about the modern history of Lucern Law School. Our point, however, is that foundationalism, as western and clearly distinct from non-western, risks operating as a false dilemma in the Turkish context that we need to steer clear of.

the last and the most important step in terms of the secularisation of the legal system by systematically internalising the Roman law rules.[5] Like elsewhere in the world, this means that Roman law lives on in modern law in the civil codes and in that capacity it was integral to a self-imposed top-down modernisation project aimed at creating a new elite and, affirming the ambiguity of our case, it was formulated as a response, a type of resistance, to growing western imperialism as it imposed itself on the Ottoman Empire in the 19th century.[6]

Of course, such lofty aspirations never came close to being fully realised, they never are. At its most basic level Foucault teaches us that politics is never simply monopolised by the powerful. This is also the case when examining the history of the contemporary predicament legal education in Turkey finds itself in. We should be cautious and instantly dismantle any notion that there was once an origin for a singular, monolithic enterprise—wherein the state and its agencies exercise control through top-down educational reforms and mandates. Certainly, state power and authority were and are omnipresent in the Turkish education system. However, there is no contrast between an idealised productive use of power in the early 20th century (to create western legal education) as opposed to today's use of power, for example when objecting to the imposition of new restrictions and prohibitions on parts of the education system.

It is in this basic Foucauldian sense that we seek to understand the predicament of legal education in Turkey, which will be elaborated in the next section, which refers to sovereignty as a 'missing foundation', first theoretically and subsequently as an observation on the early history of Turkish legal education. Within this historical context we proceed to examine various contemporary fields and specialisations. Subsequently we return to our basic Foucauldian point, drawing out our conclusion into a discussion, as made possible by our analysis. The latter revolves around our claim about the contemporary predicament: that when talking about a Turkish legal explanation one has to situate its contemporary form within the context of how law in Turkey has managed to remain at the core of the social fabric while at the same time its transgression is visible everywhere. It is in this situation that legal education is key: it shows how 'law' revolves around the education of its participants, who are might be extremely professional or even ethical in various ways, and yet are not trained in any type of consistent understanding of the nature of law nor in critique of law's role in modern society.

5 Evidence for the continuity of Byzantine law and law in modern Turkey is omnipresent in the Turkish legal literature. See, for example, Eşref Küçük (2007); Haluk Emiroğlu (2002); Gülnihal Bozkurt (1996). For a specific reference to the *Tanzimat* period, see Halil İnalcık (2006). See also below, note 23.

6 See also Adebisi in the *Biopolitics and Resistance in Legal Education* volume.

Approach

The Turkish predicament, with its legal education, is 'biopolitical' in how there is no easy distinction to be made between, on the one hand, law and lawyers as an ontological problem and, on the other hand, critique, critical methods, and their practical application as a ready-made solution. The point is not that the latter is unwelcome; there is a place for analysing such histories and practices, as biopolitics, as means of revealing an 'invisible curriculum', or as other critical ways of framing the situation that aim somehow to 'liberate' or 'emancipate' the potential of legal education.[7] However, our goal is different in that we seek to establish that it matters for today's legal education in Turkey that it continues to be premised in its practice on an 'inaccessible nucleus, origin, causality, and history' that is buried 'deep down in the dense archaeological layers of the sciences'.[8]

Approached more comprehensively such an archaeology, of law and Turkish legal education, should be studied much more extensively, especially in regard to how those in legal education are unaware of the extent that the profession is trapped in highly specific and strategically cultivated conceptions of law that are in a considerable part its own creation, a strategy that was once a choice. Within the scope of this text, our point is simply to establish this, as well as why it is not surprising that there is, currently, little space in Turkish legal education for alternatives, or if there are, that their impact will be limited. This point will be made fully in the conclusion, referencing the other texts in this volume.

Accordingly, our goal is to foreground the importance of going back to the roots of the predicament, which in its contemporary form and shape echoes many of the other texts in this volume, for example when these are pessimistically referring to the lawyer as a commodity, to how property and environmental law remain 'oblivious to local struggles and collective rights', to how the 'citizen paradigm' is 'white and male'.[9] Yet, our topic makes us hesitant to enlist Foucault in our discussion of legal education in Turkey when it would only result in a critique of the present circumstances, implicitly and nostalgically contrasted with a past wherein these problems did not exist. These and other examples that seek to challenge reductive conceptions of law tend to result in a redrawing of the same old lines in the sand in this case. These would only wash away, as Foucault pointed out with modernist categories such as 'man', or in this case a modernist understanding of the foundations of the Turkish republic as a result of the contemporary situation.[10]

7 See Souto on 'the invisible curriculum' (this volume).

8 Foucault (2002), p 275.

9 Ching refers to the commodity, Roncancio to local struggles and collective rights, Millefiorini and Caprioglio to the citizen paradigm (either in this volume or in the *Biopolitics and Resistance in Legal Education* volume).

10 Foucault (2002), p 422.

Rather than any such selective purification of either the past or the present, we understand our case of legal education as a stringent example of 'power's hold over life'—of how biopolitics should be understood as, on one hand, originating in 'the problem of sovereignty' and how its theory of right emerged from early modern traditions of political theory and legal history, while, on the other hand, today's legal reality mirrors a different type of biopolitics that continues to rely on mass education as techniques of power centred on the control of populations. To characterise our subject in these terms, as an example of 'the biopolitics of legal education', is not a complicated point. After all schools and universities in the new Turkish republic are in this sense no different than how Foucault refers to the emergence of institutions such as hospital wards, prisons, and workshops as early indications of the creation of a social fabric of public life that imposed a system of subjection and gradual objectification of individual bodies through surveillance, exercises, inspections, bookkeeping, reporting, and so on.[11]

This is a point that applies equally to today's legal education and to the nostalgia for a better past (below). Taken together the 20th-century history of legal education in Turkey brings out this general point about Foucault's theory in exemplary fashion. Legal education in Turkey was from its inception aimed at the creation of a body politic, analogous to how Foucault placed the spotlight on how power (in the 19th century) moved from disciplining bodies to the life of the population, the multiplicity of men in its relation to the population in general. The new republic accelerated this process, as the next section will outline for our case, which is to say how legal education in Turkey was (re-)introduced as a new technique of power that was inescapably tied to processes of permeation and saturation whereby sovereign rule over the multiplicity of men was to be transformed.

To Dream, for Just a Moment, of a Sovereign Republic of Law

The Turkish republic was founded in 1923 as the successor state of the Ottoman Empire. In many ways the end to the rule of the Ottoman Sultans might be seen in line with Foucault's critique of the Hobbesian monarch, which he came back to throughout his life.[12] There are many examples of how central the Hobbesian concept of sovereignty is in Foucault's works. In *The Order of Things*, he opens and concludes with a discussion of 'Las Meninas' by Velázquez, which famously revolves around the absence from the painting of

11 See Adebisi, in the *Biopolitics and Resistance in Legal Education* volume. She describes biopolitics in a relation to sovereignty that foregrounds a 'death/life' frame. While this is true at its widest scope, our interest lies in the dynamics of legal education as it reflects the problem of sovereignty. There is, therefore, not a difference, at a theoretical level, but in terms of its methodological implication. See also below where this point is made again.

12 See Tamminen and Deibel (2019).

the Spanish court of the king and the queen, whose reflection is visible in a small mirror.[13] In *Discipline and Punish*, he discusses the brutal punishment of the murderer of William of Orange (in 1584) in contrast to more 'modern' ways of controlling populations that arose shortly afterwards.[14] Similarly we could easily understand the dissolution of the Ottoman Empire in line with the famous cover of 'the Leviathan', famously showing a king whose body is made from countless figures against the backdrop of a city.[15] In this case the city would be İstanbul and the body politic would be tied to the earthly and divine right to rule claimed by any sultan who, just like the monarch on the cover of Leviathan, carries the same sword and sceptre. In such a historical model, it is only through monarchical power that the 'body politic' can be unified and any type of 'sovereign individuality' is only possible if monarchical power is exercised as its living embodiment ('I the state').

By contrast, Foucault's concern is not with the formal aspects of this model: what the sovereign looks like from on high. In this sense law and juridical institutions might at times function as instruments or strategies of power by the state, usually as an outcome of competing political circles. Instead, its various legal sovereignties are always partial in their implementation of right, they can never occupy the whole field of power relations, nor control subjectification through their incorporation into the body politic. Indeed, legal education in Turkey imagined exactly this and, unsurprisingly, failed. To examine the implications of this failure is, therefore, our goal, which is to say that we are aligning our biopolitics of legal education to how Foucault stated in his lectures that his entire point is 'to do precisely the opposite of what Hobbes was trying to do in Leviathan'.[16]

In our text, of course, our goal cannot be to explore comprehensively Foucault's references to Hobbes and the full theoretical implications of such explicit 'opposition' to Leviathan. Other texts in this book have interesting contributions in this respect, dealing with the governance of life and death, arguing that law has become detached from the preservation of life or the earth itself.[17] In our view there is no theoretical conflict with a methodological understanding of Foucault's 'problem of sovereignty'. This 'problem' remains the key to our understanding of legal education today, theoretically relevant and practically insightful for many types of legal education, inside and outside of the west, or, in our case, when it refers to an idealistic fiction that was not realistic at the time and has long since drifted out of view. Ultimately, this shows that today's changes in legal education reflect how the foundations of

13 Foucault (2002).
14 Foucault (2019).
15 Hobbes (1985).
16 Foucault (2003), p 28.
17 See Adebisi in the *Biopolitics and Resistance in Legal Education* volume.

law are removed, are missing and, sometimes, are missed (in a nostalgic sense) in the Turkish legal education system. Again, this is not a contrast between two types of biopolitics, one straightforwardly Eurocentric in its commitment to antiquity as well as western philosophy, and the other primarily opportunistic, corporate, and neo-liberal. Our analysis is Foucauldian in how it seeks to point out the importance of 'how' legal education became detached from its origin myth, an idealised notion of a rule of law that never existed even if it was much more tangible in the past as a type of biopolitics.

While it might never have been accomplished as anything more than rhetoric, its near erasure from the educational landscape goes hand-in-hand with 'how' legal education remained integral to the social fabric, even as appeals to the integrity of the 'law' have begun to sound increasingly hollow.

The Origins of Legal Education in Modern Turkey

The most sensible place to start in discussing the origins of legal education in the Turkish republic is a paper on legal education written in 1969 by Dr Özcan Karadeniz who shortly after became the foremost Turkish legal scholar of the time and one of the leading female Roman law professors in the world.[18]

In the paper she elaborated the status of Roman law in the westernisation process of Turkey and how the population was constructed according to the global values of that time. Today's Turkey is again dealing with eastern and western philosophies that are irrevocably intermingled, and is facing a very similar dilemma when it comes to the subject of legal education. Her paper, written 52 years ago, imagined a different Turkey; a country where the rule of law, democracy, and equality had become integral to its culture. The starting point for creating such a population was legal education, and the central component of legal education was legal history.

Giving such a central stage to Roman law was no coincidence.[19] After all, Roman law had been at home in the Eastern Roman Empire longer than anywhere else. While its replacement by the Ottoman Empire displaced Roman law it did not disappear entirely from the geographical area. Many of its practices remained, not in the least as means of mediating between its ethnically diverse populations and in relation to its cosmopolitan character.[20] While it is

18 Karadeniz (1969).

19 For sovereignty being embedded in Roman law, see Mommsen (1887).

20 In the later stages of the Ottoman Empire, (starting from 1850) the famous *Tanzimat* and *Islahat* reforms also included legal reformations, yet the efforts remained individual and limited. However, the adoption of the Ottoman civil code (Mejelle) in the late 19th century as *ius commune* of the eastern Mediterranean was mainly based on Code Napoleon of France. See Özsunay (1981). Mejelle only regulated contractual and property relations with economic and commercial influence and never touched the Islamic cores of the cultural values, law of persons, family, and inheritance law. See also Samy Ayoub (2015).

certainly the case that Roman law had influenced Islamic legal practices, its eventual decline followed that of the Ottoman Empire to the extent that the new republic based on western values sought to import 'law' from continental Europe, explicitly experienced and promoted as a break and a rupture from a millennium of Islamic law in Anatolia.

Roman law was therefore to form the foundation of the legal reforms pioneered by Mustafa Kemal Atatürk, the founder of modern Turkey. These had as their aim the abolishment of all the Islamic elements existing in the legal system, making it at least secular in theory. Famously the reformers described the process as: *they have not created the law for the society, but they have created a society for the law.* To modernise a former empire, it is obviously not sufficient to simply translate a European civil code. The customs and mores of Ottoman culture that were entrenched in the society for centuries were abolished in a series of legal reforms within six months. First, the *sharia* courts were abolished in 1924 alongside the Ottoman caliphate by a decree of the new Grand National Assembly of Turkey. The Ottoman caliphate had existed since the early 16th century and had been one of the primary sources of global legitimacy of the empire and its rulers. At the same time the ancient Arabic alphabet was supplanted by the Latin alphabet, which occurred with the explicit intention to create an education system that was compatible with the western world.

Furthermore, legal education was considered of the highest strategic importance for the republic, as its new capital, Ankara, needed judges, lawyers, governors, and so on.[21] To this end, the Ankara Law Faculty was established in 1925 to educate jurists to serve all over Anatolia, and the faculty was created to be the locomotive of secular and equal legal education, which meant for the first time that women had the same rights to be educated with men.[22] Indeed, Atatürk, during the inauguration speech of the faculty, described the lawyers that were to be graduated there as those who would have to '*revive the fire of the revolution as it starts to slow down*' (emphasis added).[23] A year later, in 1926, Turkey adopted the Swiss Civil Code and Code of Obligations as the official private law of the newly founded Turkish republic.[24] Two years later the clause stating that the religion of the country is Islam, which was regulated under the second article of the Constitution, was abolished. Its aim was to open the road to gender equality and freedom.[25]

Naturally such a highly idealistic attempt to create a 'new' society was selective and deeply biased in its relation to the foundations of law, as is the case with any species of biopolitics. For example, the idea of the revolutionists was

21 Cheatham (1949).

22 İstanbul Law Faculty was already active at that time but carried on many of the legal practices of the Ottoman Empire.

23 Güriz (2004).

24 Lipstein (1955); Magnarella (1973).

25 Golder and Fitzpatrick (2009).

too simple: the road to modernisation was paved by establishing a legal education that has a fully western character. A 'new' legal educational infrastructure began to be put in place, a pedagogical approach wherein the main rhetoric of the reforms was 'civilisation'. Accordingly, fully understanding the new civil code and legal culture was impossible by only reading the translations; it required internalising western values directly, for which there were few better examples than the shared history with western legal systems.

This type of legal education sought to create a class of jurists, one that would be able to comprehend the underlying dynamics of the legal system, how it was born, why it was shaped this way, how it was spread, why it was open to criticism, and so on to change the destiny of a former occidental empire. In turn, it was through legal education that a westernised Turkish population was to be created, and this dream could hardly be more biopolitical, in that it was the problem of sovereignty that gave rise to it, in its aspiration to impose a new type of discipline 'over the population as such, over men insofar as they are living beings'.[26]

Legal Education and Its Problem with Sovereignty

It is hardly unique to Turkey that there was a time when legal education was expected to form the basis of a new country and its body politic.[27] Turkey might, therefore, be only one more case that is interesting for how it strategically put Roman law into legal education curricula, aiming to create legal scholars who felt part of Europe in how they could understand the economic and social dynamics of the legal system of their nation. However, this would be nothing out of the ordinary, as many critiques of legal education in this volume foreground; there are a wide variety of places that demonstrate how frequently legal education has been used as a steam engine for political powers. This goes back as far as it can within the confines of its canon, when we recognise that the university of Bologna (the oldest in Europe) formed itself as a law faculty at first and much later adopted medicine, theology, and liberal arts.[28] Its survival was similarly sanctioned by sovereign powers of the time (the pope), no different than how Atatürk sanctioned the Ankara Law Faculty. While the content, method, and character of the new curriculum for legal education might have been influenced by academic considerations, simultaneously the 'new' required authorisation as an effective biopolitical strategy that sought to control the population. In this sense the Turkish legal education was first designed to educate lawyers, judges, governors, administrators, and so on. The underlying

26 Foucault (2003), p 247.

27 This is visible in the text by Franzoni whose study is organised around activities in a law faculty that is housed in the building that was once the senate of Brazil (in the *Biopolitics and Resistance in Legal Education* volume).

28 Grendler (1999).

idea was to provide the jurists the necessary freedom of thought and academic adequacy while also training them to take wider responsibilities. Not only would such law school graduates fill the legislative, executive, and judiciary branches, it also implied that a new type of subjectivity came into being, one that gave Roman law a key strategic place.

As Professor Karadeniz explained it: a superficial legal education would, without it, result in creating legal technicians, who do not have the necessary problem-solving mind. The state needed jurists as scientists and philosophers who had a good grasp of global legal culture and sociology of law to provide freedom of thought, freedom of expression, and independent thinking in the society.[29]

Yet, this is clearly an ambition that was never realised, and to the extent that it is remembered for a few moments in a Turkish legal course it is mostly as a symbolic origin story. Nonetheless Roman law did lend itself to such a strategy. After all, the particularity of the western continental legal system is that it is based on a shared legal culture.[30]

In this sense Roman law showed again how law, as an agent itself, was able to adjust itself to changing circumstances throughout most of its existence. Ultimately, the remnants of the Laws of the XII Tables dating back to 451 BC were still applicable in the Byzantine period and integrated in the Justinianic codification movement *Corpus Iuris Civilis*.[31] Such a mobilisation of Roman law as an agent is not unique to Turkey, and was grounded in the assumption that it would, once again, act like an *autopoietic* social system that produced and reproduced its own elements by their interactions.[32] If we acknowledge that Roman law can be more than a vague foundation for reductive ideas about law or as a precursor to today's law's 'Eurocentrism', its historical revivals demonstrate a nearly autonomous, differentiated, self-reproducing system: one that adjusted itself time and time again to social and economic realities through the works of jurists, *praetore*, emperors, and mediaeval jurists, and retained its sway over modern legal systems.

Our case, legal education in Turkey, was expected to relate to Roman law exactly like this: bridging the tired metaphorical gap between east and west by making Turkish law part of a shared legal history with the nationalised civil codes of Europe. Of course, Roman law has by now been side-lined in almost all centres of legal education.[33] This is, by itself, no different than how in the 1950s and 1960s classical legal education lost its status in Europe or even how the Nazis thought that Roman law would ideologically undermine its nationalistic direction. The contemporary situation is different once again, in

29 Karadeniz (1969), p 325.
30 Koschaker (1938).
31 Buckland (1950), p 7; Borkowski and du Plessis (2020), pp 30–1.
32 Luhmann (1988), p 18.
33 Examples would be the Beschlüsse des Tübinger Fakultätentages 1961 and Münchener Beschlüsse 1968.

how the transformation of the legal profession required the introduction of the new courses, and these were generally the products of a liberal or neo-liberal understanding of legal practice that was closely tied to free market thinking.[34]

This inevitably clashed with 'old' educational content such as Roman law, which in Turkey was highly problematic because of the symbolic value that its semi-artificial bond with the western world carried. While this project failed, the legal education system continues to be regulated today as it was before in an important respect. The overarching goal continues to be to train types of law that match the intended functions that the students 'should' have later in life. With this goal in mind, we can see how contemporary legal education in Turkey can be understood in much the same way as in most countries that have experienced trends and pressures that diminish the role of history, the philosophical foundations of law and critical thinking in general. Most notably the decline of general legal education did not extend to the foundations of private law.

The aim of the law faculties is generally perceived as the preparation of law students for practical life. The education system started to be structured around the practicalities of legal education. This is no different than in Europe, of course, in its implications: how priority began to be given to relations to the corporate world, first with commercial law, later with IP, competition law, law of capital markets, and today with AI and data protection. Initially disciplines like Roman law, legal philosophy, or legal sociology were abolished altogether in many faculties, as they came to be seen as the instruments of sovereignty of western powers.[35] This, however, received a lot of backlash, so it was decided

34 An analysis of neo-liberal transformation of Turkey is outside of the scope of this chapter, and it has been well established. This also includes education. See İnal and Akkaymak (2012), for evidence on privatisation, cuts in public spending, marketisation, as well as the transformation of curricula both in the primary, secondary, and higher education levels. This more specific point can be illustrated by the rise of private universities, from three in 1995 to 73 in 2020. This took place in a context wherein the public discussion prioritised the effectiveness and efficiency of private education and where universities re-organised the curriculum to serve the needs of the industry. Evidence is plentiful: for the statistics see the Turkish Ministry of Education (meb.gov.tr); other references include Hill (2007); Kaya (2015), pp 105–33; and in Turkish Ercan (1998), pp 14–15; Kaymak (2012), pp 4–18.

35 See Golder and Fitzpatrick (2009), p 55 on the overall Foucauldian point. The following newspaper articles (in Turkish) foreground that law faculty professors and journalists commented on the decision of the Turkish Board of Higher Education to take Roman law out of the mandatory legal curriculum in 2009 and it includes a demonstration of their commitment to the relation between law and secularism. See www.cumhuriyet.com.tr/haber/yokun-roma-hukuku-karari-94210, www.milliyet.com.tr/yazarlar/riza-turmen/hukuk-egitimine-roma-hukuku-darbesi-1153615. What these texts show is how the experts interpreted the decision of the higher educational board as a silent 'coup' in respect of the secular characteristic of Turkish legal culture, which was seen as a gateway to organise private law relations according to Islamic law. Roman law scholars and academics in Turkey challenged the decision in the administrative judiciary. The place of Roman law is still controversial. Yet, many faculties in the major Turkish cities are resisting and keep Roman law as a mandatory course in their curricula, and Roman law *de facto* fights to keep its original position. For texts that foreground these issues see: www.law.ankara.edu.tr, https://hukuk.istanbul

to give them a symbolic credit. This continues today in many places, as is also demonstrated elsewhere in this volume, both in terms of the transformation of the curriculum and wherever Eurocentrism is identified with the roots of law along with its reductive substance.[36]

When we recognise that the role of Roman law in the Turkish case was not only heavily idealised but also attached to the circuits of power, its removal is still important because of how law students and professionals thereby become ignorant of legal history in important ways. Its removal severed legal practice from any type of basic understanding of democracy and legal culture, as it was not replaced by alternatives. This has practical implications because Turkish legal education started to educate lawyers that were neither trained to solve fundamental copyright problems nor were they encouraged to contemplate the problems of the rule of law, democracy, equality, freedom, and so on. Its implication, of course, is that legal education has not accomplished its practical aims: lawyers who are not trained to think about law are blind to the social and economic realities of the era. They end up being trapped in (and reproduce) a system that taught them that positive law is an unchangeable indisputable artefact that does not transcend the boundaries of the nation-state and invariably regresses into an imaginary of sovereign power as singular and unchanging in time. To put it theoretical terms, there is no problem of sovereignty, and its foundation was, therefore, never missing (see above).

This process could provide a useful perspective on how today, in many places, and not just Turkey, there is a 'constitutive ambivalence' that characterises law in its relation to 'life', seen as the 'experiential complexity and plurality of human existence'.[37] Perhaps elsewhere the same holds as in Turkey, which is to say that more recent experiences match how the earlier focus on the foundations of law lost its status, and, more practically, how law students always already see themselves in corporate terms, as future employees of corporations or as entrepreneurs. The end result might be, just like in Turkey, the creation of a self-fulfilling prophecy, one where the only order available is one derived from geography, from control over a population with law as nothing more than a cynical instrument of established interests.[38]

.edu.tr/en/, www.hukuk.bilkent.edu.tr/en/, https://law.ku.edu.tr/en/, https://ects.gsu.edu.tr/tr/program/programmedetails/24; for others see http://hukuk.erdogan.edu.tr/tr/page/ozel-hukuk-bolumu/3922.

36 See Walter and Contarini on a transformation of a Swiss law faculty in this direction and Nwedu, Roncancio, and Adebisi for stringent critiques of law as deeply colonial. (either in this volume or in the *Biopolitics and Resistance in Legal Education* volume).

37 See Millefiorini and Caprioglio in this volume. More generally we can refer to many studies of law and technology that revolve around this same idea. See, for instance, Hurlbut and Jasanoff (2020), p 983.

38 This idea that Turkey's situation might be exemplary for others refers to the text by Walter and Contarini in this volume about Switzerland, which would be sadly ironic given how Turkey took Swiss law as its model.

The Process of Becoming Legally Educated

While there were only two law faculties in Turkey until 1970s, İstanbul and Ankara, today there are 83.[39] Despite the high number of law schools, the differences in their curricula are minor as they are centrally managed and monitored by the Turkish administrative body, the Board of Higher Education. Since the 1940s, the curricula of law schools in Turkey have followed a general pattern that is considered to be modelled on the law schools of continental European countries.[40]

In the first year, courses like constitutional law, Roman law, introduction to law, legal philosophy, history, and legal sociology are taught. Civil law courses such as law of persons, contract law, property law, family law, and inheritance law are given throughout the total length of the educational period, which is four years. Starting from the second year, commercial law, criminal law, administrative law, and international law courses are given. The general curriculum also contains economics, statistics, political science, and philosophy that ideally would give the future lawyer a formation about how to be a jurist instead of a 'legal technician'. These courses, however, often do not have the same status.[41]

More generally, the suggestion that having more law schools meets a certain social demand is clearly erroneous. An excessive amount of law faculties has led to a quantity of graduates that exceeds demand and has resulted in an obvious lack of qualified professors and academics. As a result, many scholars proposed to lengthen the educational period and increase the public funding of universities. Furthermore, there are many major problems with legal education in Turkey that cannot be solved within the confined world of law faculties and funding councils. A law student will have gone through a high school education system that prioritises subjects like natural sciences, math, Turkish language, Turkish history, and Turkish geography. There is less, if any, priority given to sociology, philosophy, world history, world geography, or any other type of 'formation' subjects.

This is reflected in the central university entrance exam that all law students will have taken. This is highly competitive; Turkey is a country of 83 million people with a young population and a rigorous ranking of fields and departments. Its outcome is a standard ranking that decides what type of university

39 According to the data of the Board of Higher Education in Turkey, https://yokatlas.yok.gov.tr/lisans-bolum.php?0094

40 Cheatham (1949), p 22.

41 The general point in these paragraphs is that there is a problem within the Turkish education system when it comes to critical thinking. This is a generally accepted point that is rarely, if ever, contested in the Turkish education system by students or educators. However, there is no readily available statistical 'evidence' that can quantify the suggested prioritisation of certain subjects over others. Aside of the already provided 'evidence' (see note 38), this will have to remain our personal observation, derived from our experience in the Turkish system, while also noting again that the general point does not depend on any individual statistical 'truth'.

education the student will follow; subject matter and the quality of school are more likely to be the outcome of the ranking than the preference of the student. A student with a talent for mathematics is likely to choose engineering because it is higher rated; a student that gets into a highly ranked law faculty might have to give up a talent for the humanities.

To get into a top law school is extremely prestigious (although not the number one, which is engineering) and implies that a student is among the very best in the country. Even getting into a university at all is extremely competitive and many students who take the entrance exam are rejected. Demographic pressures imply that existing universities are not capable of accommodating all high school graduates. Therefore, there is intense competition, which includes the selection of primary and secondary schools complemented by private courses. The preparation for this exam takes years, in schools as well as through private tutoring if the parents can afford it, although even if this is the case success is not guaranteed.

The placement test revolves around a single score, and does not (at any point) prioritise the ability to analyse, synthesise, or create, but rather seeks to train the memorisation of familiar problem types and the ability to select the right one of five options in a multiple choice exam of around 500 questions in three hours.[42] Such placement tests not only monitor and manage the population, but also, in the typical Foucauldian sense, create a population through the selective incorporation of the populace within the machinery of the state. In this case, the type of biopolitics that can be observed is strategically invested in creating a certain type of population of students. However, the Turkish university entrance exam is very intense in how it disciplines students and its effect are, consequently, felt throughout the education system. Self-evidently this is not only about the cost of education, as successful access to university education is concentrated in certain regions and population centres. What such financial and geographical parameters don't reveal, however, are the complex mix of sexual, racial, ethnic, gendered, linguistic, and religious factors involved.[43] This continues to apply to law students and to others who are to varying degrees successful when they get into university. These students bring with them their society, including their local circumstances, the characteristics of their social lives and identities, as well as the long-standing pressures on the democratic culture of Turkish society.

42 Gök (2010), pp 123–34. This includes the depressing observation that by the early 2000s the funds going into private tutoring could have funded 17 universities with a capacity of more than 3,000 students each.

43 See again Gök (2010), p 40; see Madhloom (this volume) for a comparable discussion of the power dynamics that surround the solicitors' qualification examination. The reference is also to the dynamics of class, race, and gender that are part of the Turkish university entrance exam, which is taken up more directly by Adebisi, Ashford et al., and Souto (in the *Biopolitics and Resistance in Legal Education* volume) and also by Griffin (this volume).

When law schools were first established, legal education in Turkey was seen as a mechanism of protection against the abuse of the political ideologies of religious groups.[44] Today, it is seen as a financially rewarding profession (or at least providing semi-stable income), despite the excessive number of graduates. In such a context, it is exceptional if a law school graduate aims to be a human rights lawyer or an environmental law practitioner. If the students graduate from universities that do not focus on foreign language skills, they mostly end up practising criminal law due to the high number of crimes in Turkey, or working in bankruptcy and debt enforcement claims.[45] These fields offer stable employment, as does entering into government service. The students who graduate from law schools in Ankara or İstanbul might have a more international profile and, therefore, tend to choose fields where foreign languages are required, with career paths tending towards corporate law, contract law, international commercial arbitration, and legal consultancy.[46]

Some, despite of it all, might still choose to use their legal education 'as a way to engage in the collective reconstruction' of democracy.[47] Mostly that means that after their education is over, they choose to become judges or prosecutors. Such students, however, have to pass another examination period, which begins with another multiple-choice exam that focuses on the primary legal courses such as civil law, criminal law, constitutional law, commercial law, administrative law, and so on, followed by an oral exam conducted by a jury. Another major drawback of becoming a judge or a prosecutor in Turkey is that one should be ready not to settle down for years and live in many places throughout Turkey that are far removed from the principle legal centres. The successful candidates who pass the exam will spend two years in the Turkish Academy of Justice, where mostly procedural and bureaucratic aspects of the profession are taught.[48] After this they generally start in small cities in the east or west before moving back to the more cosmopolitan areas. Nevertheless, many of the recent graduates either do not pass the exam or are not ready to take such a step in their life, so they choose to become attorneys instead.[49] Until recently this involved a mandatory one-year internship; in 2019 there

44 See Berkes (1999); Gulsci and Meyersonn (2015).

45 For the report of the Union of Turkish Bar Associations, see: www.barobirlik.org.tr/Haberler/-cmk-gorevlendirme-ve-uygulamalarindaki-sorun-ve-cozum-onerileri-calistayi-tbb-nin-ev-sahipliginde--82709

46 For example, see: http://hukuk.gsu.edu.tr/tr/aday-ogrenci, https://law.ku.edu.tr/en/academics/undergraduate/

47 See Franzoni, in the *Biopolitics and Resistance in Legal Education* volume.

48 See www.taa.gov.tr/

49 For the statistics shared by the ministry of justice, see: www.anayasa.gen.tr/adli-hakimlik.htm. For example, even in 2005 private university graduates had only a 2.8% success rate in the central exam that needs to be passed when becoming a judge or public prosecutor, whereas public universities had 15%. For the statistics of the Turkish Board of Higher Education see https://yokatlas.yok.gov.tr/mezun-basari-atlasi-tablo.php?s=5

was a judicial reform whereby admittance to the bar was yet again a matter of completing a central exam.

The Legally Educated in Their Chosen Fields of Specialisation

It would be a misconception to simply stress the shortcomings of Turkish legal education, either from the perspective of its goals at the time of the foundation of the Turkish republic or in terms of the failure of the current state of legal education to envision a functioning rule of law. Rather, these lawyers take the roles granted to them in a fabricated reality closely tied to the circuits of power that characterise their education as well as their social worlds.[50] It is expected that the professional legal expert exercises the limited and limiting power of law in their society by facilitating the discipline required by the sovereign power, both in terms of the implementation of law (as legal provisions in its technocratic sense) as well as by facilitating the normalisation of the transgression of right across the various fields of professional specialisation. After all, their daily practices are part of the preservation and production of a domain wherein life and law come together, and where they are not to be distinguished as separable life worlds.[51] Accordingly, their professional experience will expose them to constant transgressions that this premise implies, which are continuous, constantly acted out, and acted upon in its multiple relations, subjectivities, and, ultimately, throughout the social body.[52]

Nevertheless, it is also the case that one of the main concerns within established types of legal education in Turkey has always been the impartiality of the law. Considering the heterogeneity of the population of Turkey, legal education has always been directed to produce jurists who can 'distribute justice' without being affected by the individual characteristics of the subjects of the case. That is to say, the application of the legal rules should be far from the personal interests of the judges or the lawyers. This approach is reductive when seen in terms of how legal self-perception seeks to make invisible the reality of class, gender, social status, and so on. This applies to many societies and their relation to the practice of law, but their visibility would still presume a certain commitment of the legal establishment to impartiality, particularly when societies are ethnically, religiously, and economically divided.[53]

50 See Golder and Fitzpatrick (2009), p 21. See Forzani, who refers to 'the form of life of the student, including thoughts and actions, is entire absorbed—as a means to an end—into the function of learning which represents the efficacious actualisation of its governmental potentiality' (in the *Biopolitics and Resistance in Legal Education* volume). Our view is, comparatively, somewhat kinder.

51 See also Forzani, who refers to 'law's end' as presupposing 'the indistinction of law and life' (in the *Biopolitics and Resistance in Legal Education* volume).

52 Golder and Fitzpatrick (2009), p 25.

53 See Millefiorini and Caprioglio in this volume, who describe some relatively successful attempts to break through this invisibility.

In a conference held in Ankara Law Faculty in 2003 within the context of Turkey's EU harmonisation process, Prof. Hubert Rottleuthner shared his concerns on Turkish legal education.[54] His criticism was focused on Turkish legal history and the top-down adoption of western legal culture which arguably was forced on an Islamic society in an authoritarian fashion. In many ways his concerns reflect the EU's scepticism about Turkey's top-down approach to democracy, human rights, rule of law, and so on. The legal system and legal education, in this sense, were part of a wider critique coming from the EU at the time when Turkey's potential membership was still actively being discussed. Accordingly, the suggestion was made that the architecture of legal education was also part of the same top-down approach, and lacked roots in the wider society. Effectively the idea was that the Turkish legal establishment should acknowledge this tension, between the non-secular nature of Turkish Islamic culture and modern Turkish law. This would help, it was hoped, to understand the limits of western legal thought in an occidental society and the patterns of social inequalities, to have a larger picture of different cultures. However, this view had been criticised already by Turkish law professors, as for them, secularism was the fundamental value of the Turkish republic.[55] As Turkey never experienced a long period of reformation like most of Europe, French secularism was seen as the most suitable guardian of equality and impartiality.

While many countries might have faced a similar situation, the contemporary predicament should not be understood simply as another failed attempt to create a functioning rule of law. Foucault frequently refers to 'the necessary disappearance of that which is its foundation'.[56] To be precise: the foundation was never there, in Foucault's conception of sovereignty as well as in the case of the new republic and the foundation of law in Turkey. This was what the first section established, which is to say that such an appeal to the foundation of law is never realistic but its partial realisation echoes on in today's epistemic disorder, which nostalgically might 'miss' its foundations (in a chorus with a melody that also includes the complaints of concerned Europeans). Importantly, however, today's legal reality has no practical use for such foundations, beyond this type of nostalgia. In this particular instance, the defence of secularism remains strong today, even though legal education and professionals are out of touch with the inner morality of their profession, which is to say that their commitment to impartiality in its legal system has been detached from its own relation to the shared history of Roman law and there's little else than a corporate rhetoric which glorifies law and economics over justice. To illustrate this point further, however, we should briefly turn to the obvious

54 Hubert Rottleuthner (2004).

55 This is a widespread view, one that is often discussed in terms that are comparable to this particular instance. See (in Turkish): Özsunay (1978), p 334; Bozkurt (1996); Emiroğlu (2002).

56 Foucault (2002), pp 16–18.

areas of specialisation that show clearly how extensive the multiplication and normalisation of transgressions of law in modern Turkey have become.

One might, with a hopeful attitude, expect that in today's Turkey specialists in human rights law or environmental law exist in high numbers, considering the long lists of violations. However, the situation is quite the opposite. Such areas are mostly confined to doctrinal work and scholarly research. Turkey is one of the countries that are often ruled against in the European Court of Human Rights (ECHR). In 2020, ECHR decided that the Turkish republic has to pay 1.5 billion euros compensation in total for human rights violations.[57] Almost half the judgments concerned three of the 47 member states, namely the Russian Federation (185), Turkey (97), and Ukraine (86). More than 11% of the delivered judgments concerned Turkey. In 85 of the cases out of 97 at least one violation has been found. Moreover, 19% of the pending applications in 2020 that had been lodged were against Turkey.[58] Right to a fair trial, right to liberty and security, and freedom of expression were the most problematic areas. Since the Court was established in 1959, 23,406 judgments have been delivered. More than a third of these have concerned three member states: Turkey (3,742), the Russian Federation (2,884), and Italy (2,427).[59]

The situation is similar in environmental law, as the wider Turkish society has recently become aware of the climate crisis. Forest fires are turning the green Aegean and Mediterranean coast barren yellow in the summer while in the fall the same land is likely to be opened for construction, with five-star hotels rising out of the ashes of the forest. In the summer of 2021, it became clearer than it already was that the fires are more frequent, stronger, and ubiquitous in Anatolia because of climate change.[60] Yet there is, theoretically, not much wrong with Turkish environmental law. The Turkish Law of Environment was adopted in 1983, and the right to have a healthy environment is protected under Art. 56 of the Turkish Constitution. These legal tools can, of course, be criticised for adopting an anthropocentric approach rather than an ecocentric approach or some other critique of reductive legal thinking when it comes to the environment. However, this is not the main problem,

57 See https://tr.euronews.com/2021/03/31/turkiye-aihm-e-tas-nan-168-davay-kaybetti-1-5-milyon-euro-tazminata-mahkum-oldu

58 Approximately 62,000 applications were pending before a judicial formation on 31 December 2020. The European Court of Human Rights Facts and Figures (2020), p 3, at echr.coe.int/Documents/Facts_Figures_2020_ENG.pdf

59 See echr.coe.int/Documents/Facts_Figures_2020_ENG.pdf. See also the European Commission's key findings on Turkey in 2021. The topics emphasised are the organisation of the judiciary, human rights violations, and the fight against corruption, which are integral to legal education. The commission underlines 'the flaws of the legal framework and institutional architecture' as well as the country's withdrawal from the İstanbul Convention which put into question its commitment to international standards: https://ec.europa.eu/commission/presscorner/detail/en/qanda_21_5282

60 See Daşdemir et al. (2021); Ertugrul et al. (2021); Flannigan et al. (2000), pp 221–9.

as there is no environmental culture established on the basis of which the criticism could even have a footing.

Accordingly, there is a problem when calling for some of the approaches proposed in this volume, such as a 'non-anthropocentric stance', radical interdependence on 'other-than-human' beings, or even a more modest letting in of the 'more-than-human'.[61] Turkish environmental law already illustrates that even if there are provisions and protections offered by positive law, these remain too residual within the Turkish social sphere for such ambitious ways of re-imagining what law could or should be. The same applies to legal education in Turkey, which aims primarily to operate as a system and organisation that ideally enables the student to apply the law to the extent that this is still a possibility at all.[62] Turkish legal education, as a hierarchical transfer of knowledge, is aiming to be practical in that it prepares students with an in-depth knowledge of European codifications, which means that doctrinal works of European countries are taught to law school students. As a result, students graduate not only with a good knowledge of theoretical Turkish law but also Swiss law, and sometimes German, French, and Italian law. With new elective courses being introduced, like competition law, intellectual property law, or data protection law, environment and human rights is likely to rank low on the list of a student's priorities.

The end result is not surprising: the overall educational burden has increased dramatically, which results in thousands of law school graduates who have been positioned and prepared for the needs of the corporate world. Legal education has, for decades now, been acted out on its inclination towards law and economics, contract drafting, or to construction law, with each of these firmly entrenched in the mandatory curriculum as well as in the elective programme.

Legal Education Seen in Terms of Its Biopolitics

If sovereignty is a problem that defines Foucault's work, then one might very well expect that this 'problem of sovereignty' comprises the discipline of law in its entirety. After all, sovereignty is 'the great trap we are in danger of falling into when we try to analyse power'.[63] And yet he is fascinated by how 'logically the emergence of technologies of power should have led to its complete disappearance'.[64] Clearly it did not, and the case of Turkish legal education shows yet again how sovereign power persists as an organising principle, tying

61 This is a reference to the projects of Roncancio, Galloway, and Siliquini-Cinelli (either in this volume or in the *Biopolitics and Resistance in Legal Education* volume).

62 Cheatnam (1949), p 23. For the project on strengthening democratic culture and basic education see www.coe.int/en/web/education/-/strengthening-democratic-culture-for-basic-education-in-turkey-dedicated-website-available

63 Foucault (1980), p 39, Foucault (2003), p 34.

64 Foucault (2003), p 58.

together its conventional (monarchical) understanding with different types of biopolitics, such as that of Turkish legal education and the current position of 'right' in Turkish society.

Turkey is a country whose history is one in which conventional understandings of the theory of sovereignty weigh heavily, and this includes today's system of legal education. In overly simplistic terms, it would be convenient to understand today's biopolitics in contrast to a conventional theory of sovereignty, the top-down and formalised mechanism of power that used to be invoked to characterise societies. Hereby, however, we would validate a popular misconception about Foucault's concept of biopolitics as a term that simply refers to power in any other setting than the court of the sovereign and, by extension, the modern state. This, however, is not what we tried to do, as with it we follow a historical trajectory that leads Foucauldian scholarship away from critically examining social wholes towards a perspective that dissolves the individual in an ineluctably advancing 'micro-politics of power'.[65] In our view, such a generalised trend does not reflect Foucault's body of work and methodologically the early work and its relation to sovereignty still applies when doing empirical analysis that revolve around the concept of biopolitics.

Rather than separating the early work from the later work on biopolitics (by singling out passages and statements), their continuity is what keeps us focused on missing foundations. Specifically, its implication is that the case of Turkish legal education is not another micro-site, one that shows a loss of foundation and a power dynamic wherein a social space is becoming progressively less regulated, thereby foregrounding that sovereign power has its limits. Quite the opposite, 'the problem of sovereignty' implies that foundations are always already missing, which in this case refers to the role and status of legal education in the early 20th century, as discussed above. This point is, therefore, not only of theoretical relevance; methodologically this perspective allowed us to focus on what is, in our view, one of the key blind spots in today's empirical discussions of legal education.

Consequently, our end point (or empirical conclusion) cannot simply and regretfully affirm that (given a few exceptions) the new social body demands from its educators that they are re-organised around the social demands of the consumer, the corporation, and corporate-populist state interests. Even if such concerns are valid, this is not sufficient for our case (if only because it would imply something other than a Foucauldian analysis). Instead, Foucauldian thought points us towards theorising 'right' as a problem to the extent that it is

65 Said (1993), p 336. Said identifies that Foucault could be read in terms of these micro-politics and this should be avoided. This argument can, however, also be presented as part of a general disqualification of Foucauldian scholarship. See Daniel Zamora (2016) *Foucault and Neoliberalism*. Suffice to say that it is for this reason that the problem of sovereignty should remain integral to Foucauldian references to biopolitics and biopower. See Tamminen and Deibel (2019).

grounded in the theory of sovereignty that Foucault sought to get away from. This idea of 'right' was mentioned already in the introduction in theoretical terms, and at this point our case can reflect this observation in practical terms: by how transgressions of 'right' in its relation to the legal system can be normalised while the field of law retains its central role in its society. Accordingly, the transgression of law (and, of course, Foucault's 'right') occurs in many places and characterises many types of legal expertise all the time; it is reality and powerful in its effects on law as a constellation of heterogeneous layers of constant tension and confrontation. This reality is there for everyone to see, with positivist procedures and practices of law overwhelmed, crowded out, and increasingly prone to disorder in practice.

Its implication, however, is that there is not much space for alternatives. After all, the implication, within Foucauldian thought, is that legal education in Turkey continues to be premised in its practice on a missing foundation, nostalgically, and specifically in how the prevailing legal positivism is not the historical creation of its legal positivists; rather, the legal positivists are the creation of a legal positivism that was authorised to replace the earlier 'truth' about the law. Demonstrating this decisively is unlikely to be possible soon. Doing so would imply a kind of Foucauldian 'archaeology of law' that is able to uncover the layers of history, those hidden beneath the nostalgic imagination of an earlier ideal about law. However, it might also not be necessary when limiting ourselves to the question of 'how' legal education today has become detached from the (missing) foundations of law.

Certainly, this is a critique that does not preclude analysing histories and practices, as biopolitics that at the same time retain a commitment to set the law, as it is, free from the chains that bind it. Yet this implies a modernist aim that comes with an acutely experienced inability to withstand in practice how 'right' in its relation to 'justice' and 'democracy' fades away from classrooms as powerless and through a cynical normalisation of the transgression of law that is commonplace on its outside. This also applies to the status of the legal specialist, the one being educated, whose specialisation is instrumentalised but without thereby being anchored in any kind of professional ethics, some sort of 'epistemology of expert knowledge'. This refers to a different type of problem where the knowledge of the expert revolves around 'bare constructivist learning', in a reductive sense, which in our case does not go hand in hand with a need for a mostly symbolic 'experiential figure of the jurist', a status signifier for the profession.[66]

What we are left with is a sobering conclusion, one that is about the disappearance out of sight of the mythical foundation of law in Turkey. Again, this does not imply that law faded into the background, nor did the various

66 See Siliquini-Cinelli (in the *Biopolitics and Resistance in Legal Education* volume, p 172). The reference to 'epistemology of expert knowledge' is about the article by Roncancio and its suggestion of the possibility of a paradigm shift. As Roncancio's last sentence mentions, this requires that we deal with 'socio-political realities on the ground' (in the *Biopolitics and Resistance in Legal Education* volume, p 209).

associated institutions; rather 'judicial institution is increasingly incorporated into a continuum of apparatuses ... whose functions are for the most part regulatory'.[67]

This is not unique, of course, but it might be a challenge to the impressive list of suggestions that this volume contains. Who could disagree that law students would benefit from being 'more fully human', should be taught 'affective capacity', should be grounded in the present as an 'exercise in theatricality' and that this might work a lot better if teaching law becomes more reflective and even poetic. More controversial, unfortunately, would be to try and mainstream an 'outsider pedagogy', one that revolves around those who experience 'exclusion on their own skin' along with a feminist and queer 'disruptive antinormative agenda'.[68]

The same applies to 'legal clinics', which do exist in Turkey, along with other such participatory methods in other fields that are once more promising collaboration, trust, and empathy and even seeking to influence policy by being inclusive and deliberate. But, as the authors, doubtlessly, realise, there are some limitations and even tensions when it comes to these methodologies, social reality, and the goal of establishing entirely new pedagogies, like the ones aimed at affirming 'worlds otherwise', 'otherwise-ness', or 'otherness, qua immanent and unique diversity and alterity'.[69] So can we, after all, move on to a 'conclusion' that goes beyond such pessimism, ending with a typical Foucauldian flourish, observing that where there are power relations, there is resistance? After all, relations of power are nothing if not productive, and that also extends to law. Maybe such resistance could lead us to try and make visible the ongoing efforts to optimise, enhance, and renormalise what counts as legal education in Turkey? Or, perhaps, such optimism, necessary as it is, will quickly take the shape of another type of transgression.

Closing Observations

Rather than repeating the previous passages, as a conclusion, perhaps it is more useful to consider, for only a second, the many attempts of legal professionals to stand up for the integrity of their profession in recent decades.[70] This is all

67 See James (2018), p 40 (it concerns a quote from Foucault's *The History of Sexuality*).

68 Madhloom refers to 'more fully human', Franzoni to 'affective capacity', Goodrich to 'an exercise in theatricality', Ashford et al. refer to 'outsider pedagogy' and discuss queer theory and law. Vines discusses poetry. Sharp discusses reflexivity. Millefiorini and Caprioglio refer to 'exclusion' and 'skin' (all either in this volume or in the *Biopolitics and Resistance in Legal Education* volume).

69 Millefiorini and Caprioglio as well as Nwedu discuss legal clinics in these senses. 'Worlds otherwise' is from Adebisi. Forzani refers to 'otherwise-ness', aiming for 'otherness, *qua* immanent and unique diversity and alterity' comes from the contribution of Siliquini-Cinelli (all either in this volume or in *Biopolitics and Resistance in Legal Education* volume).

70 For the interviews with lawyers about the decision of the Board of Higher Education and its impact to the future of legal education, see: https://haber.sol.org.tr/devlet-ve-siyaset/roma-hukuku-neden

the more remarkable, considering our own critique, as they frequently stood up for the law and its relation to democracy in general. They do so without the benefit of having been trained in a consistent understanding of the nature of law nor in critique of law's role in modern society. Given this situation, what can we reasonably expect from making legal educators aware of the full extent that the profession is trapped in highly specific and strategically cultivated conceptions of law that are in a considerable part its own creation?

This text was motivated, initially, by our own view that some hesitation is in order when referring to biopolitics as a concept that seeks to extend a quick Foucauldian perspective to the future of Turkish legal education. This might theoretically look appealing and practically this volume contains many avenues to pursue. However, it would also be like opening 'Pandora's box'—as Puccio and Rodríguez note (this volume). They are referring to the late Foucault when considering how students and teachers should seek to construct 'the truth' about themselves as legal professionals. They rightly show awareness that this is a sensitive situation: opening the box might: 'unleash the anguish of non-meaning, the reality about one's own motivations, own incoherence and the weaknesses of frozen thoughts'. It's not for nothing that this type of truth is described by Foucault as an 'intolerable insolence' that at the same time reflects 'an extremely distinctive form of life', one that is 'the matrix, the embryo … of a fundamental ethical experience in the West'. Practically speaking it would imply placing a critical claim about (Turkish) legal education wherein the 'others are completely mistaken' in the context of their own understanding of what it means to directly experience the law and its character.[71]

Still Foucault's relation between courage and truth does help in traversing a landscape of legal objects and subjects of law while aiming to find a way back to a type of biopolitics, as a strategy that has the ability to enhance the overall good, as well as legal education, as something that could be pleasurable, form interesting knowledge, be inventive in the creation of new discourses that end up running through the whole social body. When it comes to Turkish legal education (as long as we're being hopeful) this is a long way off, but it is still a problem that is not only financial and historical. It also refers to delivering on the promise that comes with the task of seeking to formulate a critique that is not content to stay isolated from those legal educators who never had much choice when it comes to the circumstances they find themselves in. Their circumstances, including Eurocentrism, dualism, positivism, and all other such negativities, imply a distance from spaces of academic exchange where the character of law and the role of critique can be at stake. Such spaces and its agents are significant, for their own sake, but to the extent that there is a

-lazim-haberi-19957. For the opinions of the Roman law scholars see: www.ntv.com.tr/turkiye/yok-ataturkun-reformunu-kaldiriyor mu,9jH5B3oWcEiIVwq4OTHc-A

71 See Foucault (2011), p 287, 313.

suggestion of a 'new' or 'different' approach to law there is a sliver of power that comes from decisions over student admissions, teaching curricula, (aesthetic) standards for publication and so on.

Helpful in this regard, given the Turkish case, would be to re-establish an analytical relation to the investigation of the roots and foundations of law as something worthwhile in the Turkish curriculum, and not as simply reductive by comparison to what lies ahead, as disqualified by association with (the Ottoman) empire, with duality (as opposed to relationality), or any other comfort zones when it comes to critique. Ultimately critique, including that of Foucault, should not wish to detach the (ontology of) hope that it generates from the social reality it seeks to engage with but that it establishes as problematic. In this sense our contribution can be seen, in conclusion, as positing that Turkish legal education, as a case, is exemplary for the critical challenge.

Acknowledgements

The authors declare that they have no conflicts of interest.

References

Samy Ayoub (2015) 'The *Mecelle* Sharia, and the Ottoman State: Fashioning and Refashioning of Islamic Law in the Nineteenth and Twentieth Centuries' 2 *Journal of the Ottoman and Turkish Studies Association* 121.

Niyazi Berkes (1999) *The Development of Secularism in Turkey*, Routledge.

Andrew Borkowski and Paul du Plessis (2020) *A Textbook on Roman Law*, Oxford University Press.

Gülnihâl Bozkurt (1996) *Batı Hukukunun Türkiye'de Benimsenmesi, Osmanlı Devleti'nden Türkiye Cumhuriyeti'ne Resepsiyon Süreci (1839–1939)*, Türk Tarih Kurumu Yayınları.

William W Buckland (1950) *A Textbook of Roman Law from Augustus to Justinian*, Cambridge University Press.

Elliott E Cheatham (1949) 'Legal Education in Turkey: Some Thoughts on Education for Foreign Students' 2 *Journal of Legal Education* 21.

İsmet Daşdemir, Fuat Aydın and Mertol Ertuğrul (2021) 'Factors Affecting the Behavior of Large Forest Fires in Turkey' 67 *Environmental Management* 162.

Haluk Emiroğlu (2002) 'Roma Hukukunun Bilgi Kaynaklarından Corpus Iuris Civilis ve Türkiye'de Hukuk Resepsiyonu' 51 *Ankara üniversitesi Hukuk Fakültesi Dergisi* 85.

Fuat Ercan (1998) *Eğitim ve Kapitalizm: Neo-Liberal Eğitim Ekonomisinin Eleştirisi*, Bilim.

Mertol Ertugrul, Tuğrul Varol et al. (2021) 'Influence of Climatic Factor of Changes in Forest Fire Danger and Fire Season Length in Turkey' 193 *Environmental Monitoring and Assessment* 28.

Mike D Flannigan, Mike Wotton et al. (2000) 'Climate Change and Forest Fires' 262 *The Science of the Total Environment* 221.

Michel Foucault (1980) *Power/Knowledge: Selected Interviews and Other Writings, 1972–1977*, Colin Gordon (ed), Pantheon.

Michel Foucault (2002) *The Order of Things: An Archaeology of the Human Sciences*, Routledge.

Michel Foucault (2003) *Society Must Be Defended*, Picador.

Michel Foucault (2008) *The Birth of Biopolitics*, Palgrave Macmillan.

Michel Foucault (2011) *The Courage of Truth*, Palgrave Macmillan.

Michel Foucault (2019) *Discipline and Punish: The Birth of the Prison*, Penguin Books.

Fatma Gök (2010) 'Marketing Hope: Private Institutions Preparing Students for the University Entrance Examination in Turkey' in K Amos (ed) *International Educational Governance (International Perspectives on Education and Society, Vol. 12)*, Emerald Publishing.

Ben Golder and Peter Fitzpatrick (2009) *Foucault's Law*, Routledge.

Paul F Grendler (1999) 'The University of Bologna, the City, and the Papacy' 13 *Renaissance Studies* 475.

Selim Güleşci and Erik Meyersonn (2015) 'For the Love or the Republic: Education, Secularism, and Empowerment', Working Paper n. 490, Bocconi University.

Adnan Güriz (2004) 'Hukuk Eğitimine Genel Bakış' Hukuk Oğretimi ve Hukukçunun Eğitimi Sempozyumu, TBB, 21.

Dave Hill (2007) 'Critical Teacher Education, New Labour and the Global Project of Neoliberal Capital' 5 *Policy Futures in Education* 204.

Thomas Hobbes (1985) *Leviathan*, CB Macpherson (ed), Penguin Books.

Benjamin Hurlbut, Shelia Jasanoff and Krishanu Saha (2020) 'Constitutionalism at the Nexus of Life and Law' 45 *Science, Technology, & Human Values* 979.

Kemal İnal and Güliz Akkaymak (2012) *Neoliberal Transformation of Education in Turkey*, Routledge.

Halil İnalcık (2006) *Tanzimat: Değişim Sürecinde Osmanlı İmparatorluğu*, Pheonix.

Nickolas James (2018) 'Law and Power: Ten Lessons From Foucault' 30 *Bond Law Review* 4.

Özcan Karadeniz (1969) 'Hukuk Öğretimi Bakımından Roma Hukuku' 26 *Ankara Üniversitesi Hukuk Fakültesi Dergisi* 323.

Ayhan Kaya (2015) 'Critical Voices against the Bologna Process in Turkey: Neo-liberal governance in Higher Education' 52 *New Perspectives on Turkey* 105.

Murat Kaymak (2012) 'Zorunlu Kesintili Eğitim Kanunu'nun Önü-Arkası Üzerine Değerlendirmeler' 21 *Eleştirel Pedagoji* 4.

Paul Koschaker (1938) *Die Krise des römischen Rechts, und die romanistische Rechtsvvissenschaft*, München und Berlin.

Eşref Küçük (2007) 'XII. Yüzyıl Rönesansı ve Yeniden Doğan Roma'yı Günümüze bağlayan Son Halka: Pandekt Hukuku' 56 *Ankara Üniversitesi Hukuk Fakültesi Dergisi* 111.

Kurt Lipstein (1955) 'The Reception of Western Law in Turkey' 5/6 *Annales de la Faculté de Droit d'İstanbul* 225.

Niklas Luhmann (1988) 'The Unity of the Legal System' in G Teubner (ed) *Autopoietic Law: A New Approach to Law and Society*, de Gruyter.

Paul Magnarella (1973) 'The Reception of Swiss Family Law in Turkey' 46 *Anthropological Quarterly* 100.

Theodor Mommsen (1887) *Römisches Staatsrecht*, S Hirzel.

Ergun Özsunay (1978) 'Türkiye'de Yabancı Hukukun Benimsenmesi Hareketi İçinde Türk Medeni Kanununun Anlamı ve Önemi', İstanbul Üniversitesi Mukayeseli Hukuk Enstitüsü.

Ergun Özsunay (1981) 'Yabancı Hukukun Benimsenmesi Yoluyla Bir Çağdaşlaşma Modeli; Kemalist Hukuk Devrimi Üzerine Gözlemler ve Değerlendirmeler', Ankara Adalet Bakanlığı Yayınları.

Hubert Rottleuthner (2004) 'Hukuk Eğitimine Genel Bakış', Hukuk Oğretimi ve Hukukçunun Eğitimi Sempozyumu, TBB, 27.

Edward Said (1993) *Culture and Imperialism*, Chatto and Windus.

Sakari Tamminen and Eric Deibel (2019) *Recoding Life: Information and the Biopolitical*, Routledge.

Daniel Zamora (2016) *Foucault and Neoliberalism*, Polity.

Chapter 11

The Impact of Codes of Conduct on Academic Freedom

Francine Rochford

Introduction

The university is an enlightening study for indicia of new regimes and technologies of governance. It is a repository of written evidence of forms of organisation pre-dating nation-states.[1] Reporting of legal cases involving universities in dispute with their students or staff yields a sequence of visions of the university, broadly aligned with a gradual redefinition of the university *corpus* to its modern form. It thus can be a case study demonstrating Foucault's assertion that governmentality is a 'consumer of freedom'[2] since it is dependent on certain designated freedoms: the state 'can only function insofar as a number of freedoms actually exists: freedom of the market, freedom of discussion, possible freedom of expression'.[3] The contrast between the developed juridical principles defining academic freedom and the modern freedoms reinterpreted by neoliberalism can thus be demonstrated. This chapter will draw upon legal cases, focusing on management of the student and staff 'voice', but will draw more heavily on regulation of staff speech since this is more likely to lead to litigation and is thus publicly recorded. Whilst the university *corpus* in traditional universities is made up of the staff and students, in its liberal/economic manifestation the university has devolved into a conventional corporate form whose financial ends are forwarded by managerial strategies, thus dissolving individual and state interests.

The contribution of 'academic freedom' to this modern managerial university is realigned and framed within the logic of enterprise capitalism as a 'necessary pre-condition in the development of a knowledge society'.[4] The ubiquity of the application of managerial principles and processes to universities across advanced western democracies enables the delivery of educated staff to society, demonstrating the contribution of universities to 'human service

1 Scott (2006); Berdahl (1990).
2 Foucault (2008), p 63.
3 Ibid., p 63.
4 Australian Universities Quality Agency (2008).

DOI: 10.4324/9781003175193-14

markets'.[5] The Foucauldian conceptualisation of biopower,[6] or biopolitics,[7] as a technique for control of populations thus becomes relevant to universities as they move away from principled independence and ally themselves to state ends. Using this conceptualisation this chapter will trace some of the mechanisms of power that are aligning university independence, academic freedom and traditional university governance techniques with society-wide economic transformations. A conventional case analysis of disputes between university students and staff will evidence the disruption of traditional university governance techniques and reveal the complex of power relations in modern universities. Reported (legal) cases are manifestations of state power in themselves, but also evidence multiple asserted techniques of governance. Particularly in relation to cases based on disciplinary action or dismissal of staff, the evidence provided by universities as the site of authority is significant. University reliance on codes of conduct, codes of practice, and other legally ambiguous techniques is an interesting extension of Foucault's analysis of the apparatus accompanying breach. The code of conduct, instead of creating a binary relation of 'right' and 'wrong' conduct (most cogently but not exclusively illustrated in criminal law), 'establishes an average considered as optimal on the one hand, and, on the other, a bandwidth of the acceptable that must not be exceeded. In this way a completely different distribution of things and mechanisms takes shape'.[8]

This chapter reviews, critiques and synthesises legislation and case law on the topics of 'codes of conduct' in higher education and 'academic freedom' to find a new perspective on the impact of soft regulatory devices on the traditional role of the university academic and student. Based on an initial integrative literature review,[9] recent instances of Australian litigation based on codes of conduct are analysed from the perspective of Foucauldian 'technologies of governance'.

Codes of Conduct and University Relationships

Longstanding principles of employment law imply obligations on the employee, including 'duties of loyalty, honesty, confidentiality and mutual trust'.[10] In common law the duties of fidelity,[11] confidentiality[12] or compliance

5 O'Keeffe and Davidd (2020), p 939.
6 Seen, for instance in Foucault (2007), p 16.
7 Foucault (2008).
8 Foucault (2007), p 21.
9 Torraco (2016).
10 *Blyth Chemicals Ltd v Bushnell* (1933) 49 CLR 66 at 81.
11 *Federated Ship Painters and Dockers Union of Australia v Cockatoo Docks & Engineering Co Pty Ltd* (1946) 57 CAR 137.
12 c/f *Gartside v Outram* (1856) 26 LJ Ch 11 3, *Steel Corporation v Granada TV Ltd* [1981] 1 All ER 417 and *Associated Dominion Assurance Society Pty Ltd v Andrew* (1949) 66 WN (NSW) 176 in which courts qualified the duty of fidelity to the employer's interests with an overriding public interest.

with lawful direction[13] may constrain employees from public statements about the employer.[14] Contractual obligations may specifically restrict employee conduct.[15] The tempered capacity of the employer to constrain employee speech using traditional common law techniques provides a starting point for the development of other techniques of control. Not surprisingly this has coincided with an increase in disputes arising from employee speech, including university employees.[16] Most cases involving students have relied on public law as the basis for administrative relief, but many have relied on contract law in the alternative.[17]

The relative dearth of litigation involving universities and their staff and students signals the previously privileged legal position of the university. Early cases identified the relationship as non-contractual;[18] rather, students (and staff) 'enjoyed their membership of the foundation as a result of having been admitted to office therein'.[19] Consistent with a non-contractual analysis, courts had no jurisdiction.[20] The transition from a 'little municipality', where relationships arise from 'status' conferred by law rather than by agreement,[21] to a contractual relationship[22] has been conceded in case law, even if a modern approach would favour a relational contract theory,[23] acknowledging the 'matrix of social relations' within which contracts are formed.[24] The recent shift towards private law[25] was facilitated by a transformation in the private law itself. Narrative framing in terms of contractual freedom and empowered contractual parties shifted to recognition as 'a means of oppression'[26] and a tool to 'direct and coordinate'[27] the individual in their work, to make them 'compatible with industrial production, which is characterized by the use of machines and the imposition of strict hierarchies'.[28]

Whilst it is now common to recognise the university relationship with its staff and students as at least partially contractual, there is uncertainty in the nature

13 *Lane v Fasciale* (1993) 35 AILR 425 [339].
14 For a full account of the common law constraints, see Jackson (2004).
15 See generally McCarry (1981).
16 *Rigg v University of Waikato* [1984] 1 NZLR 149; *NTEIU v University of Wollongong* [2001] FCA 1069 (8 August 2001); *University of Wollongong v NTEIU* [2002] FCAFC 85 (28 March 2002).
17 See, for instance, *Griffiths University v Tang* (2005) 221 CLR 99.
18 *Thomson v University of London* (1864) 33 LJCh 625 at 638.
19 Smith (1981), p 639. Blackstone considered this to be one of the characteristics of an eleemosynary corporation which distinguished it from a civil corporation: Blackstone (1765–1769), p 471.
20 *Thomson v University of London* (1864) 33 LJCh 625.
21 MacCormack (1984); Rochford (1998).
22 Wade (1969), p 471. See also Holland (1969), p 70, quoted in Bridge (1970), p 548.
23 See, for instance, Macneil (1974); Macneil (1975).
24 Lees (2001), pp 85–6.
25 Rochford (2008), p 41.
26 Somma (2013), p 107.
27 Ibid., p 107.
28 Ibid., p 107.

and scope of the obligations arising from the relationship. In *'X' v University of Western Sydney*,[29] for instance, the 'parties conducted the matter on the basis that the relationship between the University and the plaintiff was governed by some form of contract or agreement between them'[30] along with the Policies and Codes of Conduct of the University, the *University of Western Sydney Act 1997* (NSW), and rules and by-laws made under the Act. The uncertain scope of the relationship is notable in itself: cases argued on the basis of the university–student contract have been few and limited in their scope, illustrating Macaulay's argument that relational norms and sanctions make this a relationship 'free from contract'.[31] Just as relational contract theorists cite the 'systemic stabilization'[32] of social institutions that divert individual conflicts from litigation, the university–student relationship is (historically) rarely litigated. Macneil notes that in the longer term contractual relationships may involve 'the entangling strings of friendship, reputation, interdependence, morality, and altruistic desires'.[33] Here we recognise the idea of the 'omnipresent and all-embracing biopower' in which society is subsumed into capitalist frameworks, but we also see that control is exercised by 'networks of existence' rather than disciplinary institutions.[34]

Nevertheless, the shift in the legal understanding of the university and staff/student relationships corresponds to a wider shift in the role of universities. Universities have become part of the biopolitical production system, including 'not only the constitution of manpower but also the production of bodies, intellects and affects'.[35] 'Cognitive' or 'informational' capitalism[36] requires an 'informatized, automated, networked and globalized production process and leads to a decisive transformation in the working subject'.[37] The modern 'multiversity'[38] has a central role in the creation of that subject and that subject must be prepared for the postcapitalist society in which 'knowledge—not capital, land, or labour—is the basic resource'.[39] Just as we see a globalising trend in universities in most countries, we also see 'an apparent convergence of higher education structures and policies worldwide'.[40] Biopower, the suite of practices used to control populations, provides insights into the subjugation of universities to the priorities of the state. This can be seen in a cursory history of the university, both in the alignment of university and state ends and new modes

29 *'X' v University of Western Sydney (No 3)* [2013] NSWSC 1329.
30 *'X' v University of Western Sydney (No 3)* [2013] NSWSC 1329 at [43].
31 Macaulay (2004).
32 Kagan (1984), pp 324–6.
33 Macneil (1975), p 633.
34 Lemke (2011), p 84.
35 Ibid., p 82.
36 See, for instance, Peters and Bulut (2011); Peters and Reveley (2014).
37 Lemke (2011), p 83.
38 Scott (2006), p 29.
39 Ibid., p 30.
40 Ibid., p 31.

of coordination by the state,[41] and the alignment of relationships within the university.

Codes of Conduct

Where codes of conduct, practice or ethics are developed they introduce a range of soft regulatory measures[42] which may (or may not) be incorporated into relevant contracts.[43] These add to a 'series of complex edifices … a system of correlation between juridico-legal mechanisms, disciplinary mechanisms and mechanisms of security'.[44] This body of expostulatory mores appears to be designed to work at a group or societal level;[45] however the force of codes lies partly in their uncertain reach. They are indirect methods of achieving directly enforceable ends.[46] In this process we see modern iterations of Foucault's techniques of governmentality, 'the organised practices and techniques used to produce, care for and/or dominate individual subjects'.[47]

Lack of drafting precision, potential conflict or ambiguity, and the multiple roles these documents play exacerbate disparities of power and information between parties in a relationship. Codes straddle private contractual obligations and community mores and render boundaries between promissory and non-promissory statements (even more) opaque.[48] Uncertainty about the reach of regulatory tools becomes itself a governmental technique. The 'code' can be incorporated into the contract by one of a number of conventional interpretative methods, by reference or because it is binding as a directive to employees.[49] The employee is then required either to comply or to take a defensive legal posture to protect their employment. The potential for overreach is demonstrated in *Tracey v BP Refinery (Kwinana) Pty Ltd*[50] in which the employer alleged breached policy by sharing a 'highly offensive and inappropriate'[51] meme parodying negotiations for a new Enterprise Agreement.[52] The imbal-

41 Clark (1979).

42 Kingsford Smith (2012).

43 Many of these cases are settled, including, for instance, Rugby Australia's termination of Israel Folau's contract in August 2019 on the basis of failure to comply with a Players' Code of Conduct. The Code required 'respectful use of social media'.

44 Foucault (2007), p 22.

45 Evident in, for instance, *Burns v Folau* [2020] NSWCATAD 287, in which the conduct that resulted in termination of Folau's contract of employment with Rugby Australia was also the basis for a complaint to the Anti-Discrimination Board. The complainant was not given leave to proceed.

46 Somma (2013).

47 Owens (2009), p 568.

48 See, for instance, Pärli and Vögtli (2021).

49 Ibid.

50 [2020] FWCFB 4206.

51 *Scott Tracey v BP Refinery (Kwinana) Pty Ltd* [2019] FWC 4113, [34] 'Stand Down Letter'.

52 *BP Refinery (Kwinana) Pty Ltd v Tracey* [2020] FCAFC 89; 276 FCR 9 [4]. The parody continued the *Downfall* (2004) meme, using a scene from *Der Untergang* (2004) in which Hitler reacts to news that the Nazi counter-offensive against the Soviets failed and that defeat was imminent.

ance of power between the parties was exacerbated by a statutory framework under which parties usually bear their own costs.[53]

These regulatory techniques enable scrutiny of the individual across a number of sites, including the individual's 'private' life and views. As mechanisms of control widen, cover more diverse subjects, and become less specific, the potential for the employer to assert control increases, as does the potential for conflict between values. As corporations harness normative values to their other value propositions,[54] compliance measures widen to hitherto private conduct as 'management literature sees adherence to the company's own codes of conduct [to be] part of a company's compliance policy'.[55] Reliance on legal techniques to manage this sort of risk potentially raises human rights issues and moves beyond the original 'voluntary' status of codes as methods of promoting ethics.[56] The provocative reach of this form of risk management was evidenced in Israel Folau's dispute with Rugby Australia, arising from a social media post claimed, *inter alia*, to have breached the Professional Player Code of Conduct (which may or may not have been effectively incorporated into the Player Contract). Folau's subsequent dismissal led to proceedings in the Fair Work Division of the Federal Court of Australia,[57] later settled for an undisclosed sum and an apology by Rugby Australia.[58] Folau's Amended Statement of Claim raised his Christian religion[59] and his belief that he had an evangelical duty,[60] his use of his private social media accounts in his private time,[61] and that the purported termination of his contract was contrary to public policy as against freedom of religion.[62]

53 *Fair Work Act 2009* (Cth) s 611; *BP Refinery (Kwinana) Pty Ltd v Tracey* [2020] FCAFC 89; *Scott Tracey v BP Refinery (Kwinana) Pty Ltd* [2021] FWCFB 4970.

54 Kingsford Smith (2012), p 403.

55 Pärli and Vögtli (2021), p 72.

56 Blecher (2017).

57 *Isileli "Israel" Folau v Rugby Australia Limited & Anor* MLG2486/2019. Documents were made publicly accessible by the Federal Circuit Court in view of the public interest in the case but have since been removed.

58 Rugby Australia, 'Joint statement by Rugby Australia, NSW Rugby Union and Israel Folau' available at https://australia.rugby/news/2019/12/04/if-joint-statement-dec, *Media Release*, 4 December 2019; 'Rugby Australia and Israel Folau Settle Legal Dispute over Sacking', *ABC News*, 5 December 2019 available at https://www.abc.net.au/news/2019-12-04/rugby-australia-israel-folau-mediation-settlement/11765866

59 *Isileli "Israel" Folau v Rugby Australia Limited & Anor* MLG2486/2019 Amended Statement of Claim para [14].

60 *Isileli "Israel" Folau v Rugby Australia Limited & Anor* MLG2486/2019 Amended Statement of Claim para [16].

61 *Isileli "Israel" Folau v Rugby Australia Limited & Anor* MLG2486/2019 Amended Statement of Claim para [23].

62 *Isileli "Israel" Folau v Rugby Australia Limited & Anor* MLG2486/2019 Amended Statement of Claim para [33].

Academic Freedom and the University

In the university sector recent high-profile litigation[63] has also been characterised as involving wider societal norms, instancing conflict between the protection of academic or intellectual freedom and the obligation to behave collegially in the university code of conduct.[64] These cases continue the themes seen in non-university employment cases, in which the private obligations of the employee are supplemented by normative value statements adopted by the employer. Codes of conduct or ethics are captured by evolving interpretations of the employer/employee relationship, harnessing employee conduct, potentially both public and private, to university goals. Since these goals have already been aligned with the conditioning of the subject to the economic system, what we are seeing is the further entanglement of the university and its members in a set of regulatory techniques that re-render information and communication in a restructured network of capitalist relations. Paradoxically, the domain for this entanglement is the intersection of longstanding protections of academic freedom and other regulation of employee conduct.

Academic Freedom—A Reifying Concept?

Much has been written of academic freedom, and it will not be reproduced here.[65] Like the traditional notion of the university[66] it is a contestable term, but there is broad agreement as to the existence of the freedom,[67] a matter now accepted in the High Court of Australia.[68] The broadest conception of academic freedom confers tenure of employment on academic staff, and involves interpreting statutes, policies and contracts accordingly, as

> [t]o take any other view would be to countenance a situation where … a university could exclude an academic from the ability to carry out his

63 The Australian cause célèbre is *Ridd v James Cook University* [2021] HCA 32, handed down 13 October 2021.

64 In the United States, the American Association of University Professors maintains a watching brief over cases involving academic freedom and tenure: Academic Freedom and Tenure Investigative Reports available at https://www.aaup.org/reports-publications/aaup-policies-reports/academic-freedom-and-tenure-investigative-reports.

65 See Pritchard (1998); Becker (2006); Barendt (2010); Karran and Mallinson (2017). I have written on this previously in, *inter alia*, Rochford (2003) and Rochford (2018). In *Ridd v James Cook University* [2021] HCA 32, notes 21–30, the High Court also referenced Lamont (1956); Polishook (1994); Baldwin (1995); Post (2012); Evans and Stone (2021); Brown (1900); Said (1994); Dworkin (1996).

66 *St David's College, Lampeter v Ministry of Education* [1951] 1 All ER 559.

67 See Association of American Colleges and Universities (1940), *Demers v Austin*, 746 F.3d 402 (9th Circuit Washington 29 January 2014); in the UK see Ashby (1966).

68 *Ridd v James Cook University* [2021] HCA 32 particularly para [64].

> or her duties in the academic world in circumstances where the sanction imposed (either dismissal or suspension) was in breach of statute.[69]

Traditionally academic tenure was afforded for this reason[70] and in some jurisdictions this traditional protection has been supplemented (or replaced) by constitutional[71] or statutory protection,[72] or an obligation under statute to write protection of academic freedom into institutional rules.[73]

Even on its broadest construction, however, academic freedom is subject to constraint.[74] It is the modern, inchoate forms of constraint that are the subject of this chapter. The traditional protection of academic tenure has narrowed and the realm within which academic freedom has operated has become more limited with the application of New Public Management theory to the university sector.[75] Responses to criticisms of New Public Management have prompted a 'public value discourse'[76] investing management discourse in public bodies such as universities with narratives borrowed from political philosophy. Each of these trends has acted upon academic freedom in different ways. In Australia, for instance, managerialism was linked to attenuated academic freedom in a 2001 report suggesting that 'the new managerial culture is now so entrenched that universities have an instinct to stifle uncomfortable opinions of a kind usually associated with academic institutions … [arising] from a disregard for what universities should stand for'.[77] A 2008 inquiry by the Senate Standing Committee on Education, Employment and Workplace Relations[78] considered that academic freedom included the right to 'teach, research and

69 *Cahill v Dublin City University* [2007] IEHC 20 para [10.3].

70 Cf. Bruce (2019).

71 See, for instance, *Grutter v Bollinger* 539 US 306 (2003), *Demers v Austin* 746 F3d 402, 9th Cir, 2014 c/f *Garcetti v Ceballos,* 547 US 410 (2006), *Rumsfeld v Forum for Academic and Institutional Rights, Inc* 126 S Ct 1297 (2006); Byrne (2006); Chen (2006).

72 In the United States, see O'Neil (2006), note 15.

73 See, for instance, in Australia note 88; in the UK *Johnson v Newcastle College (The Corporation)* [2001] UKEAT 1316_00_0204 (2 April 2001) which deals with the obligation to include protection of academic freedom in the Articles of Government of the College.

74 See, for instance, *Volkswagen Aktiengesellschaft v Garcia* [2013] EWHC 1832 (Ch) in which the value of academic freedom was outweighed by the security of Volkswagen cars, threatened by the publication of an algorithm enabling 'hacking' of the cars by non-owners. See also *Rigg v University of Waikato* [1984] 1 NZLR 149 in which an academic was dismissed for writing an article in a student newspaper alleging a link between an isotope laboratory and student cancer. There was no evidence supporting the claim. The academic's appeal for reinstatement on the grounds of academic freedom was not accepted. *Ridd v James Cook University* [2021] HCA 32 considers in its own context the operation of constraints, particularly the duty of confidentiality.

75 Schachter (2019).

76 Sedlačko (2020), p 161.

77 Employment, Workplace Relations, Small Business and Education References Committee, Parliament of Australia (2001), p 305 [9.40].

78 SSCEEWR (2008).

publish on contentious issues; choose their own research colleagues; and speak on social issues without fear or favour in areas of their expertise … balanced by the responsible and disciplined exercise of scholarly expertise'.[79] Conversely, academic freedom has been negatively associated with unacceptable views in relation to gender identity, thus aligning certain 'right wing' ideologies and academic freedom.[80] A 2018 audit by the Institute of Public Affairs[81] concluded that '[a] censorious culture has developed at universities'[82] giving rise to cancellation or protests against speakers, self-censorship and calls for course censorship, and trigger warnings and 'speech codes have institutionalised restrictions on free speech'.[83]

The continuing association between state interests and university education has justified regulation of the sector.[84] Higher education's importance as a 'necessary pre-condition in the development of a knowledge society'[85] has prompted regulatory authorities to articulate a requirement that universities maintain sufficient autonomy to protect academics from 'interference' from 'external government, public or private sector' influence.[86] In Australia the French Report[87] recommended the adoption by universities of a 'Model Code' for protection of academic freedom, and after some delay[88] in October 2021 all had adopted the Code or created policies in favour of free speech in the face of threats by the Federal Government that the Model Code would become law.[89] The Model Code includes the freedom to disseminate and publish research without restriction by consensus or institutional policy, to express opinions and beliefs and contribute to public debate, to express opinions about the university 'without institutional censorship or sanction', and to 'make public comment on any issue in their personal capacities, not speaking either on behalf of the university or as an officer of the university'.[90] The *Higher Education Support Act 2003* (Cth) uses conventional steering techniques to link funding to compliance by requiring universities to 'have a

79 Kayrooz et al. (2001), p 44.
80 Suissa and Sullivan (2021). See also O'Neil (2006).
81 Lesh (2018). Similar audits were carried out in previous years: Lesh (2016); Lesh (2017).
82 Lesh (2018), p 4.
83 Ibid., p 4. Several Australian events of this nature are canvassed in Evans and Stone (2021).
84 Pritchard (1998), p 101 compares the original view that 'the British tend to be sanguine about their academic freedom and values because their universities are legally independent corporate bodies', with the later view that 'older concepts of institutional autonomy have become subordinate to arguments about accountability and the right of the government to determine policy' at p 103.
85 For instance, Australian Universities Quality Agency (2008), and in the UK *Higher Education: Meeting the Challenge* (1987) para [3.4].
86 Australian Universities Quality Agency (2008).
87 French (2019).
88 Walker (2020).
89 Ferguson (2021).
90 Model Code.

policy that upholds free intellectual inquiry in relation to learning, teaching and research'.[91]

The apparent paradox—that the state feels it can usefully regulate to protect academic freedom—illustrates Berdahl's (1990) point that 'academic freedom and institutional autonomy are not the same thing'.[92] Nevertheless the conception of academic freedom as a precondition to economic interests[93] aligns the reified conception of academic freedom with the disambiguated biopolitical subject. The staff member exercises a right to academic freedom only insofar as it is in the interests of the university as a corporate body and the state. The university's interest in the protection of academic freedom maintains the residue of older conceptions, but university interests are now largely aligned with the state interest in the creation of the biopolitical subject, capable of meeting the skills and capacities required of the modern workforce.

Within the university itself, the university politic constitutes multiple subjects in place of the traditional member of the university; one as an employee defined by statute, conventional employment contracts, industrial awards and human resources policies, another as a teacher and researcher regulated largely by university policy which is, in turn, subject to governance by legislation and agency oversight,[94] and another as a 'public intellectual' with the capacity 'to contribute to public debate, in relation to their subjects of study and research'.[95] More particularly the academic subject is distinguished from the private subject engaging in 'extramural speech'.[96] Thus the private subject is defined and refined, although the process may be messy and unclear.[97] The code asserts the distinction between the role of the public intellectual and the private individual with the 'freedom … to make public comment on any issue in their personal capacities, not speaking either on behalf of the university or as an officer of the university'.[98] These personae will potentially be in internal

91 *Higher Education Support Act 2003* (Cth) subdivision 19-G, ss 19.110 and 19.115.

92 Berdahl (1990), p 172.

93 Australian Universities Quality Agency (2008).

94 *Tertiary Education Quality and Standards Agency Act 2011* (Cth) and instruments such as the *Higher Education Standards Framework (Threshold Standards) 2021*, supplemented by Policies such as the Australian Qualifications Framework, delivered through the Australian Government Department of Education, Skills and Employment through the Tertiary Education Quality and Standards Agency (TEQSA).

95 Model Code.

96 Association of American Colleges and Universities (1940).

97 See, for instance, *Dr Frank Will v Deakin University* [2015] FWC 3130 para [109] in which the Fair Work Commission noted that '[t]he University cannot accrue the accolades that flow from Dr Will's private work and at the same time direct him to properly distance his private work from his University work. If the University does not want an employee's private work to encroach on University requirements, it would appear contradictory to publicise those private matters on its website as if it had some hand in the achievement or seek to gain some benefit from it'.

98 Model Code.

conflict, but one or more may conflict with the interests of the university. As these conflicts escalate to litigation, they are resolved by reference to the legally refined and defined aspect of each subject, dissolving alternatives and reifying a single subject regulated and governed by the university and, by the process of institutional alignment, with state interests. Thus, the project of fully constituting the academic as an economic subject under new techniques of governance in fact creates multiple subjects under various suites of governance and consigns greater authority over the personal subject.

Modern Governance of Academic Speech

The French Report noted the 'rather general' or 'broad' language used by higher education rules and policies;[99] terminology inviting 'a wide range for variable judgment in interpretation and application approaching compulsion only at the limits of the range'.[100] The use of 'categories of indeterminate reference'[101] in exhortation is unremarkable. Where it is part of a suite of codes, policies and other governance documents with potential legal consequences it is more troubling, particularly where that suite is so voluminous.[102] *National Tertiary Education Industry Union v University of Sydney*[103] demonstrates the multiple forms of governance to which each academic is subject, so that their academic persona in fact constitutes multiple subjects. The Union argued that the university had breached the *Fair Work Act 2009* (Cth) in terminating the employment of Dr Tim Anderson. It alleged that the termination was a breach of a right to intellectual freedom created by the *University of Sydney Enterprise Agreement 2013–2017* (the 2013 Agreement) or the *University of Sydney Enterprise Agreement 2018–2021* (the 2018 Agreement) affirming the 'protection and promotion of intellectual freedom … [including the right] to express unpopular or controversial views, provided that in doing so staff must not engage in harassment, vilification or intimidation'.[104] The immediate legal landscape within which the dispute occurred included the *Higher Education Support Act 2003* (Cth), *Tertiary Education Quality and Standards Agency Act 2011* (Cth), the *University of Sydney Act 1989* (NSW) and the *Higher Education Standards Framework* (NSW), along with the various codes of conduct, charters, policies and associated procedures.[105] More broadly, the *Defamation Act 2005*

99 French (2019), p 217.
100 Ibid., p 218, citing Stone (1968), pp 263–4.
101 Stone (1968), pp 263–4.
102 French (2019), p 219 described a review of higher education rules and policies as like 'cleaning the Augean Stables'.
103 [2020] FCA 1709.
104 University of Sydney Enterprise Agreement 2018 cl 315 (iv).
105 Code of Conduct—Staff and Affiliates effective from 12 September 2016; Code of Conduct—Staff and Affiliates effective from 16 October 2017; Charter of Academic Freedom effective from

(NSW) was also engaged, along with various common law principles arising from the employment relationship giving rise to a range of duties. The court included amongst an employee's duties the implied duty of fidelity and duty to obey lawful directions and to carry out duties 'in accordance with his contract of employment, the 2018 Agreement, the Codes of Conduct and various other policies'.[106] At issue were Anderson's public Facebook account which identified him, at least for some period, as working at the University of Sydney, and his public Twitter account. His posts on those accounts prompted the university to allege that Dr Anderson had engaged in 'misconduct' or 'serious misconduct' under the Code of Conduct and University Policy. Further posts on social media, along with internal emails and a seminar presentation, escalated the matter, resulting in disciplinary action. In Anderson's unsuccessful action against his dismissal the court distinguished the creation and use of contested materials *as part of* teaching materials and the promulgation of that material through public social media. The 'real' reason for posting the material, according to the court, was a deliberate provocation; 'an assertion of an unfettered right to exercise what he considered to be intellectual freedom'.[107]

The recent litigation between James Cook University and physicist Dr Peter Ridd raised similar complexities.[108] The various technologies of performance involved in the control and termination of the staff member included 'breach of the JCU Code of Conduct … two speech directions, five confidentiality directions, a "no satire" direction, two censures, and … cl 14 of the JCU Enterprise Agreement 2013–2016'.[109] Ridd's case centred around his criticism, through media, of colleagues' research into the degradation of the Great Barrier Reef. Ridd was censured and given a direction under a university code of conduct which was not formally part of the relevant Enterprise Agreement. Clause 14 of the Enterprise Agreement codifies (without defining) intellectual freedom, including a constraint in cl 14.3 that there is a corollary responsibility to 'respect the rights of others' and the caveat that staff 'do not have the right to harass, vilify, bully or intimidate those who disagree with their views'. The Code of Conduct incorporates the normative generalities

6 May 2008; Public Comment Policy effective from 1 February 2007; Bullying, Harassment and Discrimination Prevention Policy 2015; Bullying, Harassment and Discrimination Resolution Procedures 2015; Resolution of Complaints Policy 2015; and Policy on the Use of University Information and Communication Technology Resources (ICT Resources) effective from 31 August 2006: *National Tertiary Education Industry Union v University of Sydney* [2020] FCA 1709 para [16].

106 *National Tertiary Education Industry Union v University of Sydney* [2020] FCA 1709 para [265].

107 *National Tertiary Education Industry Union v University of Sydney* [2020] FCA 1709 para [255].

108 *Ridd v James Cook University* [2021] HCA 32 (13 October 2021); *James Cook University v Ridd* [2020] FCAFC 123 (22 July 2020); *James Cook University v Ridd (No 2)* [2020] FCAFC 132; *Ridd v James Cook University* [2018] FCCA 3080; *Ridd v James Cook University* [2019] FCCA 997; *Ridd v James Cook University (No.2)* [2019] FCCA 2489 (6 September 2019).

109 *James Cook University v Ridd* [2020] FCAFC 123 [1].

which feature in non-binding codes ('achieve excellence', 'make a difference', 'encourage participation', 'seek … a brighter future', 'act with authenticity', 'engage in genuine dialogue') along with more concrete exhortations that replicate common law employment obligations ('act with care and diligence', 'maintain appropriate confidentiality') or general law ('not make improper use of our position, status, power or authority to gain, or seek to gain, a benefit or advantage for ourselves or any other person'). Unfortunately, as the High Court noted, the case 'was conducted by both parties on an all-or-nothing basis. JCU's position was that all of the findings against Dr Ridd were justified. Dr Ridd's position was that none of the findings made against him was justified'.[110] This had ramifications for the outcome of the Appeal, in which Ridd was unsuccessful. However, the High Court noted that Cl 14 was not constrained by a requirement of respect and courtesy. The court noted, citing Mill,[111] that

> [w]hilst a prohibition upon disrespectful and discourteous conduct in intellectual expression might be a 'convenient plan for having peace in the intellectual world', the 'price paid for this sort of intellectual pacification, is the sacrifice of the entire moral courage of the human mind'.

However, Ridd was still bound by the duties of confidentiality and the requirement to utilise internal university processes. Although Ridd's original comments, within his area of expertise, were protected by Cl 14, other conduct that attracted censure was not so protected.[112] Williams argues that the decision 'provides the strongest-ever judicial affirmation of intellectual freedom in the nation's universities'[113] and that, significantly, this would 'cut across codes of conduct in Australian universities that prioritise respectful behaviour'.[114] This presupposes that academics are willing to compromise their employment and risk litigation to challenge the censure of a university in the context of such a complex set of instruments with varying legal effect, a supposition of particular significance as academic tenure has become increasingly tenuous, and universities can find more than one way to silence academic dissent.

'Codes' are only one of the range of techniques enlarging the university's governance reach. *Zhao v University of Technology Sydney*[115] demonstrates the potential for the university to (attempt to) incorporate other tools, in this case School Academic Workload Guidelines, incorporating publication benchmarks and the academic's individual work plan, development plan and

110 *Ridd v James Cook University* [2021] HCA 32 (13 October 2021) para [63].
111 Mill (1859), p 60.
112 *Ridd v James Cook University* [2021] HCA 32 (13 October 2021) para [65].
113 Williams (2021).
114 Ibid.
115 [2020] FWC 416.

performance reviews. The academic, a Level B lecturer of 14 years standing, met other benchmarks but failed to meet a personal publication benchmark of at least one journal article published in an A* or A journal within a two-year period. Non-compliance with this benchmark was grounds for her dismissal for unsatisfactory performance. The Fair Work Commission ordered the academic's reinstatement and on appeal to the Full Bench[116] the majority[117] held that it was not in the public interest to grant permission to appeal. The decision, according to Golding, 'sent a resounding message to universities concerning the need to set careful publication benchmarks for academic staff within appropriate and reasonably achievable limits',[118] inviting the systematic reification of workload management tools and incorporation into processes of contractual onboarding, ongoing review and record-keeping. In *Cowen v Monash University*[119] the university, acting on complaints by municipal councillors about emails sent by Cowen regarding views on same-sex marriage in the Judeo-Christian tradition, discontinued his honorary appointment. The university relied upon Cowen's use of the university email address and the resulting purported implication that the Institute for Judaism and Civilisation, of which Cowen was Director, was associated with the university. The substance of the case was to obtain access to documents held by the university, but the policy relied on was the 'Information Technology Use Policy—Staff and Other Authorised Users'. The policy permitted 'reasonable use for personal purposes', where the Head of Department determined the parameters of 'reasonable use'. In *Gramotnev v Queensland University of Technology*,[120] the university also terminated the employee's contract for 'Serious Misconduct' based on use of the university email system to send '"all staff" emails containing derogatory content or [stating an intention] to defy directions or the Code of Conduct'.[121]

Litigation and the Construction of Knowledge

Law's structure is an amalgam of history, power and the process of record-keeping. Legal knowledge constructs, reinforces and replicates itself by maintaining control over categorisation, publication and legal education. At the same time litigation requires information, and control of information moulds the development of precedent, justifying efforts to facilitate free full-text access to case law and legislation along with legislation intended to enable access to information

116 *University of Technology Sydney v Ruoyun (Lucy) Zhao* [2020] FWCFB 3571.
117 Vice President Catanzariti and Commissioner Johns, President Colman dissenting.
118 Golding (2021), p 406.
119 [2018] VCAT 694.
120 [2019] QCA 108.
121 [2019] QCA 108 at para [88].

held by government and government agencies.[122] The removal of other barriers to entry through the growth of tribunals and the incidence of self-represented litigants creates the impression that individuals are empowered to navigate their own informational and legal lives. A 'hazardous undertow … [in the form of the] commercialisation of knowledge'[123] creates a significant caveat to the capacity of an individual to manage, or even calculate, the newly mercantile parameters of their lives. In the university context the paradoxical application of freedom of information principles has been the increase in litigation relating to access to information. The legislation and its processes erect narrow gates representing public interest and appoint gatekeepers regulating access, and cases involving the legislation demonstrate constructions of knowledge for the purposes of public interest in the context of freedom of information. In *Pemberton v University of New South Wales*,[124] for instance, the applicant sought information argued to 'concern matters of public interest in relation to academic freedom to express opinions, the merits or otherwise of academic research on a subject such as pornography, and workplace bullying'. The university construed the knowledge differently, arguing that there were 'public interest considerations against disclosure' including, ironically, the interest in the supply of confidential information to the university. Similarly, in *Noble v University of New South Wales*,[125] the interests of the university in 'the function of improving the performance of its staff' regulated the availability of information obtained by a consultant from staff. The consultant thus commodified and rendered confidential the words of university staff relating to 'team cohesion, behaviours and accountability, executive messaging, role and reporting clarity and leadership qualities'.[126] In this way access to information, and restrictions on access, become one of the techniques of governance regulating human service markets. In the wake of litigation the subject of the High Court proceedings appealing the termination of his employment by James Cook University, Dr Peter Ridd, argues that confidentiality and secrecy clauses chill academic conversations about academic freedom.[127]

Conclusions

The United States Supreme Court articulated a concern that diminishing academic freedom would 'cast a pall of orthodoxy over the classroom'.[128] Concerns

122 Legislation enabling access to government information exists in all Australian jurisdictions: *Freedom of Information Act 1982* (Cth); *Freedom of Information Act 1982* (Vic); *Right to Information Act 2009* (Qld); *Freedom of Information Act 1989* (NSW); *Government Information (Public Access) Act 2009* (NSW).

123 Scott (2006), p 30.

124 [2014] NSWCATAD 19.

125 [2017] NSWCATAD 2.

126 [2017] NSWCATAD 2 at para [4].

127 Ridd (2021).

128 *Keyishian v Board of Regents of the University of the State of New York*, 385 US 589 at 603 (1967).

have been expressed on both the right and the left of the political spectrum in many western democracies that academic freedom is under threat. Perhaps conceptually the threat is seen to be the homogenising force of fixed political viewpoints exercised on unformed student minds. The thesis of this chapter is that constraints on academic or intellectual freedom are not part of a grand battle of ideas, but rather the result of many menial exertions of power and control. The mechanisms of power operate through the dispersed networks of insubstantial coercions in multiple sites of influence that form grid-like over an academic's working life and beyond. In *Ridd v James Cook University*,[129] Vasta J commenced by saying:

> Some have thought that this trial was about freedom of speech and intellectual freedom. Others have thought that this trial was about the manner in which academics should conduct themselves. Some observers may have thought that this trial was about the use of non-offensive words when promulgating scientific ideas. Media reports have considered that this trial was about silencing persons with controversial or unpopular views … this trial was about none of the above. Rather, this trial was purely and simply about the proper construction of a clause in an Enterprise Agreement.[130]

The rules of construction of the clause in the Enterprise Agreement are part of an epic series of annotations on the academic role—technologies of performance that perfect the subjugation of the academic. That political views from both the right and the left demonstrate unease with the result of this manifestation of biopower suggests a full devolution of power and the self-replicating mechanisms of regulation.

In sum, the multiple exertions of regulation on the individual in the interests of the biopolitical state are proof of Foucault's 'ontology of the present'[131]—the ambiguities and complexities entrenched in our social order that render opaque the regulatory reach. The art of government in liberalism is the sleight of hand disguising the exercise of power, the recreation of the individual into *homo economicus* and the subsequent dissolution of individuality into the neoliberal state. Academic freedom, like other freedoms, is balanced against other freedoms and against security in a constantly reformulating set of processes. In place of fixed juridical understandings, academic freedom becomes a fluctuating concept 'in which action is brought to bear on the rules of the game rather than the players'.[132]

129 [2019] FCCA 997.
130 [2019] FCCA 997 para [1]–[2].
131 Foucault (2008), p 2.
132 Ibid., p 207.

References

Primary sources

Cases

Associated Dominion Assurance Society Pty Ltd v Andrew (1949) 66 WN (NSW) 176.
Blyth Chemicals Ltd v Bushnell (1933) 49 CLR 66.
BP Refinery (Kwinana) Pty Ltd v Tracey [2020] FCAFC 89; 276 FCR 9.
Burns v Folau [2020] NSWCATAD 287.
Cahill v Dublin City University [2007] IEHC 20.
Demers v Austin, 746 F3d 402 (9th Cir 2014).
Federated Ship Painters and Dockers Union of Australia v Cockatoo Docks & Engineering Co Pty Ltd (1946) 57 CAR 137.
Garcetti v Ceballos, 547 US 410 (2006).
Gartside v Outram (1856) 26 LJ Ch 11 3.
Gramotnev v Queensland University of Technology [2019] QCA 108.
Griffiths University v Tang (2005) 221 CLR 99.
Grutter v Bollinger 539 US 306 (2003).
Isileli 'Israel' Folau v Rugby Australia Limited & Anor MLG2486/2019.
James Cook University v Ridd [2020] FCAFC 123 (22 July 2020).
James Cook University v Ridd (No 2) [2020] FCAFC 132.
Johnson v Newcastle College (The Corporation) [2001] UKEAT 1316_00_0204 (2 April 2001).
Keyishian v Board of Regents of the University of the State of New York, 385 US 589, 603 (1967).
Lane v Fasciale (1993) 35 AILR 425.
National Tertiary Education Industry Union v University of Sydney [2020] FCA 1709.
Noble v University of New South Wales [2017] NSWCATAD 2.
Pemberton v University of New South Wales [2014] NSWCATAD 19.
Ridd v James Cook University [2018] FCCA 3080.
Ridd v James Cook University [2019] FCCA 997.
Ridd v James Cook University (No.2) [2019] FCCA 2489 (6 September 2019).
Ridd v James Cook University [2021] HCATrans 110 [23 June 2021].
Ridd v James Cook University [2021] HCA 32.
Rumsfeld v Forum for Academic and Institutional Rights, Inc. 126 S Ct 1297 (2006).
Thomson v University of London (1864) 33 LJCh 625.
Tracey v BP Refinery (Kwinana) Pty Ltd [2020] FWCFB 4206.
Scott Tracey v BP Refinery (Kwinana) Pty Ltd [2019] FWC 4113.
Scott Tracey v BP Refinery (Kwinana) Pty Ltd [2021] FWCFB 4970.
Steel Corporation v Granada TV Ltd [1981] 1 All ER 417.
University of Technology Sydney v Ruoyun (Lucy) Zhao [2020] FWCFB 3571.
Volkswagen Aktiengesellschaft v Garcia et al [2013] EWHC 1832 (Ch).
Will v Deakin University [2015] FWC 3130.
'X' v University of Western Sydney (No 3) [2013] NSWSC 1329.
'X' v University of Western Sydney [2014] NSWSC 82.
Zhao v University of Technology Sydney [2020] FWC 416.

Legislation

Defamation Act 2005 (NSW).
Fair Work Act 2009 (Cth).

Freedom of Information Act 1982 (Cth).
Freedom of Information Act 1982 (Vic).
Freedom of Information Act 1989 (NSW).
Government Information (Public Access) Act 2009 (NSW).
Higher Education Support Act 2003 (Cth).
Higher Education Standards Framework (Threshold Standards) 2021.
Higher Education Standards Framework (NSW).
JCU Enterprise Agreement 2013–2016.
Right to Information Act 2009 (Qld).
Tertiary Education Quality and Standards Agency Act 2011 (Cth).
University of Sydney Act 1989 (NSW).
University of Western Sydney Act 1997 (NSW).
University of Sydney Enterprise Agreement 2013–2017 (the 2013 Agreement).
University of Sydney Enterprise Agreement 2018–2021 (the 2018 Agreement).

Secondary Sources

Eric Ashby (1966) *Universities: British, Indian, African—A Study in the Ecology of Higher Education*, Harvard University Press.

Association of American Colleges and Universities (1940) *Statement of Principles on Academic Freedom and Tenure.*

Australian Universities Quality Agency (2008) *Submission to the Senate Standing Committee on Education, Employment and Workplace Relations* American Association of University Professors: https://www.aaup.org/report/1940-statement-principles-academic-freedom-and-tenure#:~:text=Teachers%20are%20entitled%20to%20full,the%20authorities%20of%20the%20institution.

Fletcher N Baldwin Jr (1995) 'The Academies, "Hate Speech" and the Concept of Academic Intellectual Freedom' 7 *University of Florida Journal of Law and Public Policy* 41.

Eric Barendt (2010) *Academic Freedom and the Law: A Comparative Study*, Hart Publishing.

Rosamunde FJ Becker (2006) *Academic Freedom in England and Germany: A Comparative Perspective*, James Nicolas Publishers.

Robert Berdahl (1990) 'Academic Freedom, Autonomy and Accountability in British Universities' 15 *Studies in Higher Education* 169.

William Blackstone (1765–1769) *Commentaries on the Laws of England*, Oxford, Clarendon Press.

Lara Blecher (2017) 'Codes of Conduct: The Trojan Horse of International Human Rights Law' 38 *Comparative Labor Law & Policy Journal* 437.

JW Bridge (1970) 'Keeping Peace in the Universities: The Role of the Visitor' 86 *The Law Quarterly Review* 531.

Elmer E Brown (1900) 'Academic Freedom' 19 *Educational Review* 209.

James E Bruce (2019) 'Does Academic Tenure Promote the Common Good?' 22 *Journal of Markets & Morality* 194.

J Byrne (2006) 'Constitutional Academic Freedom after Grutter: Getting Real About the Four Freedoms of University' 77 *University of Colorado Law Review* 929.

Alan K Chen (2006) 'Bureaucracy and Distrust: Germaneness and the Paradoxes of the Academic Freedom Doctrine' 77 *University of Colorado Law Review* 955.

Burton R Clark (1979) 'The Many Pathways of Academic Coordination' 8 *Higher Education* 251.

Ronald Dworkin (1996) 'We Need a New Interpretation of Academic Freedom' 82 *Academe* 10.

Carolynne Evans and Adrienne Stone (2021) *Open Minds: Academic Freedom and Freedom of Speech in Australia*, Black Inc Books.

Richard Ferguson (2021) 'Every Australian University has Adopted Morrison Government's Free Speech Code' *The Australian*, 26 October.

Michel Foucault (2007) *Security, Territory, Population: Lectures at the Collège de France 1977–1978*, trans. Graham Burchell, Palgrave Macmillan.

Michel Foucault (2008) *The Birth of Biopolitics: Lectures at the Collège de France 1978–1979*, trans. Graham Burchell, Palgrave Macmillan.

Gabrielle Golding (2021) 'Major Court and Tribunal Decisions in Australia in 2020' 63 *Journal of Industrial Relations* 395.

Higher Education: Meeting the Challenge (1987) 24 Cmnd 114, HMSO.

DC Holland (1969) 'The Student and the Law: Freedom and Responsibility' 22 *Current Legal Problems* 61.

Jim Jackson (2004) 'When Can Speech Lead to Dismissal in a University?' 9(2) *Australia and New Zealand Journal of Law and Education* 1.

Robert Kagan (1984) 'The Routinization of Debt Collection: An Essay on Social Change and Conflict in the Courts' 18 *Law and Society Review* 323.

Carol Kayrooz et al. (2001) *Academic Freedom and Commercialisation of Australian Universities: Perceptions and Experiences of Social Scientists*, Australia Institute.

Dimity Kingsford Smith (2012) 'Governing the Corporation: The Role of "Soft Regulation"' 35 *The University of New South Wales Law Journal* 378.

Corliss Lamont (1956) *Freedom is as Freedom Does: Civil Liberties Today*, Horizon Press.

Matthew Lees (2001) 'Contract, Conscience, Communitarian Conspiracies and Confucius: Normativism Through the Looking Glass of Relational Contract Theory' 25 *Melbourne University Law Review* 82.

Thomas Lemke (2011) *Biopolitics: An Advanced Introduction*, trans. Eric Frederick Trump, NYU Press.

Matthew Lesh (2016) *Free Speech on Campus Audit 2016*, Institute of Public Affairs.

Matthew Lesh (2017) *Free Speech on Campus Audit 2017*, Institute of Public Affairs.

Matthew Lesh (2018) *Free Speech on Campus Audit 2018*, Institute of Public Affairs.

Stewart Macaulay (2004) 'Freedom From Contract: Solutions in Search of a Problem?' 2004 (2) *Wisconsin Law Review* 777.

Geoffrey MacCormack (1984) 'Status: Problems of Definition and Use' 43 *Cambridge Law Journal* 361.

Ian Macneil (1974) 'The Many Futures of Contract' 47 *Southern California Law Review* 691.

Ian Macneil (1975) 'A Primer of Contract Planning' 48 *Southern California Law Review* 629.

GJ McGarry (1981) 'The Contract of Employment and Freedom of Speech' 9 *Sydney Law Review* 332.

John Stuart Mill (1859) *On Liberty*, Walter Scott Publishing Co Ltd.

Patrick O'Keeffe and Christina Davidd (2020) 'Discursive Constructions of Consumer Choice, Performance Measurement and the Marketisation of Disability Services and Aged Care in Australia' 57 *Australian Journal of Social Issues* 938.

Robert M O'Neil (2006) 'Bias, Balance, and Beyond: New Threats to Academic Freedom' 77 *University of Colorado Law Review* 985.

Patricia Owens (2009) 'Reclaiming "Bare Life"?: Against Agamben on Refugees' 23 *International Relations* 567.

Kurt Pärli and Jasmin Vögtli (2021) 'Control and Sanction of Employees on the Basis of Codes of Conduct – A Question of Basic Labour (Human) Rights?' 71 *Labor Law Journal* 71.
Michael A Peters and James Reveley (2014) 'Retrofitting Drucker: Knowledge Work Under Cognitive Capitalism' 20 *Culture and Organization* 135.
M Peters and E Bulut (2011) 'Introduction: Cognitive Capitalism, Education and the Question of Immaterial Labour' in MA Peters and E Bulut (eds) *Cognitive Capitalism, Education and Digital Labor*, Peter Lang.
Irwin H Polishook (1994) 'Academic Freedom and Academic Contexts' 15 *Pace Law Review* 141.
Robert C Post (2012) 'Discipline and Freedom in the Academy' 65 *Arkansas Law Review* 203.
Rosalind MO Pritchard (1998) 'Academic Freedom and Autonomy in the United Kingdom and Germany' 36 *Minerva* 101.
Peter Ridd (2021) 'Lift the Heavy Hand Smothering Academic Dissent' *The Australian*, 15 October.
Francine Rochford (1998) 'The Relationship Between the Student and the University' 3 *Australia & New Zealand Journal of Law and Education* 28.
Francine Rochford (2003) 'Academic Freedom as Insubordination: The Legalisation of the Academy' 15 *Education and the Law* 249.
Francine Rochford (2008) 'The Contested Product of a University Education' 30 *Journal of Higher Education Policy and Management* 41.
Francine Rochford (2018) 'Freedom and Control in the Constrained Modern University' in R Barnett and MA Peters (eds) *The Idea of the University: Contemporary Perspectives, Volume 2*, Peter Lang.
Edward Said (1994) *Representations of the Intellectual: The 1993 Reith Lectures*, Random House.
Hindy Lauer Schachter (2019) 'Civil Service, Academic Tenure, and Management History: How Changes in Management Theory on Professional Knowledge and Hierarchy Affected Merit Reform' 41 *Administrative Theory and Praxis* 3.
John C Scott (2006) 'The Mission of the University: Medieval to Postmodern Transformations' 77 *The Journal of Higher Education* 1.
Michal Sedlačko (2020) 'The Five Tasks of Public Value Management: Public Value as a Programme of Administrative and Societal Democratisation' 13 *The NISPAcee Journal of Public Administration and Policy* 161.
Peter M Smith (1981) 'The Exclusive Jurisdiction of the University Visitor' 97 *Law Quarterly Review* 610.
Alessandro Somma (2013) 'Private Law as Biopolitics: Ordoliberalism, Social Market Economy, and the Public Dimension of Contract' 76 *Law and Contemporary Problems* 105.
Julius Stone (1968) *Legal System and Lawyers' Reasoning*, Maitland Publications.
Judith Suissa and Alice Sullivan (2021) 'The Gender Wars, Academic Freedom and Education' 55 *Journal of Philosophy of Education* 55.
Richard J Torraco (2016) 'Writing Integrative Literature Reviews: Using the Past and Present to Explore the Future' 15 *Human Resource Development Review* 404.
HWR Wade (1969) 'Judicial Control of Universities' 85 *The Law Quarterly Review* 468.
Sally Walker (2020) *Review of the Adoption of the Model Code on Freedom of Speech and Academic Freedom*, Department of Education, Skills and Employment.
George Williams (2021) 'Peter Ridd's Lost Battle a Key Win in War for Academic Freedom' *The Australian*, 17 October.

Reports

Employment, Workplace Relations, Small Business and Education References Committee (2001) *Universities in Crisis*, Parliament of Australia.

Hon Robert French AC (2019) *Report of the Independent Review of Freedom of Speech in Australian Higher Education Providers.*

Terence Karran and Lucy Mallinson (2017) 'Academic Freedom in the UK: Legal and Normative Protection in a Comparative Context' *Report for the University and College Union*, University of Lincoln.

Senate Standing Committee on Education, Employment and Workplace Relations (2008) *Allegations of Academic Bias in Universities and Schools: Report*, Commonwealth of Australia.

Workplace Relations, Small Business and Education References Committee (2001) *Universities in Crisis*, Parliament of Australia.

Part 3

Meta-Structures

Chapter 12

Loneliness in Legal Education and the Legal Profession

Chin Chin Sia

Introduction

In recent years, the issues of loneliness and social isolation have gained increased attention and focus,[1] especially with the outbreak of Covid-19 globally. The first ever joint online meeting was held between the British Minister for Civil Society and Loneliness, Baroness Barran, and the Japanese Minister for Loneliness and Isolation, Tetsushi Sakamoto, on 17 June 2021 during Loneliness Awareness Week.[2] Both countries will share data and information on how loneliness is affecting their citizens, their policy and measurement approaches, and the learning shared between government, academics, and other stakeholders in order to increase global awareness of loneliness, and always be informed by the views of people who have experienced loneliness.

Among the various professions and occupations,[3] in 2018, lawyers were ranked as the loneliest profession in the US in a longitudinal survey published in *Harvard Business Review*.[4] Lawyers outranked other professionals on a 'loneliness scale' in a survey of more than 1600 workers. In a breakdown of loneliness and social support rates by profession, legal practice was the loneliest kind of work, followed by engineering and science. In the same study, graduate degree holders in the sample reported higher levels of loneliness and less workplace support than respondents who had only completed undergraduate or high school degrees. Law and medical degree holders were the loneliest by far, scoring 25% lonelier than other degrees, and 20% lonelier than PhDs. The phenomenon of loneliness among law students and legal professions is closely linked to the concept of biopolitics in legal education. The concept of biopolitics has been used and developed in social theory by Michel Foucault[5] to examine the strategies and

1 Cacioppo and Cacioppo (2018), pp 391–2.
2 Department for Digital, Culture, Media & Sport, Office for Civil Society, and Baroness Barran MBE, 'Joint message from the UK and Japanese Loneliness Ministers', www.gov.uk/government/news/joint-message-from-the-uk-and-japanese-loneliness-ministers, 17 June 2021.
3 Murthy (2017), pp 9–10.
4 Achor et al. (2018).
5 Foucault (1982), pp 777–95.

DOI: 10.4324/9781003175193-16

mechanisms through which human life processes are managed under regimes of authority over knowledge, power, and the processes of subjectivation. The problem of loneliness in the context of the politicisation of 'life' within the sphere of legal education is to be critically analysed in order to demonstrate how current legal education systems and the nature of the legal profession incentivise, normalise, and reward a winner-take-all mentality and mindset by law school in general.[6] This is one of the major malaises and existential crises in legal education systems,[7] despite variance in course design which occurs in different jurisdictions across the UK, Germany, and the US.[8] It is striking how characteristics of 'thinking like a lawyer' parallel the state of excessive vigilance: an increased emphasis on self-preservation, risk-aversion, and contribution to the feeling loneliness. The traditional methods of teaching law are one of the major causes leading to psychological distress in law students according to some studies.[9] With the widespread use of digital platforms during and post-pandemic, the teaching and learning of law is seen as an instrument which could cause law students to further slip down the scale of loneliness, resulting from automated analysis of data profiles, rather than recognition of individuality.[10]

An Analysis of the Definition and Features of Loneliness

Loneliness is defined as a state of emotional distress from lacking desired interpersonal relationships. It focuses on internal or perceived social isolation which refers to the person's perceptions of loneliness, trust, and satisfaction with their relationships. A person can have the subjective experience of being isolated and lonely even when they have regular contact with other people. Conversely, they may not feel isolated even when their contact with others is restricted. The 2020 Cigna survey[11] suggests that—Generation Z (adults ages 18–22) and Millennials (adults ages 23–37) are lonelier and claim to be in worse health than older generations; students have a higher loneliness score than retirees; and this survey indicate no major difference in the level of loneliness between women and men or between races (Figure 12.1).

Loneliness impacts both physical and psychological health.[12] Loneliness is a concern for our economy since it has been found that lonely workers perform more poorly, are more likely to quit, and have lower job satisfaction.[13] On 19 August 2018, a local fellow lawyer in Malaysia committed suicide in Solaris

6 Giulia Walter and Filippo Contarini (this volume).
7 Luca Siliquini-Cinelli, in the *Biopolitics and Resistance in Legal Education* volume.
8 Jane Ching (this volume).
9 Sheldon and Krieger (2007), pp 883–97.
10 Bruce Baer Arnold (this volume).
11 Cigna (2020).
12 Rubinstein (1986).
13 Bowers et al. (2022), pp 18–19.

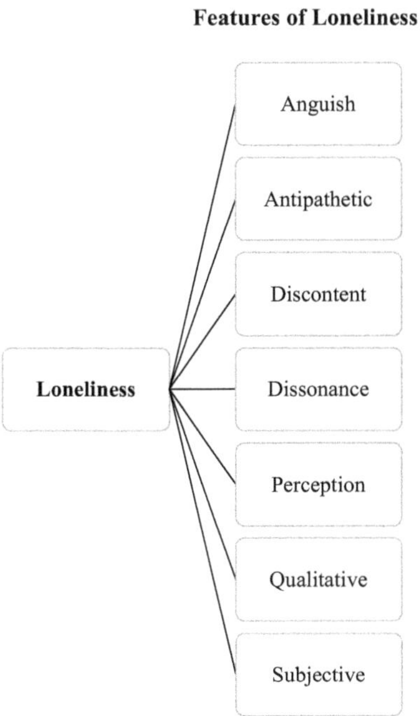

Figure 12.1 Features of Loneliness. Figure adapted from Ash (2019).

Dutamas, Kuala Lumpur. He was only 45 years old, leaving behind his two children.[14] Loneliness and social isolation can increase the risk of suicide and, conversely, having strong human bonds can be protective against it. Currently in Asia, there is a lack of data in relation to loneliness among law students, and within the legal profession. This chapter aims to explore the following from the lens of biopolitics:

(1) What is loneliness, who is lonely, and how does it impact an individual?
(2) Current research on well-being and loneliness in the legal profession
(3) Results from a loneliness survey of law students conducted in July 2019

Loneliness Research as an Evolution

A leading researcher in the field of loneliness, John T Cacioppo of the University of Chicago,[15] evaluated the science behind behaviours common to and driving

14 Praktis, 'Suicide and lawyers', www.praktis.com.my/all-articles/suicide-and-lawyers#_ftn1, 28 September 2018.

15 Spithoven et al. (2019), pp 376–96.

loneliness. Cacioppo's theory of loneliness is based on principles of evolution. In addition, he also studied the neuroendocrinology associated with loneliness. The literature also indicates loneliness may contribute to the next public health crisis resulting from the pandemic. In the US, a study estimated lawyers report the highest rates of depression among professionals.[16] Judges suffer mental health challenges too, citing daily stressors such as endless caseloads, severe time limitations, social isolation, lack of privacy, and the weight of deciding others' fates. An American Bar Association study indicated 28% of lawyers exhibited some type of depression within the year, four times the rate of the general population. Furthermore, 61% of lawyers reported struggling with depression at some time in their career, nearly ten times the general population.

Based on the Foucauldian theory of the subject and power, the empirical analysis of certain disciplines, including law and education, shows the way in which systems of objective finality and systems of communication and power can be welded together. In the legal education and profession, these models of articulations are visible in the following phases of life of a lawyer:

(1) Finalising educational activities (as in undergraduate or postgraduate legal education)
(2) Relationships of communication (as in the sphere of pupillage or traineeship)
(3) Giving pre-eminence to power relations and obedience (as in partner and junior associates of a legal firm, or as in counsel and judge in the courtroom)

From the analysis above in the context of biopolitics, in legal education and the profession, the interplay of subject and power is ever present, from the birth of a law student till the death of a legal practitioner.

To be a good lawyer, one has to be a healthy lawyer. Sadly, our profession is falling short when it comes to well-being.[17] The American Bar Association's report revealed that too many lawyers and law students experience chronic stress and high rates of depression and substance use. The reasons for this are complicated and varied, but some include the reluctance of lawyers to ask for help when they need it, high levels of depression amongst legal professionals, and the stressful nature of the job. These findings are incompatible with a sustainable legal profession,[18] and they raise troubling implications for many lawyers' basic competence.

In the US, Larry Krieger and Ken Sheldon[19] researched law student well-being at two separate law schools, publishing their initial results in 2004, with

16 Bruce et al. (2019).
17 Lawson (2021).
18 Hellberg and Knutsson (2018), pp 93–107.
19 Sheldon and Krieger (2014), pp 219–26.

further results published in 2007. Sheldon and Krieger measured law students' subjective well-being (referred to as SWB), by assessing their mood, life satisfaction, and physical health. The results indicated that at the start of law school, students tend to have a positive SWB as compared with undergraduates. One year into law school, the results indicated a decline in SWB and an increase in physical health problems. When the study was expanded to include students from more than just one law school, the results supported the previous findings of an overall decline in law student well-being after a year in law school.

Similarly, in 2014 the Yale Law School Mental Health Alliance published a report on the mental health of Yale Law students.[20] Half of the respondents agreed that mental health challenges impaired law school academic performance, and just over half agreed that mental health challenges affected them socially.[21] In Asia, large gaps remain in the literature and the empirical data on the loneliness of law students and their well-being. Only a handful of studies have been published on the issue on loneliness among general university students in China and Japan,[22] and none specifically on law students. The loneliness issue is underexplored specifically within the context of biopolitics, which concerns the administering and regulating the conditions of life at the aggregated level of the law student population.

What Is Loneliness, Who Is Lonely, and Power Struggles of an Individual

What Is Loneliness?

Loneliness is a subjective, unwelcome feeling of lack or loss of companionship, which happens when we have a mismatch between the quantity and quality of social relationships that we have, and those that we want. It is often associated with social isolation, but people can and do feel lonely even when in a relationship or when surrounded by others.[23] The evolutionary model of loneliness[24] posits that perceived social isolation or loneliness is a serious risk factor, which increases hypervigilance for social threat accompanied by physical and mental health consequences (e.g., stress, negative thinking and expectation of negative social information and interaction, anxiety, and depression).[25] From the perspective of biopolitics, loneliness could be seen as the effect of struggle by the minority (i.e., those who are experiencing more loneliness) against the

20 Organ et al. (2016), pp 116–56.
21 Ayres et al. (2017), pp 118–19.
22 Xie at al. (2020), pp 20–1.
23 Office for National Statistics (2018), pp 2–6.
24 Cacioppo and Cacioppo (2018), p 426.
25 Ypsilanti (2018), pp 144–6.

domination of the majority in the mainstream (i.e., those who are experiencing less loneliness).

Who Is Lonely?

Loneliness affects people of all ages and from all backgrounds—from the schoolchild who struggles to make friends, to the new parent coping alone, to the older person who has outlived her friends and immediate family.[26] Feelings of loneliness affect us all at some point, but being lonely can become a serious problem when it becomes chronic.[27]

For law students, there are specific factors that impact their well-being.[28] Some have suggested that law students may have certain inherent personality characteristics[29] that exacerbate levels of anxiety such as perfectionism and competitiveness.[30] Others have speculated as to whether the traditional methods of teaching law cause psychological distress[31] in law students. Or that perhaps law students acquire, through their law school education, certain values and attitudes that exacerbate levels of anxiety such as excessively high value placed on status and materialism.[32] Based on some of these factors, the impact of loneliness is likely to be more significant among law students[33] and young lawyers.[34] In 2018, a British study of 2393 participants with ages ranging from 15 to 97 years old indicated the highest levels of loneliness are in those younger than 25 years and older than 65 years of age.[35]

Even back in 1966, a study in the US demonstrated that in a classification of law students as 'thinkers' and 'feelers', students classified as 'thinking' types made up 72% of the law school, compared to only 54% of other undergraduates.[36] Of these 'thinking' types, only 11% eventually dropped out of law school, compared to 20% of the 'feeling' types. The 'thinker' is dependable and practical with a realistic respect for facts, who absorbs and remembers great numbers of facts while able to cite cases to support evaluations, and who emphasises logical analysis and decisiveness. The 'feeler' is chiefly concerned with people who value harmonious human contact, is friendly, tactful, sympathetic, and loyal, who is warmed by approval and bothered by indifference

26 Williams and Braun (2019), pp 7–14.
27 Barreto et al. (2021), pp 169–71.
28 Organ et al. (2016), pp 116–56.
29 Counts and John-Henderson (2020).
30 Counts and John-Henderson (2019), pp 1–6.
31 Scott (2018), pp 635–72.
32 Skead and Rogers (2015), pp 81–90.
33 Ash and Huang (2021).
34 Hurley (1987), pp 9–12.
35 Macdonald (2018), pp 88–94.
36 Miller (1966), pp 460–2.

and tends to idealise those he or she admires. This inherent characteristic of 'thinker' may have a higher tendency of falling into the trap of loneliness, as depicted by the one and only sculpture of *Le Pensuer* by Auguste Rodin.

From the lens of biopolitics, the law school is seemingly a 'block' in which the adjustment of abilities, resources of communication, and power relations constitute a regulated and concerted system. A law school constitutes a block of capacity-communication-power by providing its space, governing its internal life through meticulous regulations, organising different activities, and letting people with their own functions and well-defined characters meet or live with one another. Certain types of behaviour are developed there by means of a whole ensemble of regulated communications, for instance through lectures, seminars, questions and answers, coded signs of obedience, differentiation of scores of the 'value' of each person, and of the level of knowledge.[37]

Loneliness and Power Struggles of an Individual

Research indicates that loneliness is often associated with behavioural and mental health problems.[38] In clinical problems such as suicide, alcoholism, or depression, loneliness is often involved.[39] The available evidence suggests that loneliness is associated with poor mental health. Research found that lonely respondents scored higher on Eysenck's neuroticism scale and were more frequently judged in a structured psychiatric examination as having mental symptoms needing treatment.

Among undergraduates, loneliness was associated with indices of poor personality integration,[40] neurosis, and general maladjustment derived from the Tennessee Scale.[41] Studies also reported a strong relationship between loneliness and a checklist of psychosomatic symptoms such as headaches, poor appetite, and feeling tired. Loneliness is strongly correlated with anxiety[42] and a strong correlation is found between loneliness and Zung's Clinical Index of Potential Suicide.

A number of studies have documented an association between loneliness and aggressive tendencies. More research suggests that loneliness in males is associated with aggression towards women and proclivity towards rape.[43]

Further evidence linking loneliness with social problems can be seen in studies showing loneliness is associated with poor grades,[44] expulsion from

37 Foucault (1982), p 787.
38 Counts and John-Henderson (2019), pp 1–6.
39 Perlman and Peplau (1981), pp 31–56.
40 Oakley (2020) pp 29–30.
41 Lobdell and Perlman (1986), pp 589–95.
42 Russel et al. (1980), p 472.
43 Check et al. (1985), pp 243–52.
44 Nicpon et al. (2006), pp 345–58.

school,[45] running away from home, and engaging in delinquent acts such as theft, gambling, and vandalism.[46] The literature clearly indicates that loneliness is often associated with behavioural and mental health problems.

The evidence cited above comes from studies that have focused specifically on loneliness. It seems likely that studies of clinical problems such as suicide, alcoholism, or depression would find that loneliness is often involved.

Upon graduation from university or dropping out from college, lonelier workers[47] reported lower job satisfaction, fewer promotions, more frequent job switching,[48] and a higher likelihood of quitting their current job in the next six months. Feeling a lack of workplace social support was associated with similar negative business outcomes. The economic impact of loneliness is indeed staggering.[49] The US government spends almost US$7 billion on loneliness-related healthcare expenses per year.

In the context of power struggles, based on Foucault, generally there are three types of struggles, firstly against domination (ethnic, social, and religious), secondly against exploitation which separates individuals from what they produce, and lastly against that which ties the individual to himself and submits him to others in this way (struggles against subjection, subjectivity, and submission). Social struggles created by loneliness are akin to that of the last type of struggle, in which it is a struggle against that which ties the individual to themselves and submits them to others in this way. This occurs when the individual struggles to be subjected to the mainstream work or study culture in legal education and in the profession.

Current Research on Well-Being and Loneliness in the Legal Profession

Lawyers (along with physicians) are among the most isolated of professionals, reporting levels of loneliness 25% higher than the average population in the US.[50] The legal profession is, by nature, high stress and high stakes—often with clients' livelihoods or liberty on the line, and frequently involving confrontational interactions with adversaries, government agencies, and in court.[51] Additional stresses include rigid and competitive law firm hierarchies, long work hours and clients' growing expectations of 24-hour service, a work hard/play hard after-work culture, and a profession where reputations are built on demonstrated toughness, high ethical standards, and perfectionism.

45 Rönkä et al. (2017), pp 93–106.
46 Elran-Barak et al. (2022).
47 Bruce et al. (2019).
48 Moens et al. (2021).
49 McDaid et al. (2017).
50 Greenawald (2020), pp 20–4.
51 Buchanan et al. (2017).

In 2016, a study commissioned by the American Bar Association, in conjunction with the Hazelden Betty Ford Foundation,[52] was published in the *Journal of Addiction Medicine*. This report elaborates the widespread and pervasive problems of mental health, substance use, and lawyer well-being, and has captured the public's attention. The study analysed data gathered from 12,825 lawyers, presented some unsettling statistics, particularly with respect to young lawyers: 20.6% of respondents exhibited signs of problem drinking, with the rate of problem alcohol use markedly higher among younger associates (31.9% of attorneys aged 30 and under reported alcohol-related issues). Among those who used drugs (both legal and illicit), 74.1% used stimulants, 51.3% used sedatives, and 21.6% used opioids. Notably, only a fraction of respondents (6.8%) stated that they had sought treatment for drugs or alcohol—and many cited concerns about confidentiality as the main obstacle to seeking help.

The study also found that 28% of lawyers suffer from depression, 19% reported problems with anxiety, 23% suffer from stress, and that lawyers exhibit increased levels of suicide, work addiction, and sleep deprivation. These sobering findings, especially with respect to young lawyers, have raised serious concerns about the health and competence of lawyers in an increasingly demanding profession.

Results from a Loneliness Survey of Law Students Conducted in July 2019

Methodology

Before recruiting participants to the study, approval was granted by an institutional review board. To obtain a sample of students within the law school, recruitment was coordinated through the module leaders in the law school. Among them, five module leaders were requested to email the survey to their students and acquaintances in the legal profession. Those module leaders were instructed to send three recruitment emails over a one-month period to all students who were currently law students or graduated less than five years ago. The email provided a brief synopsis of the study and past research in this area, described the goals of the study, and provided a URL directing people to the consent form and an electronic survey via Google Form. Participants completed the survey (Appendix 1) with 28 questions in total (adapted from the Revised UCLA Loneliness Scale, Russell and Peplau (1980)). There were 20 closed (four-point Likert) questions, seven demographic questions (Age, Gender, Ethnicity, Enrolled Course) and one open-ended question (Suggestions to reduce the negative effects of loneliness). Participants were not asked for identifying information, thus allowing them to complete the survey anonymously.

52 Krill et al. (2016), pp 46–7.

Because of concerns regarding potential identification of individual students, email addresses were not tracked.

Findings and Analysis

The findings of the survey are shown in Table 12.1.

For question 1, around one-third of the participants rarely find themselves to be in tune with the people around them. This can be a significant issue if this becomes a prolonged phenomenon.

Around 42 per cent of participants feel they are sometimes/often lacking in companionship. As for whether or not there is someone to turn to, again around 40 per cent of the students sometimes/often find there is no one they can turn to.

Pertaining to question 4 on the feeling of being alone or not, around 38 per cent of the participants never/rarely do not feel alone. As to whether or not the participants feel they are part of a group of friends, around 33% never/ rarely feel they are part of a group of friends.

On the question of whether or not the participants have a lot in common with the people around them, 45% rarely/ feel they have a lot in common.

Table 12.1 Percentages of participants' answers to the questions posed

No.	*Questions*	*% of 1 (Never)*	*% of 2 (Rarely)*	*% of 3 (Sometimes)*	*% of 4 (Often)*
1	I feel in tune with the people around me	3.5	29.8	61.4	5.3
2	I lack companionship	7.0	50.9	29.8	12.3
3	There is no one I can turn to	14.0	45.6	28.1	12.3
4	I do not feel alone	12.3	26.3	45.6	15.8
5	I feel part of a group of friends	7.0	26.3	43.9	22.8
6	I have a lot in common with the people around me	7.0	38.6	36.8	17.5
7	I am no longer close to anyone	28.1	22.8	33.3	15.8
8	My interests and ideas are not shared by those around me	8.8	35.1	43.9	12.3
9	I am an outgoing person	1.8	36.8	38.6	22.8
10	There are people I feel close to	1.8	15.8	49.1	33.3
11	I feel left out	12.3	26.3	43.9	17.5
12	My social relationships are superficial	10.5	42.1	31.6	15.8
13	No one really knows me well	8.8	28.1	36.8	26.3
14	I feel isolated from others	14.0	38.6	33.3	14.0
15	I can find companionship when I want it	8.8	17.5	47.4	26.3
16	There are people who really understand me	7.0	22.8	45.6	24.6
17	I am unhappy being so withdrawn	12.3	54.4	24.6	8.8
18	People are around me but not with me	8.8	36.8	40.4	14.0
19	There are people I can talk to	1.8	15.8	45.6	36.8
20	There are people I can turn to	7.0	19.3	42.1	31.6

Moving on to question 7, approximately 49% of participants feel they are sometimes/often no longer close to anyone. In addition, 64% of participants feel their interests and ideas are sometimes/often not shared by those around them. As to whether or not the participant considers themselves as an outgoing person, around 40% never/rarely think they are outgoing at all.

On question 10 regarding feeling close to others, around 18% never/rarely feel there are people they feel close to. For the feeling of being left out, an alarming 61% of the participants sometimes/often feel left out.

In a nutshell, based on the findings of the survey, it can be seen that loneliness is a real issue which is being neglected among Asian law students. However, it is encouraging to observe that some meaningful suggestions were made by the participants to overcome loneliness (see Table 12.2).

Conclusion

The results of the loneliness survey of law students at our law school reinforce the well-documented fact that law students experience higher levels of loneliness, stress, anxiety, and depression than university students not in law school. Through analysis of survey data from 57 law students, it is clear that our students in the law school do suffer from loneliness.

Whilst feelings of loneliness among peers and in the wider university community may impact on student well-being, some law students—about half of the respondents—were able to be proactive in suggesting ways to reduce loneliness.

There is an urgent need within law schools to start to tackle the phenomena of loneliness in the legal profession. If the current legal education regime, which has led to the formation and perpetuation of unhealthy identities in the lives of the students and profession, remains unchallenged, this is likely to lead to a downward spiral of severe power struggles to combat this phenomenon. Loneliness is not only harmful for our health, but also for the legal profession itself. Loneliness can contribute to a constellation of physical and psychiatric dysfunctions and psychosocial risk factors that may include depression, anxiety, aggression, impulsivity, alcoholism, and suicidal thoughts. A well-developed understanding of the biopolitics, biology and psychology of the loneliness epidemic is essential. It is necessary to recognise this and aid in the creation of supportive authentic social connections among fellow learned friends. People who have strong social connections with their colleagues are more likely to be resilient, more productive, and less likely to suffer loneliness-related illness. These strong connections also foster increased self-efficacy and self-esteem, which buffers us when we face stressful situations, such as the pandemic. If loneliness is not recognised and is left to grow, there will be increased health-related expenditures, including for illness, missed days, and treatment. All the law schools which have great aspirations[53] for the health and well-being of

53 Talib et al. (2017), pp 134–50.

Table 12.2 Some suggestions by participants of how to overcome loneliness

More open and honest conversation about the struggles dealt with in the legal industry and less judgement/prejudice towards mental health, as well as a change in mindset—working together as opposed to competing against each other
Mutual understanding with friends
Supervised group work and or individual assignments
Reach out, there is always someone …
Surround yourself with people that makes you feel like home
De-romanticise the idea of having a partner/other half and single being equivalent to loneliness
As an international student I can understand why I feel loneliness it might be because we as students we came from different back grounds and especially in Taylor's I do feel alone and I used to it. I can't wait to finish my studies and go back home.. but this made me stronger …
Nothing the institution can do. It's more of a cultural/social problem with uni students in Malaysia
Even in law school, I can't find people with the same thoughts and feelings as I do. Many students are too childish for my taste and possess an aversion for anything intellectual, contrary to popular stereotypes
Go out and socialise sometimes
I don't know but tell me once you know
Talk to more people. Find more friends. Play musical instruments
Force law students to participate in more social activities which are fun and stimulating at the same time—but not competitive, as most law students are already very competitive in nature
Everybody needs to stop being ego to themselves and to one another
I can't seem to find a way myself
More group assignment
Mindfulness and meditation
Improve the counselling facilities on campus
Law schools should prioritise more in a work–balance lifestyle. Too often students are cooped up in their rooms to finish up tutorials (and some have 12 long questions that are *All* required to be answered!) thus not being able to spend time on other things
Talk less about legal issues and government policies
Talk to family when you're feeling alone. They will be your best listener and also they are the best companion ever
Plan your time wisely and put some time away to get out and try something new which you could be interested in
Reaching out to people
Being yourself and be less dependent on others in daily life
Listening to music and watching drama
Open up to people around you
Focus less on law, more balancing in social life
Accept that being alone is not a bad thing—then we feel less lonely
Keep yourself busy with other things, e.g. exercising, go out for a walk, explore nature, talk to friends/family

the legal profession, especially in the Southeast Asian region, should start to look at loneliness from a biopolitical perspective. Loneliness, as an acute health epidemic among our students, ought to be prioritised in order to achieve the holistic goal of the well-being of the legal profession in the post-pandemic era. The current legal education regime is to be further critically analysed from the lens of biopolitics to combat the struggle against the loneliness phenomena which prevails in law schools across the globe.

Human Ethics Approval

The study was conducted with the approval of the author's university in accordance with the institutional human ethics policy.

References

Shawn Achor et al. (2018) 'America's Loneliest Workers, According to Research' *Harvard Business Review*, https://hbr.org/2018/03/americas-loneliest-workers-according-to-research.

Ian Ayres Ian et al (2017) 'Anxiety Psychoeducation for Law Students: A Pilot Program' *Journal of Legal Education* 118.

Olivia Ash (2019) 'The Prevalence and Effects of Loneliness in the General Population, Lawyer Well-being, and a Survey of Law Students', https://papers.ssrn.com/sol3/papers.cfm?abstract_id=3390457.

Olivia Ash and Peter H Huang (2021) 'Loneliness in COVID-19, Life, and the Law', https://papers.ssrn.com/sol3/papers.cfm?abstract_id=3793900.

Manuela Barreto et al. (2021) 'Loneliness Around the World: Age, Gender, and Cultural Differences in Loneliness' 196 *Personality and Individual Differences* 110066.

Anne Bowers et al. (2022) 'Loneliness Influences Avoidable Absenteeism and Turnover Intention Reported by Adult Workers in the United States' 9 *Journal of Organizational Effectiveness: People and Performance* 312.

John T Cacioppo and Stephanie Cacioppo (2018) 'The Growing Problem of Loneliness' 391 *The Lancet* 426.

James VP Check, Daniel Perlman and Neil M Malamuth (1985) 'Loneliness and Aggressive Behaviour' 2 *Journal of Social and Personal Relationships* 243.

Cigna (2020) 'U.S. Loneliness Index', https://newsroom.cigna.com/loneliness-in-america.

Cory J Counts and Neha A John-Henderson (2020) 'Risk in Childhood Family Environments and Loneliness in College Students: Implications for Health' 68 *Journal of American College Health* 381.

Cory J Counts and Neha A John-Henderson (2019) 'Diminished Cardiovascular Stress Reactivity is Associated with Lower Levels of Social Participation'118 *Journal of Psychosomatic Research* 12.

Liana DesHarnais Bruce et al. (2019) 'Loneliness in the United States: A 2018 National Panel Survey of Demographic, Structural, Cognitive, and Behavioral Characteristics' 33 *American Journal of Health Promotion* 1133.

Roni Elran-Barak et al. (2022) 'Neighborhood Violence and Health: The Mediating Role of Loneliness Among Two Ethnic Groups in Israel' *Health Promotion International*, https://doi.org/10.1093/heapro/daac028.

Michel Foucault (1982) 'The Subject and Power' 8 *Critical Inquiry* 777.

Mark H Greenawald (2020) 'Creating Intentional Professional Connections to Reduce Loneliness, Isolation, and Burnout' 27 *Family Practice Management* 20.

Dan Hurley (1987) 'Why are Young Lawyers the Loneliest People in the Profession' 14 *Barrister* 9.

Sofie Hellberg and Beniamin Knutsson (2018) 'Sustaining the Life-chance Divide? Education for Sustainable Development and the Global Biopolitical Regime' 59 *Critical Studies in Education* 93.

Patrick R Krill, Ryan Johnson and Linda Albert (2016) 'The Prevalence of Substance Use and Other Mental Health Concerns Among American Attorneys' 10 *Journal of Addiction Medicine* 46.

Nicholas D Lawson (2021) 'To Be a Good Lawyer, One Has to Be a Healthy Lawyer: Lawyer Well-Being, Discrimination, and Discretionary Systems of Discipline' 34 *Georgetown Journal of Legal Ethics* 65.

Judith Lobdell and Daniel Perlman (1986) 'The Intergenerational Transmission of Loneliness: A study of College Females and their Parents' 48 *Journal of Marriage and the Family* 589.

Stephen J Macdonald, J Nixon and L Deacon (2018) '"Loneliness in the City": Examining Socio-Economics, Loneliness and Poor Health in the North East of England' 186 *Public Health* 88.

David McDaid, Annette Bauer and A-La Park (2017) *Making the Economic Case for Investing in Actions to Prevent and/or Tackle Loneliness: A Systematic Review*, London School of Economics and Political Science, www.lse.ac.uk/business/consulting/reports/making-the-economic-case-for-investing-in-actions-to-prevent-and-or-tackle-loneliness.

Eline Moens et al. (2021) 'Does Loneliness Lurk in Temp Work? Exploring the Associations Between Temporary Employment, Loneliness at Work and Job Satisfaction' 16 *PloS One*, https://doi.org/10.1371/journal.pone.0250664.

Vivek Murthy (2017) 'Work and the Loneliness Epidemic' 9 *Harvard Business Review* 3.

Megan Foley Nicpon, et al (2015) 'The Relationship of Loneliness and Social Support with College Freshmen's Academic Performance and Persistence' 8 *Journal of College Student Retention: Research, Theory & Practice* 345.

Lee Oakley (2020) *Exploring Student Loneliness in Higher Education*, Springer International Publishing.

Jerome M Organ, David B Jaffe, and Katherine M Bender (2016) 'Suffering in Silence: The Survey of Law Student Well-being and the Reluctance of Law Students to Seek Help for Substance use and Mental Health Concerns' 66 *Journal of Legal Education* 116.

Daniel Perlman and L Anne Peplau (1981) 'Toward a Social Psychology of Loneliness' 3 *Personal Relationships* 31.

Anna Reetta Rönkä et al. (2017) 'Associations between School Liking, Loneliness and Social Relations Among Adolescents: Northern Finland Birth Cohort 1986 Study' 22 *International Journal of Adolescence and Youth* 93.

Robert L Rubinstein (1986) *Singular Paths: Old Men Living Alone*, Columbia University Press.

Dan Russell, Letitia A Peplau and Carolyn E Cutrona (1980) 'The Revised UCLA Loneliness Scale: Concurrent and Discriminant Validity Evidence' 39 *Journal of Personality and Social Psychology* 472.

Charity Scott (2018) 'Mindfulness in Law: A Path to Well-being and Balance for Lawyers and Law Students' 60 *Arizona State Law Journal* 635.

Kennon M Sheldon and Lawrence S Krieger (2007) 'Understanding the Negative Effects of Legal Education on Law Students: A Longitudinal Test of Self-Determination Theory' 33(6) *Journal of Personality and Social Psychology* 883.

Kennon M Sheldon and Lawrence S Krieger (2014) 'Service Job Lawyers are Happier than Money Job Lawyers, Despite their Lower Income' 9 *The Journal of Positive Psychology* 219.

Natalie K Skead and Shane L Rogers (2015) 'Do Law Students Stand apart from Other University Students in their Quest for Mental Health: A Comparative Study on Wellbeing and Associated Behaviours in Law and Psychology Students' 42 *International Journal of Law and Psychiatry* 81.

Annette WM Spithoven et al (2019) 'Genetic Contributions to Loneliness and their Relevance to The Evolutionary Theory of Loneliness' 14 *Perspectives on Psychological Science* 376.

Talib et al. (2017) 'Aspirations of a Young Law School: Process, Content and Direction' 1 *The Law Review* 134.

Sue E Williams and Bonnie Braun (2019) 'Loneliness and Social Isolation—A Private Problem, a Public Issue' 111 *Journal of Family and Consumer Sciences* 7.

Ying Xie et al. (2020) 'Comparison of Causes of Loneliness and Coping Behaviors Among Japanese and Chinese University Student Sample' 67 *Juntendo Medical Journal* 46

Antonia Ypsilanti (2018) 'Lonely but Avoidant—The Unfortunate Juxtaposition of Loneliness and Self-Disgust' 4 *Palgrave Communications* 1.

Reports

Bree Buchanan et al. (2017) 'The Path to Lawyer Well-Being: Practical Recommendations for Positive Change (The Report of the National Task Force on Lawyer Well-Being), Part II, Recommendations for Law Schools'.

Office for National Statistics (2018) 'Loneliness – What Characteristics and Circumstances are Associated with Feeling Lonely?' *Analysis of Characteristics and Circumstances Associated with Loneliness in England Using the Community Life Survey, 2016 to 2017*, www.ons.gov.uk/peoplepopulationandcommunity/wellbeing/articles/lonelinesswhatcharacteristicsandcircumstancesareassociatedwithfeelinglonely/2018-04-10.

Appendix 1: Loneliness in Law Survey 2019 Questions

You are invited to complete this survey in investigating the interaction between loneliness and the law; more specifically, the extent to which law students and legal professionals feel lonely. You were selected as a participant because you are a current law student, legal academic, lawyer, or in the legal profession. There are a total of 28 questions and it takes less than 10 minutes to complete them. The questions are adapted from the Revised UCLA Loneliness Scale (Russell and Peplau, 1980). Many thanks for your time and active participation!

Feel free to contact Sia Chin Chin from Taylor's University, Faculty of Business and Law, Taylor's Law School for further information or details.

Your ethnic group

- Chinese
- Eurasian
- Indian
- Malay
- Other:

Your gender

- Female
- Male

What is the highest degree of education you have earned?

- High School Diploma
- Undergraduate Degree
- Master's Degree
- Doctorate Degree
- Other:

Which of the following BEST describes your current status with respect to the legal profession?

- Law Student—Full Time
- Law Student—Part Time
- Practising Lawyer
- Non-Practising Lawyer
- Law Academic
- Paralegal
- Other:

Please choose the law programme you are currently enrolled on, or if you are no longer a student, the most advanced law programme you have completed. (Note: If you did not complete any of the programmes listed, please choose 'Other')

- BPTC (Bar Professional Training Course)
- CLP (Certificate of Legal Practice)
- JD
- LLB
- LLM
- Other:

If you *Are* a law student, what is your year of school? (Note: If you are *Not* a law student, choose 'N/A')

- Year 1
- Year 2
- Year 3
- Year 4 and above
- N/A

If you are *Not* a current law student, how many years have you been in the legal field? (Note: If you *Are* a current law student, please choose 'N/A')

- 0–5 years
- 5–10 years
- 10–15 years
- 15–20 years
- 20–25 years
- 25–30 years
- 30 years and above
- N/A

I feel in tune with the people around me

- 1=Never
- 2=Rarely
- 3=Sometimes
- 4=Often

I lack companionship

- 1=Never
- 2=Rarely

- 3=Sometimes
- 4=Often

There is no one I can turn to

- 1=Never
- 2=Rarely
- 3=Sometimes
- 4=Often

I do not feel alone

- 1=Never
- 2=Rarely
- 3=Sometimes
- 4=Often

I feel part of a group of friends

- 1=Never
- 2=Rarely
- 3=Sometimes
- 4=Often

I have a lot in common with the people around me

- 1=Never
- 2=Rarely
- 3=Sometimes
- 4=Often

I am no longer close to anyone

- 1=Never
- 2=Rarely
- 3=Sometimes
- 4=Often

My interests and ideas are not shared by those around me

- 1=Never
- 2=Rarely
- 3=Sometimes
- 4=Often

I am an outgoing person

- 1=Never
- 2=Rarely
- 3=Sometimes
- 4=Often

There are people I feel close to

- 1=Never
- 2=Rarely
- 3=Sometimes
- 4=Often

I feel left out

- 1=Never
- 2=Rarely
- 3=Sometimes
- 4=Often

My social relationships are superficial

- 1=Never
- 2=Rarely
- 3=Sometimes
- 4=Often

No one really knows me well

- 1=Never
- 2=Rarely
- 3=Sometimes
- 4=Often

I feel isolated from others

- 1=Never
- 2=Rarely
- 3=Sometimes
- 4=Often

I can find companionship when I want it

- 1=Never
- 2=Rarely

- 3=Sometimes
- 4=Often

There are people who really understand me

- 1=Never
- 2=Rarely
- 3=Sometimes
- 4=Often

I am unhappy being so withdrawn

- 1=Never
- 2=Rarely
- 3=Sometimes
- 4=Often

People are around me but not with me

- 1=Never
- 2=Rarely
- 3=Sometimes
- 4=Often

There are people I can talk to

- 1=Never
- 2=Rarely
- 3=Sometimes
- 4=Often

There are people I can turn to

- 1=Never
- 2=Rarely
- 3=Sometimes
- 4=Often

Suggestions to reduce the negative effects of loneliness? Please elaborate your answer.

Chapter 13

The 'Politics' of Responsible Social Media Use in Universities

Cautionary Tales for Student Experience?

Kim Barker and Olga Jurasz

Introduction

The rise of the internet and information and communications technologies has transformed teaching and learning, making it connected, accessible, and flexible. In doing so, higher education has followed the overall trend of the digitalisation of society which has also seen people's lives become increasingly intertwined between offline and online spaces, including social media. The experience of the COVID-19 pandemic has further reaffirmed the rise in demand for online forms of teaching and learning, rapidly forcing most of the higher education institutions in the UK—as well as worldwide—to transform their working and teaching practices in order to facilitate teaching online and at a distance.[1] Equally, this unprecedented disruption to the 'traditional' methods and spaces of teaching,[2] learning, and experiencing university brought to the fore a number of problematic issues facing higher education institutions today, prompting reflection about the practices within them, and the norms they foster. In particular, the changes to the higher education sector arising from the pandemic opened up questions about the current state of the biopolitics of higher education, including student welfare online,[3] not only under exceptional circumstances such as the pandemic.[4]

The increase in everyday use and reliance on social media has also been reflected amongst the demographic of university students—it is estimated that 88% of 16–24-year-olds had a social media profile in 2020,[5] with Facebook and Instagram being the most often used platforms amongst 16–24-year-olds.[6] Consequently, the broader social changes affecting university students and their experience of higher education is reflective of both positive and negative

1 It ought to be noted that certain institutions in the UK, such as The Open University, adopted this model years before the pandemic outbreak.
2 Barn (2020).
3 Scottish Women's Rights Centre (2020); Sladdin (2020); Phippen and Bond (2021).
4 Foucault (2003), p 244.
5 Statista (2021).
6 Ofcom (2021), p 31; 78% of 16–24-year-olds report using Instagram and 69% use Facebook.

DOI: 10.4324/9781003175193-17

impacts of the migration to online spaces. Amongst the latter, there has been a noticeable rise in recent years in cases of online abuse[7] and online hate[8] amongst university students, which also reflects the prevalence of such abusive behaviours on social media platforms more generally. Importantly, however, it is a bitter reminder that the higher education environment and its spaces are not immune to or separate from other socio-political changes, events, and phenomena. For instance, movements such as #MeToo or #BlackLivesMatter have prompted student voice and activism, speaking out against the prevalence of sexual harassment and violence in universities[9] (#MeTooOnCampus, #MeTooPhD) as well as about racial structural inequalities in higher education.[10]

This chapter reflects on the experiences of online abuse and online hate amongst university law students and places them in the broader context of the contemporary biopolitics of higher education in the UK, as well as social and legal developments addressing these phenomena. It problematises the issue of online abuse and online hate not only as a factor affecting students' experience in a modern marketised university landscape,[11] but also as an issue which highlights the need for a robust, meaningful, and modern approach towards social media regulation.

Old Problems, New Environments but Old Solutions?

In 2019, the Annual Review of English higher education carried out by the Office for Students identified hate crime, sexual violence, and harassment (both on and off campus) as 'significant issues for student wellbeing and safeguarding'[12] which also affect the student experience. Whilst the increased transparency in institutional and sectoral recognition of these abusive and violent behaviours is certainly a welcome step, these are—worryingly—not new findings. There have been long-standing concerns over the scale and commonality of harassment, hate, and violence experienced by students in university settings.[13] In particular, the prevalence of sexual harassment in higher education has been well documented in the literature and powerfully spoken

7 The term 'online abuse' is used here as an umbrella term which includes abusive and/or violent behaviours online which are communicated to the recipient online, typically using social media or other internet-based platforms. It includes, but is not limited to, online harassment, online bullying, online threats, online misogyny—including the racialised and/or religion-based and/or sexualised and/or gendered forms thereof.

8 Universities UK (2016), p 5, 10, 44; Universities UK (2019).

9 Zhou (2018); UN Women (2018), p 30; Das and Griffiths (2019); Hardy (2018); Duong et al. (2020).

10 Advance HE (2021); NUS (2020); Pittam (2020).

11 Nixon et al. (2018).

12 Office for Students (2019), p 46.

13 Perry (2010); Aljazeera Investigative Unit and Howlett (2021); Howlett and Aljazeera Investigative Unit (2021).

about following the #MeToo movement.[14] The National Union of Students has campaigned on this issue since 2010,[15] including the 'I heart consent' campaign which set out to combat rape culture by subverting problematic notions and myths surrounding sexual consent, questioning 'lad culture' and educating students about consent to sexual activity.[16] Equally, the concerns about experiences of hate among university students have been officially voiced for more than a decade,[17] with the NUS Reports[18] highlighting the impact of hate incidents on students, deficiencies in reporting systems and the need for the development of a cross-sectoral strategy 'to tackle hate and prejudice experienced by students in the UK'.[19]

In contrast, the issue of students being subjected to online abuse and online hate has only relatively recently been raised at the sectoral and policy levels in the UK, despite early indicators of these problems in the literature.[20] Undoubtedly, online spaces have become spaces of violence and abuse for a number of university students.[21] For example, Universities UK noted 'the growing prevalence of online harassment and hate crime' only in 2016[22] whilst acknowledging the complexity of managing this problem given the extensive and everyday use of social media by students.[23] In 2019, a further report specifically addressing online harassment and online welfare was issued by Universities UK, coinciding with the launch of the 2019 Online Harms White Paper (now the Online Safety Bill 2021).[24] The report, whilst paving the way towards addressing the issue at a sectoral level, is symptomatic of the broader issues affecting policies aiming at tacking online abusive behaviours: inconsistent and erroneous use of terminology (subsuming a number of different abusive behaviours under the umbrella term of harassment, which has a specific legal meaning and threshold), increasing visibility of some forms of online abuse whilst suppressing others (e.g. text-based (sexual) abuse), and significantly underestimating and misunderstanding the types and nature of harms arising from online abuse.[25] For instance, the infamous example of the female students at the University of Warwick being targeted by a male undergraduate

14 Phipps and Smith (2012); Tutchell and Edmonds (2020). Furthermore, see the website of Universities Supporting Victims of Sexual Violence: https://usvreact.eu/
15 Universities UK (2016).
16 NUS (2010); NUS (2015).
17 Universities UK (2005); Michael (2015), pp 157–9.
18 NUS (2011a); NUS (2011b); NUS (2012).
19 NUS (2011a), p 5.
20 Finn (2004).
21 Marsh (2019).
22 Universities UK (2016), p 5.
23 Ibid., p 30.
24 Universities UK (2019); HM Government (2019).
25 Barker and Jurasz (2020); (2021).

students' 'rape chat'[26] containing violent and sexual comments illustrates this detrimental dynamic which is replicated within policies on tackling online abuse and violence. Even though many UK universities have harassment and/ or abuse policies, their applicability is limited when abuse happens online due to the specific nature of online environments, applicable legal frameworks,[27] and unique nature of online harms arising from these forms of abuse.[28] For instance, the law has been reformed in recent years in England and Wales, and Scotland, to criminalise, for example, the non-consensual sharing of intimate images through the Criminal Justice & Courts Act 2015 s33(1) and the Abusive Behaviour and Sexual Harm (Scotland) Act 2016. These are not isolated examples—other examples include changes made to the stalking legislation in England and Wales through stalking protection orders via the Stalking Protection Act 2019, and legislation to prosecute 'downblousing' and 'upskirting'. These legal tweaks do not offer a comprehensive approach to the harms of online abuse(s) facilitated through social media, with the Online Safety Bill failing to include specific gendered protections. Similarly, piecemeal alterations to legal provisions do not, in isolation, address the harms caused by the behaviours the legislation is designed to tackle. The impact of online abuse via social media is significant and particularly harmful to women and girls' participation in society,[29] something especially damaging in educational settings. The harms are multifaceted and crosscutting, affecting all aspects of life. Universities are often ill-equipped to deal with such abuses not least because of their online aspect—traditional policies relating to sexual harassment often omit or overlook the digital aspect of abuse. Similarly, even where policies are general and *could* be applied to the online environment, there persist issues of reporting and signposting.

In addition, the universities' practices of (mis)handling and silencing[30] reported cases of violence and abuse—both online and offline[31]—further compounds the problem, contributing to injustice and the lack of appropriate and effective avenues for redress for students. The latter has also been a key reason why students have taken to share their stories of harassment, violence, and abuse at universities via social media and on the internet, recognising these spaces as more inclusionary than those offered through the formal institutional routes.[32] The lack of investigation(s), and lack of recognition is symptomatic of the general attitude towards instances of violence, and hate, evidenced most recently by the approach of some elite higher education institutions in respect

26 Batty (2019).
27 Barker and Jurasz (2019), Chapters 3 and 4.
28 Barker and Jurasz (2021).
29 Ibid.
30 Bradford (2020).
31 Cowan and Munro (2021).
32 See, for example: Jokic (2020); Oppenheim (2019); McGlynn and Furgalska (2019).

of sexual harassment in particular, with the University of Oxford adopting a policy of non-investigation unless or until there is an accompanying police report.[33] This approach does little to build confidence that institutions are concerned about instances of harassment, violence, and abuse—neither offline nor online.

Whilst a 2021 survey carried out by the Universities UK suggests progress in the institutional tackling of harassment and hate crime,[34] research from the UK as well as from Canada confirms significant deficiencies in universities' approaches to tackling online abuse (including online harassment) and online hate. Hodson, Gosse and Valetsianos found that only 41 out of 232 Canadian universities and colleges had policies which acknowledged online abuse and harassment, which proved to be limited in their scope.[35] Results of a study by Phippen and Bond confirm that UK universities pay lip service to tackling online abuse and harassment, with the overarching focus across the sector falling on 'the protection of the institution, rather than the support of students'.[36] For instance, almost 60% of the policies analysed in the study had no mention of 'online' whatsoever despite the institutions claiming coverage of online harassment and abuse,[37] with further worrying patterns of universities failing to provide specialist training on online abuse and showing very low levels of recorded incidents of online abuse.[38]

This raises a significant question: are universities well placed to protect students from online abuse and to respond to its reported instances? Whilst the policies tackling online abuse and harassment are likely to work their way into UK universities over time, the experience thus far indicates severe shortcomings in universities' understandings of the uniqueness of online abuse and, consequently, specific measures that need to be deployed to address online harms arising from it. However, apart from very few examples of good practice, the sector's policy approach is merely treating 'online' forms of abuse as an 'add-on' to the existing policies on harassment and other forms of abuse. This is evident in the Statement of Expectations by the Office of Students[39] which outlines recommendations to higher education providers in the UK regarding harassment and sexual misconduct: in a seven-page document, the word 'online' appears only once, to reaffirm that harassment and misconduct can be 'carried out through any medium, including online'.[40] Similarly, there are no references to online forms of abuse regulated by English law, such as image-based

33 Aljazeera Investigative Unit and Howlett (2021).
34 Universities UK (2021).
35 Hodson et al. (2021).
36 Phippen and Bond (2020), p 18.
37 Ibid., p 12.
38 Ibid., p 18.
39 Office for Students (2021); Phippen and Bond (2021).
40 Office for Students (2021), p 2.

sexual abuse, which does not feature under examples of 'sexual misconduct' outlined in the statement. Not only are the policies of institutions deficient in this area, but the broader policy approach from the Office for Students is remarkably naïve about the realities of encounters in modern society.

The current approach can be best described as a version of what Ahmed refers to as institutional polishing.[41] In this context, the 'institutional polishing' takes the form of creating inadequate policies on tackling online abuse to create an external image of a 'happy and safe institution' despite these disturbing occurrences of abuse and violence. This is particularly the case where gendered and racialised forms of online abuse are concerned whereby universities' public commitments to diversity, equality, and inclusion (also reflected in policies on these matters) clash with the lived experiences of online abuse by students. The created imagery of equality and diversity in universities is effectively undermined by online abuse (including manifestations of online hate) but even more so by the lack of direct, fair, and transparent action being taken by universities to provide justice to the affected students, leaving the language of equality and diversity as little more than a public relations exercise.[42]

Social Media and Student Experience

The rise, prevalence, and impact of social media abuse has been startling in recent years. The university sector has been somewhat late to recognise and address instances of online abuse, with full attention only being paid in the last two or three years. Given the rise in discussions relating to online abuse in other sectors such as professional sport, politics, and journalism, and the seriousness of such issues, the higher education sector must also pay attention to these problems, and at the very least investigate their prevalence and their impact upon the student body.

Given the difficulties with the recognition of online harassment, violence, and abuse in higher education institutions, there is a growing need to establish a body of data which gives insights into the reactions and experiences of students of social media abuse. The current research[43] was designed to explore some of that gap in knowledge, focusing specifically on online and/or technologically facilitated forms of such behaviours.

To identify further the impact on the student experience of issues arising on social media that include sexual violence, harassment, hate, and abuse, a pilot study was designed to capture some initial impressions from the student body. The small-scale study that has informed this research involves two phases. The first phase is designed around online surveys of students from six

41 Ahmed (2017), p 102.

42 Ahmed (2012), p 151.

43 The survey was generously funded by the British and Irish Law, Education and Technology Association, without whom this work would not have been possible.

law schools—two from England, two from Scotland, and two from Wales (Northern Ireland was excluded on the basis of geographical access and funding limitations), but also due to the legal distinctions and differences in educational operations). The first phase of the data collection involved online surveys targeted at students enrolled on taught law programmes, and was designed to ask respondents to consider their usage of social media, their university's approach to social media, and the problems associated with social media. While initially designed to allow for follow-up focus groups at the same six institutions, the second phase of data collection, and this research project, has been disrupted due to Covid-19.

The survey included a range of questions exploring uses of social media, and experiences of abusive behaviours on social media, through multiple-choice and free-text-box responses. The pilot study resulted in a low number of respondents, 30 in total across undergraduate and postgraduate taught programmes, but the insights offered in response to the questions posed remain valuable, as the data indicates. The data is particularly revealing as to the attitudes of students based on their experiences of social media problems.

The data shows that the majority of respondents use some form of social media on at least a daily basis (Figure 13.1), with the most popular sites proving to be Facebook (now Meta), Twitter, Instagram, and Snapchat (see discussions above). Of those surveyed, 23 use Facebook and Instagram, with Snapchat and LinkedIn proving to be the next most popular. Surprisingly, Twitter features lower in the list of popularity—an intriguing finding given the prevalence of abusive and hateful content that appears on its platform. The data does not (in phase 1) reveal why Twitter is less popular amongst the respondents surveyed, though it is a working hypothesis of the researchers that the problems prevalent on Twitter are at least—in part—some of the reasons for the dip in popularity compared to other interactive social platforms. It is also much more likely that

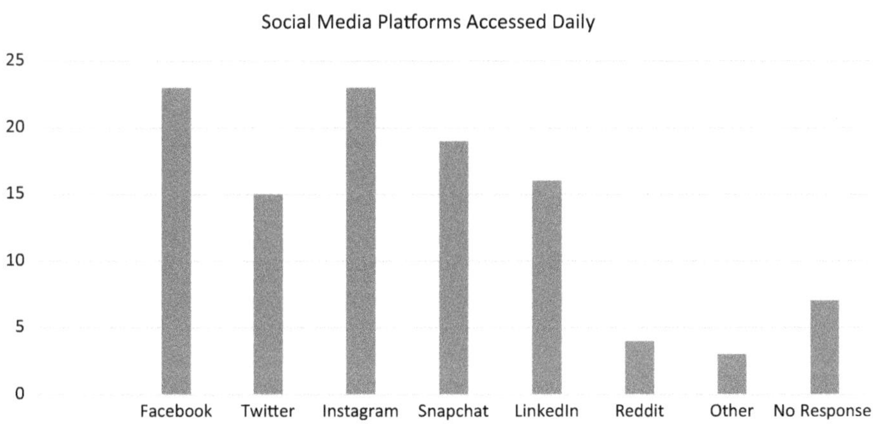

Figure 13.1 Social Media Daily Use.

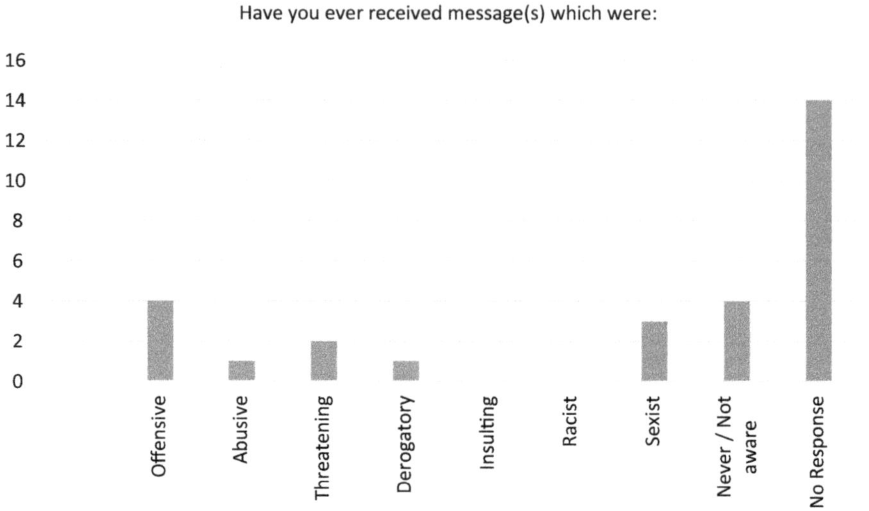

Figure 13.2 Messages Received.

Facebook and/or Snapchat are likely to form the cornerstones of the 'social' aspect of student life.

The level of social media engagement does not appear to be connected to the prevalence (or otherwise) of abusive messages received. Of the respondents, almost 40% had received some kind of message which was offensive, abusive, threatening, derogatory, sexist, or insulting (Figure 13.2). This is, in some respects, unsurprising given the reported levels of abuse, harassment, and threatening communications received on social media by other groups, including politicians,[44] journalists,[45] and sports stars.[46]

The prevalence of problematic messages received on social media is perhaps unsurprising in light of other data, but nevertheless indicates that the problems experienced by other groups are shared across the student body too. It is however noteworthy that despite the rise in racist abuse on social media,[47] none of the respondents indicated having received such a communication. While this is a small-scale study, the respondents represented a diverse group of students, with a spread of ethnicity (including 13% of respondents from an Asian background and 10% from a black background), age, and gender being captured. The responses also indicate that there is no age cut-off point at which problematic messages are not received, with respondents recording an age range of

44 Dhordia (2017).
45 Observer Sport (2021).
46 MacInnes (2020).
47 Thompson (2021).

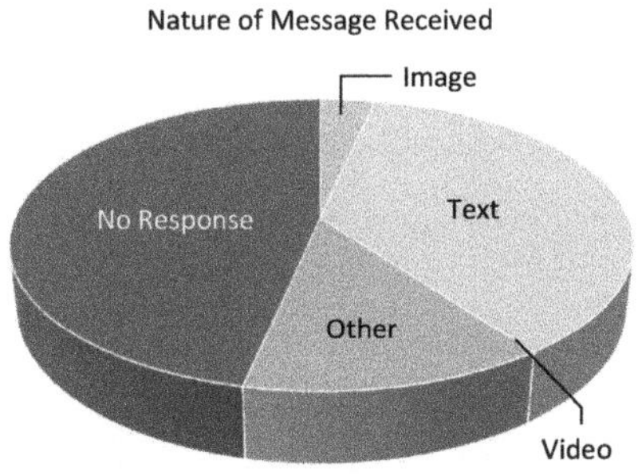

Figure 13.3 **Nature of Messages Received.**

between 16 and 74. The range of categories in which problematic messages have been received is striking, with messages received that include threats and abuse, as well as sexist messages. While not all of these are necessarily serious enough to meet the threshold for criminal investigation,[48] they are all noteworthy as to the harm caused and the impact they have on the recipients. This is particularly detrimental where messages serve to drive people away from engaging with and through social media platforms. It is also likely to be a negative factor impacting upon the educational experience of students where these messages are linked to their university, or to university life (see Figure 13.3).

The category of problematic message received is not the only aspect worthy of comment in terms of the substance of the communications. It is striking to note that 37% of respondents indicating a problematic message received that message in textual form—particularly because the law does not per se capture text-based abuses as a form of harassment or stalking.[49] The overwhelming majority of responses were textual rather than image based here—noteworthy given the specific legislation introduced to address image-based forms of online harassment (to tackle both so-called 'revenge porn' and upskirting).

While respondents indicated that messages are received, the reporting of such messages and reacting to them receives less attention (Figure 13.4). Only three respondents, representing 10%, reported the issue to the social media platform on which it was received, while the same number blocked or hid the sender who had sent the post initially. Intriguingly, where reports were made, these were made—according to respondents—only to social media platforms. None of the respondents who had received a problematic message on social media indicated that they reported the matter to the police. Similarly, no reports were made to universities, student committees, students' unions, or to student societies. It is not clear from the data whether this is due to the fact

48 Barker and Jurasz (2019), Chapters 3 and 4.
49 Barker and Jurasz (2021).

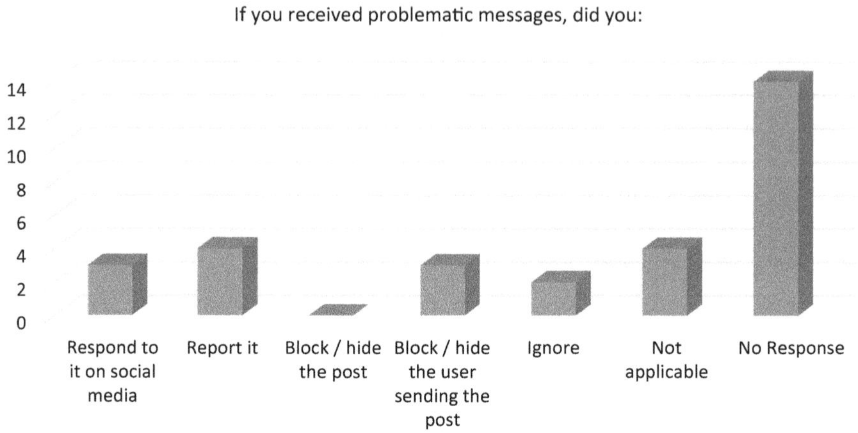

Figure 13.4 Problematic Messages Follow-Up Action.

that the messages were not educationally connected, or whether respondents feel that the onus to act is on social media platforms—something very much evident in the policy and law reform landscape in the UK through the Online Safety Bill (2021). That said, the policies themselves may well be contributing factors in the non-reporting to universities or students' unions. Equally, where policies are silent as to the digital dimension of abuse and harassment online or problematic messages, it is unsurprising that students and victims may believe that the policies do not extend to online conduct. The Online Safety Bill provides a unique opportunity to clarify its applicability to educational contexts. Similarly, it also offers a chance to educational institutions to address—via their policies and support mechanisms—the digital dimension of modern student life and the issues that can (and do) arise.

Perhaps the most interesting element of the data collected from the respondents at this point, though, relates to the reported impacts of the messages received through social media platforms, irrespective of whether they were reported or not. Respondent 13 was particularly shocked by the response she got to posting on Reddit about being single over 30, when met with a reaction that was unexpected. Respondent 13 reports being 'deeply hurt' that strangers and anonymous online posters 'saw fit to hurl abuse at [me] online'. This is a similar reaction to that of Respondent 15, who also reported being 'shocked' and 'upset' at the offensive message received online. These responses to problematic online messages are not isolated, with the harm recorded by Respondent 17 going beyond the raw emotion, and resulting in a 'more isolationist attitude', with less engagement, and a reduced inclination to participate fully online being the outcome of threatening messages in this instance. Other respondents report a more pragmatic but resigned approach to the impact of the messages received, with Respondent 23 highlighting that the offensive message received was something that they would 'not take … seriously'. Respondent 18 echoes this, stating that there was 'little actual risk IRL'. These reactions are not the norm though, and are outliers in the data recorded here, with other respondents indicating the impact was profound, 'distressing' (Respondent 14), or led to being 'annoyed' (Respondents 26, 36, and 37), or 'pissed' (Respondent 28). Respondent 26's reaction to the offensive message offers an insightful snapshot of the generally reported dismay at the ways in which social media seem to be used now, stating that it made them 'sad that someone could be so small minded and angry towards someone they did not know'.

These comments take on a slightly different dimension when the university context is considered more broadly: 43% of respondents indicated that they believe offensive or abusive messages on social media to be a problem, whereas only 17% had an awareness as to the contents of their university's policy on social media use; 33% of the respondents had no awareness of their students' union / NUS policy on social media use, but the same percentage reported that this lack of awareness had no impact on how they used such platforms. That said, 43% were of the opinion that their institution should have guidance on the responsible use of social media platforms. Opinions on what this guidance should address (Figure 13.5) was much more widespread than considerations of reporting problematic messages, or the need for institutional guidance.

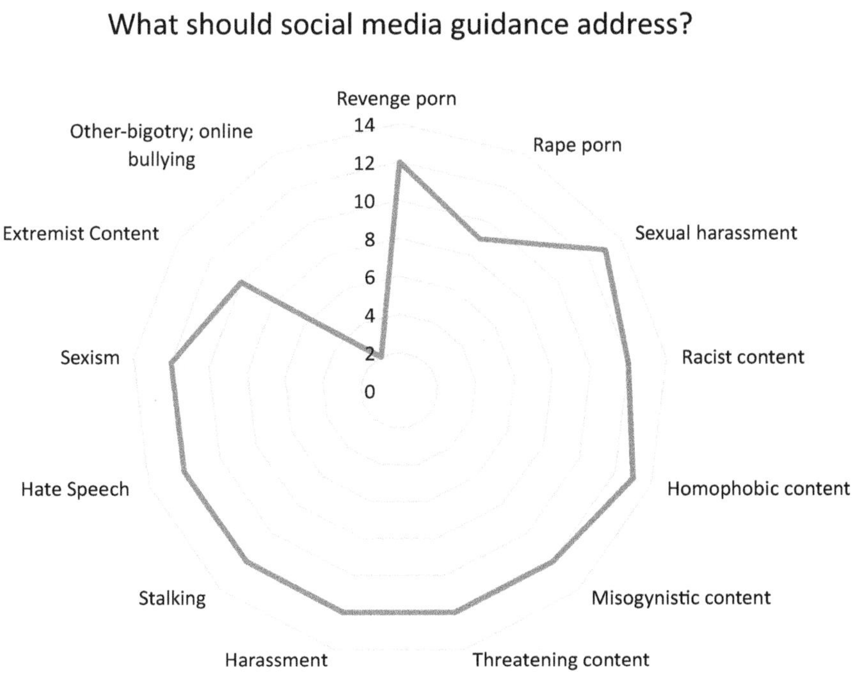

Figure 13.5 What Type of Online Behaviour Should Social Media Guidance Address?

The responses indicate that while reporting—to institutional authorities—or others may not be the predominant response of all students who receive or suffer online abusive, harassing, or threatening messages, the impact is still significant. Ultimately of course, there are some categories of online abuse which are criminal in nature, and which fall outside of a university's remit when it comes to taking action—in such instances, it is not reasonable to expect universities to tackle what could amount to the basis of a criminal prosecution. The common themes from these snapshots indicate that the real harm rests in losing faith in interacting with others through online media, but also the emotional impact that the personal touch can have when receiving offensive, abusive, or threatening messages—even where there is (allegedly) no real risk.

Conclusions

Ultimately, while there is a need for further work and further exploration of student experiences of social media, particularly in educational contexts, there are clear indicators from this small-scale study that the impact of abuse, harassment, and hate has spread to students too. This is unsurprising given the prevalence of reports of similar incidents which have affected other groups. What is very much apparent from this data and the vignettes, though, is the lack of reporting, and that social media abuses can have a significant impact. More work is required to explore why there is a lack of reporting to universities and educational institutions. While some of the problems on social media may be the responsibility of educational institutions, particularly where they occur in respect of student societies and are between members of the institution, not all problems encountered will be directly traceable to universities. It is therefore particularly important to remember that while universities have a wellbeing responsibility to their students, not all of the impact of social media lies within their remit. Similarly, merely amending policies will not address the issue(s) posed by social media abuse in textual or image form. For much of the social media experience—impacting on student experience or otherwise—there is little that universities can tangibly do. They can offer support to victims, and they can pursue disciplinary action against identifiable perpetrators, though it must be noted that this is often resource intense, and difficult for universities (and support mechanisms) to grapple with. This is in spite of the expectation from those surveyed here that guidance be introduced, and that guidance be wide ranging to cover a number of behaviours which can lead to social media abuse, harassment, and violence. Interestingly, respondents were clear that this should be the situation (Figure 13.5), even where they confessed to not knowing if their institution or union had similar guidance. More can—and must—be done to raise awareness of reporting options and the available support for victims.

Universities are not responsible for regulating social media platforms or social messaging apps, and yet the ubiquity of social media in student life poses challenges for students and for universities alike. Fundamentally, the platforms themselves are private entities and are regulated outside of the educational sector—there is therefore a need to distinguish between types of abuse suffered by students where universities can be expected to act, and where they cannot be expected to act. That said, the way in which responsibility for social media plays out will remain an unknown for the foreseeable future. Policy developments at Whitehall have emphasised the online safety elements of platform regulation—but that emphasis imposes a duty on the platform provider. For students, and for universities, this is likely to mean that despite the plaudits of the proposed Online Safety Bill (2021), there will still be a shortfall between what the law requires and what students expect.

Acknowledgements

This research was made possible through the funding offered by the British and Irish Law, Education and Technology Association (BILETA), without whom the study here would not have taken place. The authors thank the association for their support.

Ethics Statement

Research project, 'Online Hate and Responsible Social Media Use: A Preliminary Analysis' (No: GUEP465) approved by the ethics committee at University of Stirling (2018).

References

Advance HE (2021) 'Black Lives Matter and the Student Voice', www.advance-he.ac.uk/knowledge-hub/black-lives-matter-and-student-voice, June 2021.

Sara Ahmed (2012) *On Being Included: Racism and Diversity in Institutional Life*, Duke University Press.

Sara Ahmed (2017) *Living a Feminist Life*, Duke University Press.

Kim Barker and Olga Jurasz (2019) *Online Misogyny as a Hate Crime: A Challenge for Legal Regulation*, Routledge.

Kim Barker and Olga Jurasz (2020) 'Online Violence Against Women as an Obstacle to Gender Equality: A Critical View from Europe' 1 *European Equality Law Review* 47.

Kim Barker and Olga Jurasz (2021) 'Text-based (Sexual) Abuse and Online Violence Against Women: Toward Law Reform?' in J Bailey, A Flynn and N Henry (eds) *The Emerald Handbook of Technology-facilitated Violence and Abuse*, Emerald Publishing.

Balbir Barn (2020) 'The Digitalisation of the University' *Wonkhe*, https://wonkhe.com/blogs/the-digitalisation-of-the-university-2/, 29 April 2020.

Danielle Bradford 2020 'I Learned Firsthand How British Universities are Silencing Abuse Survivors' *The Guardian*, www.theguardian.com/commentisfree/2020/feb/18/universities-silencing-abuse-survivors-students, 18 February 2020.

David Batty (2019) 'Warwick University Not Safe, Says Woman Targeted by "Rape Chat"' *The Guardian*, www.theguardian.com/education/2019/jul/14/warwick-university-not-safe-says-woman-targeted-by-chat, 14 July 2019.

Sharon Cowan and Vanessa Munro (2021) 'Seeking Campus Justice: Challenging the "Criminal Justice Drift" in United Kingdom University Responses to Student Sexual Violence and Misconduct' 48 *Journal of Law and Society* 308.

Shanti Das and Sian Griffiths 2019 'University is Protecting My Rapist' *The Times*, www.thetimes.co.uk/article/university-is-protecting-my-rapist-3lpzzqt95, 6 July 2019.

Azmina Dhordia (2017) 'Unsocial Media: Tracking Twitter Abuse Against Women MPs', https://medium.com/@AmnestyInsights/unsocial-media-tracking-twitter-abuse-against-women-mps-fc28aeca498a, 4 September 2017.

Viet Duong, Phu Pham, Ritwik Bose and Jiebo Luo (2020) '#MeToo on Campus: Studying College Sexual Assault at Scale using Data Reported on Social Media', https://arxiv.org/pdf/2001.05970.pdf, 16 January 2020.

Jerry Finn (2004) 'A Survey of Online Harassment at a University Campus' 19 *Journal of Interpersonal Violence* 468.

Michel Foucault (2003) *'Society Must Be Defended': Lectures at the Collège de France, 1975–1976*, Allen Lade.

Kieran Hardy (2018) '#MeTooPhD Reveals Shocking Examples of Academic Sexism' *The Guardian*, www.theguardian.com/commentisfree/2018/feb/04/metoophd-reveals-shocking-examples-of-academic-sexism, 4 February 2018.

Jaigris Hodson, Chandell Gosse and George Veletsianos (2021) 'Analog Policies in a Digital World: How Workplace Harassment Policies Need to Adapt to an Increasingly Digital Education Environment' *Academic Matters*, https://academicmatters.ca/analog-policies-in-a-digital-world-how-workplace-harassment-policies-need-to-adapt-to-an-increasingly-digital-education-environment/, 19 May 2021.

Natasha Jokic (2020) 'I Told My University I Was Harassed Online. They Asked Me What a Hashtag Was' *The Guardian*, www.theguardian.com/education/2020/apr/20/i-told-my-university-i-was-harassed-online-they-asked-me-what-a-hashtag-was, 20 April 2020.

Paul MacInnes (2020) 'Sky Sports Tries to Tackle Online Abuse after Lockdown Surge', www.theguardian.com/football/2020/oct/01/sky-sports-online-abuse-lockdown-surge-sexism-racism, 1 October 2020.

Sarah Marsh (2019) 'Hundreds of Students in UK Sanctioned Over Racist or Offensive Online Posts' *The Guardian*, www.theguardian.com/education/2019/may/06/hundreds-of-students-in-uk-sanctioned-over-racist-or-offensive-online-posts, 6 May 2019.

Clare McGlynn and Magdalena Furgalska (2019) 'What Does Campus Justice Mean for Survivors of Sexual Violence?' *Social and Legal Studies Blog*, https://socialandlegalstudies.wordpress.com/2019/10/23/what-does-campus-justice-mean-for-survivors-of-sexual-violence/, 23 October 2019.

Lucy Michael (2015) 'Hate Crimes Against Students: Recent Developments in Research, Policy and Practice' in N Chakraborti and J Garland (eds) *Responding to Hate Crime: The Case for Connecting Policy and Research*, Policy Press.

Elizabeth Nixon, Richard Scullion and Robert Hearn (2018) 'Her Majesty the Student: Marketised Higher Education and the Narcissistic (Dis)satisfactions of the Student-consumer' 43 *Studies in Higher Education* 927.

Maya Oppenheim (2019) 'Students Share Sexual Abuse Allegations Online Because they Feel Ignored by University Staff' *The Independent*, www.independent.co.uk/news/uk/home-news/student-sexual-abuse-assault-harassment-university-social-media-a8927201.html, 23 May 2019.

Barbara Perry (2010) '"No Biggie": The Denial of Oppression on Campus' 5 *Education, Citizenship and Social Justice* 265.

Andy Phippen and Emma Bond (2021) 'Is Online Delivery Placing Students at Greater Risk of Abuse?' *Times Higher Education*, www.timeshighereducation.com/opinion/online-delivery-placing-students-greater-risk-abuse, 15 January 2021.

Alison Phipps and Geraldine Smith (2012) 'Violence Against Women Students in the UK: Time to Take Action' 24 *Gender and Education* 357.

David Pittam (2020) 'Black Lives Matter: Students "Need Support" Over George Floyd Death' *BBC News*, www.bbc.co.uk/news/uk-england-nottinghamshire-53024298, 17 June 2020.

Julian Sladdin (2020) 'Covid-19 Should Be Driver for Higher Education to Tackle Online Risk' *Pinsent Masons Out-Law Analysis*, www.pinsentmasons.com/out-law/analysis/covid-19--higher-education-online-risk, 13 November 2020.

Rachel Thompson (2021) 'Twitter Shares Analysis of Racist Abuse Against Football Players after Euro' https://mashable.com/article/twitter-analysis-football-euro-racist-abuse, 10 August 2021.

Eva Tutchell and John Edmonds (2020) *Unsafe Spaces: Ending Sexual Abuse in Universities*, Emerald Publishing.

Naaman Zhou (2018) '#MeToo Campaign May Change University Culture, Students Say' *The Guardian*, www.theguardian.com/australia-news/2018/mar/01/metoo-campaign-may-change-university-culture-students-say, 28 February 2018.

Reports

Aljazeera Investigative Unit and Alex Howlett (2021) '"What We Fear as Women": Sexual Abuse in UK Universities' *Aljazeera*, www.aljazeera.com/features/2021/11/2/what-we-fear-as-women, 2 November 2021.

Aljazeera Investigative Unit and Alex Howlett 2021, 'UK Universities Do Not Probe Bulk of Sexual Misconduct Reports' *Aljazeera*, www.aljazeera.com/news/2021/10/26/uk-universities-fail-to-review-bulk-sexual-misconduct-complaints, 26 October 2021.

HM Government (2019) *Online Harms White Paper*. www.gov.uk/government/consultations/online-harms-white-paper.

NUS (2010) 'Hidden Marks: A Study of Women Students' Experiences of Harassment, Stalking, Violence and Sexual Assault', www.nusconnect.org.uk/resources/hidden-marks-a-study-of-women-students-experiences-of-harassment-stalking-violence-and-sexual-assault.

NUS (2011a) 'No Place for Hate: Hate Crimes and Incidents in Further and Higher Education: Sexual Orientation and Gender Identity', www.nusconnect.org.uk/resources/no-place-for-hate-hate-crimes-and-incidents-in-further-and-higher-education-sexual-orientation-and-gender-identity.

NUS (2011b) 'No Place for Hate: Hate Crimes and Incidents in Further and Higher Education: Disability', www.nusconnect.org.uk/resources/no-place-for-hate-hate-crimes-and-incidents-in-further-and-higher-education-race-and-ethnicity.

NUS (2012) 'No Place for Hate: Hate Crimes and Incidents in Further and Higher Education: Race and Ethnicity', www.nusconnect.org.uk/resources/no-place-for-hate-hate-crimes-and-incidents-in-further-and-higher-education-race-and-ethnicity.

NUS (2015) 'I Heart Consent Pilot Report', www.nusconnect.org.uk/resources/i-heart-consent-pilot-report, 17 August 2015.

NUS (2020) 'NUS Repsonds to the Murder of George Floyd', www.nus.org.uk/articles/nus-responds-to-the-murder-of-george-floyd, 10 June 2020.

Ofcom (2021) 'Online Nation. 2021 Report', www.ofcom.org.uk/__data/assets/pdf_file/0013/220414/online-nation-2021-report.pdf, 9 June 2021.

Office for Students (2019) 'English Higher Education 2019: The Office for Students Annual Review', www.officeforstudents.org.uk/media/53fd78d2-6388-4540-b622-3e73be0434c8/ofs-annual-review-2019.pdf.

Office for Students (2021) 'Office for Students Statement of Expectations for Preventing and Addressing Harassment and Sexual Misconduct Affecting Students in Higher Education', www.officeforstudents.org.uk/media/d4ef58c0-db7c-4fc2-9fae-fcb94b38a7f3/ofs-statement-of-expectations-harassment-and-sexual-misconduct.pdf, 19 April 2021.

Andy Phippen and Emma Bond (2020) *Online Harassment and Hate Crime in HEIs – Report from FOI*, Univeristy of Suffolk, www.uos.ac.uk/sites/www.uos.ac.uk/files/FOI-Report-Final-Jan-2020-rgb_0.pdf, January 2020.

Scottish Women's Rights Centre (2020) 'Abuse at University/College During COVID-19: Support for Students', www.scottishwomensrightscentre.org.uk/news/covid-19coronavirus-info/abuse-at-university--college-during-covid-19--support-for-students/.

Statista (2021) 'Share of Respondents Who Had Set Up Their Own Social Network Profile in the United Kingdom (UK) from 2010 to 2020, by Gender', www.statista.com/statistics/271892/social-network-profile-creation-in-the-uk-by-gender/, 14 July 2021.

Universities UK (2005) 'Promoting Good Campus Relations: Dealing with Hate Crimes and Intolerance'.

Universities UK (2016) 'Changing the Culture: Report of the Universities UK Taskforce Examining Violence Against Women, Harassment and Hate Crime Affecting University Students', www.universitiesuk.ac.uk/sites/default/files/field/downloads/2021-07/changing-the-culture.pdf, October 2016.

Universities UK (2019) 'Changing the Culture: Tackling Online Harassment and Promoting Online Welfare', www.universitiesuk.ac.uk/sites/default/files/field/downloads/2021-07/tackling-online-harassment.pdf, August 2019.

Universities UK (2021) 'Survey Demonstrates Positive University Progress in Tackling Harassment and Hate Crime, but Highlights Areas for Improvement', www.universitiesuk.ac.uk/topics/equality-diversity-and-inclusion/survey-demonstrates-positive-university, 29 July 2021.

UN Women (2018) *Guidance Note on Campus Violence Prevention and Response*, www.unwomen.org/en/digital-library/publications/2019/02/guidance-note-on-campus-violence-prevention-and-response.

News

Observer Sport (2021) 'BBC's Sonja McLaughlan Reveals Online Abuse Over Owen Farrell Interview', www.theguardian.com/sport/2021/feb/27/bbcs-sonja-mclaughlan-reveals-online-abuse-over-owen-farrell-interview, 27 February 2021.

Chapter 14

'A Personal University'

Lifelong Learning and a Certain Kind of Fiction in the Swiss Law Educational System

Giulia Walter and Filippo Contarini

It's great that you formed a critical students association. We too, would like to be more critical in the classroom, but the students won't let us.

(Two professors to us, 2017)

Introduction

At the beginning of the 2000s, universities around the world began experiencing a process of entrepreneurialisation.[1] In Europe this was linked to the transition to the so-called 'Learning Society', which laid down the foundations for the coveted self-entrepreneurship of every citizen and adapted the academic system to the needs of the knowledge-based economy.[2] This shift also affected the young University of Lucerne, where both authors happily received our legal training. In several documents available on its recent history,[3] we found rather homogeneous visions about this evolution.[4] Since we witnessed, during our own education in Lucerne, an actual personal atmosphere, something will necessarily be lost in our analysis: after all, scientific observation excludes at least one point; namely, the origin of the observation.[5] Our aim with this chapter is, nonetheless, to give an alternative contribution to the legal-academic discussion about the 'learning society'.[6]

1 Marginson (2002); Marginson and Considine (2000), p 4; Huber (2008); Huber (2012).

2 Hammer (2016), p 47.

3 Our main sources are: annual reports (cited as 'Jahresbericht', available at www.unilu.ch/universitaet/portraet/jahresbericht/), university magazines ('UniluAktuell', from 2018 on 'Cogito', available at www.unilu.ch/magazin/), other sources published on special occasions (like the Dies Academicus), presidents' speeches and legislative materials. Our analysis considers sources up to the beginning of 2021.

4 We identified here 'discourses', i.e., crystallisations into stable statement patterns that disintegrate after a certain amount of time: Sarasin (2020), p 110. For a joint lecture of the Foucaultian discourse analysis and the Luhmanian systems theory, see Siri and Robnik (2016).

5 Luhmann (1998), p 187, 538; see also Luhmann (1987a), p 395.

6 On the evolution in Lucerne see also Schmid (2017); e.g., for the Faculty of Law of the University of Zurich see 'Study Reform 2021', www.ius.uzh.ch/en/studies/bologna21.html

DOI: 10.4324/9781003175193-18

The 'Hunt' for Students and Other Marketing Strategies

From Rural Canton to Academic Canton

In Lucerne, the core of Switzerland, a fervent humus of institutional actors succeeded, in 2000, in finally bringing a university to a region traditionally hostile to academism.[7] The arguments used to convince the population were that the university would benefit the area and that the law faculty would be self-financing:[8] 72% of voters approved this project,[9] explicitly constructed according to New Public Management logic.[10]

While the first 15 years taken altogether were clearly oriented towards expansion and growth,[11] in the first five years alone the focus was set on the present; as a consequence, growth and the narrative around it were moderate.[12] In 2005, a shift in self-representation occurred. On the one hand, there were efforts to bring more attention to research.[13] On the other hand, the concept of 'competitivity' entered the semantic realm used by the university[14] and became something to strive towards, which has continued ever since.[15] With the initial stabilisation phase over, the academic discourse evolved towards a well-grounded assertiveness, where the university—with headlines such as 'From rural canton to academic canton'[16]—spoke of itself as being the institution carrying central Switzerland into the future, responsible for the rejuvenation of the canton.[17]

Even if in the very first years, the intention was to stabilise student numbers at around 900,[18] in 2005 the university began to show a real urge to extend its offer, become larger, more prestigious and more competitive. Already in that year the number of students was 1200.[19] By interpreting this success as

7 Fuchs (2011); (2020).

8 Botschaft des Regierungsrates an den Grossen Rat zum Entwurf eines Gesetzes über die universitäre Hochschulbildung, p 5, 7.

9 The democratic vote about a university was a world-premiere, see Mattioli and Ries (2000), p 133.

10 Richli (2011), p 5.

11 Schatz (2020).

12 The founding dean explained that having 'happy students' was the most important good of the university, UniluAktuell 12/2005.

13 As sociologist Rudolf Stichweh became president, he tried to pursue a new financing approach through research funding, UniAktuell 12/2005. In UniluAktuell 15/2006, professors of private law focused on the fact that 'there is life after study', recalling the importance of opening up to enterprises in the economic world.

14 First time in Jahresbericht 2005 and UniluAktuell 11/2005.

15 For example, in the annual reports, see Jahresbericht 2011, 2012 and 2015.

16 Jahresbericht 2010.

17 Jahresbericht 2009 and 2010.

18 Botschaft des Regierungsrates an den Grossen Rat zum Entwurf eines Gesetzes zur universitären Hochschulbildung of the 28 September 1999, p 2, 6, 8.

19 UniluAktuell 11/2005.

affirmation of their choices, a new target was rapidly set at 2600 students by 2012.[20] In 2006, the population approved with an 80% majority the acquisition of a new building to house the university, thereby legitimising the expansionist verve.[21] In 2010, there were 2400 students, and the university began complaining about the maximum limit of 2600 set by the cantonal policy, calling it 'not adequate' for the financing of the university.[22] The university's strategic board was already brooding on the next target of 3500–4000, to be reached by 2020.[23] Now, in 2021, the number of enrolled students is 3155.[24]

This rush is not astonishing. The canton of origin of the student must pay a certain amount for every student that goes to study in another canton.[25] In Lucerne's total budget, intercantonal funding represents the highest percentage,[26] which means that the university is economically dependent on the fact that students choose Lucerne as their place of study, and not the university in their own or in another city. This percentage is the highest among all Swiss universities. The founding dean of the law school, who later became the university president, explained that the need for more students was part of the university's strategy for self-financing.[27] This became even more urgent with the cantonal austerity plans put in place after the 2008 crisis.[28]

From the Autonomous Student to the 'Personal University' Tagline

At the inauguration of the new university building in 2011, the Swiss Head of the Federal Department of Home Affairs reiterated the strong competiveness credo for the Swiss academic system in the third millennium.[29] In this environment, Swiss universities increasingly describe themselves through a 'marketing culture'.[30] Lucerne is no exception: even if in 2003 a professor still declared himself happy about the growing number of students despite low faculty marketing,[31] in the following years the need for a new 'corporate identity'

20 UniluAktuell 9/2004.
21 UniluAktuell 18/2006.
22 UniluAktuell 33/2010.
23 Fuchs (2011), p 99, 105; see also UniluAktuell 33/2010.
24 Of which 1287 are law students, www.unilu.ch/universitaet/portraet/zahlen-und-fakten/
25 Art. 3 Interkantonalen Universitätsvereinbarung vom 20. Februar 1997.
26 Statistics by the Federal Statistical Office (Finanzen der universitären Hochschulen: Basistabellen, 26.11.2019, su-d-15.06.03.01-2018).
27 UniluAktuell 33/2010.
28 The university expresses discontent towards and a fairly sharp critique of the austerity measures of the canton in the Jahresbericht 2010, 2011, 2012, 2014 and 2015.
29 The portal of the Swiss government, 'Eröffnung des neuen Uni-PHZ-Gebäudes Luzern—"Luzern, der dynamische Herausforderer". Luzern, 01.09.2011—Rede von Bundesrat Didier Burkhalter', www.admin.ch/gov/de/start/dokumentation/medienmitteilungen.msg-id-40936.html
30 A feature of the enterprise university according to Marginson (2002); see Hafner (2021), critical of this development at the University of Berne.
31 UniluAktuell 5/2003.

had emerged.[32] In Lucerne the marketing efforts are primarily justified by the 'hunt' for students.

In their 1999 legislative project, cantonal politicians mentioned that the university would be 'personal'.[33] Since its establishment as a small institution, the university has thus insisted on the intimate atmosphere it has been able to create, where the student is at the centre and their contact with professors is assured.[34] Indeed, in our student years, we experienced this proximity. The initial representation of the law student was that of the student as a partner, not as a client.[35] The idea was not only that the university was small and capable of offering an intimate atmosphere, but also that students supposedly knew what they wanted. So, between 2001 and 2005, the law faculty actually asked its students what they wanted their academic curriculum to look like. The university knew the results could not actually be used (how could students *really* know what subjects are more important for their professional future?),[36] but it was a way of communicating to students that the faculty took seriously their desire of being autonomous persons.[37] Moreover, the bachelor study regulation of 2001 allowed for a good amount of freedom in the composition of one's own curriculum: 10 ECTS had to be obtained by attending non-juridical subjects (either economy or sociology), another 4 ECTS had to be obtained by experiencing the professional world (not only the legal), and two juridical subjects, equivalent to 12 ECTS, could be picked from a list of six alternatives.[38] The faculty was actually a 'personal' one.

At a certain point, the representation of the bachelor student as capable of wilful actions, despite the fact that it had previously been crucial for the nationwide success of the newborn law faculty, was lifted.[39] The last university student survey published in UniluAktuell was in 2005.[40] Therein, the university

32 The new visual strategy was presented in the UniluAktuell 20/2007.

33 Botschaft des Regierungsrates an den Grossen Rat zum Entwurf eines Gesetzes zur universitären Hochschulbildung (Universitätsgesetz), 28 September 1999, p 7.

34 One of the founders of the law faculty said at the university's opening ceremony in 2001 that the personal contacts between professors and students would have been fostered and 'emotional intelligence put in the syllabus': Gauch (2001), p 12.

35 Richli (2001), p 16.

36 Marginson (2002) asks the same question.

37 In 2009 students in Lucerne refused to take part in the protests against Bologna. Ironical voices maintained that the managing board of the university feared reputational damage because of this refusal, see Jonas (2009).

38 Studien und Prüfungsordnung der Fakultät III für Rechtswissenschaft der Universität Luzern vom 27. Juni 2001.

39 In a 2005 international ranking in which the opinion of the students was asked, the university was at the top, UniluAktuell 12/2005. When in another type of ranking, based on professors' opinions, Lucerne arrived last, the ex-dean—then university president—affirmed that rankings are irrelevant and 'it is much more important that students find jobs', see Gautschi (2013). On rankings, see Esposito and Stark (2019).

40 UniluAktuell 10/2005; Jahresbericht 2005.

managing board had asked the students where they would have liked the new main building to be placed. The students' answer—to leave the university in the city centre—was then ignored by both the university and the canton, who decided to put the new large building behind the train station,[41] thus encouraging commuting. A few months later, the tagline—'a Personal University'[42]—was introduced.[43]

The university was relentlessly changing the way it understood students' wishes: from what they could want to what they *needed to* want. It began to anticipate their will, focusing on the product sold, caring about the successfulness of their future career.[44] It is also worth noticing that, at the same time as its marketing was exalting this kind of 'new personality', the law faculty was standardising its curricula. In the new Exam and Study Regulation of 2008, the possibility to obtain ECTS with experience in the professional world was eliminated and the obtainable ECTS for non-juridical subjects was reduced. In 2011, the ECTS for non-juridical subjects were substituted with a 'pass or fail' exam. With the latest reform, which came into force in 2018 and was called 'Bologna 2.0',[45] non-juridical subjects are no longer worth any ECTS, and bachelor students can no longer choose their curriculum. Subjects taught at the bachelor level are back within the traditional professional canon and training for specific fields takes place directly in the professional world.[46] A new professorial discourse, according to which students need, first and foremost, to learn how to solve 'legal cases', has crept in.[47]

The professional world refers to this uniformisation of the curricula as a positive for students, which allows them to be generalists at the beginning of their career.[48] But what is left today is the students' fungibility at the end of their curriculum. Degrees thus become central for selection in the professional

41 Menrath (2020) praises the building; we personally never liked its cold and unwelcoming architecture.

42 Other institutions use similar taglines, e.g., 'The UAS Grisons is digitally personal in study and research', www.fhgr.ch, 20 April 2021.

43 The founding dean accompanied this communicative breakthrough affirming that the university's personal approach was engraved in its mission statement, UniluAktuell 13/2005. In April 2021, the University of Lucerne's website showed a new slogan: 'personal and unique'.

44 Cf. Stichweh (2010a). The marketing strategy of using a personality for branding has proven to be effective in influencing consumer attitudes and behaviours. Issues such as building positive brand image, developing brand trust and loyalty and influencing consumer behaviours are important concerns in commercial marketing, Ross et al. (2016); on the McDonaldisation of the university, see Arnold (in this volume).

45 Schmid (2017).

46 Schwarz (2016), p 213, 218; Haegi (2017), p 101; Eicker and Bosshart (2019), p 114, 116; with BGE 146 II 309, the Swiss Federal Supreme Court decided in 2020 that to become a lawyer one also needs a Bachelor of Law (and not only a Masters). Schwarz (2021) criticises this development.

47 Eicker and Bosshart (2019), p 115; critical: Hesse (1982), p 276.

48 Haegi (2017), p 102.

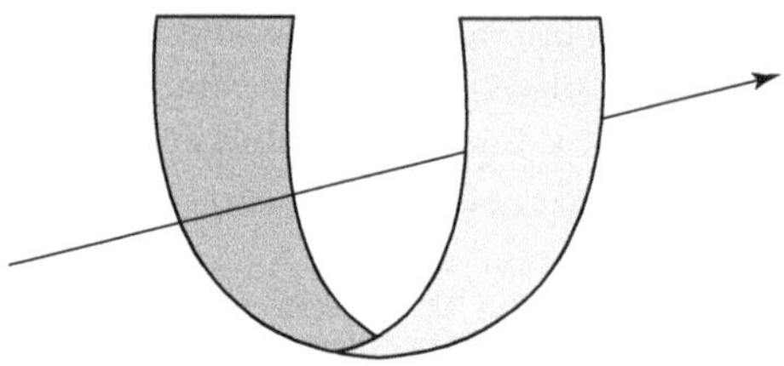

Figure 14.1 A Schematic representation of the dynamics explained in the text: the crescent moon represents the oscillation of the professorial discourse; the arrow represents entrepreneurial rationality.

world.[49] At the same time, the old references to the independence of lawyers[50] and to their ability to make a manipulative use of law,[51]—still seen in the 1990s as strong attributes of a *persona* and related to the archetype of the liberal professions to which the training of the jurist tended[52]—seem to have disappeared from the academic discourse. What is now demanded are rather values such as 'networked thinking, argumentation ability, interdisciplinarity, teamwork, good time management and organisation'.[53]

The Interaction between the Professorial Self-Description and the Professional World

In the legal-academic discourses we are observing, two fields are detectable. On one side the professorial self-description, on the other the administrative-entrepreneurial. These two fields overlap in the personalities of the faculty dean and the university president, who are at once professors *and* administrative headmen and who mostly interact with the political contracting parties. In turn, the self-descriptive discourse within the group of professors takes on a form of an oscillating[54] halfmoon, crossed on the bias by an arrow, i.e., the governance of the enterprise university, that heads towards the future (see Figure 14.1).[55]

49 Locher (2014); Luhmann (1991), p 437.
50 Gauch (1991); Drolshammer (1994), p 78.
51 '*Zu diesem manipulativen Potential gehört auch die bewusste oder unbewusste Vermengung der Wertungen des Gesetzes mit persönlichen Wertungen*', Arzt (1994), p 12.
52 Fellmann (2017), p 651.
53 Eicker and Bosshart (2019), p 114; see also Schwarz (2016), p 211. University should also prepare students for the next educational step: Eicker and Bosshart (2019), p 115, and Schwarz (2016), p 221; Senn (2013), p 86, remarks how the Bologna reform is shifting away from the intellectually free human being towards conditioned and dependent people; the depersonalisation of the profession is thematised also by Fellmann (2017), p 9 f.
54 For the concept of oscillation in the humanities, see Gumbrecht (2014), pp 73–9.
55 Marginson and Considine (2000) p 7 f.: 'Governance does not contain in itself the sum of teaching and research, but it affects them … Governance sits between government … and academic work.

In the discursive oscillations of the **professorial halfmoon**, two subfields are oscillating: one between theory/practice and one between research/teaching.[56] These debates, recognisable already in the academic juridical professorial self-description of the 19th century,[57] also concern the general question of what profile should be given to students:[58] a more practical one, or a more scientific-theoretical one.[59]

The **arrow**, or enterprise university, can be clearly observed in the evolution of the composition of the faculty assembly.[60] Since 2005, the weight of the professorial vote in the assembly has been progressively reduced. In the most recent version of the faculty regulation, dating 2007, the faculty manager was given more operative powers and a right to vote, whereas before they just had advisory competencies.[61] Progressively, the decisional process about the study curriculum has been 'corrupted' (in a very systems theoretical sense) with external rationales.[62]

In Lucerne, the consequence of this entrepreneurialisation seems to be a particular cognitive openness for the legal-professional discourse. As Stichweh explains, particularly in Switzerland, studying law means receiving a professionally rather than a scientifically oriented education.[63] When in 2010 a loud cry came from the forensic professions—including judges—aimed towards the law faculty, the faculty board was easily 'irritated' (again in a systems theoretical sense). The complaint concerned the supposedly excessive freedom enjoyed by law students in the choice of study subjects, which allegedly resulted in the worsening of the examinees' results at the cantonal bar exams. This cry was used by the faculty board as leverage for a more paternalistic approach by the law faculty towards its students.[64]

It also mediates the expanding relationships with business and industry, and between teaching and research'.

56 See: Eicker and Bosshart (2019), p 113 ff., Schwarz (2016), p 216, and Martino Mona in an interview by David and Schmid (2016). They move in the context of strong academic traditions, cf. Huber (2012).

57 See Siegrist (1996).

58 Hesse (1991), p 129 f. considers this debate 'intelligent but futile' and based on fictions.

59 Stichweh (2010b), p 14, refers to this as an 'interorganisational System' at the crossroads between education and science systems.

60 Namely the organ responsible for the enactment of the study and exam regulations, § 9 lit. d Reglement der Fakultät III für Rechtswissenschaft der Universität Luzern vom 27. Juni 2001.

61 § 8 para. 1 lit. e Reglement der Fakultät III für Rechtswissenschaft der Universität Luzern vom 27. Juni 2001, in its version of the 15 January 2007; see also UniluAktuell 21/2007: allegedly, the role has been introduced to relieve the dean. In our lecture, instead, it has the aim to underline the functional differentiation.

62 This development is highly similar to that described, e.g., in Australia by Marginson (2002), or in Austria by Burtscher et al. (2006).

63 Stichweh (2011); Luhmann (1995), p 9.

64 The first stone was thrown by the cantonal Chief Justice and President of the Bar Examination Commission of the Canton of Lucerne Marianne Heer (2010); the criticism was repeated again in

It is worth noting that this phenomenon has been seen before. Every decade, the professional world insists that students' quality is worsening[65] but no evidence has ever been provided to substantiate this claim.[66] We suggest that the cry from the practitioners was a symbolic affirmation of the relevance of the structural coupling between the law faculty and the legal profession. This 'irritation' allowed the faculty board to reflect on the image of the future lawyer it ought to give its students.[67]

The 'Futurisation' of Academic Education

A Breakthrough: The New Lifelong Learning Paradigm

In the past, Swiss law faculties conceived the studies they offered as an academic moment in one's life span.[68] This approach has changed in the context of continental evolutions. In 1995, the White Paper 'Teaching and Learning—Towards the Learning Society' coupled the European education policy with the exigencies of the knowledge-based economy for the first time, with a focus on the development of competences for the improvement of one's own employability.[69] The following discussions culminated in the establishment of the 'European Area of Lifelong Learning'.[70] Switzerland absorbed this policy with the adoption, in 2005, of Art. 63a of the Federal Constitution. In the accompanying report of the parliamentary commission, lifelong learning is described as a 'growing integral part of a coherent masterplan of academic education'.[71] The commentators denote the market-oriented character of this new education format.[72]

Nowadays, it seems that people need to continue studying their whole life to fuel their careers, and this futurisation[73] of student life has been completely

2018: 'The great freedom comes at the expense of solid basic knowledge', in Pastega (2018), para. 9. On the concept of 'employability' for describing the expectations of the academic system, see Haegi (2017), p 100.

65 As Schwarz (2016), p 212, states: 'the criticism of the Cantonal bar examination boards according to which universities do not prepare students well enough, is constant'; see also Gauch (1991) and Schott (1992).

66 Schwarz (2016), p 211 f; Haegi (2017), p 106.

67 Cf. Eicker and Bosshart (2019).

68 Drolshammer (1994), p 68.

69 See Hammer (2016), p 47.

70 In Commission of the European Communities, A European Area of Lifelong Learning, Bruxelles 2002, p 9.

71 Parlamentarische Initiative Bildungsrahmenartikel in der Bundesverfassung Bericht der Kommission für Wissenschaft, Bildung und Kultur des Nationalrats vom 23. Juni 2005, BBl 2005 5479, p 5531.

72 Ehrenzeller and Konrad (2014), N 50 ad Art. 63a BV; given this political agenda, the subjects themselves—i.e., the students—now absolutely want to be educated for life. This is a typical liberal symbolic dispositif, see also Čuroš (in this volume).

73 Morrissey (2013).

internalised by the university. In this context, even the admission to the bar is now seen as a mere step among many in the long path of advanced education.[74] Even if conceived as emancipatory by the neoliberal, globalised[75] world, where people are 'free to constantly reinvent themselves',[76] it has in fact become inevitable necessity for the individual to constantly obtain new degrees in order to remain employable.[77]

The Entrepreneurialisation of Continuing Education

In Lucerne, the enterprise university observed these discourses and inserted them into its operational chords, letting lifelong learning become a solid point of reference in the struggle to find financial means. The semantic shift from continuing education to a more market-oriented lifelong learning itself is paradigmatic of this evolution.

The initial aim of continuing education ('*Weiterbildung*') was that of anchoring the institution to its role of updater and engine for small and medium-sized enterprises established in the region. In the legislator's mind, bachelors and masters prepared students for professional lives.[78] Only in 2011 was '*Weiterbildung*' suddenly called lifelong learning and presented as 'duty' by a professor-lawyer.[79] The president of the Swiss Bar Association explained in 2017 that *Weiterbildung* is part of the lawyer's deontological care and diligence and is therefore imperative (Art. 12 let. a BGFA).[80] As all other Swiss universities, the faculty in Lucerne entered the national *Weiterbildung* market through a series of academic-professional courses, upon completion of which a Certificate of Advanced Studies (CAS) is issued.[81] In 2020, the cantonal minister for education praised this 'additional effort' of the law faculty[82] and the university president expressed the aim to have more students in the 'advanced' curriculum in order to gain a better proportion between the two numbers.[83] His approach

74 Schwarz (2016), S. 218.
75 Ash (2021).
76 Gumbrecht (2014), p 24.
77 See Forzani, in the *Biopolitics and Resistance in Legal Education* volume.
78 Botschaft des Regierungsrates an den Grossen Rat zum Entwurf eines Gesetzes über die universitäre Hochschulbildung vom 28. September 1999, p 9.
79 UniluAktuell 37/2011. Then again in 50/2015 and in the Jahresbericht 2019, where it is stated that 'knowledge gets old fast' and in an English-written pamphlet of 2018, where it is stated that 'the *necessity* of lifelong learning is accommodated through the provision of postgraduate study and continuing education'.
80 Haegi (2017).
81 UniluAktuell 23/2008, the first 'course certificate' was established in 2009.
82 Jahresbericht 2019, p 2.
83 Interview by Troxler (2020). It was the canton in the first instance pushing for this strategy through its 'achievement agreement' with the university for the years 2015–2018: www.unilu.ch/fileadmin/universitaet/unileitung/dokumente/reglemente_uni/Leistungsvereinbarung_2015-2018.pdf, p 8;

was clearly an economic one. While enrolment fees for bachelor and master are modest, ca. 800 CHF per semester, CAS cost between 5000 and 15,000 CHF, for a total of 15–20 days.

The Coupling of Lifelong Learning and the Corporate Legal World

In the first decade of the millennium, Swiss lawyers began following the organisational example of large multinational consulting firms and clustered together in the legal form of companies limited by share ('AG').[84] The Swiss Federal Court retroactively legitimised this tendency in 2012.[85] In that year only 14% of Swiss lawyers were working for a big law firm, but in 2017 that percentage had already reached 31%.[86] The model in which lawyers either work alone or in horizontally organised collectives is gradually disappearing.[87]

These law firms are characterised by a rigorous preordained path, where both experience and extra qualifications are prerequisites for accessing higher positions.[88] We are witnessing a gradual shift: lawyers with a university degree project themselves more and more as members of these corporations and not as self-employed professionals.[89] In the internal academic discourse, this shift is addressed only in passing, and in the professional discourse, lawyers tend to obscure the fact that they are increasingly part of pyramidal structures and instead exalt their affiliation to the profession ('Stand').[90] Nonetheless, the top-down logic of enterprises is the reference the student is taken along. As sociologists explain, universities train people who are seen by the elite as already accustomed to being at the top of economic structures,[91] so the whole university structure mimics that of the enterprise and communicates that students should go work for such.[92] Unsurprisingly, the advertising used by the University

Drolshammer (1994), p 64, remembers that this behaviour to attract more and more students in a competitive fashion was absent in the period after World War II. See also Kieserling (2010), pp 259–76.

84 For example, www.nkf.ch/firm/history/2008/. On the development of societies towards the organisation form, see Luhmann (2011).

85 BGE 138 II 440; see Nater (2011); Fellmann (2017), p 668.

86 Bergmann and Nietlispach (2019), p 294.

87 Ibid., p 294: between 2003 and 2017, the percentage decreased from 34% to 12%.

88 Ching (in this volume).

89 The generation of lawyers who are now retiring instead chose the bar explicitly because it allowed them to be self-employed: Drolshammer (1994), p 78.

90 Within the profession, a rigid hierarchy with multiple layers (Partner, Counsel, Senior Associate, Associate, Of Counsel, Junior Associate) is in force, but this is rarely mentioned. E.g., it does not emerge from the words of the Swiss Bar Association's president, Haegi (2017). See also Sethe (2017); Fellmann (2017), p 9 f.

91 Hartmann (2008), p 91 ff, 140–1; see also Luhmann (1998), p 774.

92 Luhmann (1987b); Holzer (2010), p 422; Kurtz (2011), p 48 f.

of Lucerne since 2014—'Your talent has future'[93]—is similar to 2006 UBS's slogan 'Your exceptional talent drives our success. It starts with *you*' and Ernst & Young's 'Take charge of your career. *Now*', both figuring as the only two advertisements in the university official magazine of 2006.[94]

Thus, the concept of lifelong learning becomes an element of structural coupling between the law faculty and the professional world. So partners from big law firms are invited as speakers at graduation ceremonies, and once there, they explain to the laurel-crowned graduates that the new approach to a legal career is precisely one of 'lifelong learning'.[95] The same firms, together with the legal services of big multinational enterprises, are also the main sponsors of the programme Primius for 'talented students'.[96] The university lets those firms *swarm* into the networking events organised by career services,[97] knowing that these firms will issue an invitation for a job interview only to those with a high grade point average.[98]

Conclusion

Let us briefly return to the opening quote of the chapter: '*It's great that you formed a critical student association. We too, would like to be more critical in the classroom, but the students won't let us*'. We understand this sentence as symptomatic of today's enterprise university, where there seems to be a gap between the professors' ideals and what the university actually provides. In the discourses between professors, it seems to us that everyone focuses on the old *topos* of theory/practice-related didactical problems: they always talk about the Bologna reforms and never about those that introduced the concept of lifelong learning.

Through a wide analysis of contextual sources, we found out that what the university seems to be doing is training efficient students, who function well in the top-down corporate system of big law firms. Through this communication, disguised under discourses on the importance of lifelong learning, the university seeks to ensure that students are attracted to study in its classrooms,

93 In UniluAktuell 47/2014 in the form of 'My talent has a future'; it has become 'your' in UniluAktuell 60/2017.

94 UniluAktuell 15/2006. In the era of depersonalisation, enterprises tend to market using personal pronouns to surrogate empathy, see Packard et al. (2018); by operating on the unconscious level of desire and personalisation, the university thus constructs its neoliberal object, see also Čuroš (in this volume); as Arnold (in this volume) recalls, 'contemporary universities have been characterised as exemplifying a hegemonic neoliberalism'.

95 For example, Peter Forstmoser, UniluAktuell 60/2017; there is a similar celebration of lifelong learning in Haegi (2017), p 117.

96 Primius looks to be the successor of the 'coaching programme' started in 2005 by two students. The professors charged by the faculty with its management called themselves 'ashamed for not having thought about it before', UniluAktuell 15/2006; see also UniluAktuell 37/2011.

97 For example, the 'Connext—The Legal Career Fair', see UniluAktuell 34/2010.

98 Buschor (2019).

therefore guaranteeing its own self-financing. If the legal-academic apparatus promises students to become legal executors in big firms, why should students be grateful to professors when they try to train critical graduates?

Just as the continuing education format has evolved and changed, so too has the concept of personality. The enterprise university shows with its marketing how it understands itself and its students. For the university, speaking of personality means certifying the importance of the student as a warrantor of its own operativity, while the structural coupling with the profession allows the university to externalise responsibility for its choices on the study curriculum. The university can ultimately justify itself by declaring that it is just doing what the professional market is asking, whilst concurrently not having to decide who this *person* really is.

References

Primary sources

Decision of the Swiss Federal Supreme Court *146* II 309 (2020).

Decision of the Swiss Federal Supreme Court *138* II 440 (2012).

Botschaft des Regierungsrates an den Grossen Rat zum Entwurf eines Gesetzes über die universitäre Hochschulbildung vom 28. September 1999.

Parlamentarische Initiative Bildungsrahmenartikel in der Bundesverfassung Bericht der Kommission für Wissenschaft, Bildung und Kultur des Nationalrats vom 23. Juni 2005, BBl 2005 5479.

Commission of the European Communities, A European Area of Lifelong Learning, Bruxelles 2002.

Verordnung des Hochschulrates über die Koordination der Lehre an den Schweizer Hochschulen vom 29. November 2019.

Studien und Prüfungsordnung der Fakultät III für Rechtswissenschaft der Universität Luzern vom 27. Juni 2001.

Interkantonalen Universitätsvereinbarung vom 20. Februar 1997.

Secondary sources

Gunther Arzt (1994) 'Strafrecht: ein dogmatischer Tyrannosaurus Rex?' in Gunther Arzt et al., *Juristenausbildung als Denkmalpflege? Berner Ringvorlesung 1992 aus Anlass der Reform des juristischen Studiums*, Haupt Verlag 9.

Timothy Garton Ash (2021) 'Für einen Liberalismus der Hoffnung', *NZZ* Online, www.nzz.ch/feuilleton/timothy-garton-ash-so-gelingt-die-zukunft-des-liberalismus-ld.1596438.

Heiko Bergmann and Lucca Nietlispach (2019) 'Zentrale Ergebnisse der SAV-Studie Praxiskosten' 6–7 *Anwaltsrevue* 293.

Christian Burtscher, Pier-Paolo Pasqualoni and Alan Scott (2006) 'Universities and the Regulatory Framework: The Austrian University System in Transition' 20 *Social Epistemology* 241.

Dario R Buschor (2019) 'Recruiting von Substituten in den grössten Schweizer Wirtschaftskanzleien' *Jusletter* 11 March 2019.

Gjon David and Gian Andrea Schmid (2016) 'Juristen sind keine Ingenieure des Rechts' 6 *Plädoyer* 40.

Jens Drolshammer (1994) *Internationalisierung der schweizerischen Rechtskultur nach 1945. Gespräche mit Zeitzeugen – Ein phänomenologisches Erkundungsbuch*, Schulthess.

Bernhard Ehrenzeller and Konrad Sahlfeld (2014) 'Art. 63a BV', in B Ehrenzeller et al. (eds) *St. Galler Kommentar der Schweizerischen Bundesverfassung*, 3rd ed., Schulthess/Dike.

Andreas Eicker and Stefan Bosshart (2019) 'Rechtswissenschaft an der Universität Luzern: Juristische Bildung mit Praxisorientierung' *Anwaltsrevue* 113.

Elena Esposito and David Stark (2019) 'What's Observed in a Rating? Rankings as Orientation in the Face of Uncertainty' 36 *Theory, Culture & Society* 3.

Walter Fellmann (2017) *Anwaltsrecht*, 2nd ed., Stämpfli.

Hanns Fuchs (2011) *Der Aufbruch: Wie das Luzerner Volk zu seiner Universität kam*, Luzern.

Hanns Fuchs (2020) 'Der Aufbruch in den 1990er Jahren', in A Mattioli and M Ries (eds) *Weg der Universität Luzern. historische Meilensteine der universitären Bildung und Forschung in Luzern*, Luzerner Universitätsreden 35, Universität Luzern.

Peter Gauch (1991) 'Über die Ausbildung der Juristen', H Hausheer (ed) *Richter und Verfahrensrecht. 150 Jahre Obergericht Luzern. Festgabe als Sonderband 127bis der «Zeitschrift des Bernischen Juristenvereins»*, Stämpfli.

Peter Gauch (2001) 'Ansprache von Prof. Peter Gauch', in Rektor der Universität Luzern (ed) *Eröffnungsfeier der rechtswissenschaftlichen Fakultät der Universität Luzern vom 22. Oktober 2001*, Luzerner Universitätsreden 15, Universität Luzern.

Manuel Gautschi (2013) Luzerner Uni fällt durch, *Zentralplus* Online, www.zentralplus.ch/luzerner-uni-faellt-durch-682241/.

Hans Ulrich Gumbrecht (2014) *Our Broad Present. Time and Contemporary Culture*, Columbia University Press.

Urs Haegi (2017) 'Aus- und Weiterbildung der Anwältinnen und Anwälte' 136 *ZSR II* 85.

Urs Hafner (2021) Universität Bern: Wenn Marketing Forschung besiegt, *NZZ* Online, www.nzz.ch/feuilleton/universitaet-bern-wenn-marketing-forschung-besiegt-ld.1608077?reduced=true.

Edith Hammer (2016) *Lebenslanges Lernen in der Mediengesellschaft. Eine diskursanalythische Untersuchung*, Springer.

Michael Hartmann (2008) *Elitesoziologie. Eine Einführung*, 2nd ed. Campus Verlag.

Thomas Heer (2010) 'UNIVERSITÄT LUZERN: Selbst die Besten fallen am Schluss durch', *LZ Online*, www.luzernerzeitung.ch/zentralschweiz/luzern/universitaet-luzern-selbst-die-besten-fallen-am-schluss-durch-ld.22489.

Hans Albrecht Hesse (1982) 'Die Praxis der juristischen Berufe und der Juristenausbildung' 37 *JZ* 272.

Hans Albrecht Hesse (1991) 'Juristenausbildung im Reich der Fiktionen' 46 *JZ* 129.

Boris Holzer (2010) 'Was man an der Uni lernt' 16 *Soziale Systeme* 419.

Michael Huber (2008) 'Die Zukunft der Universität' 37 *Soziologie* 275.

Michael Huber (2012) 'Die Organisation Universität', in M Apelt and V Tacke (eds) *Handbuch Organisationstypen*, Springer.

Jonas (2009) 'Eklat an der Universität Luzern', *NZZ Online*, www.nzz.ch/eklat_an_der_universitaet_luzern-1.4048817.

Thomas Kurtz (2011) 'Der Professionsansatz von Niklas Luhmann', *Soziale Systeme* 17.

Martino Locher (2014) 'Kanzleien bewerben sich um Talente', 2 *Plädoyer* 25.

Niklas Luhmann (1987a) *Soziale Systeme – Grundriss einer allgemeinen Theorie*, Suhrkamp.

Niklas Luhmann (1987b) 'Zwei Quellen der Bürokratisierung in Hochschulen', in A Kieserling (ed) *Universität als Milieu*. Kleine Schriften, Haux.

Niklas Luhmann (1991) 'Der Gleichheitssatz als Form und Norm' 4 *Archiv für Rechts- und* 77 *Sozialphilosophie* 435.

Niklas Luhmann (1995) *Das Recht der Gesellschaft*, Suhrkamp.

Niklas Luhmann (1998) *Die Gesellschaft der Gesellschaft*, Suhrkamp.

Niklas Luhmann (2011) *Organisation und Entscheidung*, 3rd ed., Springer.

Simon Marginson (2002) 'Towards a politics of the Entreprise University' 17–18 *Arena Journal* 109.

Simon Marginson and Mark Considine (2000) *The Enterprise University: Power, Governance, and Reinvention in Australia*, Cambridge University Press.

Aram Mattioli and Markus Ries (2000) *'Eine höhere Bildung thut in unserem Vaterlande Noth'*, *Steinige Wege vom Jesuitenkollegium zur Hochschule Luzern*, Chronos.

Manuel Menrath (2020) 'Das neue UNI/PH-Gebäude an der Frohburgstrasse', in A M and M Ries (eds) *Weg der Universität Luzern: Historische Meilensteine der universitären Bildung und Forschung in Luzern*, Luzerner Universitätsreden 35, Universität Luzern.

John Morrissey (2013) 'Governing the academic subject: Foucault, governmentality and the performing university' 39 *Oxford Review of Education* 797.

Hans Nater (2011) 'Zulässigkeit der Anwalts-AG: Stunde der Wahrheit' 107 *SJZ* 211.

Grant Packard et al. (2018) '(I'm) Happy to Help (You): The Impact of Personal Pronoun Use in Customer–Firm Interactions' 55 *Journal of Marketing Research* 541.

Nadja Pastega (2018) 'Jus-Studium schützt vor Unkenntnis nicht', BZ online, www.bernerzeitung.ch/sonntagszeitung/jusstudium-schuetzt-vor-unkenntnis-nicht/story/22758744.

Paul Richli (2001) 'Das Luzerner Universitätsgesetz im Fokus der Rechtswissenschaft', in Rektor der Universität Luzern (ed) *Das Luzerner Universitätsgesetz im Fokus der Rechtswissenschaft*, Luzerner Universitätsreden 12, Universität Luzern.

Paul Richli (2011) 'Die Universität als rechtlicher Raum' in Rektor der Universität Luzern (ed) *Die Universität als rechtlicher Raum*, Luzerner Universitätsreden 20, Universität Luzern.

Gordon Ross et al. (2016) 'Unlocking the Potential of Branding in Social Marketing Services: Utilising Brand Personality and Brand Personality Appeal' 30 *Journal of Services Marketing* 48.

Philipp Sarasin (2020) *Michel Foucault zur Einführung*, Junius.

Wolfgang Schatz (2020) 'Die Universität Luzern – von der «Geburt» bis heute', in A Mattioli and M Ries (eds) *Weg der Universität Luzern: Historische Meilensteine der universitären Bildung und Forschung in Luzern*, Luzerner Universitätsreden 35, Universität Luzern.

Gian Andrea Schmid (2017) 'Universität Luzern startet Bologna 2.0' 3 *Plädoyer* 30.

Clausdieter Schott, Juristenausbildung und Rechtsgeschichte. Gedanken zu Studienreformen, NZZ 35 12.02.1992, p 19.

Jörg Schwarz (2016) 'Einige Gedanken zur Juristenausbildung' in J Schmid (ed) *Hommage für Peter Gauch*, Schulthess.

Jörg Schwarz (2021) 'Die fachlichen Voraussetzungen für die Zulassung zum Anwaltspraktikum und zur Anwaltsprüfung' in K Müller and J Schwarz (eds) *Auf zu neuen Ufern! – Festschrift für Walter Fellmann*, Stämpfli.

Marcel Senn (2013) *Rechtswissenschaft und Juristenausbildung. Fünf kritische Beiträge zu Grundlagenfragen der Wissenschaft des Rechts nach Einführung der Bologna-Reform*, Schulthess.

Rolf Sethe (2017) 'Die juristische Ausbildung an den Universitäten der Schweiz. Probleme und Herausforderungen' 136 *ZSR* 7.

Hannes Siegrist (1996) *Advokat, Bürger und Staat*, Vittorio Klostermann.

Jasmin Siri and Tanja Robnik (2016) 'Systemtheorie und Diskursanalyse' in K Möller and J Siri (eds) *Systemtheorie und Gesellschaftskritik. Perspektiven der Gesellschaftskritik*, Transcript.

Rudolf Stichweh (2010a) 'Universität nach Bologna. Zur sozialen Form der Massenuniversität' in Rektor der Universität Luzern (ed) *Universität nach Bologna. Zur sozialen Form der Massenuniversität/Universität in der Weltgesellschaft*, Luzerner Universitätsreden 19, Universität Luzern.

Rudolf Stichweh (2010b) 'Universität in der Weltgesellschaft', in Rektor der Universität Luzern (ed) *Universität nach Bologna. Zur sozialen Form der Massenuniversität/Universität in der Weltgesellschaft*, Luzerner Universitätsreden 19, Universität Luzern.

Rudolf Stichweh (2011) 'Zur Funktion der Schweizer Universität' in Europa Forum Luzern (ed) *Bildung, Forschung, Innovation. Der Industriestandort Schweiz in Europa und der Welt*, Europa Forum Luzern.

Roseline Troxler (2020) 'Rektor der Universität Luzern setzt künftig auf Weiterbildung', *Luzerner Zeitung online*, www.luzernerzeitung.ch/zentralschweiz/luzern/unirektor-setzt-auf-weiterbildung-ld.1182233.

Reports

Jahresbericht, www.unilu.ch/universitaet/portraet/jahresbericht/

UniluAktuell, www.unilu.ch/magazin/

Chapter 15

A Tyranny of Metrics in the Age of Legal Big Data

Bruce Baer Arnold

Introduction

How do we understand life, the activity and inactivity of individuals and groups of individuals?[1] By extension how does our understanding shape life, potentially determining both an individual's self-perception and that person's opportunities for self-fulfilment? How do the state and its proxies such as universities form, alter and erase identities in ways that might be administratively rational and expressed as fair, facilitative or socially beneficial but embody a technocratic subjectivity founded on an unstated (and thus rarely contested) biopolitics?

This chapter explores contemporary legal education as a matter of digital analytics, in other words the automated observation and appraisal of both learners and educators. It argues that digital panopticism[2] in online law teaching, where students might only have a virtual presence and teachers may be precarious,[3] conflates seeing with understanding. That panopticism embodies an imperative, fostered by solutions vendors and by a 'big data' governmentality in society at large, to minimise costs by tacitly and automatically collecting data at every opportunity. The imperative is typically legitimated through reference to enhancement of the 'student experience', with students being construed as consumers in a market for legal education and as abstractions—data profiles—rather than individuals.[4] It interacts with appraisal of legal academics on the basis of digital 'teaching scores' that are potentially misunderstood and misused by managers.[5] It also interacts with a governmentality on the basis of publication indices construed as objective indicators of merit, a 'truth in numbers' that erodes dignity by regarding scholars as units of production for a global marketplace.[6]

1 Lemke (2011), p 119; Dean (2013), p 38.
2 Gandy (1993), p 29.
3 Cross and Goldenberg (2009); Mauri (2019), p 185.
4 For an overview of the 'market university', see Molesworth et al. (2011), and Marginson and Considine (2000).
5 Hayes and Cheng (2020), p 493.
6 Becker (2009); Peck (2010); Bunds (2012).

DOI: 10.4324/9781003175193-19

The chapter begins by considering digital learning platforms as a manifestation of biopolitics.[7] Those platforms are increasingly prevalent as universities across the globe respond to the ongoing Covid-19 pandemic, whether autonomously or in partnership with commercial entities such as Keypath[8] and 2U[9] whose raison d'etre is exemplary return on investment by offering 'online programme management' (OPM) services. Those services differ from university-operated platforms such as Moodle,[10] Canvas[11] and Blackboard.[12] They instead extend from student recruitment through to highly standardised curriculum design and assessment in ways that refashion traditional understandings of the university,[13] with the institution's commercial partner providing the teaching and the university providing certification of that product. Arnold characterised that relationship as a matter of surveillance machines in ivory towers,[14] a neoliberal manifestation of surveillance capitalism.

The chapter considers the tyranny of metrics in relation to the legal academy's generation and critique of knowledge,[15] in other words institutions that deserve a privileged position as enablers of individual agency and of civil society. The chapter concludes by looking beyond specific criticisms of metrics and concerns with a 'metrics tide'[16] to offer a critique from the perspective of theorists such as Nussbaum and Gewirth who are concerned with flourishing rather than life as a matter of markets.[17] It suggests some responses by students, academics and regulators.

The chapter is written from an Australian perspective, drawing on practice in public and private institutions, but is applicable to the legal academy in the United States, Canada, the United Kingdom and elsewhere.

Seeing Like a University

Contemporary universities have been characterised as exemplifying a hegemonic neoliberalism—a soft biopolitics—that understands public/private institutions in terms of markets, consumers and competition.[18] It is hegemonic because global, apparent in both the public and private sectors, and so prevalent

7 Rose (2007); Foucault (2010); Mirowski (2013); Cohen (2018), p 213; Blencowe (2012).
8 www.keypathedu.com.au
9 www.2u.com. 2U in 2021 absorbed EdX, a massive open online course (MOOC) provider created by Harvard and MIT.
10 www.moodle.com
11 www.instructure.com
12 www.blackboard.com
13 Williamson (2021), p 50; Hall (2021), p 77.
14 Arnold (2022), pp 69–71.
15 Muller (2018).
16 Wilsdon et al. (2015), p 1.
17 Nussbaum (1997) and (2011); Gewirth (1998).
18 Thornton (2012); Whelan (2015); and Cheney-Lippold (2011).

as to be largely unremarked. What is unrecognised or regarded as inevitable is unlikely to be successfully contested. Although there are differences in the autonomy of institutions, the relationship between professional training and each academic curriculum, and broader legal frameworks regarding human rights such as privacy, overall we can construe law faculties and their parent universities as information machines. They collect, process and act upon data regarding students and staff. As such they are counterparts of many public/private sector entities, with universities increasingly embracing a private/private sector managerialism that encompasses use of external service providers, restructuring of work practices through use of digital technologies and reference to 'clients' or 'customers' as determinants of both an institution's financial viability and legitimacy.

That market orientation involves standardisation of what is taught and how it is taught, with reliance on what are characterised as learning management systems (LMS), content management systems (CMS) or digital learning platforms. The 'platforms' characterisation adopts language used by entrepreneurs and consumer protection regulators in identifying social media and other digital platforms such as Twitter, Facebook, LinkedIn, Google and YouTube where consumers interact with each other as part of an 'attention economy'[19] in which the platform operators track those interactions and thus profile users in ways that may not be apparent to or desired by those consumers.[20]

Those processes are a manifestation of surveillance capitalism,[21] a radical extension of the profiling by marketers and credit referencing bodies evident since at least the 1850s. They are also an extension of the more traditional exercise of authority by governments engaged in 'seeing like a state'[22]—a matter of abstraction in identification and deployment of human and other resources on a grand scale with inadequate regard for the diversity inherent in human dignity. Concerns regarding dignity are noted below.

Australian universities assist the national government to see as a state, in other words to understand human needs and interactions on a population scale, through the digital provision of statistical data about student demographics that include age, gender, nationality, place of residence and previous/intended qualifications. Some of that data is aggregated. Some is individual-specific, facilitated for example in Australia by a Unique Student Identifier that is independent of the particular institution or qualification and thus underpins efforts by policymakers to make sense of education as a dynamic, complex but single market across an individual's lifespan and accordingly embracing tertiary, vocational and secondary education. Universities also seek to see in their own right,

19 Hendricks and Vestergaard (2019); and Simon (1971), p 41.
20 Yu and Couldry (2022), p 127.
21 Zuboff (2019); and Komljenovic (2021), p 320.
22 Scott (1999).

mapping cohorts and individuals through individual-specific identifiers, often referred to as student numbers, that are only used by the particular institution and any partners. Those identifiers enable the institution to both see the student's presence on its digital platform and associate that presence with other sources of data.

Digital learning platforms are mechanisms for panopticism, observation that is pervasive and that disciplines observed individuals—abstracted as data subjects, manifestations of particular traits.[23] That observation is typically non-reciprocal. The platforms are administratively convenient. However, like other technologies, they are not value neutral[24] and should be actively critiqued within a dignitarian framework of human rights rather than reinforcing a biopolitics that is soft because it does not feature physical force valorised by theorists such as Schmitt. They enable law faculties (and the universities of which faculties are a part) to see like a state, including building and parsing rich stores of data about individual students and about broader demographics such as gender, nationality, age and prior qualifications. As universities come to rely on OPM providers those for-profit entities also engage in panopticism regarding law students and law teaching, potentially in a more sophisticated and more challenging way than the partner institutions. Some challenges are discussed below.

Platforming and Panopticism

In many countries, legal education, centred on building capability for activity as a solicitor or advocate or administrator, has taken two forms over the past 70 years. One form has been the provision of doctrine and skills building in law schools within public/private universities, consistent with an embrace by the professions of tertiary qualifications as both a quality assurance mechanism and a basis for assertion of professional autonomy.[25] It has complemented the other, more traditional form: practice-oriented training by legal practitioners through for example pupillage to a barrister.

The first has often been a matter of 'chalk and talk', in other words face to face lectures in which an academic expounds principles to a student audience, tutorials in which there is a Socratic dialogue with/between students to deepen understanding of what was presented in the lectures, and assessment on the basis of written exercises such as invigilated exams. Exams have traditionally been justified as mechanisms for ensuring integrity, testing understanding through problem-solving and tacitly building self-reliance through experience in a stressful environment analogous to an appearance in court or negotiation with an adversary.

23 Marachi and Quill (2020), p 418.
24 Kranzberg (1986), p 544; O'Shea (2019).
25 Abel (2020), p 77.

That model is disrupted or simply reoriented by digital platforms that have been adopted by universities across the globe, with increasing uptake as a response to Covid-19 as institutions shifted to a partly or fully online content delivery and assessment model because of concerns regarding the pandemic.[26] Those platforms might be developed *de novo* within an institution, involve integration of a range of off the shelf 'learning tools' and integrity mechanisms (such as plagiarism checkers) provided by non-profit/commercial entities, or involve a partnership between the institution and OPM business as discussed below.

Key features of the platforms are typically online provision of lecture content on a synchronous or asynchronous basis (usually involving the PowerPoint tool that is ubiquitous for corporate presentations in the public and private sectors), online tutorials in 'virtual rooms' and online submission of text/video assessment items that are automatically checked using plagiarism software that compares the particular submission with published material and other assessment items. Some universities have sought to strengthen integrity by using specialist assessment invigilation service providers such as Proctorio that involve the provider undertaking a video scrutiny of both the student and the location in which the student is undertaking an exam,[27] for example that person's bedroom, an invasiveness that raises ethics questions.[28] In future platforms are likely to move beyond automated quiz marking and feedback to automated essay marking, with algorithms replacing human involvement but embodying norms that are discussed below.[29]

Platforms, irrespective of whether they are social media services such as Twitter and Facebook or enable law teaching, involve systemic observation by the platform operator of those people who are using the platform.[30] In considering digital learning platforms (LMS or OPM systems), it is useful to recognise that the observed and therefore managed users are both students and academics, with the latter including people who might be highly skilled and certified on the basis of their own academic achievement but have a precarious employment status.

The language used to characterise the systems is revealing: they are indeed concerned with management of people. Seeing on a large scale, through abstraction that elides individual variation and dignity, and through integration with (or benchmarking against) other data sources, is a feature of contemporary 'truth in numbers' managerialism. It is not restricted to universities. Historically it is not remote from the authoritarian observational states critiqued by James Scott,[31] with radical centralised decision-making about lives, infrastructure and

26 Selwyn (2019b), p 11.
27 Silverman et al. (2021), p 115; Harwell (2020).
28 Coghlan et al. (2021), p 1581.
29 Selwyn (2019a); Hall (2021), p 77.
30 Reidenberg and Schaub (2018), p 263.
31 Scott (1999).

ecosystems by authorities remote from those affected by their decisions and indifferent to the human impacts epitomised by the apocryphal 'the death of one man is a tragedy, the death of a million is a mere statistic'.[32]

Platforms vary in sophistication and globally there is uncertainty about the extent to which law faculties (and more broadly universities) have embraced the 'featuritis' that may or may not be used by specific institutions.[33] In principle students might 'live' on the platform, the academic version of a walled garden, and accordingly be open to pervasive surveillance. Their virtual presence potentially encompasses the downloading or viewing of pre-recorded or synchronous lectures (on occasion in the binge mode evident in consumption of television series), the drafting and submission of assessment items on an individual or group basis, chatting with academics and peers, reading and contributing to discussion fora, and the viewing of text or video course material such as articles and chapters. It might also encompass identification and viewing of publications through an interface between a specific course/unit on the platform and an associated library database that provides access to content held by that library or to content accessed via the library's subscription to commercial publisher databases.

In many law faculties, Covid-19 appears to have resulted in a normalisation of reliance on digital platforms, an inflection point in which 'talk' occurs in virtual classrooms and 'chalk' has moved to a laptop, mobile phone or other networked device. That might be embraced by students and teachers alike as necessary on public health grounds or as convenient, with for example interaction outside traditional time frames and accordingly promoted as 'student centric'.[34] It might be regarded by students and academics as alienating, whether because face to face interaction was richer or because administration of the particular platform requires a reductive standardisation.[35] Managers might regard it as beneficial and inevitable,[36] presenting an opportunity for restructuring of course content[37] and even tacitly for a change in the university workforce. Those managers, who typically do not teach, might more subtly regard implementation and enhancement of platforms as a justification of their existence[38] and source of institutional pride, analogous to rulers of developmental states understanding the establishment of pervasive official data collection mechanisms as a badge of modernity. Awareness and endorsement of platforms as observation machines thus varies.[39]

32 Exenberger (2009), p 163.
33 Bender (2005), p 109; Teräs (2020), p 863.
34 Raffaghelli and Stewart (2020), p 435; Hall (2021), p 77.
35 Shibania (2020), p 100730; Teräs (2020).
36 Essa (2019), p 35.
37 Brown (2020), p 384.
38 Sun et al. (2019).
39 Stewart and Lyons (2021), p 54.

In considering digital platforms in legal education as an enabler of a particular biopolitics there is another perspective. Platforms function as dynamic sets of data points—representations of moment by moment attributes, actions, capabilities—that generate data profiles and objectify people in ways that are erosive of dignity.[40]

Norms, Observation, Identities

Foucault claimed, at odds with the biopolitics of Schmitt and Agamben,[41] that modern politics is

> no longer a matter of bringing death into play in the field of sovereignty, but of distributing the living in the domain of value and utility. Such a power has to qualify, measure, appraise, and hierarchize, rather than display itself in its murderous splendor; it does not have to draw the line that separates the enemy of the sovereign from his loyal subjects. It effects distributions around the norm.[42]

Learning platforms build and reinforce norms in ways that may not be recognised and are not necessarily beneficial. One way, predating digital networks, is that law teaching involves social sorting. People who perform gain admission; continued performance is rewarded with graduation or with opportunities for further employment as an academic. In that process particular traits such as resilience and attention to detail may be fostered. Conversely values such as a commitment to social justice might be discouraged, reinforcing both a class system (including for example co-option of talented members of minorities)[43] and a way of thinking about law.[44]

As with traditional teaching, that performance may be as much a function of social capital (including family or peer expectations and support) as it is of intellect and diligence. Abstraction of students and academics, exemplified for example by use of student numbers rather than names or faces and by automated marking, might be perceived as providing equality for everyone on the platform, a neutrality that mitigates potential biases in legal education. That equality however is likely to be formal rather than substantive.

One issue with norms regarding learning platforms is that they may not be consistent with the needs and capability of individual law students. Some institutions, for example, in making inferences from the frequency with which students visit the platform and the duration of time on that platform, have

40 Nussbaum (1995), p 249.
41 Schmitt (1997); Agamben (1998); Blencowe (2010), p 113.
42 Foucault (1980), p 144.
43 Markovits (2019).
44 Granfield (1992); Mertz (2007); Wizner (1998), p 583.

concluded that infrequent short term engagement is definitively a marker of weak performance that requires intervention by a tutor or lecturer to support someone who is 'at risk'.[45] In some instances the intervention has been mechanistic, with students receiving an automated alert about the need for greater engagement. Engagement statistics might however be misleading, given that students have a range of learning styles and operate in different environments such as working full time rather than accessing content during standard hours. Some for example may have a highly structured approach, downloading content at the beginning of each teaching period rather than on a 'drip feed' basis. That approach is facilitated by a teaching style in which academics 'front load' course material and clearly articulate expectations, so that in following weeks the emphasis is on exegesis and discussion rather than introduction of new content.

Platform architects who influence and in some instances determine decisions by faculty executives might, however, impose different norms regarding how law is taught using the platforms.[46] A strength of traditional law teaching has been variation, with academics as individuals within a non-Fordist culture using different teaching styles to impart knowledge and build skills. That variation is consistent with differing student learning styles and with differing professional needs: many legal practitioners work collaboratively rather than in isolation, all practitioners require skills in persuasion but not all are advocates in a courtroom or tribunal, and a law degree might be of social and personal benefit in roles other than that of a practitioner.

One tendency in the design and maintenance of learning platforms is to inhibit variation by emphasising standardisation in how content is delivered and how performance is assessed. That norm might accordingly result in reliance on a template approach that extends beyond the appearance of content, for example requires each academic to provide students with quizzes in a specified format in a weekly or fortnightly progression. Such standardisation enables administration of the overall platform and disciplining of academics, discussed below, but exclusion of teaching outside the norm results in a sameness that does not engage students. It also potentially reinforces social divides, with elite institutions offering customised teaching and their poorer peers—who in the past have relied on courseware (digital textbooks, guides, tutorial exercises and even lectures) from vendors such as Cengage—providing offerings that are weakly indistinguishable from other universities and from one course to another. A McDonaldisation of teaching is administratively convenient but reinforces social divides and the status of law faculties as vendors of teaching as a commodity.[47]

45 Sun et al. (2019).
46 Williamson (2016); Williamson et al. (2020).
47 Hayes (2017).

A preceding comment noted the scope for students, in particular students who are time poor or lacking diligence and initiative, to 'live' on a platform rather than exploring outside the walled garden. Assessing academics on the basis of student satisfaction metrics may result in a norm where students expect to receive everything they need via that platform, analogous to the traditional 'if it is not in the exam it does not matter'. That norm potentially results in assessment that is biased towards a lower-ranked cohort rather than those students who are exceptional and to retention rather than achievement metrics, given that academics and faculties might be evaluated on the percentage of students who progress through a course to graduation rather than on a bell curve regarding distribution of grades. Automated tracking of proficiency in 'marking to the curve' (and by extension to assessment design in order to meet metrics-based understanding of student capability) reinforces evaluation of individual academics against a production norm, in other words an abstraction relative to statistics relating to the performance of their peers.

Seeing Like a Consumer and a Surveillance Subject

Legal education involves dialogue, an engagement with authority in which both students and academics draw on lived experience and literature (practice-based, historical and theoretical) to identify and critique principles, precedent and practice. That dialogue might liberate students and academics alike from preconceptions, for example that law is necessarily a representation of morality[48] (in other words a traditional biopolitics based on punishment or elimination of those whose behaviour was contrary to norms founded on religious texts) or that female working class students are less capable. It also fosters professionalism, including habituation to norms about courtesy and cogency in asking and responding to questions. Those norms are fundamental for legal practitioner interaction with peers, courts, clients and others. They are however a potentially awkward fit with student feedback regarding teaching.

The awkwardness reflects four facets of the anonymous feedback mechanisms embedded in several platforms. The first is that there is a potential dissonance between institutional rhetoric for students about the status of those students as customers and academic expectations regarding professional communication. The second is that anonymity fosters the disinhibition that has been noted in studies of online anonymous/pseudonymous communication, with students performing a culture of complaint that on occasion amounts to upwards bullying.[49] Institutions have typically sought to reduce oppressive behaviour, gendered or racist expression and bullying by academics in face to

48 Hart (1963).
49 Tucker (2014), p 347; Lee et al. (2021), p 1; Tucker (2021), p 261.

face or virtual modes. There has been less recognition of bullying by 'customers' directed at those delivering content and appraising capability.

As a corollary, the third facet is that feedback may be guided through prompts that skew answers, for example a yes or no to the question asking 'is this unit (or your teacher) giving you everything you need' or 'what you need for professional practice'. Qualitative rather than quantitative feedback mechanisms may also encourage students to comment on the quality of content delivery/assessment at a stage when they have unrealistic expectations about what the legal profession requires or about the effort that they need to put in for high marks in the more challenging subjects. First year law students who are not employed as paralegals rarely have much sense of the realities of legal practice but may be unaware of their ignorance or their gender bias.[50] The final facet is that irrespective of the subjectivity of the feedback it may be misinterpreted by managers, particularly if a small number of strongly negative comments is misread as representative of a class as a whole. That misreading might not be offset by recurrent online surveys, typically undertaken by students on a voluntary basis but on occasion recognised as resulting in survey fatigue that leads to student disengagement.[51]

If, paraphrasing Foucault, data is power, we can identify two consequences of such online feedback activity. Given student resistance to engagement with metrics generation that they construe as misplaced or onerous, some institutions are responding by assessing academics on the percentage of students in each class who provide feedback. Higher rates of feedback might be attributable to encouragement by a respected teacher or by inducements such as free cookies in face to face sessions or online badges, dismissed by later year law students in particular as an infantilisation of their cohort. A more pernicious consequence, to which precarious academics might be particularly susceptible, is an effort to 'game the system' by teaching and assessing at a level that elicits positive student responses.[52] Peers might however dread the numbers and there appears to be no comprehensive cross-institutional study about the impact of rule by numbers on the wellbeing of those employees.[53]

That impact is obfuscated by promotional language used by managers, with an Australian university for example unpersuasively referring to its 'award-winning' data collection tool as 'one of the institution's arsenal of new tools supporting progressive, adaptive learning' that 'uses learning analytics to provide both students and staff with relevant, real-time data and feedback on their learning and teaching'.[54]

50 Hornstein (2017).
51 Hoel and Dahl (2019), p 361.
52 Stroebe (2020), p 276; Berezvai et al. (2021), p 793.
53 Murphy (2021), p 108; Jones (2014), p 37.
54 Lazaroo (2018).

A Rights Critique

In discussing the 'regime of truth', i.e. power, Lemke asks:

> In what vocabulary are processes of life described, measured, evaluated and criticised? What cognitive and intellectual instruments and technological procedures stand ready to produce truth?[55]

Preceding paragraphs contended that law faculties and more broadly universities in embracing digital platforms are relying on a truth in numbers derived from pervasive observation and graphing of performance by students and academics. The use of platforms for the delivery of content, strengthening of capability and assessment of proficiencies is not inherently pernicious.[56] It is remote from the biopolitics espoused by legal theorist Schmitt, in which the 'enemy' was to be excluded from learning, teaching or life itself. Given ostensible blindness to some attributes, it is also remote to the exclusionism evident in the ethno-religious quotas used by elite United States law schools last century.[57]

Financial pressures on universities, concerns about contagion through endemic Covid and the hegemonic status of neoliberal managerialism as the only way to successfully administer a university means that digital platforms are here to stay. Few institutions, particularly those with a large and financially disadvantaged student body, are likely to reject them. As indicated above, many universities are likely to enter into for-profit platform providers whose business model is founded on rigorous standardisation and even more rigorous use of precarious academics who are simply units of production. Institutions are similarly unlikely to disregard global, national and sectoral performance metrics such as the Times Higher Education Index or Quacquarelli Symonds given that those indices may be tied to funding and to student enrolment, irrespective of credibility.[58]

A rights critique, drawing on work by theorists such as Nussbaum, might offer an alternative understanding of platforms as tools rather than outcomes, emphasising legal education as a matter of personal and social development that fosters individual/collective flourishing and that necessitates looking beyond metrics to engage with human frailties, diversities and aspirations. That education might avoid mechanistic platform-based quizzes, reductive rubrics and a drift to automated marking. It might instead emphasise close engagement between students and academics in ways that emphasise dignity, and learning for citizenship. Such engagement is not utopian. It requires investment in infrastructure, in staff and in support for disadvantaged students. It is

55 Lemke (2011), p 119.
56 Goldsworthy (2020), p 243; Kwet and Prinsloo (2020), p 510.
57 Wechsler (1977).
58 Pusser and Marginson (2013), p 544.

possible however, given that, from the market perspective questioned above, law faculties typically generate more revenue than they cost and that systemic problems such as the Global Financial Crisis or inadequate responses to Covid indicate a need to reorient the state.

Against the Panoptic Sort

Foucault, in an unconscious echo of Max Weber's iron cage,[59] construed understandings as inherently repressive. In embracing Nussbaum's more positive view of knowledge as a potential basis for agency by people who are the subjects of understandings, we might recognise that data subjects—students and academics—have some scope to refashion panopticism.[60] Gaining knowledge about panoptic practices and outcomes is consistent with the emphasis in law teaching and research on principle- and fact-based critique as a basis for justice through law reform.

This chapter began by commenting that the biopolitics of legal education is rarely articulated (and even more rarely understood) through explicit reference to the use of LMSs or dominant publishing indices such as Scimago, h-index and i10-index. Few academics in the course of teaching appear to explain what data is collected, who has access and how that data is or might be used. Many academics and students may be sceptical about the subjectivity of qualitative surveys about performance. Some may note inconsistent panopticism: academics are observed by managers but have less scope to observe those managers and no scope to go to the market by buying in services from outside their institution.

A lack of understanding of the realities of panopticism reinforces the norm of acceptance by 'consumers' of surveillance capitalism in life outside legal education, with people taking as a given that they will be surveilled, that they have little scope as individuals to mitigate their status as data subjects and that governments are indifferent to—if not complicit in—pervasive data collection/analysis in the private sector. One response is accordingly that law academics in their teaching should expressly identify learning platform data collection processes/uses and relate that panopticism to what students experience in dealing with Facebook, Twitter, LinkedIn and online retail services.[61]

If students are understood as customers in a market for legal education, where axiomatically the customer is right and has agency, they might go further and require restraints on potential abuse of data by universities and OPMs, irrespective of any intervention by consumer protection agencies and privacy regulators.[62] Such activism is consistent with Nussbaum's understanding of

59 Maley (2004), p 69.
60 Cecez-Kecmanovic (2019); Ulrich (2019); Silverman et al. (2021), p 115.
61 Zuboff (2019).
62 Cohney (2020).

education as facilitation of autonomy, self-awareness and embrace of responsibility.[63] It might be centred on an express commitment by institutions to not collect data absent a compelling need to do so, something that in the first instance would reduce survey fatigue. It might involve a nuanced approach to the appraisal of performance by law academics and students. It might most directly involve the abandonment of integrity mechanisms that involve videoing students in their bedrooms or other private spaces during examinations on the basis that they are suspects who have agreed to waive rights in order to undertake a law degree.[64]

Academics also have a role to play, something that requires individual and collective awareness of how their participation in panopticism (and more broadly in an increasingly Fordist culture) deepens a data-driven biopolitics. In August 2021, Australia's national tertiary education union approached the Fair Work Commission—the employment regulator—to stop publication of course evaluation data at the University of NSW and the potential for that data to be misused to create league tables of academics. Law faculties provide teaching and independent research; they are not a reality television show and should be prepared to show leadership in contesting managerialism.

Universities are part of a global surveillance economy. They might however set an example. In Australia and other jurisdictions that provide weak human rights protection, the law faculties for example might step beyond minimal requirements by embracing the principles of the European Union's General Data Protection Regulation regarding everyone's rights to be informed, to rectification, to erasure, to restrict processing, to data portability, to object, and access. That is one way of signalling to the community that law teaching is not simply a servant of the market and that faculty autonomy is one basis for resisting the drift to a justice system where outcomes are determined by automated decision-making on the basis of data profiles.

References

Richard Abel (2020) 'Legal Pedagogy and Its Discontents' 16 *International Journal of Law in Context* 77.

Giorgio Agamben (1998) *Homo Sacer: Sovereign Power and Bare Life*, trans. Daniel-Heller Roazen, Stanford University Press.

Bruce Baer Arnold (2022) 'Surveillance Machines in Ivory Towers? Surveillance Capitalism, Dignity and Learning Management Systems' 19 *Canberra Law Review* 69.

Gary Becker (2009) *Human Capital: A Theoretical and Empirical Analysis, With Special Reference to Education*, The University of Chicago Press.

Bob Bender (2005) 'Learner Engagement and Success in CMS' in Colleen Carmean and Ali Jafari *Course Management Systems for Learning: Beyond Accidental Pedagogy*, Idea.

63 Nussbaum (2011).

64 Grant (2020); Harwell (2020).

Zombor Berezvai, Gergely Dániel Lukáts and Roland Molontay (2021) 'Can Professors Buy Better Evaluation with Lenient Grading? The Effect of Grade Inflation on Student Evaluation of Teaching' 46 *Assessment and Evaluation in Higher Education* 793.

Claire Blencowe (2010) 'Foucault's and Arendt's 'Insider View' of Biopolitics: A Critique of Agamben' 23 *History of the Human Sciences* 113.

Claire Blencowe (2012) *Biopolitical Experience: Foucault, Power and Positive Critique*, Palgrave Macmillan.

Michael Brown (2020) 'Seeing Students at Scale: How Faculty in Large Lecture Courses Act Upon Learning Analytics Dashboard Data' 25 *Teaching in Higher Education* 384.

Kyle Bunds (2021) ''Please Let It Stop': Fear, Anxiety, and Uncertainty on the Neoliberal Tenure Track' 27 *Qualitative Inquiry* 1040.

Dubravka Cecez-Kecmanovic (2019) 'The Resistible Rise of the Digital Surveillance Economy: A Call for Action' 34 *Journal of Information Technology* 81.

Simon Coghlan, Tim Miller, and Jeannie Paterson (2021) 'Good Proctor or "Big Brother"? Ethics of Online Exam Supervision Technologies' 34 *Philosophy and Technology* 1581.

John Cheney-Lippold (2011) 'A New Algorithmic Identity: Soft Biopolitics and the Modulation of Control' 28 *Theory, Culture and Society* 164.

Julie Cohen (2018) 'The Biopolitical Public Domain: The Legal Construction of the Surveillance Economy' 31 *Philosophy and Technology* 213.

Shaanan Cohney et al. (2020) 'Virtual Classrooms and Real Harms' arXiv:2012.05867.

John Cross and Edie Goldenberg (2009) *Off-Track Profs: Nontenured Teachers in Higher Education*, The MIT Press.

Mitchell Dean (2013) *The Signature of Power: Sovereignty, Governmentality and Biopolitics*, Sage.

Alfred Essa (2019) 'Is Data Dark? Lessons from Borges's "Funes the Memorius"' 6 *Journal of Learning Analytics* 35.

Andreas Exenberger (2009) 'One Death is a Tragedy, One Million is a Statistic', in Christopher Hamilton et al. (ed) *Facing Tragedies*, Lit.

Michel Foucault (1980) *The History of Sexuality. Vol 1*, Vintage.

Michel Foucault (2010) *The Birth of Biopolitics (Lectures at the Collège de France 1978–79)*, Picador.

Oscar GandyJr (1993) *The Panoptic Sort: A Political Economy of Personal Information*, Westview.

Alan Gewirth (1998) *Self-Fulfillment*, Princeton University Press.

Daniel Goldsworthy (2020) 'The Future of Legal Education in the 21st Century' 41 *Adelaide Law Review* 243.

Robert Granfield (1992) *Making elite lawyers: Visions of Law at Harvard and Beyond*, Routledge.

Kara Grant (2020) 'College Students Are Learning Hard Lessons About Anti-Cheating Software' www.voiceofsandiego.org/topics/education/college-students-are-learning-hard-lessons-about-anti-cheating-software/.

Stephanie Hall (2021) 'Getting Online Higher Education Right', in H Han, J H Williams, and S Cui (eds) *Tackling Online Education: Implications of Responses to COVID-19 in Higher Education Globally*, Cambridge Scholars.

HLA Hart (1963) *Law, Liberty, and Morality*, Stanford University Press.

Drew Harwell (2020) 'Cheating-detection Companies Made Millions During the Pandemic. Now Students are Fighting Back' *The Washington Post* 12 November

Aneta Hayes and Jie Cheng (2020) 'Datafication of Epistemic Quality: Advancing Understandings of Teaching Excellence Beyond Benchmarked Performativity' 25 *Teaching in Higher Education* 493.

Dennis Hayes (2017) *Beyond McDonaldization: Visions of Higher Education*, Routledge.
Vincent Hendricks and Mads Vestergaard (2019) *Reality Lost*, Springer.
Henry Hornstein (2017) 'Student Evaluations of Teaching are an Inadequate Assessment Tool for Evaluating Faculty Peormance' 4 *Cogent Education* 1304016.
Anniken Hoel and Tove Irene Dahl (2019) 'Why Bother? Student Motivation to Participate in Student Evaluations of Teaching' 44 *Assessment and Evaluation in Higher Education* 361.
Edward Jones (2014) 'Handle with Care! An Exploration of the Potential Risks Associated with the Publication and Summative Usage of Student Evaluation of Teaching (SET) Results' 38 *Journal of Further and Higher Education* 37.
Janja Komljenovic (2021) 'The Rise of Education Rentiers: Digital Platforms, Digital Data and Rents' 46 *Learning, Media and Technology* 320.
Melvin Kranzberg (1986) 'Technology and History: "Kranzberg's Laws"' 27 *Technology and Culture* 544.
Michael Kwet and Paul Prinsloo (2020) 'The 'Smart' Classroom: A New Frontier in the Age of the Smart University' 25 *Teaching in Higher Education* 510.
Suzanne Lazaroo (2018) 'UC's InterFace App Scores Top Marks' (28 September 2018) www.canberra.edu.au/about-uc/media/newsroom/2018/september/ucs-interface-app-scores-top-marks.
Megan Lee, Rosanne Coutts, Jann Fielden, Marie Hutchinson, Richard Lakeman, Bernice Mathisen, Dima Nasrawi and Nichole Phillips (2021) 'Occupational Stress in University Academics in Australia and New Zealand' 44 *Journal of Higher Education Policy and Management* 1.
Thomas Lemke (2011) *Biopolitics: An Advanced Introduction*, trans. Eric Frederick Trump, NYU Press.
Terry Maley (2004) 'Max Weber and the Iron Cage of Technology' 24 *Bulletin of Science, Technology & Society* 69.
Roxana Marachi and Lawrence Quill (2020) 'The Case of Canvas: Longitudinal Datafication Through Learning Management Systems' 25 *Teaching in Higher Education* 418.
Simon Marginson and Mark Considine (2000) *The Enterprise University*, Cambridge University Press.
Daniel Markovits (2019) *The Meritocracy Trap*, Penguin.
Christian Mauri (2019) 'Formulating the Academic Precariat' in Fabian Cannizzo and Nick Osbaldiston (eds) *The Social Structures of Global Academia*, Routledge.
Elizabeth Mertz (2007) *The Language of Law School: Learning to 'Think like a Lawyer'*, Oxford University Press.
Philip Mirowski (2013) *Never Let a Serious Crisis Go to Waste: How Neoliberalism Survived the Financial Meltdown*, Verso.
Mike Molesworth, Richard Scullion and Elizabeth Nixon (2011) *The Marketisation of Higher Education and the Student as Consumer*, Routledge.
Jerry F Muller (2018) *The Tyranny of Metrics*, Princeton University Press.
Brendon Murphy (2021) 'Against Wellbeing: The Problem of Resources, Metrics and Care of the Self' 46 *Alternative Law Journal* 108.
Martha Nussbaum (1995) 'Objectification' 24 *Philosophy & Public Affairs* 249.
Martha Nussbaum (1997) *Cultivating Humanity: A Classical Defense of Reform in Liberal Education*, Harvard University Press.
Martha Nussbaum (2011) *Creating Capabilities: The Human Development Approach*, Harvard University Press.

Lizzie O'Shea (2019) *Future Histories*, Verso.
Jamie Peck (2010) *Constructions of Neoliberal Reason*, Oxford University Press.
Brian Pusser and Simon Marginson (2013) 'University Rankings in Critical Perspective' 84 *The Journal of Higher Education* 544.
Juliana Raffaghelli and Bonnie Stewart (2020) 'Centering Complexity in 'Educators' Data Literacy' to Support Future Practices in Faculty Development: A Systematic Review of the Literature' 25 *Teaching in Higher Education* 435.
Joel Reidenberg and Florian Schaub (2018) 'Achieving Big Data Privacy in Education' 16 *Theory and Research in Education* 263.
Nikolas Rose (2007) *The Politics of Life Itself*, Princeton University Press.
Carl Schmitt (1997) *The Concept of the Political*, The University of Chicago Press.
James Scott (1999) *Seeing Like A State: How Certain Schemes to Improve the Human Condition Have Failed*, Yale University Press.
Neil Selwyn (2019a) *Should Robots Replace Teachers*, Polity.
Neil Selwyn (2019b) 'What's the Problem with Learning Analytics?' 6 *Journal of Learning Analytics* 11.
Antonette Shibania, Simon Knight and Simon Buckingham Shum et al. (2020) 'Educator Perspectives on Learning Analytics in Classroom Practice' 46 *The Internet and Higher Education* 100730.
Sarah Silverman, Autumm Caines, Christopher Casey, Belen Garcia de Hurtado, Jessica Riviere, Alfonso Sintjago and Carla Vecchiola (2021) 'What Happens When You Close the Door on Remote Proctoring? Moving Toward Authentic Assessments with a People-Centered Approach' 39 *To Improve the Academy: A Journal of Educational Development* 115.
Herbert A Simon (1971) 'Designing Organizations for an Information-Rich World', in M Greenberger (ed), *Computers, Communication, and the Public Interest*, Johns Hopkins Press.
Bonnie Stewart and Erica Lyons (2021) 'When the Classroom Becomes Datafied' 29 *Italian Journal of Educational Technology* 54.
Wolfgang Stroebe (2020) 'Student Evaluations of Teaching Encourages Poor Teaching and Contributes to Grade Inflation: A Theoretical and Empirical Analysis' 42 *Basic and Applied Social Psychology* 276.
Kaiwen Sun, Abraham H Mhaidli, Sonakshi Watel, Christopher A Brooks, and Florian Schaub (2019) 'It's My Data! Tensions Among Stakeholders of a Learning Analytics Dashboard' CHI 2019, 4–9 May 2019, Glasgow, Scotland.
Marko Teräs, Juha Suoranta, Hanna Teräs and Mark Curcher (2020) 'Post-Covid-19 Education and Education Technology "Solutionism": A Seller's Market' 2 *Postdigital Science and Education* 863.
Margaret Thornton (2012) *Privatising the Public University: The Case of Law*, Routledge.
Beatrice Tucker (2014) 'Student Evaluation Surveys: Anonymous Comments that Offend or are Unprofessional' 68 *Higher Education* 347.
Beatrice Tucker (2021) 'Disruptive Trends in Student Experience Evaluations and Implications for Academic Staff Wellbeing', in M Shah, J T E Richardson, A Pabel, and B Oliver (eds), *Assessing and Enhancing Student Experience in Higher Education*, Palgrave Macmillan.
Peter Ullrich (2019) 'In Itself But Not Yet For Itself—Organising The New Academic Precariat', in Walter Baier et al. (eds), *The Radical Left in Europe: Rediscovering Hope*, Merlin Press.
Harold Wechsler (1977) *The Qualified Student: A History of Selective College Admission in America*, Wiley.

Andrew Whelan (2015) 'Academic Critique of Neoliberal Academia' 12 *Sites: A Journal of Social Anthropology and Cultural Studies* 1.

Ben Williamson (2016) 'Digital Education Governance: Data Visualization, Predictive Analytics, and "Real-time" Policy Instruments' 31 *Journal of Education Policy* 123.

Ben Williamson, Sian Bayne and Suellen Shay (2020) 'The Datafication of Teaching in Higher Education: Critical Issues and Perspectives' 25 *Teaching in Higher Education* 351.

Ben Williamson (2021) 'Making Markets Through Digital Platforms: Pearson, Edu-business, and the (E)valuation of Higher Education' 62 *Critical Studies in Education* 50.

James Wilsdon et al. (2015) *The Metric Tide: Report of the Independent Review of the Role of Metrics in Research Assessment and Management*, Sage.

Stephen Wizner (1998) 'Is Learning to "Think Like a Lawyer" Enough?' 17 *Yale Law & Policy Review* 583.

Jun Yu and Nick Couldry (2022) 'Education as a Domain of Natural Data Extraction: Analysing Corporate Discourse About Educational Tracking' 25 *Information, Communication and Society* 127.

Shoshana Zuboff (2019) *The Age of Surveillance Capitalism: The Fight for a Human Future at the New Frontier of Power*, Public Affairs.

Index

Page numbers in *italics* reference figures and **bold reference tables

For Product Safety Concerns and Information please contact our EU
representative GPSR@taylorandfrancis.com
Taylor & Francis Verlag GmbH, Kaufingerstraße 24, 80331 München, Germany

www.ingramcontent.com/pod-product-compliance
Ingram Content Group UK Ltd.
Pitfield, Milton Keynes, MK11 3LW, UK
UKHW020143200926
475702UK00005B/893

* 9 7 8 1 0 3 2 0 0 6 9 2 5 *